THE ILLUSTRATED HISTORY OF THE

AZTECS & MAYA

THE ILLUSTRATED HISTORY OF THE

AZTECS & MAYA

LEGENDS, MYTHS AND CULTURE OF THE ANCIENT NATIVE PEOPLES OF MEXICO AND CENTRAL AMERICA, WITH MORE THAN 500 PHOTOGRAPHS

CHARLES PHILLIPS

LORENZ BOOKS

CONTENTS

THE GLORY THAT WAS MESOAMERICA

In 1519, a group of Spanish soldiers on an exploratory voyage from the Spanish colony in Cuba encountered a great civilization in full flower in the Valley of Mexico. From a cold mountain pass between the awe-inspiring snow-capped peaks of Popocatépetl and Ixtaccíhuatl, the nervous Spaniards looked down on a remarkable series of interconnected lakes in the Valley, with well-ordered towns and raised fields on the shores, and a great city built on islands and causeways towards the western edge of the largest of the lakes. They knew something of the Aztec people who built this city, Tenochtitlán, for earlier in the adventure the Spaniards had encountered the Aztecs' allies and enemies and heard tales of their vast empire. As the Spaniards marched down on to the plain and neared the city, they went across one of the causeways linking the island metropolis to the mainland and were astounded by Tenochtitlán's size and beauty. The great temples and palaces rose from the water like a vision. One member of the Spanish force, Bernal Díaz del Castillo, later likened it to a city from a fairytale, a vision of enchantment.

Below: The builders of Maya cities such as Tikal, in Guatemala, raised towering stone temples in the midst of thick jungle.

EARLY BEGINNINGS

The city of Tenochtitlán and the culture of its Aztec builders was the product of more than 22,000 years of human activity, which stretched back to the arrival of the first hunter-gatherers in America in 21,000BC.

Descendants of these ancient settlers who left their mark in the area included the Olmec builders of the great cities of La Venta and San Lorenzo in *c.*1200BC, the Zapotec architects of Monte Albán in *c.*500BC and the Toltec founders of Tollán in AD950. They also included the Maya, who built their remarkable jungle cities in the lands to the east of the Valley of Mexico in the first centuries of the Christian era. At the time of the Conquest they were still thriving in the northern part of the Yucatán peninsula.

Above: Mictlantecuhtli, the Aztec 'Lord of the Dead', was worshipped in this form by the people of Teotihuacán in c.*100BC.*

WHAT WAS MESOAMERICA?

Scholars give the name Mesoamerica to this 22,000-year timespan and to the lands settled by these peoples; it is both a cultural and a geographical label. Geographically, Mesoamerica runs from the area of desert north of the Valley of Mexico across Guatemala and Honduras to western Nicaragua and Costa Rica.

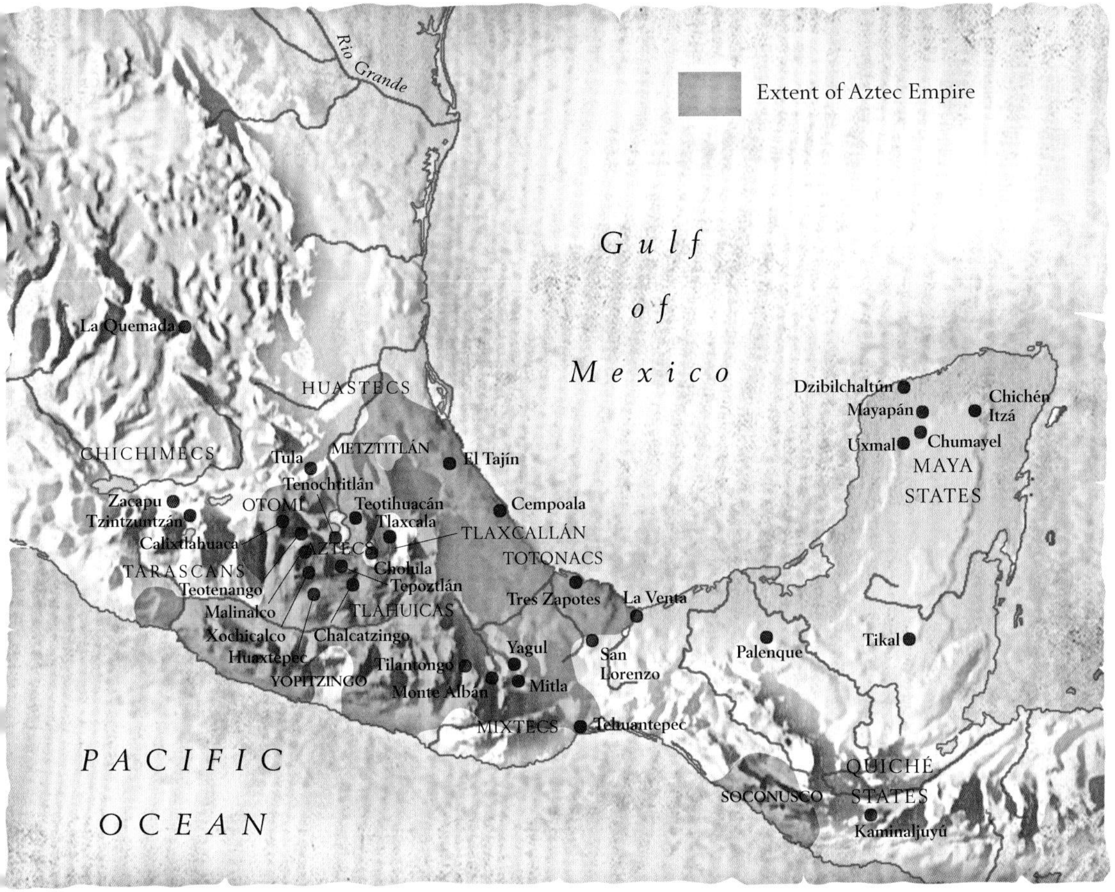

Above: Map showing the main sites of the successive Mesoamerican cultures and the size of the Aztec empire in 1510.

It largely coincides with what we call Middle America, including areas of some modern Central American countries. Other Central American countries, such as Panama, were not settled by Mesoamericans. Mexico, most of which was an important part of Mesoamerica, is geographically part of North America. Historically, Mesoamerica covers all events between the arrival of the first human settlers in the region in *c.*21,000BC and the Conquest of the Mesoamerican empire in 1521.

Scholars use an additional set of chronological divisions to divide Maya history. The years *c.*AD250–900 that represent the fullest flowering of Maya civilization are labelled the Classic Period. The Classic years are the ones in which the Maya set up dated stone columns celebrating the achievements of their holy kings. The 20,000-odd years before are called the Archaic (20,000–*c.*2500BC) and Preclassic (*c.*2500BC– AD250) periods. The 600-odd years after are known as the Postclassic Period (AD900–1500s).

This book covers the historical achievements and mythology of all these cultures, concentrating on the cultures of the Maya and the Aztecs because we know most about them. Succeeding cultures inherited a great deal from their predecessors.

Right: Tall stone warrior figures carved by Toltec craftsmen in the 11th century AD celebrated a fierce, militaristic culture.

Above: This court in Xochicalco, Mexico, was built in AD700–800 for playing the ball game revered by Mesoamericans.

Religious rituals, cultural achievements and mythological elements are common to most of the peoples of the Mesoamerican region and historical period, so that it is possible to talk of 'Mesoamerican civilization'.

CALENDARS

Foremost among these common elements was the use of a complex ritual calendar. Among the Maya and Aztecs, priests marked the passing of time and predicted the future with two calendars, one a solar count of 365 days linked to the passing seasons, another a ritual calendar of 260 days, thought to be based on the length of a human pregnancy. The two calendars combined to make a longer measure. The period needed for a particular day in the 365-day calendar and a particular day in the 260-day calendar to coincide was 18,980 days, or 52 365-day years. This measure, called the 'bundle of years' by the Aztecs, was invested with great significance. The end of each 52-year period was seen as a moment of great danger, at which the gods might end the world. The preoccupation with measuring and recording time went far back into Mesoamerican history – the earliest surviving writing from the region may be a Zapotec calendrical note from *c.*600BC – and the calendar was very widely used throughout the region. Indeed, the scholar Michael Coe has suggested that one good way of defining Mesoamerica would be to draw a line around the area known to have used the ritual calendar.

Left: The long-nosed Maya rain god Chac – carved here at Sayil, Mexico – had his counterpart in Tláloc, the Aztec god of rain.

BLOOD SACRIFICE

Another important central element of Mesoamerican civilization – at least as far back as the Olmecs in *c.*1200BC – was the use of human blood sacrifice to honour and propitiate the gods. Among the Aztecs, vast lines of prisoners of

war were paraded up steep temple pyramids to be sacrificed by having their hearts ripped from their chests. The Classic-Period Maya more commonly decapitated their victims. Both Maya and Aztec worshippers also offered their own blood to the gods. Women and men drew blood from wounds in their cheeks, ears, arms and legs while men also made cuts in the penis.

The Mesoamericans worshipped a vast pantheon of gods and goddesses in the course of their civilization. These deities often have alternative names and animal or human twin forms. The cult of one god in particular was enduringly popular across centuries and cultures. The Plumed Serpent Quetzalcóatl, known to the Maya as Kukulcán, was associated with wise rulership and revered as a creator, a wind god and as the morning star. In myth, he was said to have departed by sea on a raft of snakes, promising to return. It is a popular theory that some among the Aztecs may have interpreted the coming of Hernán Cortés and his Spanish troops in 1519 as the promised return of Quetzalcóatl from exile.

THE BALL COURT

One of the basic common elements of Mesoamerican civilization was a ball game played on a court shaped like a capital 'I'. The court, which formed part of the ritual complex in cities, had sloping or vertical side walls. The object appears to have been to get the ball into the end sections, rather like the 'endzones' on an American football pitch or the areas where tries are scored on a British rugby pitch. Some courts had rings high on the side walls and extra points may have been scored by getting the ball through the hoop. This would have been difficult since players could not direct the ball with their feet or hands, only their hips, elbows and knees. The game seems to have been understood as an enactment of cosmic struggles; by the Aztecs as a clash between light and dark, between Quetzalcóatl and his dark brother Tezcatlipoca, by the Maya as a re-enactment of the myth cycle in which the Hero Twins go to the underworld to overcome the gods of that fearsome realm.

Above: On the steep steps of temples, the Aztecs made human sacrifices to the gods.

Left: Tezcatlipoca played a part in the ball game as an enactment of cosmic struggles.

UNCOVERING THE SECRETS OF THE PAST

There was great excitement in Europe when the conqueror of the Aztecs, Hernán Cortés, sent a consignment of gold, featherwork and other rare treasures from Mesoamerica to the court of Charles V. The German artist Albrecht Dürer, who viewed the collection of objects, wrote in his journal, 'I have seen nothing that has so thrilled my heart as these artefacts, for I saw in them strange and wonderfully worked objects and marvelled at the subtle genius of men in far-off lands.'

Europeans had a tantalizing introduction to the 'subtle genius' of Mesoamerican civilization. Almost six centuries after Dürer wrote these words and following more than a century of excavations and interpretations, today we know much more about ancient Mesoamerican civilization. Weather and land conditions often did not favour the survival of early remains. Local practice before the Conquest meant that much of Mesoamerican mythology and history was transmitted orally from generation to generation and never written down. But the major part of the blame for the paucity of surviving remains must be shouldered by the Spanish conquerors themselves. After they had captured Tenochtitlán in 1521, they vandalized the city, breaking images of the gods, melting down treasures into ingots to be sent back to Europe, tearing down buildings and using the materials for the foundations of their colony, New Spain.

Left: The imposing Pyramid of the Moon in Teotihuacán contains a hidden burial chamber with a sacrificial victim.

FRAGMENTS OF HISTORY

The Spanish missionaries who arrived in Maya lands after the conquest of Tenochtitlán were responsible for burning many of the locals' bark-paper books or codices. One of the most enthusiastic of these was Bishop Diego de Landa, author of *Report of Things in Yucatán*, who wrote, 'These people used certain letters with which they wrote in their books about ancient subjects ... We found many books written with these letters and since they held nothing that was not falsehood and the work of the evil one, we burned them all'.

THE CODICES

As far as we know, only four Maya codices survived the attentions of the monks. Three of these codices are now known after the names of the European cities in which they are kept – the Dresden, Madrid and Paris Codices – while the fourth, the *Grolier Codex*, is in North America. They contain many images of Maya deities, as well as information used by priests for divining the future, timing sacred rituals and monitoring the movements of Venus and the eclipses of the sun and moon.

THE POPOL VUH

Other surviving accounts of Maya history and mythology were written down after the Conquest. The *Popol Vuh* ('Book of Advice') was a sacred text of the Quiché, a group of southern Maya inhabiting highland Guatemala. It survived for posterity through a combination of Quiché determination and good fortune. The original book, in Maya hieroglyphs, was secretly translated into the Roman alphabet by members of the Quiché nobility in the mid-1500s. This was part of an attempt to preserve the book at a time when the Spaniards, who had conquered the region in 1523–24, were seeking to exterminate native culture. The manuscript was not found until later in the century, by which time some members of the Catholic Church had begun to see some merit in recording and preserving accounts of ancient Mesoamerican culture and history and so allowed it to be preserved. This version was discovered in 1703 by Francisco Ximenez, a Franciscan friar who could read Quiché and who was therefore able to translate the text into Spanish.

Left: This funerary urn was used by the Quiché, southern Guatemalan Maya, whose holy book, the Popol Vuh, *contains a detailed account of the creation of the world.*

Above: An unknown 4th-century Maya ruler adorns a jade belt pendant found in the Petén region.

NATIVE HISTORIES

Two other native histories survive. The first, *The Annals of the Cakchiquels*, contains entries up to 1604 and decribes the history of the Cakchiquels, neighbours of the Quiché, from mythical beginnings onwards. Like the *Popol Vuh*, it was first transcribed into the Roman alphabet in the 1500s. The second, *The Books of Chilam Balam*, contains a mixture

Right: Spanish conquistadors prepare to land in Mexico in 1519. The invaders' unfortunate belief that the local books and religious rites were wicked led to a terrible cultural loss.

of prophecy and history-myth of the Maya of Yucatán. These accounts were kept from the early 16th century onwards, but were rewritten, with additions, until the 19th century. They take their name from a Maya seer who is said to have predicted the coming of 'bearded men of the east' who would bring violence and force the Maya to speak another language. Both these sources give eyewitness accounts of the Spanish conquest and the many changes that followed it.

Below: Information concerning Maya cosmology and details of the gods associated with the four principal directions are to be found in the Madrid Codex.

AZTEC HISTORY AND MYTHOLOGY

Most of the written evidence we have of Aztec customs, beliefs, history and mythology was recorded after the Conquest, in manuscript books or codices written by young natives educated in Spanish schools and in reports written by the Spanish chroniclers, based on what they saw and heard from locals.

WRITTEN SOURCES

An important example is the *Codex Mendoza*, commissioned *c.*1525 by the first Spanish Viceroy, Don Antonio de Mendoza. It contains an account of the growth of the Aztec empire illustrated and written by native Mesoamericans based on older pictorial records.

The movements of the Méxica/Aztec and other tribal groups prior to the establishment of Tenochtitlán are described in 16th-century manuscripts such as the *Codex Aubin* and the *Codex Xólotl* and also in the 17th-century history recorded by Fernando de Alva Ixtlilxóchitl. All were based on oral histories and earlier codices, now lost.

Among the Spanish chroniclers' accounts is Friar Bernardino de Sahagún's compendious 12-volume *General History of the Things of New Spain*, completed in 1569. His fellow Churchman Diego Durán compiled both the *History of the Indies of New Spain* and the *Book of the Gods and Rites and the Ancient Calendar*. First-hand accounts of the Conquest itself survive in the letters written by Hernán Cortés to Charles V and in *True History of the Conquest of New Spain*, written by Bernal Díaz del Castillo, a member of Cortés' force.

Above: Serpents writhe round the neck of the Aztec earth goddess Coatlícue. Ritual victims were decapitated in her honour.

REWRITING THE PAST

Scholars treat all the surviving written evidence with caution as many accounts blend history and mythology in a dense combination that is difficult to interpret, not least because it is full of repetitions and contradictions. A good example is that of the Aztecs' treatment of Tula, which combines knowledge handed down by oral tradition of the historical city (flourished *c.*AD950–1150) with the myth of Tollán ('the Place of the Reeds'), home to wondrous craftsmen, where the god Quetzalcóatl ruled in the guise of the prince Topiltzin. In general, Mesoamerican peoples looked to the past for justification of the present. The

Left: The Palace of King Yaxchilán contains a sculpture honouring the 8th-century AD Maya monarch Bird Jaguar.

Above: Aztec codices are more numerous than their Maya counterparts. The Codex Magliabechano *is a late 1500s copy of a pre-Hispanic manuscript. It contains valuable information on Aztec worship and the use of the ritual calendar.*

Aztecs, for example, rewrote their own history to establish that their destiny was to dominate other peoples and expand their own territories. The Aztecs often presented events or themes that were common to many cultures as unique 'historical' happenings. The Aztecs claimed they found their origin in the 'Place of the Seven Caves', but this origin story was common to the beliefs of many Mesoamerican groups.

Yet the Mesoamericans themselves viewed these accounts as history, even though the narratives contain non-sequential episodes and metaphorical accounts of events. Because of the Mesoamericans' willingness to blend fact with what the modern mind would class as myth in historical accounts, we know nothing for certain of events that took place more than 400 years before the Conquest. All scholars can do in the circumstances is to gauge the meaning of surviving buildings and ruins in the light of the latest knowledge.

Left: Mesoamerican societies had an enduring fascination with the jaguar. This clay model was made by an Aztec artist.

STELAE

Many carved inscriptions survive in Maya lands, notably on stelae, stone columns set up during the Classic Period in the 3rd to 9th centuries AD. They bear portraits of the 'holy kings' of Maya city-states and commemorate the rulers' accessions and jubilees, battle victories and important religious sacrifices, which sometimes included the humiliation and slaughter of a rival king.

One stela, erected in honour of King Cauac Sky in Quiriguá, south-eastern Guatemala, is 10m (33ft) tall and weighs 10 tons. It was set up in AD771. The Maya stopped erecting carved stelae in the 9th century AD and scholars believe that after this point they probably kept their records in books. The books were destroyed by the Spanish, but the stelae survive, providing an invaluable source of information about Maya history and culture in the Classic Period.

UNLOCKING THE SECRETS OF MAYA SOCIETY

In the mid-20th century, a breakthrough in the interpretation of Maya hieroglyphs led to a major reappraisal of the very nature of Maya society. Earlier scholars thought that the hieroglyphs combined a picture-image (rebus) and a symbol representing a word or idea (logogram). But in 1952 Soviet language specialist Yuri Knorosov showed that Maya hieroglyphs were also phonetic: different signs represented combinations of vowels and consonants and were used to spell out words. Phonetic signs, he argued, were written or carved alongside logograms. Maya experts resisted Knorosov's theory for some years , but in time they came to realize that he was right. Now they could begin to read the inscriptions, with results that helped to turn our understanding of the Maya on its head.

NEW UNDERSTANDINGS

In the early 20th century, scholars had recognized that the inscriptions contained a great deal of information about the ritual calendar and astronomy. They thought the carvings on the stelae were of priests rather than kings, and that images of beheaded victims represented sacred rites. They argued that the Maya were a peaceful people led by priestly astronomers. However, later scholars who could read the writing began to see that the inscriptions were about events in a king's reign. They understood that the carvings were of kings and that the sacrificial victims were often rival kings put to ritual death after defeat. A new, more accurate image emerged of the Maya as a martial people living in city-states that were almost constantly at war.

Another major breakthrough in our understanding of the Maya also occurred in 1952, with the discovery of a great royal tomb beneath a mortuary monument in the Maya city of Palenque. Mexican architect Alberto Ruz Lhuillier was excavating the vast Temple of Inscriptions there when his curiosity was aroused by one of the slabs on the temple floor. This particular stone slab was cut with a double row of holes that could, he conjectured, be used as finger grips to raise the stone. When he had the stone lifted, he discovered a narrow stairway leading downward. The stairway had been deliberately blocked with rubble, which Lhuillier painstakingly cleared over the following four years. In June 1952 he discovered the stairs led to a chamber, beyond which he found a great funerary crypt 9m long and 7m in height (30ft by 23ft). The crypt held a carved stone sarcophagus in which lay a body later identified from inscriptions as that of King Pacal, ruler of Palenque in the 7th–8th centuries AD. Prior to Lhuillier's breakthrough, scholars had generally understood that the Maya built stepped pyramids as temples, but the discovery of Pacal in his magnificent royal tomb suggested that some of the pyramids were erected primarily as funerary monuments to honour deceased monarchs.

Above: The Chiapas rainforest crowds in on the ruins at Bonampak of the court of Lord Chan Muan, who reigned AD776–795.

ARCHAEOLOGIST AND LITERARY SLEUTH

Mexican archaeologist Alfonso Caso y Andrade (1896–1970) bridged the gap between the interpreters of ancient literature and the investigators of ruined sites. Not only did Andrade decipher a number of Mixtec codices in the course of his work, he also performed a painstaking archaeological study at Monte Albán, establishing a chronology for the occupation of the site in the Oaxaca valley and demonstrating that the Mixtec people occupied Monte Albán in the wake of the Zapotecs. Andrade published the celebrated *El Mapa de Teozacaoalco* in 1949 and *Kings and Kingdoms of the Mixteca* in 1970.

'PAINTED WALLS'

Six years earlier, in 1946, an American photographer called Giles Healey made another remarkable discovery deep in the rainforest of the Mexican state of Chiapas. Healey, who was searching for Maya ruins in the area, was led by locals to a city they referred to as Bonampak ('Painted Walls'). There he found a three-roomed building

Above: The murals at Bonampak depict court life and celebrations marking a battle won by Lord Chan Muan in AD790.

whose walls were decorated with a remarkable series of murals that contain vivid images of life at a Maya royal court in the 8th century AD, including royal accessions, battles, musical performances and other ceremonies. In recent years, scholars have used digital technology to enhance photographs of the images and restore their original bright colours. The natives' name stuck: the city, about 30km (18 miles) from Yaxchilán, became known as Bonampak.

Archaeological work on Tenochtitlán was complicated by the fact that the capital of the Spanish colony of New Spain and later the vast metropolis of Mexico City were built on top of Aztec ruins. Important discoveries were made in the course of building work. In 1790, workers laying flagstones in the main square of Mexico City discovered the 24-ton Sun Stone, which commemorates the five Aztecs 'suns' or ages, together with a remarkable sculpture of Coatlícue, the earth goddess. A carving of the earth lord Tlaltecuhtli was found in 1968 during digging for a metro line. In 1978, an electrical company worker uncovered part of a 3.25m- (10ft 9in) diameter monolith depicting the dismembered goddess Coyolxauhqui, who in myth was killed by her brother Huitzilopochtli. Scholars knew that the foundations of the Aztecs' Great Pyramid were adjacent to the spot where the monolith was found. The discovery of what became known as the 'Coyolxauhqui Stone' resulted in a major excavation of the foundations of the Great Pyramid over the following years.

Archaeologists' investigations brought many valuable insights into Teotihuacán, the site in the north-east Valley of Mexico that was revered by the Aztecs as the 'place of the gods'. The city was surveyed systematically in the 1960s and 1970s by American archaeologist René Millon. One of the major breakthroughs came by accident. In 1971, digging during preparations for a *son et lumière* ('sound and light') show uncovered a cave in volcanic lava beneath the city's most sacred building, the vast Pyramid of the Sun. Offerings found there have been dated to many centuries before the Pyramid was built in the 2nd century AD, suggesting that the city had been built on an ancient site of pilgrimage. The Aztecs frequently visited ruined sites such as Teotihuacán, sometimes taking artefacts from the site and sometimes adding others of a different period.

Right: In Mexico City the Aztec past is never far away. A subway station is home to a temple honouring the wind god Éhecatl.

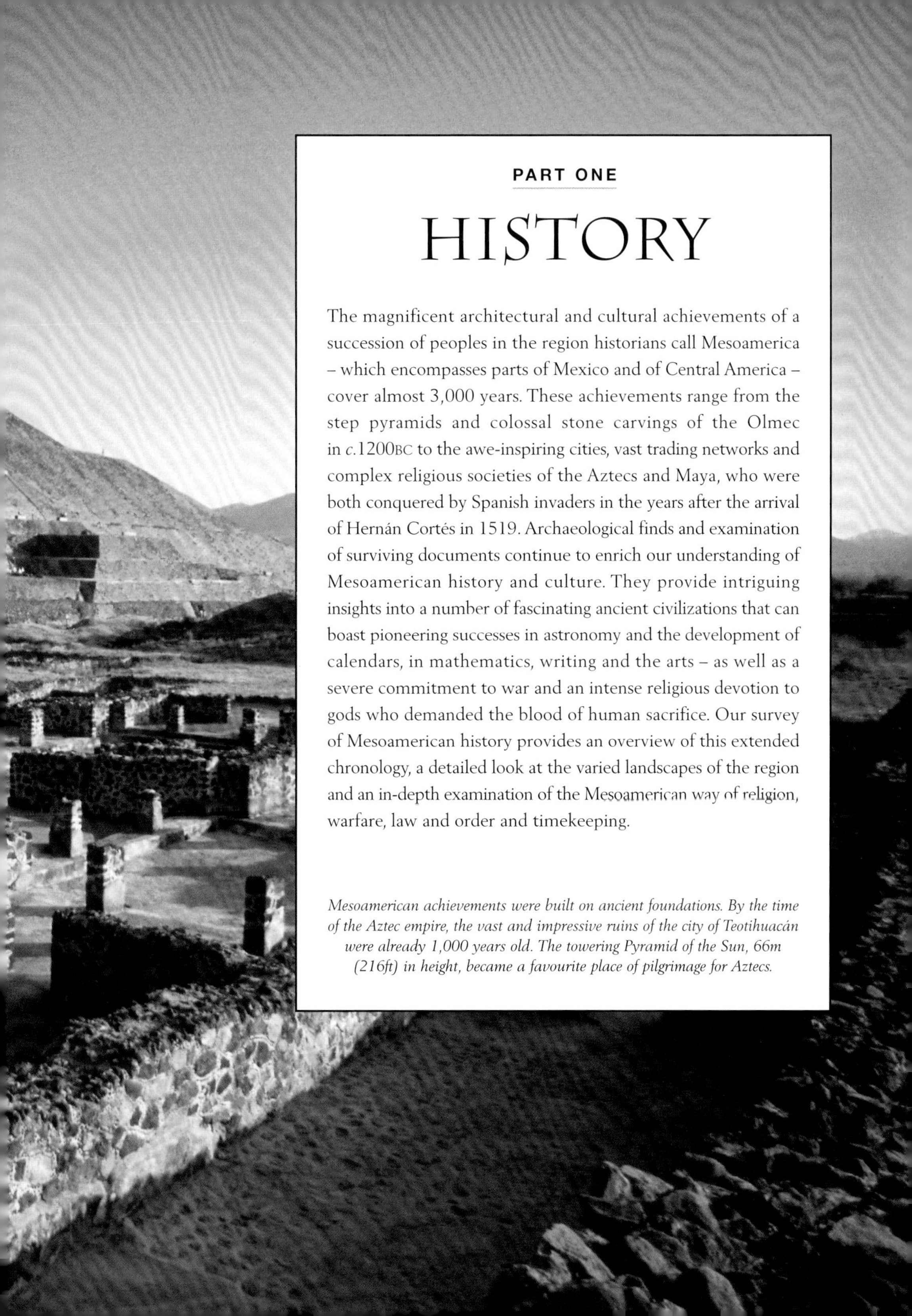

PART ONE

HISTORY

The magnificent architectural and cultural achievements of a succession of peoples in the region historians call Mesoamerica – which encompasses parts of Mexico and of Central America – cover almost 3,000 years. These achievements range from the step pyramids and colossal stone carvings of the Olmec in *c.*1200BC to the awe-inspiring cities, vast trading networks and complex religious societies of the Aztecs and Maya, who were both conquered by Spanish invaders in the years after the arrival of Hernán Cortés in 1519. Archaeological finds and examination of surviving documents continue to enrich our understanding of Mesoamerican history and culture. They provide intriguing insights into a number of fascinating ancient civilizations that can boast pioneering successes in astronomy and the development of calendars, in mathematics, writing and the arts – as well as a severe commitment to war and an intense religious devotion to gods who demanded the blood of human sacrifice. Our survey of Mesoamerican history provides an overview of this extended chronology, a detailed look at the varied landscapes of the region and an in-depth examination of the Mesoamerican way of religion, warfare, law and order and timekeeping.

Mesoamerican achievements were built on ancient foundations. By the time of the Aztec empire, the vast and impressive ruins of the city of Teotihuacán were already 1,000 years old. The towering Pyramid of the Sun, 66m (216ft) in height, became a favourite place of pilgrimage for Aztecs.

TIMELINE OF MESOAMERICA

ARCHAIC AND PRECLASSIC PERIODS TO AD250

Above: Stepped temple-pyramids at Monte Albán give on to a large plaza.

21,000BC Hunter-gatherers enter the New World across the Bering Strait and a few thousand years later live in the Valley of Mexico near where the Aztecs will build their capital, Tenochtitlán.

7000–5000BC Mesoamerican settlers develop farming skills and domesticate wild plants – including maize.

2500–1500BC The first farming villages in Mesoamerica appear. Settlers raise maize, chilli peppers, squash and cotton.

1500–1200BC Olmecs build San Lorenzo.

1350BC A major urban settlement is built at San José Mogote.

1100BC A second Olmec city is built at La Venta.

1000BC The Ocós and Cuadros village-farming cultures thrive on the Pacific coast of Guatemala.

900BC The Olmec site of San Lorenzo is destroyed.

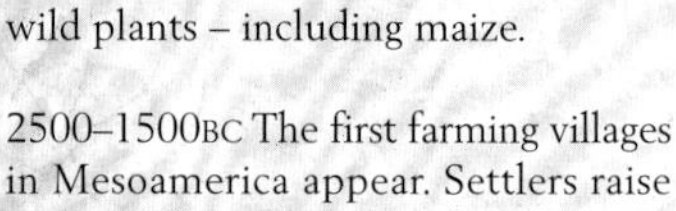

800BC Settlers build the first villages in the lowland Maya region.

600BC Carving on a monument at San José Mogote may be the earliest Mesoamerican writing.

*c.*600–400BC Maya build a living and ceremonial centre at Nakbé.

*c.*500BC Zapotecs build Monte Albán.

*c.*400BC The Olmec site of La Venta, on the Gulf coast, is destroyed. In the Valley of Mexico, Cuicuilco becomes an important city.

300BC Decline sets in at Nakbé.

300BC–AD100 Maya craftsmen build ceremonial and living centres at Tikal and Uaxactún, northern Guatemala.

*c.*100BC Volcanic eruption drives settlers from Cuicuilco, Valley of Mexico, to the city of Teotihuacán.

36BC The earliest Pre-Maya Long Count inscription is carved at Chiapa de Corzo in the Chiapas region of southern Mexico.

AD150 The Pyramid of the Sun is built at Teotihuacán.

AD199 The Hauberg stela, the earliest piece of writing in the Maya system, is carved.

AD200 The Zapotecs are at the peak of their powers.

CLASSIC PERIOD C.AD250–900

Above: Temples at Palenque stand in the forested foothills of the Sierra Madre.

c. AD300–650 Peak of Maya building: pyramids, temples and ballcourts are put up in many Maya lowland cities.

c. AD350 Teotihuacán becomes the pre-eminent Mesoamerican city.

c. AD400 Copán expands from a farming settlement to a major city.

c. AD750 Northern tribes sack Teotihuacán.

AD700–900 Decline in Maya lowlands is perhaps caused by overpopulation.

AD799 Last stela carved in Palenque.

c. AD800 Murals painted at Bonampak.

AD820 Last dated stela is put up at Copán.

AD879 Last dated stela at Tikal.

c. AD850–950 Many Maya centres in Guatemala and Mexico are abandoned.

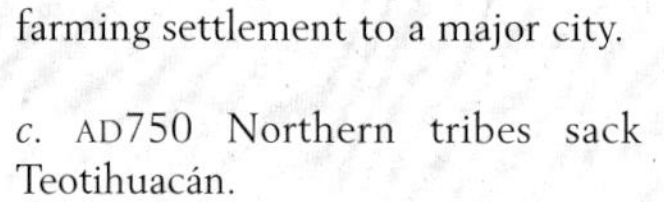

POSTCLASSIC PERIOD AD900–1521

AD 900–950 The Toltecs build their capital at Tula.

*c.*1000 Mixtec people carry out royal burials at Monte Albán.

*c.*1150 The city of Tula is destroyed by Chichimec tribesmen.

*c.*1200 The Méxica/Aztecs make their way southward into the Valley of Mexico.

1263 The city of Mayapán is founded.

1325 The Méxica/Aztecs found the city of Tenochtitlán.

Below: Toltec stone warriors at Tollán were originally painted in bright colours.

1375 Acamapichtli, the first historical ruler of the Méxica/Aztecs, is elected *tlatoani* ('speaker') in Tenochtitlán.

1428 The cities of Tenochtitlán, Texcoco and Tlacopán form the Triple Alliance and begin to build the Aztec Empire.

1441 Mayapán falls and is abandoned.

1481 The Aztec Sun Stone is erected in Tenochtitlán.

1487 Ahuitzol, *tlatoani* in Tenochtitlán, oversees the rededication of the city's Great Temple.

1492 Spanish explorers land in the West Indies.

1502 Christopher Columbus meets Maya traders in the Gulf of Honduras.

1502 Moctezuma II, the last independent Aztec ruler, becomes *tlatoani* in Tenochtitlán.

1507 A new 52-year cycle begins for the Aztecs with a New Fire ceremony.

1517 The first of three Spanish exploratory missions to Mesoamerica from Cuba is led by Francisco Hernández de Córdoba.

1519 Spanish explorers, led by Hernán Cortés, land in Mexico.

1521 Tenochtitlán falls to Cortés and his Spanish troops on 13 August after a siege of 93 days.

Above: The Aztec Sun Stone is an ancient calendar revealing much about the past.

1523–4 Spanish under Pedro de Alvarado conquer southern Maya lands in the highlands of Chiapas and in southern Guatemala.

*c.*1550 Members of the nobility among the Quiché, a group of southern Maya, secretly translate the Maya sacred book *Popol Vuh* ('Book of Advice') into the Roman alphabet in a bid to save it from the book-burning zeal of Spanish monks.

1566 Bishop Diego de Landa completes his *Report of Things of Yucatán*.

1569 Friar Bernardino de Sahagún completes his *General History of the Things of New Spain*.

1697 The last independent Maya centre – at Tayasal, on an island in Lake Flores, Guatemala – falls to the Spanish.

1703 Quiché-speaking Franciscan friar Francisco Ximenez finds *Popol Vuh* and translates it into Spanish.

1790 The Aztec Sun Stone is discovered in Mexico City.

CHAPTER ONE

3,000 YEARS OF CIVILIZATION

Civilization was born in the lands of Mesoamerica when the region's early farmers began to settle in villages around 2500–1500BC. The ancestors of these first villagers had spent perhaps 5,000 years in more or less nomadic farming and many millennia as hunter-gatherers. However, they took very quickly to the settled life and within a few centuries a major culture had arisen in the fertile, low-lying lands of Veracruz and Tabasco, adjoining the Gulf of Mexico. The creators of the Olmec civilization produced corn, squashes and other foodstuffs in such quantities that they could divert their energies into building and artistic activities. At La Venta and San Lorenzo they left behind large and impressive ceremonial centres and enigmatic carvings in stone. They laid the foundations for the great Mesoamerican civilization that would follow them: their pyramids, open plazas and rites of human sacrifice can all be found among the Zapotec, Teotihuacano, Toltec, Maya and Aztec societies that came in their wake. Other aspects of Mesoamerican religious and cultural life, including a deep reverence for the fleet-footed jaguar, were also first seen in Olmec lands. The essentials of a civilization that would endure for 3,000 years until the sudden and bloody arrival from the east of Hernán Cortés appear to have been laid in just a few hundred years by the inventive Olmec.

Left: Grass and stunted trees grow at high altitude beneath the vast, magnificent Popocatépetl. Rising 5,452m (17,900ft) above sea level, the volcano dominates the Valley of Mexico, where a succession of Mesoamerican cultures flourished.

THE BIRTH OF THE OLMEC

The first inhabitants of Mexico were probably descendants of Siberian immigrants to North America. Scholars do not know for sure when the first nomads arrived in the region we call Mesoamerica, but radiocarbon dating of bone fragments found at Tlapacoya (south-east of Mexico City) proves that by 21,000BC people were living in a region close to where the Aztecs would construct their magnificent capital city, Tenochtitlán.

EARLY INHABITANTS

For another 14,000 years, these early Mesoamericans lived as hunter-gatherers. The climate in the region was cooler than today's, and large herds of grazing animals thrived on lush grassland vegetation. Around 7000–5000BC, the settlers began to develop farming skills, gradually domesticating the plants that they had gathered in the wild. One of these in particular would become crucial to Mesoamerican civilization. A wild cereal of the region, maize, became the staple food over many centuries of selective breeding. Settlers had domesticated this grass by 5000BC.

A major climate change may have encouraged this change of lifestyle for the Mesoamerican settlers. Around 7000BC, temperatures rose worldwide and in Central America many grassland areas gave way either to desert or to tropical jungle. Animals were fewer and hunting became more difficult, so people turned to more intensive food cultivation.

People in the 'New World' of the Americas began to cultivate food in roughly the same era as the first farmers in the 'Old World' of the Near East and Europe, but in some ways the Mesoamericans had a harder time of it. Where the Old World farmers had cows, pigs and sheep, the peoples of Mesoamerica had only small dogs and turkeys to supplement the meat and fish they hunted. Another major difference was that the Mesoamericans had to manage without beasts of burden – they had no oxen or horses and did not even use the llamas and other camelids that were animal pack-carriers for the peoples of the central Andes who developed the Inca civilization. Partly as a result of this, Mesoamericans did not develop wheeled vehicles. Although small wheeled objects have been found in graves, it is clear that the early Mesoamericans did not have the benefit of animal-drawn vehicles or even handcarts for moving food and materials.

Over many centuries, these early farmers gradually abandoned their nomadic existence. By the time that the first Mesoamerican villages appeared, about 2000–1500BC, the farmers were raising crops of corn, chilli peppers, squashes and cotton. They were using flint knives, stone axes and very sharp cutting blades made from the volcanic rock obsidian, inhabiting thatched cane huts, weaving cloth, making pottery and fashioning evocative female figures thought to be images of an archaic fertility goddess. They appear to have lived essentially as equals in self-contained

Above: Six monoliths and 16 figures, made of jade and serpentine, were buried in this position as an offering by Olmec worshippers.

Below: This Olmec stone from La Venta was probably a royal throne. The carving above the ruler's head is of a jaguar pelt.

settlements. Then, in about 1500–1200BC, the first major Mesoamerican civilization was born in the jungles of Mexico's southern Gulf coast.

THE RISE OF THE OLMEC

Labourers built awe-inspiring ceremonial centres on the banks of the region's slow-moving rivers. In the Veracruz rainforest, at San Lorenzo, men working with handbaskets raised a towering earthen platform 45m (150ft) high, topped by a cone-shaped earthen mound, by *c.*1200BC. At La Venta, around 50km (30 miles) downriver towards the coast, they built an earthen pyramid mound 32m (106ft) high and a ceremonial plaza in *c.*1000BC. The San Lorenzo complex contained the earliest stone drainage system to have been discovered in the Americas.

Craftsmen carved remarkable stone heads up to 3m (10ft) in height. These ancient works of art have characteristic flattened faces, thick lips and headgear reminiscent of a helmet. Their creation is a matter of enduring wonder. To make the carvings found at San Lorenzo, stone-cutters and labourers transported huge rocks on sledges and water-rafts over 80km (50 miles) from the Tuxtla Mountains.

The people behind these astonishing achievements lived in a more hierarchical society than their immediate ancestors. Scholars believe that the vast stone heads they carved were a homage to their rulers. Great armies of labourers were needed to build their vast ceremonial centres.

Below: The priest in this Olmec carving wears a jaguar helmet. The Olmec revered the jaguar as the supreme predator.

This ancient culture is now called Olmec from the Aztec word for the area in which it originated. The Olmecs developed a wide-ranging trading network. At its height, their civilization had a very wide sphere of influence. Olmec-style grave objects have been found in the north-western area of Mexico City, while stone carvings exhibiting an Olmec influence were made some 1,200km (750 miles) to the south in El Salvador. However, there is no evidence that there was an Olmec empire and the civilization gradually faded in the early part of the first millennium BC. The site at San Lorenzo was destroyed in 900BC and, within 100 years, Olmec cultural and stylistic influences began to wane, although they would continue to survive for many years. The culture's full span was probably *c.*1500–*c.*400BC.

Above: Olmec sacred buildings had a major influence on those erected by their Mesoamerican descendants, such as this pyramid at the Maya site of Uaxactún.

The Olmec had lasting influence, for they bequeathed many distinctive religious ideas and practices to their descendants in the region. They developed religious rites involving human sacrifice and blood-letting, pioneered the use of ceremonial centres and invented the ball game that would remain popular right through Aztec times. They propounded the idea that the universe was divided into four directions and often carved a divine figure that combines the features of a human baby with those of a jaguar. Some scholars claim the Olmec may also have invented the writing system later developed by Mesoamerican peoples, notably the Maya. Archaeologists examining Olmec works of art have identified more than 180 symbols that may have been used as glyphs.

THE ZAPOTEC AND THE MAYA

The distinction of developing the Mesoamerican writing system is more often claimed for the Zapotec people of the Oaxaca Valley who, less than 200km (125 miles) from the centre of Olmec power, established a distinctive civilization that endured for more than 1,000 years. At the height of Olmec influence, in about 1350BC, the peoples of southern Mexico near the modern city of Oaxaca constructed a ceremonial and possibly living centre at San José Mogote. They were clearly engaged in trade with the Olmec region, for archaeologists in San José have found turtle-shell drums and conch-shell trumpets from as far north and east as the Gulf of Mexico.

Above: From early days rival Maya leaders won respect through warfare. Soldiers fought at close quarters with spears and darts.

DAILY LIFE

By *c.*1000BC, the settlement's central area covered almost 50 acres (20 hectares) and boasted imposing temples and tall platforms of stone. What we know of religious and daily life at San José indicates that the city's inhabitants shared many features with the Olmec and engaged in practices that would characterize Mesoamerican culture for centuries to come. Finds of fish spines suggest that they practised blood sacrifice, for these objects are known to have been used at Maya sites for the sacred rites of autosacrifice – the letting of a person's own blood. They were also – like the Olmec – initiates of the cult of the jaguar. They made pottery that was decorated with the distinctive jaguar imagery that is associated with shamanism and Aztec worship of Tezcatlipoca. They understood the importance of measuring and marking the passage of time and, by *c.*600BC, they had begun to cut calendar symbols and early hieroglyphs at the site.

Below: The Zapotec were keen traders. This incense vase may have been made for sale or exchange with the people of Teotihuacán.

MONTE ALBÁN

Around 500BC, the peoples of the Oaxaca region built a major centre at Monte Albán. Labourers carried out vast earthworks to construct a flattened mountaintop 1km (3/5 mile) in length, raising stone pyramids, temples and

Below: A stepped pyramid at Monte Albán gives on to a large plaza. The city has a ball court, and 170 tombs have been found there.

Right: In later years Maya lands stretched from Palenque in the west to Mayapán and Uxmal in the north and Copán in the east.

palaces around a vast ceremonial plaza. The site, which commands a magnificent view over the valleys below, was almost certainly built as a symbol of local power. It may have been occupied only by the political and religious elite, while the bulk of the population lived below in the valleys.

Monte Albán grew rapidly. By 200BC as many as 15,000 people lived there. Buildings spread on to painstakingly terraced lands on adjoining hills. At the height of the city's size and prestige in the period 200BC–AD200 there were 15 residential areas, each with its own plaza. Scholars do not know for sure who founded Monte Albán, but by 200BC it was occupied and controlled by the Zapotec people, who had risen to pre-eminence in the region. Monte Albán thrived as the Zapotec capital for another 1,000 years. Its people traded with the merchants of the more powerful city of Teotihuacán to the north-west.

By the 8th century AD, 25,000 people lived in Monte Albán, but in the following century the city, which had endured for more than a millennium, declined rapidly in power. The city – or its Zapotec elite – lost its hold over the people, who appear to have spread into surrounding communities.

THE MAYA

While the culture of the Olmec and Zapotec and of Teotihuacán was blooming in central Mexico, another great civilization was flowering in the jungles to the south and east, in lands that now form south-eastern and eastern Mexico, Guatemala and Belize.

Little is known of the earliest history of the Maya, partly because the tropical lands they occupied did not provide a good base in which archaeological remains could survive. But we know that village settlements with clear cultural connections to the later Maya way of life had been established by the second millennium BC on the Pacific coast of Guatemala close to the Mexican border.

Village farmers established settlements in the southern highland and central lowland regions of what were later to be the Maya homelands in the centuries after 800BC. Curiously, they do not appear to have been dominated or even influenced by the powerful Olmec culture of Mexico, perhaps because as essentially peasant villages they were not drawn into trade or cultural exchange. The Maya began to build larger ceremonial and urban settlements by *c*.600BC–400BC and in the four centuries after 300BC, many of the villages expanded into notable settlements as the culture thrived. A village at Tikal, in the tropical rainforest of northern Guatemala, became an important ceremonial centre. Its builders erected temples and pyramids in the years 300BC–AD100. Ceremonial buildings were also put up at Uaxactún, 20km (12 miles) to the north, before AD100. They contain giant masks that suggest a definite Olmec influence. A great city was built at El Mirador just to the north of Nakbé, with vast limestone temple pyramids on huge basalt bases.

TEOTIHUACÁN: CITY OF THE GODS

In the 1st century BC, a new power arose in the Valley of Mexico. Unknown builders laid out a magnificent city at a site 50km (30 miles) north-east of Lake Texcoco, where the Aztecs would build their capital, Tenochtitlán. The imposing ruins at Teotihuacán so overwhelmed the Aztecs that they incorporated the site into their mythology as the place where the sun and moon were created at the beginning of the current era, the 'fifth sun'. They named it Teotihuacán ('The Place of the Gods'). Historians use the name 'Teotihuacanos' for the unidentified people who built Teotihuacán.

TWO CENTRES

The inhabitants of the Valley of Mexico thrived through trade with the great Olmec civilization, exchanging highly prized local green obsidian and other goods for exotic bird feathers and sea shells. In the first millennium BC the population of the Valley grew rapidly and two centres were established, at Teotihuacán and at Cuicuilco in the south-western part of the Valley, in an area now covered by southern Mexico City.

But Cuicuilco had an unhappy destiny, for it was situated close to an active volcano. In *c.*100BC the volcano erupted, destroying buildings and burying the fertile agricultural lands around the city beneath rock. This natural disaster sent waves of refugees travelling north-east from the wasteland of Cuicuilco. Teotihuacán, made rich by trade in obsidian and its position on a mercantile route between the Valley of Mexico and the Gulf of Mexico, was able to take them in and the city expanded very rapidly.

PLANNED GROWTH

By AD1 Teotihuacán had upwards of 40,000 inhabitants, and it had as many as 100,000–200,000 in AD500. At this point it covered more than 20sq km (8sq miles) and was one of the largest cities in the world – far larger than the London of that era. Remarkably, its growth was not haphazard, for its architects followed an established layout to create a landscape of manmade foothills and mountains with a powerful symbolic meaning for Mesoamerican peoples. Scholars believe that it was built on a site of ancient

Above: The carved head of the Plumed Serpent Quetzalcóatl adorns the pyramid built in his honour at Teotihuacán.

Below: The awe-inspiring Pyramid of the Moon in Teotihuacán measures 130m by 156m (426ft by 511ft) around its base.

Right: The doorway of this Maya temple at Hochob, Campeche, represents the mouth of a monster. Carvings of human figures are visible on the roof.

religious significance that may have been a place of pilgrimage long before the construction of the towering Pyramid of the Sun and Pyramid of the Moon and many centuries before the awe-inspiring Street of the Dead was laid out.

The people of Teotihuacán appear to have been cosmopolitan and to have thrived as much by trade as by war. Around two-thirds of the vast population farmed the fields that surrounded the urban development, while others worked as potters or carved tools, ornaments and weapons from the volcanic glass obsidian.

They may not have been known for their military prowess, but the Teotihuacanos engaged in religious practices that were bloodthirsty in the extreme and had a lasting effect on the rites of the Maya and Aztecs. At its height, the Teotihuacanos' influence was felt throughout Mesoamerica and left an enduring symbolic legacy in the creation of an evocative city of the divine that was to be a place of pilgrimage and worship for generations of Aztecs.

MAYA EXPANSION AND COLLAPSE

In this era, in the lands to the south and east of Teotihuacán's sphere of influence, the Maya continued to thrive. The 650 years after *c.*AD250 – the era dubbed the Classic Period by scholars – saw the Maya culture at its zenith. Important settlements were founded or expanded at Chichén Itzá, Copán, Uxmal and Palenque. At the height of the Classic Period of Maya civilization there were more than 40 Maya cities, with populations of between 5,000 and 50,000 in each, giving a total of perhaps two million people. Most of these lived in the area known as the Maya lowlands, now in Guatemala.

Maya city-states existed in a state of almost constant conflict. Each had its ruling family and these dynasties made and broke alliances with rival rulers as the demands of conflict dictated. At the same time, Maya civilization produced a magnificent flowering of culture that produced imposing temples, pyramids and palaces, advanced irrigation systems, a sophisticated calendar for timekeeping, elegant mathematics, detailed astronomical science and a highly developed writing system.

Around the 9th century AD, the great Maya lowland cities were suddenly abandoned. Scholars are still debating what caused this sudden change and why Maya cities situated further north in the Yucatán peninsula such as Chichén Itzá and Uxmal continued to thrive.

Right: Maya cities such as Uxmal in Yucatán continued to thrive at the time of the great Maya 'collapse' in lands further south.

THE MIXTECS AND THE TOLTECS

The glory of Teotihuacán was not destined to last forever and the city's very grandeur may have contributed to its downfall. Its inhabitants laid waste to large areas of countryside to manufacture the lime needed for the mortar and stucco used in Teotihuacán's fine buildings. This may have caused erosion and reduced the amount of land available for agriculture. When food was short, a severe drought or other natural disaster may have been enough to undermine the once-unchallengeable authority of Teotihuacán's rulers. Parts of the city's complex were torched, perhaps by angry Teotihuacanos, perhaps by outsiders. At some point in the 7th or 8th centuries AD, nomads poured south into the Valley of Mexico, probably driven by changes in the climate of northern Mesoamerica that made a farmer's lifestyle unsustainable. Teotihuacán was too weak to repel them.

Above: The Plumed Serpent Quetzalcóatl, a Toltec and an Aztec deity, protects this back-shield worn by a Toltec nobleman.

Below: A beautifully fashioned gold and turquoise disc bears witness to the Mixtecs' high reputation for working precious metals.

A POWER VACUUM

The collapse of the city, which had stood proud and pre-eminent for many centuries, created a power vacuum in which various groups competed for position. One group, the Mixtecs, rose to prominence in the Oaxaca Valley, settling and flourishing in the Zapotecs' former centre at Monte Albán. As well as winning a reputation for martial prowess, the Mixtecs made a name as refined craftsmen, excelling as potters, mosaic artists and goldsmiths.

THE TOLTECS

To the north-west, the Toltecs became a pre-eminent group. In about AD950 they founded the city of Tollán ('the Place of the Reeds') near modern Tula, about 80km (50 miles) north of the site of the later Aztec capital of Tenochtitlán. The Aztecs later viewed the Toltecs with great reverence, mythologizing them as tall, peerless warriors, ruthless conquerors, pioneers of the finest arts and sciences, developers of the Aztec calendar and year count, writers of just and lasting laws. In the Aztec account they were led in their southward expansion by Mixcóatl ('Cloud Serpent') whose son Topiltzin became identified with the god Quetzalcóatl and presided at Tollán over a city of wonderful architecture, a peaceful golden era of magnificent artistic progress, before being tricked and driven out by the warrior devotees of the war god Tezcatlipoca.

TOLLÁN

In reality, the city of Tollán was far less grand than its predecessor Teotihuacán. The exact position of Tollán was unknown for many years – indeed the Aztecs at some points identified Teotihuacán as the urban centre of the revered Toltec forebears. However, an archaeological site near Tula was identified as the remains of the Toltecs' principal city by Mexican archaeologist Jimenez Moreno in 1941. His work and further excavations have established that Tollán grew to be a centre of great importance and some size, but even at its height it was home to no more than 30,000 people, less than one-sixth of Teotihuacán's estimated population peak of some 200,000.

A MARTIAL PEOPLE

The Toltecs engaged in trade with distant regions, notably in turquoise with parts of what is now the southern USA, but they were also a martial race who, through war, expanded their territories to include the

Above: Toltec stone warriors, which stand impressively on a pyramid in Tollán (Tula), were originally painted in bright colours.

bulk of the modern Mexican state of Hidalgo and the northern areas of the Valley of Mexico. Within their empire, the Toltecs settled a number of tribute areas, where garrisons kept the peace and oversaw the collection of produce; a pioneering development from which the Aztecs would learn a good deal.

Toltec culture, religious imagery and architecture celebrated ritual bloodshed and war: the capital is filled with warlike imagery. Forbidding stone columns carved in the shape of warriors stand atop one of the pyramids at Tollán and at one time held up the roof of the temple that stood there. The walls of the city's temples are decorated with soldiers wearing armour and shields on their backs and carrying spear-throwers and clumps of darts.

The temples are also adorned with gruesome *chacmools* – reclining stone figures with a bowl on the stomach in which the heart of a sacrificial victim was flung – and also contain skull racks on which heads were displayed. Scholars see in the fiercely militaristic culture of the Toltecs a reflection of a demanding political reality; a world in which tribal groups had to compete desperately for land, scarce resources and trade.

Right: Stone carvings featuring Toltec-style death's-head decorations are found in the Maya city of Chichén Itzá in Yucatán.

THE COLLAPSE OF TOLLÁN

A highly competitive environment lay behind the collapse of Tollán. The city of the Toltecs was destroyed in the mid- to late 12th century in the era of a ruler called Huemac, of whose depravity and failings many tales were later told. Migrations of nomads from the north had continued and the Toltecs may have met their match. The city was sacked. According to later Aztec accounts, the roof columns were torn down from Quetzalcóatl's temple, the buildings were torched and the people driven out. Many Toltecs moved on, some settling elsewhere in the Valley of Mexico, others as far to the east as the Maya city of Chichén Itzá in northern Yucatán, where architectural details such as death's-head decorations echo those in Tollán.

Following Tollán's collapse, many nomadic groups known by the name of Chichimec ('Sons of the Dog') flooded into the Valley of Mexico, competing for the most fertile territories and for strategic positions. The myth of the Toltecs' golden achievements was amplified as competing groups claimed descent from the people of Tollán. Among these peoples was a small group, the Méxica or Aztecs, who would become celebrated in history as the builders of great Tenochtitlán and rulers of a glorious empire.

THE RISE OF THE AZTECS

The details of the Aztecs' origins are shrouded in myth, for this proud people told many tales that legitimized their supremacy, their use of human sacrifice and their devotion to the tribal god Huitzilopochtli. Their mythologized history told how the first Aztecs or Méxica found their origin in the island-town of Aztlán, from which they set off on a long, hazardous migration across northern landscapes, guided by Huitzilopochtli, before they came to the place on Lake Texcoco at which they were destined to found their capital, another island site identified by the divinely ordained vision of an eagle perched on a prickly cactus making a meal of a writhing serpent.

Above: A mask of Xochipilli, later worshipped by the Aztecs as the god of flowers, was found at Teotihuacán.

NAMING THE AZTECS

The founders of Tenochtitlán had three names in their original language, Nahuatl: Aztecs, Méxica and Tenochcas. According to the chronicler Hernando Alvarado de Tezozómoc, they were known as Aztecs because of their place of origin, the mysterious island-city of Aztlán (meaning perhaps 'White Land' or 'Land of the Cranes'), which has never been identified. The second name, Méxica, was given to the wandering tribes by their patron god Huitzilopochtli, and scholars believe it either comes from Méxi, one of the god's secret titles, or derives from Metzliapán ('Moon Lake'), a name for Lake Texcoco. The tribe was also called Tenochnas after Tenoch, the ruler who led it under the guidance of Huitzilopochtli in the final parts of its wandering journey. The name of their capital, Tenochtitlán, came from Tenocha while the divinely delivered appellation, the Méxica, gave its name to the great metropolis of Mexico City that grew on that site and to the country of Mexico itself.

The founders of the empire based on Tenochtitlán called themselves 'Méxica' and were known by this name by their Spanish conquerors. But scholars brought the name Aztec back into use in the 18th and 19th centuries and it is now the generic title for all the tribes of the Valley of Mexico in the era of the Spanish Conquest. In this book, 'Méxica' is used where it is necessary to distinguish the people of Tenochtitlán from other tribes in the Valley of Mexico, but otherwise 'Aztec' is used to discuss the achievements and governance of the empire and the culture shared by these people.

WANDERINGS

The Méxica wandered throughout the 12th and 13th centuries in search of a safe place to put down roots. It was a lawless time; scholars compare the southward incursions of Chichimec groups that followed the fall and collapse of Toltec civilization to the waves of barbarians that took advantage of the collapse of the western Roman empire in 5th-century Europe. A group of Chichimec – said to be led by a ruler named Xólotl, who is probably a legendary figure or a conflation of several

Left: The Toltecs cast a long shadow. Many details in the Maya city of Chichén Itzá suggest Toltec influence or conquest.

Above: The Codex Boturini, *an Aztec account of their travels, depicts ancestors leaving their original homeland, Aztlán.*

historical rulers – established themselves in the Valley of Mexico, first at Tenayuca and later at Texcoco, and formed an alliance with dispersed members of the Toltecs who were settled at Culhuacán. A group named the Tepanecs intermingled with the inhabitants of the Valley of Mexico and settled at Azcapotzalco near Lake Texcoco. The migrations of a third group, named the Acolhua, led them to eastern regions of the Valley.

The Méxica's mythical account of their origins has it that in this period they were temporarily settled in ruins near Tula or, in some accounts, Teotihuacán. Here they learned the skills of irrigation and agriculture and developed the religious culture, including sun worship and human sacrifice, under which they later thrived. But Huitzilopochtli, diviner of the tribe's destiny, would not let them settle there and set them once more on their wanderings.

Toward the end of the 13th century, the Méxica passed to the west of Lake Texcoco and settled at Chapultepec near some highly prized springs in a region under the control of the city of Culhuacán. The people of Azcapotzalco and Culhuacán attacked the incomers to safeguard their control of the spring waters and sacrificed the Méxica leader. The Méxica threw themselves on the protection of Culhuacán and were allowed to settle in the stony area of Tizapán, which was infested with poisonous snakes. Here their presence was tolerated and they stayed for perhaps a quarter-century, using all their growing agricultural skills to raise crops in the unfriendly landscape and, according to one account, roasting the snakes to supplement their meals.

SETTLEMENT

The Méxica intermarried with the locals and began to call themselves Méxica-Culhua to emphasize their connection with that city's Toltec inheritance. They won honour in battle supporting the Culhua against nearby Xochimilco. However, in 1323, after a dramatic fallout with one of Culhuacán's leading nobles, they were forced to move on and to explore Lake Texcoco's marshes. Two years later, on an island around 3km (2 miles) out in the lake surrounded by marshes, they founded their new settlement, the future capital of a glorious empire that would be blessed by the bloodthirsty gods with wealth and enduring fame.

Above: The first pages of the Aztecs' Codex Boturini *detail their long migration across Mexico before founding Tenochtitlán.*

THE TWIN CITIES

Shortly after establishing Tenochtitlán, the Méxica founded a second settlement, Tlatelolco, on another island nearby. For around 30 years, the Mexica developed their twin towns, trading with their neighbours and perfecting the science of building the *chinampa*, or artificial islands called 'floating gardens'. With careful irrigation these produced invaluable crops. The two Méxica cities strengthened their links with the most powerful local peoples in an astute manner.

A SOCIAL CONTRACT

Tezozómoc, the brilliant Tepanec empire builder and military ruler of Azacoalco, cast a long shadow and, in the times of high tension following his death, the people of Tenochtitlán were understandably nervous about waging war against the Azcapotzalcans.

The warrior Tlacaélel delivered a declaration of war to the Azcapotzalcán leader Maxtla but, according to Méxica accounts, the news was not well received by all at home. A public debate brought the warriors, who wished to pursue the war, into conflict with the common people, who wanted to avoid the risk of defeat. The warriors, it is said, then made a remarkable pledge in an attempt to win popular support for an attack on Maxtla. 'If we fail', they declared, 'we are yours to feast on. You will be able to slice our bodies limb from limb and eat us in your dinner pots. The war will be lost but there will be food in plenty.' This moved the people to give their agreement. 'Let it be so,' they said,'and we will pledge that if you deliver victory in this fearful encounter we will honour you with tribute. You will be our lords. We will serve you in the sweat of our bodies and build you fine houses.'

The story legitimizes the increasing social hierarchy that accompanied changes in granting land following victory over the Azcapotzalcán leader Maxtla and the establishment of the Triple Alliance. The warriors' offer of themselves for self-sacrifice reflects the fact that it was considered an honour to be sacrificed if defeated in war and a shame to be spared or kept as a prisoner.

THE RISE OF THE AZTECS

TLATOANI 'HE WHO SPEAKS'

The chieftain at the time of the foundation of the twin cities was Tenoch. He lived for many years after 1325. He was identified as *tlatoani* ('He Who Speaks') and this was the title of the supreme ruler of the Méxica/Aztecs until the fall of the empire. Following Tenoch's death, the Méxica of Tenochtitlán approached the leaders of Culhuacán to ask for one of the nobles of that city, Acamapichtli, to become *tlatoani* of Tenochtitlán. There had been intermarriage between Méxica and Culhua when the Méxica were living near Culhualcán at Tizapán, and Acamapichtli was descended from both Culhua and Méxica families. At the same time, the Méxica of Tlatelolco asked for the son of a Tepanec ruler of Azcapotzalco to become their lord. Acamapichtli and the Tepanec prince were both installed as rulers with full ritual and ceremony in 1375.

Above: With Huitzilopochtli and Tezcatlipoca, the Plumed Serpent Quetzalcóatl was foremost among Aztec deities.

A SUCCESSION OF RULERS

Under the leadership of Acamapichtli, who legitimized his rule by claiming descent from the blessed Topiltzin-Quetzalcóatl of Tollán, the Méxica started to take a more significant part in local political events. During this period, Azcapotzalco, the Tepanec city-state, was ruled by Tezozómoc, who built up an empire through ruthless military skill and a genius for intrigue. The Méxica people began by serving as mercenaries for Tezozómoc in his struggles against the Chichimec of Texcoco and against the Toltec of Culhualcán. In time, they built up a measure of independent power, and even expanded their territories by managing to gain *chinampa* lands in the area of Lake Xochimilco to the south of Lake Texcoco.

Acamapichtli was ruler until 1396 and he became the founder of a dynasty in Tenochtitlán, while his younger sons and favoured followers established a ruling class in the city. He was succeeded by his son Huitzilíhuitl although, in keeping with ancient tradition, Huitzilíhuitl was elected by a council of elders rather than simply by accession to his father's place. Huitzilíhuitl strengthened the Méxica's ties to Tepanec by marrying a granddaughter of Tezozómoc. They continued to fight as vassals in Tepanec wars and were rewarded with grants of land, notably after wars against Xaltocán.

In the years leading up to 1426, the Méxica made a significant advance in power and status. They fought alongside Tezozómoc against the city-state of Texcoco. The Texcocan leader Ixtlilxóchitl was forced to abandon his city and flee to the mountains, where he was killed as his young son Netzahualcóyotl looked on.

In the same year, the death of Tezozómoc further changed the balance of power in the region. Tezozómoc was succeeded, after a reign of 55 years, by his less able son Maxtla, sparking

Left: An Aztec eagle carving celebrates Tenochtitlán's foundation in 1325. The Aztecs were told they would know they had found the right spot to settle when they saw an eagle on a cactus clasping a serpent.

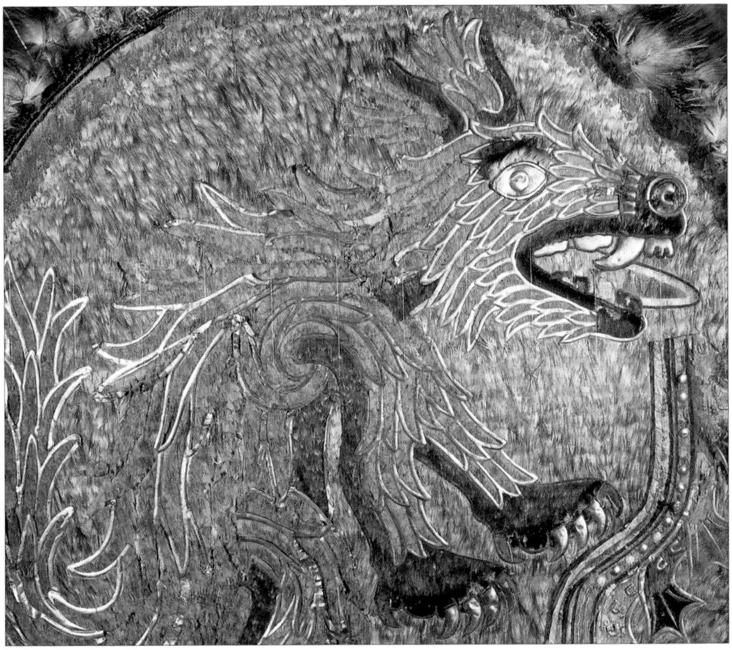

Above: The animal on this Aztec shield of c.1500 may be a coyote, a fierce creature associated with warriors and warfare.

a number of conflicts between Méxica and Tepanec that led to the assassination of Chimalpopoca, ruler of Tenochtitlán. Tensions rose to breaking point between the two cities. Maxtla prepared for war and demanded tribute from his Méxica neighbours, while opinion was sharply divided in Tenochtitlán about the wisdom of provoking the might of Azcapotzalco.

In the end the Méxica, now led by Itzcóatl, formed a coalition of sufficient might to let them defeat Maxtla. Netzahualcóyotl, the Texcocan prince who had witnessed the slaughter of his father was prominent in this grouping. He led a force from Huexotzingo to the southeast, where he had twice fled for his life from Tepanec attacks. Another significant coalition member was the Tepanec town of Tlacopán, which rose up and took part in the revolt against Azcapotzalco. After a siege of 114 days, Azcapotzalco fell and Maxtla was captured. The historian Fernando de Alva Ixtlilxóchitl reports that the defeated ruler was hauled from his place of refuge in a ritual sweat-bath and handed over to Netzahualcóyotl, who dispatched him by cutting out his heart in sacrifice.

Below: The Plumed Serpent Quetzalcóatl was one of many gods the Aztecs inherited from their forerunners in Mesoamerica.

THE TRIPLE ALLIANCE

The Tepanec empire created by Tezozómoc was no more. The three main players in the victorious coalition – Tenochtitlán, Texcoco and Tlacopán – formed a triple alliance in 1428 and divided the spoils. Tlacopán took control over land in the western region of the Valley of Mexico, Texcoco was granted much of the eastern part of the Valley, while Tenochtitlán now had power over the lands to the south and north.

This balance of power would remain essentially unchanged until the Spanish Conquest. The Aztec empire was a confederation of these three city-states, each drawing tribute from its own lands. Tenochtitlán was of prime importance: the Méxica were the largest and most significant grouping and their capital was dominant. Next in significance was the capital of the Acolhua, Texcoco, which gained a reputation for learning, goldwork, jewellery and fine picture-manuscripts. Third, but still an enduring member of the alliance, was Tlacopán.

THE COMING OF THE SPANIARDS

Moctezuma II ruled over a great empire, but he was troubled by ill portents. In 1509, ten years before the arrival of the Spanish conquistadors, a comet appeared in the skies over Lake Texcoco. According to Friar Bernardino de Sahagún, author of *General History of the Things of New Spain*, it thrust into the sky like a tongue of flame and spilled a rain of small fiery drops as if it had broken through the canopy of the heavens. The priests and astronomers either would not or could not provide an interpretation, but the Texcocan ruler Netzahualpilli, who was believed to be able to see the future, declared that terrible events lay ahead that would usher in the destruction of the cities of the lake and of their empire. Many tales were told of unhappy omens that preceded the collapse of the Aztecs – some probably seeking with the benefit of hindsight to establish the inevitability of the Spanish triumph. Yet it appears that when the Spaniards arrived, the Aztec ruler was unsettled by doubt and ill equipped for decisive action.

REPORTS OF STRANGERS

The Aztecs must surely have known of European visitors, perhaps by word of mouth through merchants, many years before the conquistadors landed in Mexico in 1519. In 1492, the Spaniards landed in the West Indies and afterwards left their mark around the region in Hispaniola, Cuba, Venezuela and Panama. In 1502, Christopher Columbus encountered Maya traders, probably near the place now known as the Bay Islands in the Gulf of Honduras. In 1508, two Spanish sailors from Seville landed in the Maya region of Yucatán and may have inspired a drawing of what appears to be three temples borne on the sea in canoes that was seen by Moctezuma and his advisers in Tenochtitlán. Three years later, several Spanish survivors of a shipwreck off Yucatán were taken prisoner by the Maya.

In 1518, a labourer came to the imperial court reporting that he had seen mountains floating on the sea – a reference to the large Spanish ships – and Moctezuma sent advisers to the coast to investigate. They discovered reports of men with long beards and fair skin, of fishing vessels and of floating mountains.

RETURN OF THE GOD?

The most intriguing aspect of these reports was the possibility that they were portents of the return of the god Quetzalcóatl, the Plumed Serpent.

Below: Cortés and his men first explored the coast, then cut boldly inland towards Popocatépetl to find the Aztec capital.

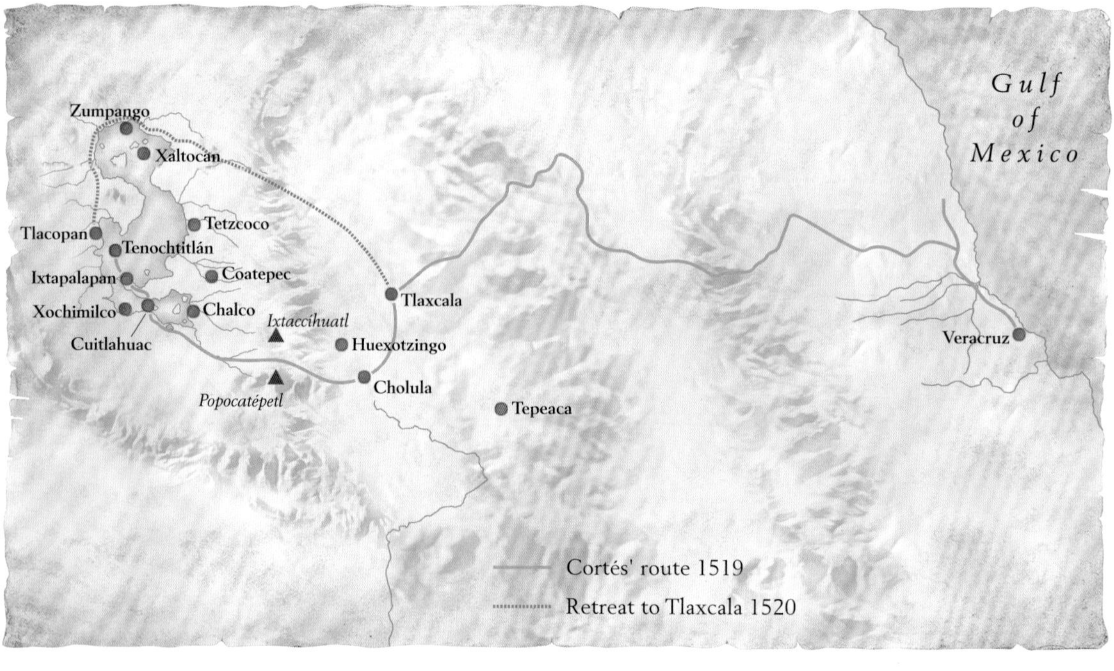

Above: A lookout sees the Spaniards near landfall in what Moctezuma's informers considered to be a 'floating mountain'.

According to myth, he had departed by sea heading east following the collapse of his power in Tollán and had vowed to return from that direction in order to usher in a new age. When Moctezuma was told in April 1519 that ships belonging to these sailors had made landfall in the region that would become Veracruz, it confirmed his impression, for they landed at the exact spot where Quetzalcóatl was said to have made his departure and vowed to make his second coming, and also came in the very year (1-Reed according to the Aztec reckoning) prophesied for the Plumed Serpent's return.

WELCOME VISITORS?

The Spanish expedition was led by Hernán Cortés and came from the Spanish colony in Cuba to explore the coast of Mexico. It was in fact the third exploratory Spanish trip from Cuba; the first, in 1517, had been led by Francisco Hernández de Córdoba and the second, in 1518, by Juan de Grijalva.

Moctezuma seems to have been uncertain whether to treat the incomers with reverence, as gods, or with violence, as invaders. First he sent supplies, together with magnificent offerings including large discs of gold and silver representing the sun and moon, and ritual costumes that had been worn by performers impersonating the gods in ceremonies at Tenochtitlán. Some of the food he sent had been ceremonially doused with the blood of a sacrificial victim as was customary in the Aztec capital. Upon the rejection of his envoys by Cortés he changed his mind and dispatched sorcerers to cast spells capable of keeping the intruders in their place. However, the Spaniards proved resistant to local magic and Cortés led them inland from the coast towards the imperial capital.

He came first to the high plateau of Tlaxcala, where the locals attempted to drive the Spaniards back but were defeated. Cortés persuaded the Tlaxcaláns, who had resisted attempts to persuade them into the Aztec empire and who were determined enemies of Tenochtitlán, to join in his campaign. The invaders came next to Cholula, which was allied to the Aztecs. As part of a plan hatched by Moctezuma, the Choluláns invited the army into the city. Hidden warriors were supposed to emerge later and put the foreigners to death. The plan was revealed to the Spaniards, however, and they slaughtered the Cholulán chiefs.

When the Spanish force and its allies came to Tenochtitlán, Moctezuma went out to meet Cortés on a palanquin carried by four noblemen and greeted the Spaniard with the utmost respect.

Below: This turquoise and shell mosaic figure formed the handle of a knife used by Aztec priests to despatch sacrificial victims.

THE COMING OF THE SPANIARDS

Moctezuma gave Cortés a necklace of snail shells and shrimps fashioned from solid gold and in return was presented with a string of Venetian glass beads. Then, in a fateful moment, he invited the Spaniards into the Aztec capital.

Above: Moctezuma presented Cortés with a splendid quetzal feather headdress like this. Priests wore these magnificent feathers when impersonating the gods during rites.

HOSTILITIES BEGIN

The visitors were quartered in the palace of Axayácatl near the ritual enclosure at the heart of the city. They soon saw the need to act swiftly, and were well aware that the plot that had failed in Cholula might be tried again. In an act of great simplicity and audacity, they took the Aztec emperor prisoner and kept him in guarded apartments in their palace of Axayácatl. The Aztec nobility began to prepare for violent resistance but Moctezuma urged cooperation.

Cortés had enraged the governor of Cuba by exceeding the brief of his expedition and dealing directly with Charles V in Europe. Now he was called away from Tenochtitlán to face a Spanish force sent from Cuba to arrest him. Cortés defeated the new arrivals and he persuaded the bulk of the force to return to the Aztec capital under his command. They found the city silent, but primed for explosion. In Cortés' absence, the Spaniards had attacked and slaughtered a group of Aztec nobles in order, the officers said, to put down a conspiracy.

Desperate for revenge, the Aztecs attacked the Spanish and their allies in the palace of Axayácatl. Moctezuma was persuaded to climb on to the palace roof to call for peace, but although the Aztecs obeyed their emperor, they lost their respect for him in that moment. Shortly afterward they elected Moctezuma's brother, Cuitláhuac, *tlatoani* and attacked once more. Again Moctezuma climbed to the palace parapet to calm the enraged warriors, but this time they would not hear him. They greeted his words with jeers and then with a storm of arrows and stones. He was injured and later died, either from his wounds or secretly strangled by his Spanish captors, according to differing accounts.

Afterwards the Spaniards, led by Cortés, stormed the Great Pyramid itself, set fire to the shrines and threw down the Aztecs' revered idols. At every level of the pyramid the invaders were met by ferocious defenders, who hurled burning missiles down on their heads, but the well-organized Spanish force prevailed. To the people of Tenochtitlán, this defeat, and the sight of the column of smoke that rose mournfully from the ruined shrines above their once apparently invincible city, was the greatest of humiliations. In Mesoamerican warfare, the capture and sacking of an enemy temple was proof of total victory.

HASTY RETREAT

Another wave of Aztec violence was inevitable and Cortés decided to quit the city with his troops. Under cover of a moonless night and a storm of rain on 30 June 1520, Cortés' men attempted to retreat across the causeway that led westward to Tlacopán, but their movements were discovered and the Aztecs launched furious assaults on them.

Below: The ashes of Moctezuma's predecessor Ahuítzotl (1486–1502) were stored in this stone casket, which is carved with a relief of the Aztec rain god Tláloc.

Right: An illustration from Diego Durán's account of the Spanish invasion depicts Aztec warriors attacking beleagured Spaniards in Tenochtitlán.

The Spaniards and their allies lost many men in this bloody encounter. As dawn rose at the end of what was to become known as the *Noche Triste* ('Sad Night') the remnant of the Spanish army was left to lick its wounds as the Aztecs retreated, bearing booty and their partially restored honour, to Tenochtitlán.

FINAL ASSAULT

Cortés prepared for another assault on the Aztec capital. He made allies in Tlaxcala and Texcoco and a new contingent of Cholulans also joined his army. In the hour of their greatest need, the Aztecs' much-vaunted 'empire' fell apart. Even as Cortés had made his first approach to Tenochtitlán he had encountered subjects only too willing to overthrow the pride of Moctezuma.

Cortés planned to besiege the lake city of Tenochtitlán and so force its surrender. He placed armies at the head of each of the three causeways, while armed vessels or barques prevented the defending Tenochtitláns from using their usual shoreline landing places. Fighting was prolonged and bloody, but gradually the besiegers began to gain ground, pinning the defenders down in Tlatelolco. The Tlaxcaláns seized the opportunity to avenge themselves on the Aztecs with ferocious enthusiasm, piling up the bodies of their victims.

Finally, on 13 August 1521, after a siege of 93 days, the *tlatoani* Cuauhtemoc and his leading warriors were captured as they attempted to flee to a new base from which to carry on the fight. They made a dignified surrender. The Aztec empire was no more.

CONQUEST OF THE MAYA

The Spaniards found the more dispersed Maya a harder enemy to bring under control than the Aztecs.

Francisco Hernández de Córdoba, leader of the first exploratory expedition sent to Mesoamerican lands from the Spanish island of Cuba, died of wounds inflicted by Maya warriors in 1517 near what is now Champotón. The clash was the Maya's first encounter with gunpowder, but it was not their first contact with the Europeans, for Maya traders had met Christopher Columbus as early as 1502.

The second and third Spanish-Cuban voyages, led by Juan de Grijalva in 1518 and Hernán Cortés in 1518–19, largely bypassed Yucatán. It was not until 1528 that the Spaniards turned their attention to the 'northern Maya' of Yucatán. Francisco de Montejo, who led the campaign, faced a tough task. Cortés had succeeded against the Aztecs partly because he was able to isolate and undermine the authority of their emperor, but among the Maya there was no comparable figure of central authority. In addition, the pragmatic Maya fought a campaign reminiscent of modern guerrilla warfare, attacking by night and setting traps and ambushes in the difficult jungle terrain. It took the Spaniards 14 years to establish a colonial capital, at Mérida in 1542, and four years later they put resistant Maya tribes to the sword.

Above: Hernán Cortés moved with great directness and simplicity against the Aztecs.

The southern Maya area, incorporating the Quiché and Cakchiquel kingdoms, was conquered by Pedro de Alvarado between 1523 and 1541. However, one pocket of Maya independence survived until 1697, when their lands were found to be in the path of a proposed roadway that would link Guatemala and Yucatán. When Martin de Ursua, Governor of Yucatán, sailed across Lake Flores to demand the surrender of the people of Tayasal, his ship was surrounded by Maya canoes, and when one of the Spanish soldiers fired his arquebus at the canoes it unleashed a hail of Spanish gunshot that crushed the Maya and terrified the remaining defenders into fleeing the city. The last pocket of Maya independence was defeated.

CHAPTER TWO

DESERT, MOUNTAIN, LAKE AND JUNGLE

Mesoamerica was a region of great contrasts. Its landscapes range from the snowcapped volcanoes of Popocatépetl and Ixtaccíhuatl to the swampy Tabasco Plain that borders the Gulf of Campeche; from the dusty sagebrush of the northern Mexican plateau to the humid lowland jungles of El Petén in northern Guatemala.

Varied climates and landscapes called for different survival strategies. The northern Mexican plateau could only support bands of nomads; the southern part of the plateau in which lies the Valley of Mexico, was a well irrigated, fertile highland area of 800,000 hectares (2 million acres). Over many centuries, several major cultures established themselves in the Valley of Mexico, including the Teotihuacanos and the Méxica/Aztecs. Throughout this period, warlike northern groups were a threat to their southerly neighbours and on more than one occasion they flooded southward, either to overrun local peoples or simply to settle. The Méxica themselves came originally from the north. According to their own account of their origins, it was only after they had come south and been settled for some time near Tollán that they picked up 'civilization' in the form of the skills needed to raise crops and to irrigate the land.

Left: Tall trees and strong tropical creeper grow on the hills surrounding the ceremonial structures at the Maya city of Palenque in Chiapas, Mexico.

MANY LANDSCAPES

The variety of the Mesoamerican landscape had a significant influence on the type of civilization that developed area by area. In many parts of the region, such as the Valley of Mexico and the tropical forests of Maya lands, the peoples of Mesoamerica were blessed with fertile soil. Fed and protected by the land, they were nevertheless always at the mercy of drought and the famines it brought. The Maya and Aztecs, and their cultural predecessors, were drawn into an intense, spiritually charged relationship with the natural world. They saw the gods everywhere: in the earth, the crops that grew from it, the rain that fed the plants, the mountains where the rainclouds gathered and the wind that carried the clouds to their fields.

Above: In the tropical woodlands of El Petén in Guatemala, Maya cities such as Tikal and Uaxactún once defied the dense jungle.

TOPOGRAPHY

To the east and west of the Mexican plateau rise the great mountains of the Sierra Madre Oriental and the Sierra Madre Occidental, while to its south lie the spectacular peaks of the Transverse Volcanic Axis, including Popocatépetl, Ixtaccíhuatl and Toluca. Beyond the mountains to east and west lie coastal lowlands bordering the Pacific Ocean and the Gulf of Mexico. Further south of the plateau lie more mountains, the Southern Highlands, which include the ranges of the Sierra Madre del Sur. These run down almost to the coast of the Pacific Ocean. To their east lies the lowland area of the Isthmus of Tehuantepec, beyond which the land rises to the south-east in the Sierra Madre de Chiapas and runs to the north-east into the Tabasco Plain, filled with swamps and slow-moving rivers.

Below: In the rainforests of Veracruz, bordering the Gulf of Mexico, the Olmec set up basalt columns to mark sacred places.

MAYA LANDS

The highlands of Chiapas run eastward, linking up with the volcanic mountains in Guatemala that form the southern limit of the territories occupied by the Maya. In these uplands, where the volcanic soil is highly fertile, the Maya raised their crops with comparative ease. They also found materials that were highly valuable both for trade and their own use. These included obsidian, the hard volcanic glass used throughout Mesoamerica for the blades of knives and spears, flint and jade, the latter prized as a precious stone and often found in grave offerings. The Maya also mined basalt, which they used to make grinding stones for processing maize. In the mountain forests they tracked the quetzal bird, whose long green feathers were worn in costumes and headdresses by kings and priests.

To the north of the volcanic mountains, the land runs down to the lowlands of El Petén, where the first Maya settlers encountered areas of highly fertile

Below: Despite the harsh terrain of the mountainous landscape of Oaxaca's peaks, the Zapotec built a great civilization there.

tropical forest interspersed with low-lying seasonal swamps and areas of tall bush. In this unlikely setting they built the early ceremonial centre of Nakbé and the great cities of Calakmul, Tikal, Uaxactún and Yaxchilán. Here they felled great cedar trees that were carved into canoes 24m (80ft) in length that carried traders as far as Panama, a distance of 2,400 sea miles. They found brazil wood, which they processed as a dye for staining cloth, and collected copal, a resin exuded by tropical trees, which was burned in religious ceremonies.

Further north, Maya settlers found that the land spread out in a flat expanse covered with scrub forest, which is now known as the northern Yucatán peninsula. The name came originally from a misunderstanding, for when early Spanish explorers from Cuba first asked the Maya what their country was called, the natives replied 'Ci-u-than' ('We cannot understand you'), which in time became 'Yucatán'. According to Bernal Díaz del Castillo, at the time of the Conquest the Maya had accepted the use of Yucatán but among themselves still called the land by its old name, which he reports was 'Land of the Deer and the Turkey'.

On the north-western edge of the lower Yucatán peninsula is a forested region known as Campeche, and to its west, bordering the Gulf of Campeche, lies the tropical area of Tabasco, filled with swamps and sluggish rivers. Here the Maya grew cacao, which was very highly prized and traded as a luxury item throughout Mesoamerica.

Above: A map of Mesoamerican terrains indicates how mountains and expanses of ocean hem in areas of very fertile land.

AREAS OF OCCUPATION

Scholars identify three areas of Maya occupation. The 'Southern Maya' were those living in the volcanic mountains of Guatemala and the highlands of Chiapas. The 'Central Maya' occupied the region stretching from Tabasco and the southern part of the Campeche through the lowlands of El Petén to Belize and part of western Honduras. This is the area largely abandoned in the 'Maya collapse' of the 9th century. The 'Northern Maya' lived in northern Campeche and towards the tip of the Yucatán peninsula. This region includes great settlements such as Chichén Itzá, Uxmal and Mayapán.

JUNGLE CITIES OF THE MAYA

We cannot know why the Maya built their cities where they did. Some are close to rivers, lakes or waterholes, but many are far from natural water sources. The lands of El Petén, which had thick tropical growth, high bush and seasonal marshes, would appear to present a daunting challenge to builders, but it was here that the first ceremonial centres and cities of the emerging Maya civilization were built. It may be that the sites were chosen by priests claiming divine inspiration; with the Aztecs and the founding mythology of their capital, Tenochtitlán, the city rose in the place that had been chosen by the gods.

Differences in farming techniques and attitudes to land between the lowlands of El Petén and the highland southern Maya regions may have had a significant impact on the types of settlement and kinds of rule that developed in the two places.

THE FARMER'S FIELD

The sacred book of the Quiché Maya, the *Popol Vuh*, tells how the sky and sea gods brought the Earth into being from the primordial waters at the dawn of time. They had only to speak the word 'Earth' and it rose up like a great mist, unfurling and clearing to reveal the mountains and the plain. Dense vegetation spread over the terrain. The holy text likens the miraculous event to the process a Maya farmer followed to measure out a field. This was a 'fourfold siding, fourfold cornering, measuring, fourfold staking, halving the cord, stretching the cord, in the sky, on the earth, the four sides, the four corners.' Farmers across the Maya realm used a measuring technique like this, but they cleared and used the land differently in the Guatemalan highlands where the Quiché lived and the jungle-covered lowlands of El Petén, with corresponding effects on their feeling for the land and perhaps also their loyalty to their ruler.

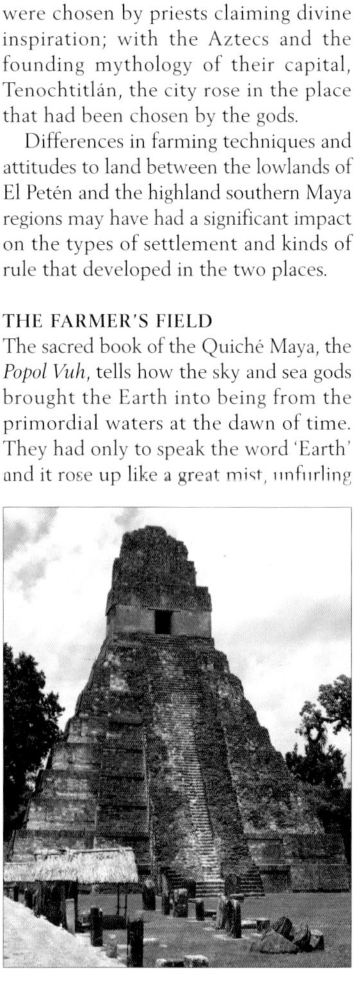

Left: The great heights to which Maya builders aspired in cities such as Tikal outdid even the towering jungle trees.

Left: Shrieking monkeys were the Mayas' neighbours in the Guatemalan jungle. This pot dates from around the 9th century AD.

SETTLEMENT PATTERNS

In the jungle, farmers traditionally practised 'slash and burn' agriculture. During the dry season, a farmer would use a stone axe to clear the dense growth of trees and set them ablaze. He would measure out his plot with the fourfold cornering and plant seeds of maize and other crops in the ash-enriched earth in good time for the beginning of the rainy season in May or early June. Ten years or so would usually exhaust the land on a particular plot, so after that period the farmer would move on to clear and burn another area of jungle.

In the highlands the volcanic earth was deeper and richer and farmers did not need to move their fields periodically. There, settlements were more rooted; in the jungle, farmers did not feel themselves tied to a particular piece of the land in the same way. Scholars believe that this contributed to the long-term instability of the jungle city-states. The cities were close together, often no more than a day's march apart. As farmers moved further away from the stone towers of their own settlement, they may have felt increasingly vulnerable to interference or attack.

Kings commanded loyalty by military ability, charisma and their capacity to demonstrate power through great public sacrificial rituals on the temple-pyramids of their ancestors. This type of loyalty could quickly melt away if a king was defeated, captured and sacrificed – and the next member of his dynasty was weak. The result was that a succession of kingdoms rose to brief pre-eminence, then were conquered or faded away.

INTENSE COMPETITION

Recent archaeological work has transformed our idea of what the jungle and the jungle cities would have looked like in the 8th or 9th centuries AD. At one

time, scholars thought that the Maya of the lowland jungles were relatively few in number and that there was plenty of land for clearance and sowing. But the latest evidence indicates that in the 8th century the Maya population in the jungle lowlands was extremely high and that the Maya at this time were farming the land intensively. We now know the Maya jungle farmers cleared slopes and built terraced fields and even constructed raised fields in the region's low-lying swamps.

It appears that by the 8th century the Maya had cleared the jungle almost completely. The lush vegetation that now almost swamps many of the jungle cities is secondary rather than primary growth. Modern tourists climb the towering pyramids of sites such as Tikal and look down beyond the city limits on the tall green towers of the forest, but a Maya priest in the same position in the 8th century would have looked down on land that had been cleared and set aside for farming.

Many scholars now believe that this state of affairs holds the key to the 'Maya collapse' – the abandonment of the cities of the region in the 9th century that marks the end of the Classic Period. They argue that the overuse of the land caused an ecological catastrophe. There was no longer enough land to go round and what territory there was was not highly fertile. The Maya city-states fought bitterly over the last available areas of good land.

Above: The temples of Palenque stand on the densely forested foothills of the Sierra Madre, overlooking the plain of Chiapas.

Below: In the mid-20th century the lush forest of El Petén swamped Tikal. Clearing work, beginning in 1956, uncovered the city.

SACRED MOUNTAINS IN THE JUNGLE

Mountains were revered throughout Mesoamerica. To the Maya, they were the place where deceased ancestors lived on and even today the Maya peoples of the Chiapas region hold to this belief. The architects of the El Petén region and northern Yucatán lived many miles north of the Chiapas highlands and the volcanic mountains of southern Guatemala, but in cities such as Tikal, Palenque and Uxmal they created their own sacred mountains in the form of the stepped stone pyramids that today still tower above great ceremonial plazas.

Above: Access to the Temple of the Masks, Tikal, at the top of the staircase and halfway to heaven, was restricted to the priesthood.

THE PYRAMIDS

Pyramids were identified by the word *witz*, which could also mean 'mountain'. A pyramid was a sacred building with a temple at its summit, used for ceremonial processions and religious rituals. However, they were also, and perhaps primarily, mortuary monuments, erected to honour the memory of a dead king. Both symbolically (as a stone mountain) and literally (as a giant tomb) they were homes to deified royal ancestors.

It may be that the temples on top of the pyramids were architectural versions of the natural caves in which Mesoamericans had left offerings from time immemorial. Some – such as those at Tikal and Yaxchilán, for example – had large vertical roofcombs that reinforced the impression that they were openings in a rockface close to the sacred sky. Many of the pyramids, like mountains, presented a forbidding challenge to those seeking to climb them. They towered to great heights, their stepped sides were very steep and the steps themselves so narrow that the members of the religious procession mounting to the holy places on high would have had to put their feet sideways on each step.

Below: The ceremonial centre at Uxmal, in Yucatán, is bounded to the right by the soaring Pyramid of the Magician.

SACRED STRUCTURES

Other architectural elements of the Maya city were representations in stone of the sacred structures of the universe and of the natural world around them. In Maya culture, water was linked to the underworld; a number of surviving carvings represent royal passengers in a canoe on their final voyage to the spirit world. Scholars believe the great ceremonial plazas of Maya cities represented lakes or

Above: The steep incline of the steps – as here at Palenque – made it a demanding task to climb to the holy places above.

seas that offered a way to the underworld. Some scholars believe the Maya thought the ball court, specifically, represented an entry to the underworld, while the ball used in the game represented the sun. Even the stone columns or stelae on which rulers recorded their dates of accession, anniversaries of their rule and political or military triumphs were associated with the natural world. The Maya word for the stela was *te tun* ('tree rock'). The stelae at Yaxchilán, for example, rise toward the sacred sky in the same way as the trees of the forest in which the city stands.

UNDERWORLDS AND HEARTHSTONES

The structures of pyramids, temples and plazas had detailed religious and mythic significance. For example, temples at Palenque and Tikal with nine levels suggest the nine regions of the underworld the king encounters as his soul makes its voyage through the spirit realm. One construction at Tikal, Temple II, has three layers. At Izapa, in the Pacific coastal region of Chiapas, a plaza contains three pillars, each 1.3m (4ft 3in) tall and supporting a circular stone. Both the Tikal temple and Izapa pillars are symbolic references to the three hearthstones of the Maya creation myth, which the Maya believed were visible in the night sky as the three stars in Orion's belt.

In man-made versions of natural holy places, the gods could be honoured with sacrifices designed to recycle spiritual and cosmic energy (largely in the form of life-blood) on behalf of the city state. Maya kings, priests and people hoped that the sacrifices would safeguard the flow of divine power needed to keep the natural world functioning; the sun rising, the rain clouds forming and unloading their cargo, the land giving birth to maize plants.

Below: At Cobá, in Quintana Roo, a rounded pyramid rises like a natural mountain peak from the jungle floor.

WATER: A SCARCE RESOURCE

Because of the physical characteristics of their lands, the Maya often had to come up with ingenious solutions to provide water for their cities and their people.

Below: Some cenotes *or underground waterholes, such as this well at Dzitnup, are accessible only through a small opening.*

FRESH WATER

In the northern part of the Yucatán peninsula there are no large rivers and early in the dry season, which can last six months, all streams disappear. The land is porous limestone; water runs through the rock and collects below ground. In places, the land has collapsed, forming vast holes – some 60m (200ft across) and 30m (100ft) deep – which are fed by underground rivers. These holes, called *cenotes*, are used as wells.

Above: The city of Tulum on the cliffs of eastern Yucatán is battered by ocean winds and washed by Caribbean spray.

CENOTES

Chichén Itzá was built around two *cenotes*. The earliest settlers constructed the city in the 5th century around the southernmost of the two wells. They built two stairways of masonry 20m (65ft) down to the water. The city was 'refounded' by the Itzá in the years after AD987, based on a second *cenote* further north. This second well is around 60m (200ft) across, while its rim is 22m (73ft) above the surface of the water. While they continued to use the southern *cenote* for drawing water, they used the northern one for religious rituals. A sacred causeway 275m (900ft) in length runs from the Great Plaza northward to the 'Well of Sacrifice'.

According to Bishop de Landa, the Maya held sacrifices to the rain god Chac during droughts, in which priests threw

Right: With two wells, Chichén Itzá had a plentiful water supply. This is the northern waterhole, set aside for religious rites.

human victims into the well with offerings of precious gold and jade. De Landa suggests that the Maya did not think that the victims died, although they did not see them again once they had been cast into the well. A colourful 19th-century addition to the folklore surrounding the sacred well suggested that beautiful virgins were cast into its water to please Chac. Edward Thompson, US Consul to Merida, bought the site of Chichén Itzá in 1901 and had the well dredged, turning up precious offerings and the remains of human sacrifices. Biological anthropologist Ernest Hooton examined skulls found in the well and found them to include skulls of men, women and children.

Another celebrated *cenote* existed at Bolonchen ('Nine Wells') in the Campeche, where water lies 135m (450ft) below the surface. The American traveller and archaeologist John Lloyd Stephens, author of *Incidents of Travel in Central America, Chiapas, and Yucatán* (1841), visited the site and described how, by the light of pine torches, the Maya descended over crumbling rock deep into the earth using a long ladder made from great planks of wood lashed together, with earthen pots for carrying the water tied to their backs and heads. His companion Frederick Catherwood made a celebrated lithograph of the Bolonchen well in use, showing heavily laden natives clambering down to the water and up to the light.

Below: At Labná, near Uxmal in the Puuc region of Yucatán, rainwater was collected in a specially constructed cistern.

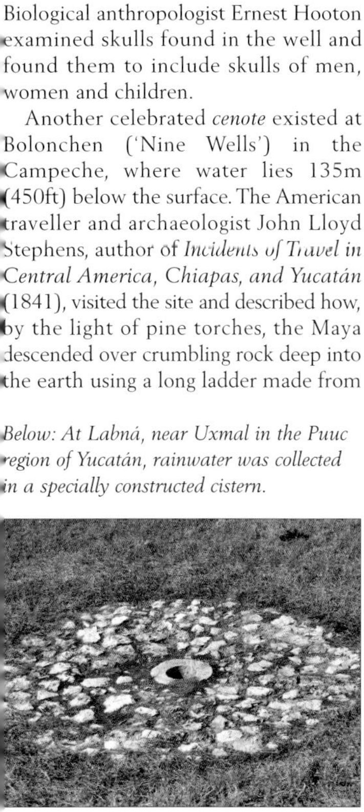

RESERVOIRS AND RIVERS

In some places the Maya made their own reservoirs. The city of Tikal had no access to water from springs, rivers or wells but rainfall was plentiful. Its inhabitants relied on the water collected in a great reservoir situated just off the city's ceremonial centre. Its builders lined two natural ravines with clay and left them to dry in the sun, thus creating a water-tight area. They added a causeway across the reservoir that also functioned as a dam. Rainwater could flow in freely from the ceremonial area: the builders laid the plaza so that its surface tilted at an angle of five degrees from level to encourage water-flow into the reservoir. The Maya also built wells that collected rainwater as it ran off the roofs of houses and ceremonial buildings. The wells had their own roofs to limit evaporation of the precious liquid during hot weather.

Some Maya cities were built within convenient reach of water. Yaxchilán and Piedras Negras, for example, were built alongside the River Usumacinta. At Palenque, which lies just above the floodplain of the Usumacinta, the River Otulum runs right through the site: here the builders diverted the river into an artificial waterway that passes beneath the palace. Cobá, in north-eastern Yucatán, was situated between two lakes.

SALT WATER

Some Maya cities were built on the coast, facing the ocean. The builders of Tulum erected their city atop a 12m (40ft) limestone cliff on the coast of eastern Yucatán looking down on the Caribbean Sea. Built in the 6th century AD, it was still occupied by the Maya at the time of the Conquest. The city's name means 'fence' or 'wall' and came into use after the arrival of Europeans because Tulum is enclosed on its inland sides by high walls. Its ancient name may have been Zama ('dawn') because it faces east to greet the jaguar sun god each morning on his emergence from the underworld.

Tulum greatly impressed Europeans when they first encountered it. The 1518 Spanish exploratory mission led by Juan de Grijalva sailed down the coast and Juan Díaz, the mission chaplain, reported he had seen three great towns, one as large as Seville with a great tower. Tulum contains a tall building known as El Castillo ('the castle'), with a temple on its top. The city was connected by a stone causeway which led to Xelha and to Chichén Itzá.

CITY OF AWE: TEOTIHUACÁN

The impressive setting, the towering architecture and the vast grid layout of Teotihuacán struck awe into Aztec hearts. They knew nothing of the historically distant peoples who erected this symbolic urban landscape and became convinced that its architects must have been the gods themselves.

CITY OF THE GODS

Teotihuacán lies in a side valley running off the Valley of Mexico, around 50km (30 miles) north-east of the Aztec capital Tenochtitlán. Its unknown founders may have chosen the setting because of its proximity to a rich source of the highly prized volcanic glass obsidian and to the San Juan river, which provided water for agriculture. The site also lay on a significant trade route that ran to the Gulf Coast from the Valley of Mexico.

The Aztecs were deeply impressed by the architecture and stylized grid pattern of Teotihuacán. Their powerful mythological imagination saw in the Pyramids of the Sun and Moon the setting for the divine rituals that set the modern era in motion and raised the life-giving sun and his pale companion the moon in the skies. However, to the Aztecs who made pilgrimages to the site to gaze in awe at the vast buildings, to make sacrifices and offerings to the gods, to consult oracles and to put criminals to a bloody death, this city of man-made mountains laid out against a backdrop of natural peaks was a deeply moving statement of religious devotion and its power to safeguard a world that could at any moment be brought to an abrupt end by the gods.

Above: Goggle eyes and fanged mouth identify this Teotihuacán carving as the rain god. The Aztecs worshipped him as Tláloc.

SITE OF ANCIENT PILGRIMAGE

As well as being the imagined setting for primal mythological events, Teotihuacán had other deeply seated religious and spiritual associations. At some points in their history, the Aztecs identified Teotihuacán with the revered civilization of Tollán, whose golden age of fertile lands, divine leaders and just laws represented an earthly paradise. The Aztecs believed that the people of Tollán had flourished in the era immediately before their own rise in the 14th century, and so imagined the flowering of Teotihuacán to have taken place more than 500 years after the city's actual primacy (*c*.100BC–AD650).

Moreover, the great Pyramid of the Sun was erected atop a natural cave that was a site of ancient religious observance. The cave, discovered during architectural investigations in 1971, contains remains of religious offerings made many centuries before the pyramid was raised in honour of the gods in around AD150. From time immemorial, Mesoamerican peoples saw caves as gateways to the world of spirit; scholars suggest that these offerings may have been part of rituals that were based on archaic shamanistic practice and that the cave and surrounding area may long have been an area visited by the devout. This holy site was the natural spot for the construction of the Pyramid of the Sun, the most sacred of the buildings in Teotihuacán.

SACRED LANDSCAPE

The Pyramid of the Sun stands 66m (216ft) high, a great man-made mountain containing 765 million cubic metres

Left: Priests standing atop the Pyramid of the Moon would have been able to look directly down the 'Street of the Dead'.

Above: Teotihuacán made an evocative setting for Aztec religious rites. The moon hangs above the wide 'Street of the Dead'.

(1,000 cubic yards) of laboriously quarried rock that dominates the centre of the city. It stands to the east of the ceremonial roadway that was dubbed the 'Street of the Dead' by the Aztecs. This roadway, 40m (130ft) wide, runs for 2.4km (1.5 miles) and lies 16 degrees to the east of true north, so that it runs exactly towards Cerro Gordo, an extinct volcano revered as a sacred mountain. The road, which forms the basis of the city's grid pattern, is lined with lower buildings that the Aztecs believed were the tombs of ancient kings, but which are now known to have been palace residences. At the northern end of the road, situated so that it is framed by Cerro Gordo, stands the city's second largest construction, the Pyramid of the Moon, 43m (140ft) tall. The pyramid's main stairway gives directly on to the Street of the Dead. The Pyramid of the Sun and the Pyramid of the Moon probably had temples on their flattened tops.

The southern part of the Street of the Dead gives to the east on to a 15-hectare (38-acre) sunken square courtyard called the Citadel, which contains the temple of Quetzalcóatl, a stepped pyramid-platform whose decorated walls bear numerous stone sculptures representing Quetzalcóatl and Tláloc. Many burials have been found near the temple, including a ceremonial interment dated to AD200 of 18 men, probably captured soldiers put to sacrificial death.

The vast city of Teotihuacán amazes even the modern visitor with its grandeur and scale. The city contained 2,000 apartment buildings, 600 pyramids and many other temples, plazas, administrative buildings and palaces used by nobles and priests. There were 500 areas of workshops where craftsmen made pots or worked in obsidian and a vast marketplace served by merchants from many parts of central America. Its construction must have been the work of generations of Teotihuacanos and is an astonishing, enduring proclamation of the power of the city's rulers. The city's great stone peaks honour and echo the natural mountains that range against the sky behind them. It is not difficult to understand the Aztecs' reverence for its architects.

Right: Heads of Quetzalcóatl flank the steep stairs of a Teotihuacán temple. One of the god's aspects was as the wind deity Éhecatl.

'WATER MOUNTAIN': TENOCHTITLÁN

Above: The Aztecs' reliance on causeway or boat to connect to the lake's shore is clear in this schematic image of Tenochtitlán.

The Spanish conquistadors encountered Tenochtitlán at the height of its glory, a vast metropolis on the water with more than 150,000 and perhaps as many as 300,000 inhabitants. They were moved to compare it to the Italian city of canals, Venice, or even to the enchanted cities described so colourfully in medieval chivalric romances. Yet the Aztecs constructed what appeared to be a city of dreams from the most unlikely of beginnings.

FOUNDING OF A CITY

The Méxica/Aztec incomers who founded Tenochtitlán were latecomers in the Chichimec incursions that followed the collapse of Toltec power in the 12th century. When they arrived in the Valley of Mexico in the mid-13th century, the best territories had already been settled and the Méxica were not made welcome by the Alcohua, Tepanec and other groups who had already made their homes there. Moreover, the newcomers were driven out of the places where they did settle. When they finally brought their wanderings to an end in 1325, the Méxica had to take what lands they could get. The twin islands on which they were to found their great city were some of the least attractive lands in the vicinity, so unpromising that none of the three powers in the region of Lake Texcoco – Texcoco to the east, Azcapotzalco to the west and Culhuacán to the south – had bothered to lay claim to them.

Left: 'Floating fields' such as these created in Lake Xochimilco were needed to support the burgeoning population of Tenochtitlán.

The city had to be designed to fit the setting and its island situation and marshy surroundings were crucial shaping factors from the start. Certainly there were some benefits to the site. For food, the settlers had their pick of the fish, birds and plentiful waterlife. Indeed, the Aztecs came to view the lake as a mother who had given them refuge at her breast. In fertility rites held on the lake each year, the water was addressed as Tonanueyatl ('Mother Vast Water'). The watery setting was also an advantage in terms of transport. In a country where men and women made no use of beasts of burden or wheeled carts, it was easier to move things by canoe. The islands were also in a central position, within a triangle formed by the lake's three foremost cities. This was important strategically and was also of benefit to the Méxica when they established marketplaces in Tenochtitlán and Tlatelolco.

LAYOUT AND DESIGN

The Aztecs laid their city out in four quarters to match the four cardinal directions and built a sacred precinct at its centre. Each of the *capultin* or tribal clans was assigned its own area and its own temple within the city; the clans held their land communally. The Great Pyramid and ritual precincts that developed here were understood by the Aztecs to be the centre of the universe. The pyramid itself was a holy mountain, a reproduction within the city of

Above: Netzahualcóyotl built a 16-km- (10-mile) dyke to seal off the freshwater part of the lake containing Tenochtitlán.

the sacred heights of Popocatépetl, Ixtaccíhuatl and Mount Tláloc. The city itself was a mountain on the lake – indeed the Nahuatl word for 'city', *atl tepetl*, translates as 'water mountain'. They built three long causeways, said by Hernán Cortés to be 3.5m (12ft) wide, to link the islands to the mainland. An aqueduct carried water in from mainland springs at Chapultepec hill.

CHINAMPA

Agricultural land was initially in short supply until the Aztecs developed their own *chinampa* or 'floating fields'. In shallow water, these fields were built up in the lake bed with layers of mud and plants, fixed in place by tall posts. In deeper water, fields were made by filling 'floating' reed-beds with earth and anchoring them to the lake bed. The plots were laid out in pairs with a central footpath and canals on either side from which the farmers could draw water to irrigate the crops. Canoes used the canals to transport goods. *Chinampa* varied in size from 100sq m to 850sq m (1,100 to 9,000 sq ft). A typical *chinampa* might be farmed by 10–15 people. The available land was greatly increased after the Aztec under Itzcóatl took control in 1428 of the large *chinampa* plantations in the freshwater lakes of Xochimilco and Chalco that lay to the south of Lake Texcoco.

The city's location and design made it vulnerable. It could easily be flooded. A flood in 1500 destroyed many houses. Netzahualpilli, son of Netzahualcóyotl of Texcoco, told the Aztec *tlatoani* Ahuítzotl that the gods must be enraged. A great reconstruction project was launched: the nobles built palaces, dykes were strengthened and willows and poplars planted along the canals. The second, ultimately disastrous, drawback was that the city was not self-sufficient and could be cut off, making it vulnerable to siege. Sadly for the Aztecs, Hernán Cortés saw this. He blocked the three causeways and used a fleet of armed barges to prevent food being brought in any other way. The three-month siege led to the city's fall and the end of the Aztec empire.

Right: An illustration from the manuscript of the Codex Mendoza *(c.1541) represents Tenochtitlán as a city founded on water.*

ON THE EDGE: COPÁN AND JAINA ISLAND

The city of Copán, which lay close to the Guatemala–Honduras border, was the most easterly of the large Maya cities. For the Maya, Copán lay at the eastern limits of their civilization.

The site at Copán was occupied from 1000BC onwards, but for many centuries it was only a small farming settlement. Copán developed into a major city *c.*AD400, when a group of public buildings and a ball court were erected.

Above: *These figures on Altar Q at Copán represent Yax Pak (centre) receiving a sceptre from his ancestor Yax K'uk Mo'.*

OPENING TO THE UNDERWORLD

By the 9th century, the city had as many as 20,000 inhabitants. It covered 100 hectares (250 acres) and contained two large pyramids, as well as several plazas, stairways and stone temples, most arranged on a central raised platform called the Acropolis by archaeologists. In the 7th century, King Smoke Imix made the city a leading power in the world of the Maya.

Through architecture, the king also sanctified Copán: the arrangement of his stelae in the city and the valley around it identify the place as a sacred opening to the underworld. His descendant Smoke Shell built a magnificent dynastic stairway 15m (50ft) wide and with 1,250 hieroglyphs on the risers of its 72 steps, from which scholars have been able to trace a dynasty of 16 kings who ruled the city from Yax K'uk Mo' ('Blue Quetzal Macaw') in *c.*AD435 to Yax Pak ('First Sunrise') in AD820.

Left: King 18 Rabbit, subject of several stelae at Copán, oversaw a major building programme in the city in the early AD700s.

For many years, scholars believed that the city had a special significance for Maya civilization as a centre for study of astronomy and astrology. There is no doubt that astronomy fed strongly into the city's development. Many of the buildings and stelae erected in the reign of the 9th-century monarch King 18 Rabbit are arranged to mirror the sacred patternings of the sky. The stelae bear many detailed carvings of the king. One shows him as both a young man and an older king, while another depicts him wearing both the jaguar-skin garment associated with kings and a beaded dress of the kind usually seen in depictions of women. As Maya scholar John S. Henderson has noted, the images, their positioning and the hieroglyphic inscriptions suggest a number of highly significant symbolic oppositions, including left–right, young–old and female–male – as well as the three realms sky–world–underworld and the four directions east–north–west–south.

ALTAR Q

Much of the scholarly debate about the significance of Copán was generated by misinterpretation of a square structure with 16 figures carved on its sides. The object, called Altar Q by archaeologists, was built by King Yax Pak in the 9th century. Historians used to believe that the figures on the altar were those of

Above: A stela honouring King Smoke Imix, 12th ruler in Yax K'uk Mo's dynasty, overlooks part of the ball court at Copán.

Below: This figurine from Jaina Island wears a fine cotton blouse, suggesting that she is a woman of high rank.

astronomers called to Copán to adjust the Maya calendar. We now know that the individuals are Yax Pak and his 15 ancestors in the dynasty of Yax K'uk Mo'. Copán might have been at the limit of Maya realms, but it had dynastic links with other Maya cities. Scholars believe that the dynasty descended from Yax K'uk Mo' had connections among the royal family at Tikal – the Copán emblem glyph has been found in texts at Tikal. The mother of the dynasty's final king, Yax Pak, was from Palenque.

At the other end of the Maya realm lay the enigmatic Jaina, a limestone island off the coast of Campeche that the Maya used as a burial ground in the late Classic Period (during the 7th–9th centuries AD) and where archaeologists have found a wealth of small clay figurines in graves. The island's westerly location made it a natural choice for a cemetery. Viewed from the mainland, the sun would have set behind Jaina on its nightly journey to the spirit realm. Its setting in the ocean also made it appropriate, for lakes, seas and expanses of water were considered to offer a passage to Xibalba. The clay figures represent women and men of different social levels and may be portraits of the deceased. Some of them certainly depict deities, notably the sun and moon gods, who in mythology survived the frightful realm of the underworld to rise immortal into the sky.

THE JEWEL OF THE CEREN

To the south of Copán lies a farming village that was of little importance in Maya times, but which is of great interest to archaeologists because a volcanic eruption in c.AD590 buried its buildings in ash, so preserving them in perfect condition for future generations to explore and analyse.

The village, now known as Joya del Ceren ('Jewel of the Ceren'), was discovered in 1976 by the American anthropology professor Payson D. Sheets. It appears that the inhabitants of the village were able to flee the disaster, but they left behind a treasure trove of tools, materials, household furniture and even food, enabling Professor Sheets and other scholars to build up a convincing picture of life in a Maya farming village during the Classic Period. Surviving structures include adobe houses, public and religious buildings and a communal bathhouse.

CHAPTER THREE

APPEASING THE GODS

In 1428, Maxtla, ruler of the once-dominant Tepanec city of Azcapotzalco, was decisively defeated by a coalition of Tenochtitlán, Texcoco and Tlacopán. He was taken prisoner and put to ritual death in a ceremony that is revealing of the many ways in which war and blood sacrifice served to legitimize political power and safeguard the natural order in Mesoamerica.

The ceremony was a graphic demonstration of the triumph of the new Triple Alliance of Tenochtitlán, Texcoco and Tlacopán at the expense of the waning Tepanec empire. Maxtla's sacrifice was also a symbolic appropriation of Tepanec lands into the domain of the Triple Alliance and an expression of Netzahualcóyotl's primacy in his own city-state; he would become ruler of Texcoco three years later. However, the sacrifice had a number of more general, and more significant, symbolic meanings. First was its link to fertility. Netzahualcóyotl and all those present trusted that the offering of the victim's lifeblood would safeguard the richness of the soils, guarantee the return of the rains and therefore promote a good harvest. Second, the ritual was a renewal of the state itself, validating the power of the ruler and the war that was his weapon, keeping chaos and dissolution at bay. Third, the killing of Maxtla was an act of respect, for Mesoamericans considered it shameful for a warrior or ruler to be captured and kept alive and believed it was an honourable fate to be despatched as a human sacrifice.

Left: In sacrificial rites, the victim's heart was flung into the container on the flat belly of a chacmool *figure. This* chacmool *reclines outside the Temple of the Warriors in Chichén Itzá.*

MANY TYPES OF BLOOD OFFERING

For Mesoamerican peoples, offering human blood in sacrifice was a religious duty, necessary to sustain the world by maintaining the fertility of the land and the power of the ruler. It was also vital for satisfying the gods, who might at any moment determine to bring the present age to a violent end. Humans, gods and the natural world were part of a cosmic pattern of energy in which ritual and sacrifice were the means by which energy was recycled or passed on. Among the Aztecs, the two most common forms of sacrifice were extracting the victim's heart from his chest and burning to death.

Above: In a carved lintel at Yaxchilán, King Shield Jaguar's wife Lady Xoc draws a blood offering from her tongue.

REMOVING THE HEART

The extraction of the heart was performed with great ceremony on a special sacrificial block known as a *quauhxicalli* ('Stone of the Eagle'). The stone was pointed in the centre, so that a victim thrown down on it would be forced to arch his back and so thrust up his chest ready for the sacrificial knife.

Post-Conquest Spanish accounts report that naked victims were grouped at the foot of the temple steps as a priest descended from the sacred heights of the temple with an image of the god in whose honour the sacrifice was to be made. He showed the divinity to each victim, saying, 'this is your god', before the victims were led up to the sacrificial stone. Six priests of the highest rank (*chachalmua*) performed each sacrifice: four to hold the victim's feet, one to hold his throat and one to cut his chest. The foremost of these priests, dressed in a splendid red tunic and his head adorned with a helmet of yellow and green feathers, sliced the victim's chest with a flint knife known as a *técpatl*. He tore the heart from the chest, held it up to the sun, then cast it steaming before the image of the god. The six priests together pushed the corpse off the sacrificial stone and down the bloodstained temple steps. Bodies gathered at the foot of the steps in a bloody pile. Later on, they were collected, prepared and eaten in a respectful and devout ritual.

BURNING

Sacrifice by burning was mainly reserved for ceremonies in honour of the fire god Xiuhtecuhtli, who was sometimes worshipped as Huehuetéotl ('The Old God'). The rite represented the rebirth of the god, the rising of new life from death in the same way the sun was born when the god Nanahuatzin cast himself into the flames in an act of divine self-sacrifice. Other sacrificial methods were similarly

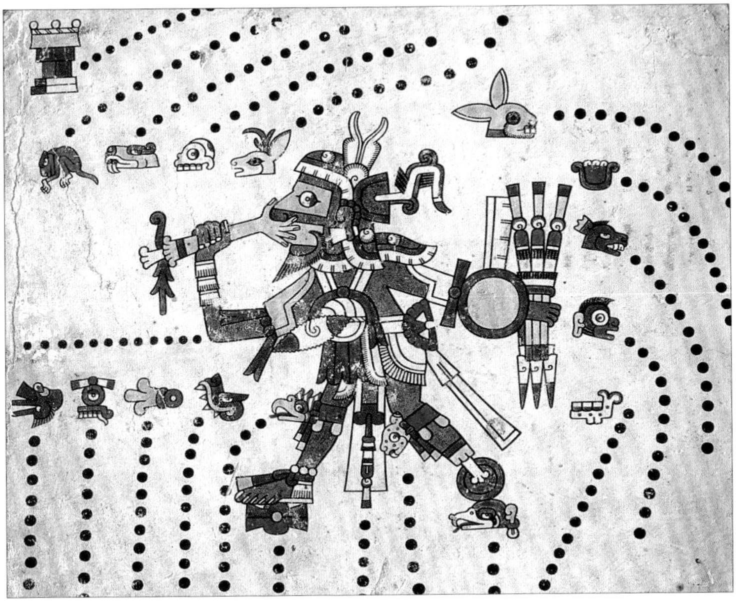

Above: A 16th-century codex illustration depicts Tezcatlipoca, dark lord of fate, feasting on the body of a sacrificed prisoner.

associated with particular gods. Victims killed in honour of Xipe Totec, the god of planting and vegetation, were shot with arrows so that their blood flowed into the earth like life-giving waters. Indeed, the Aztecs called human blood *chalchiuatl* ('precious water'). The corpse was then flayed and a priest would wear the skin in honour of the god, who was known as 'Our Lord the Flayed One'. The rite was a celebration of the splitting of seeds that makes possible the growth of new vegetation each spring.

MAYA METHODS

The Maya also used the primary Aztec method of slicing the victim's chest and extracting his dripping heart to offer to the gods. The priest oversaw the rite. Four aged men, called *chacs* in honour of the Maya rain god, were positioned to hold the body of the victim on the sacrificial stone while a specialist named the *nacom* cut open the victim's chest. In the Classic Period, however, many Maya sacrificers preferred to decapitate their victims. They also cast victims into the waters of their sacred wells or *cenotes* to drown. The American archaeologist Edward H. Thompson found the skeletons of many men, women and children in the *cenote* at Chichén Itzá.

Autosacrifice or offering one's own blood to the gods was practised. The Maya used a string threaded with thorns to cut their cheeks, lower lips, ears and tongues. They collected blood and then smeared it on images of the god or on their own body or hair. Men also used sharp knives or the spines of stingrays to cut and draw blood from their penises for offering in the same way. Among the Maya, ritual bloodletting of this kind was considered a privilege and was performed by members of the nobility. At important times, such as the passing from one calendrical cycle to another, the king and his family would perform the ritual in honour of his ancestors and on behalf of himself, the city-state and his people. There are also illustrations in Maya codices, on door lintels and on ceramics, of the gods themselves letting their blood in this way. A vase unearthed at Cahal Pech near Belize depicts a figure with the appearance of the sun god drawing blood from his penis.

Among the Aztecs, the offering of one's own blood was the preserve of priests. They would perform the rite prior to important state events and at auspicious and inauspicious dates in the calendar. They used maguey spines or blades of the volcanic glass obsidian to cut their earlobes and prick their legs and arms, or would run a thorned cord across their tongue or penis. In the rites prior to investiture as *tlatoani*, the new ruler would offer his own blood – drawn in this way from his earlobes, calves or arms – before the shrine of Huitzilopochtli atop the Great Temple in Tenochtitlán.

Animal sacrifices were also made. The Aztecs slaughtered many quails, ripping their heads off before images of the gods. Quails were associated with the myth of Quetzalcóatl, in which the Plumed Serpent descended to the underworld at the end of the previous age of the world, in order to take the bones of a previous race of men and use them to create a new tribe of humans to inhabit the current age. The underworld god Mictlantecuhtli was angry and ordered quails to chase him. Both Aztecs and Maya also sacrificed turkeys, dogs and, on special religious or state events, jaguars. In the Maya city-state of Copán, 16 jaguars were killed to mark the accession of the 16th king, Yax Pak. The bones of a jaguar were also placed among the foundations of the Great Temple in Tenochtitlán.

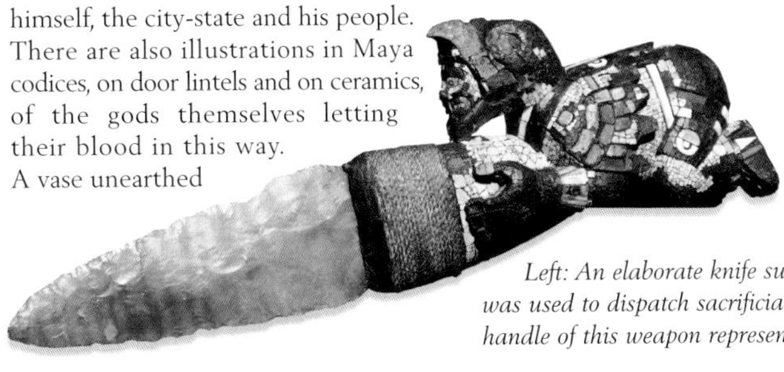

Left: An elaborate knife such as this was used to dispatch sacrificial victims. The handle of this weapon represents a warrior.

MESOAMERICAN DIVINITIES

CREATORS

AZTEC

Ometecuhtli, dual nature male and female as Ometeotl and Omecihuatl. Also took form of Tonacatecuhtli and Tonacacihuatl.
Tezcatlipoca, sometimes seen as supreme creator god.

MAYA

Itzamná, also known as Hunab Ku. In *Popol Vuh* Huracán (Hurricane or Sky Heart, sky god creator) and Gucumatz or Kukulcán (Sovereign Plumed Serpent, sea god creator). Kukulcán is the Maya equivalent of the Aztec god Quetzalcóatl.

Tezcatlipoca

Itzamna

SUN, MOON AND VENUS

AZTEC

Tonatiuh, sun god.
Metzli, moon god.
Tlahuizcalpantecuhtli (god of dawn, Venus as Morning Star), a form of Quetzalcóatl.
Xólotl (double of Quetzalcóatl), associated with Venus as Evening Star.

MAYA

Kinich Ahau, sun god by day. Jaguar god of the Underworld, sun god by night.
Ix Chel (Goddess Rainbow), goddess of the moon.
Lahun Chan, god of Venus.

Xipe Totec

Xochipilli

EARTH AND FERTILITY

AZTEC

Xipe Totec (god of vegetation and spring, transitions and oppositions) also known as Red Tezcatlipoca, linked with east.
Chicomecóatl, maize goddess.
Cihuacóatl, fertility goddess.
Cintéotl, maize god.
Coatlícue, earth goddess.
Tlatecuhtli, earth god/goddess.
Xilonen, maize goddess.
Xochipilli, the flower prince.
Xochiquetzal, flower goddess, also goddess of weaving.
Toci, earth goddess, also childbirth.
Teteoinnan, earth goddess.
Mayahuel, maguey plant goddess.
Ilamatecuhtli, ancient mother goddess.
Tepeyollotl, regeneration.
Tonantzin, mother goddess.
Tlazoltéotl, goddess of love and filth.

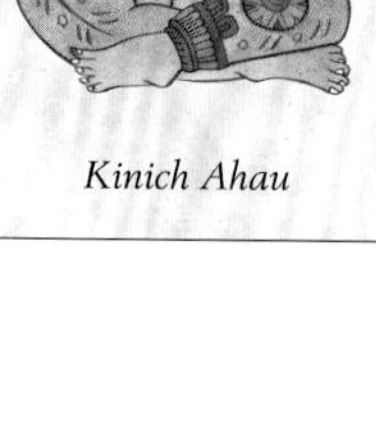
Kinich Ahau

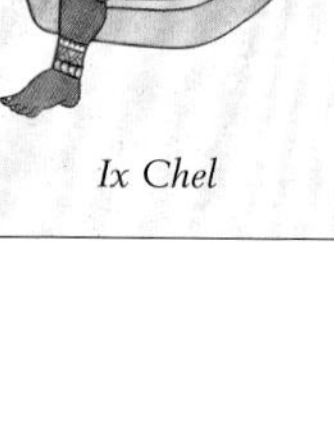
Ix Chel

MAYA

Yum Caax, sometimes Young Maize God; in *Popol Vuh*, One Hunahpú.

DEATH AND DESTINY

AZTEC

Tezcatlipoca, god of night and destiny, also associated with kingship, creation, destruction, deception, war.

MAYA

Ah Puch, death god.
Ixtab, goddess of suicide.

Tlazolteotl

Yum Caax

MOUNTAINS

AZTEC

Popocatépetl.
Ixtaccíhuatl.
Mount Tláloc.
Tetzcotzingo.
Matlalcueye.

ANIMAL/BIRD DEITIES

AZTEC

Xólotl, dog-double of Quetzalcóatl.

MAYA

Hun Batz and **Hun Chouen**, Monkey-man gods, half-brothers of Hero Twins.
Vulture god.
Fox god.
Rabbit god.
Jaguar god figures worshipped from Olmec times onward.
Seven Macaw.
Zotz, bat god.

Tláloc

Chalchiúhtlicue

Chac

Yacatecuhtli

RAINS, WINDS, WATERS

AZTEC

Tláloc, rain god.
Tlaloques, rain gods.
Quetzalcóatl, storms and wind, also known as White Tezcatlipoca, linked with west, amid many other attributes.
Tepictoton, rain god.
Éhecatl, wind god, form of Quetzalcóatl.
Chalchiúhtlicue, goddess of springs, rivers and the sea.
Huixtocíhuatl, salt goddess.
Atl, god of water.

MAYA

Chac, rain god.

HUNTING

AZTEC

Camaxtli, hunt god.
Mixcóatl, ancient hunt god.

Huitzilopochtli

Quetzalcóatl

FIRE

AZTEC

Huehuetéotl, old fire god.
Xiuhtecuhtli, fire god.
Chantico, earth goddess.

WAR

Huitzilopochtli, Méxica tribal god, also associated with sun and war. Also known as Blue Tezcatlipoca, linked with south.
Tezcatlipoca, associated with north.

TRADERS

AZTEC

Yacatecuhtli, god of traders and travellers.

MAYA

Ek Chuah, god of merchants.

ANCESTRAL GODS/CULTURE HEROES ETC

AZTEC

Quetzalcóatl-Topiltzin, god of storms, wind and rain, among many other attributes.
Huitzilopochtli, tribal god of México.
Mixcóatl, hunt god worshipped in both Huexotzingo and Tlaxcala.
Camaxtli, hunt god of Chichimec origin, worshipped particularly in Huexotzingo.

MAYA

Hero Twins Hunahpú and **Xbalanqué**.

MEDICINE AND FOODS

AZTEC

Octli, deities of pulque drink.
Patécatl, medicine god.

MAYA

Ix Chel, moon goddess, also goddess of medicine.

UNDERWORLD

AZTEC

Mictlantecuhtli, god of underworld or Mictlán.
Mictlantecacihuatl, goddess of underworld or Mictlán.

MAYA

Cizin, underworld god.
Lords of Xibalba.

Hero Twins Hunahpú and Xbalanqué

ONE ABOVE ALL OTHERS: THE SUPREME GOD?

Mesoamericans worshipped a bewildering number of gods. Each deity could simultaneously take many forms. For example, a Maya divinity might be old and young, male and female, have both spiritual and bodily forms and have animal, human and divine characteristics.

WHY SO MANY GODS?

Mesoamericans happily took on the forms of worship of previous generations. Peoples did this partly in order to legitimize their own standing. The Méxica, for example, were keen to associate themselves with the deities and achievements of their Toltec forerunners. In addition, new gods regularly joined the pantheon. The idea of converting new worshippers to the faith, so central to Christianity, was alien to Mesoamerican thought. When the Aztecs conquered lands during the expansion of their empire, they did not suppress the gods of the native peoples. They would occasionally impose the worship of their own warlike tribal god Huitzilopochtli, but they usually let their new subjects to continue their traditional forms of worship.

Right: Itzamná, the supreme Maya god, holds a vision serpent in this limestone tablet, c.100BC–AD250.

Many deities of the Aztecs and Maya had their origins far in the distant Mesoamerican past. The Aztec cult of the earth mother, worshipped as Tonantzin ('Our Sacred Mother') and Toci ('Our Grandmother'), might have grown from ancient rites in honour of figures of fertility goddesses, which have been found in many parts of the Mesoamerican region and dated to as far back as *c.*2000BC. In the era of the Olmec civilization (*c.*1500–400BC) Mesoamericans were already worshipping primitive forms of Tláloc (the Aztec rain god), Tezcatlipoca (the Aztec god of night and bringer of discord), Quetzalcóatl (the Aztec Plumed Serpent, known as Kukulcán to the Maya) and Huehuetéotl (the Aztec fire god). The Olmec were devotees of a cult of the jaguar that seems to have been associated both with fertility and royalty and which had a major influence on Maya and Aztec religion. The jaguar was later a major manifestation of Tezcatlipoca.

The builders of Teotihuacán, the city so revered by the Aztecs, worshipped Quetzalcóatl, Tláloc and the rain god's consort Chalchiúhtlicue. The cult of the rain god was also strong among the Zapotec, who worshipped him as Cocijo; the Preclassic Maya knew him as Chac.

Below: Builders of Classic Maya cities paid frequent homage to Chac, god of rain, as here in the 'nunnery quadrangle' at Uxmal.

A SUPREME DIVINITY?

Certain Maya and Aztec traditions held that a supreme creator existed behind the massed ranks of the gods. According to some Maya sources, the supreme god was Itzamná ('Lizard House'), sometimes

TEMPLE TO THE HIDDEN GOD

Netzahualcóyotl, ruler of Texcoco, made a remarkable break with religious orthodoxy when he decided to order the construction of a temple to an abstract creator god, the source of life.

Netzahualcóyotl was the same royal figure who, as a prince, had witnessed the slaughter of his father Ixtlilxóchitl by Tepanec forces after a failed revolt and who later enthusiastically performed the ritual sacrifice of his Tepanec enemy Maxtla. He was no stranger either to bloodshed or to conventional Aztec religious life. However, he must have been touched by visions of a serene divinity, for he built in his city-state a nine-storey temple to an abstract god he named Ipalnemoani ('The One By Which We Live') or Tloquenahuaque ('The One Who is Always Near').

The shrine to this deity, situated at the top of the temple, was empty of statues or other conventional decoration, for the Texcocan ruler believed the god he wished to celebrate could not be ascribed a visible form. Netzahualcóyotl showed a typically Mesoamerican openness to divergent religious approaches by allowing the other major Aztec gods to be worshipped on the lower levels of his temple.

known also as Hunab Ku ('Only Spirit'). He was depicted as a great sky serpent or as an old man, toothless and with a hooked nose, and was believed to be patron of writing and divination. His consort was Ix Chel ('Lady Rainbow'), goddess of childbirth, medicine and weaving.

Similarly, one Aztec creation myth told of a supreme creator, Ometéotl, who brought the Earth into being. Ometéotl had dual male-female aspects, was known as 'Lord of Duality' and could manifest as separate deities, Tonacatecuhtli ('Lord of Our Sustenance') and Tonacacíhuatl ('Lady of Our Sustenance'), who were entwined in a fruitful embrace. In different versions of the myth, either Ometéotl created the family of Aztec gods or Tonacatecuhtli made the Plumed Serpent Quetzalcóatl from his breath.

Another prominent Aztec ruler, Netzahualcóyotl, King of Texcoco, is reported to have been drawn to the worship of an abstract and supreme deity. However, both cultures were, in general, polytheistic. The concept of one god above or encompassing all others was largely foreign to the Mesoamerican imagination.

CHANGING SIGNIFICANCE

Scholars have shown the Maya worshipped different supreme deities in different eras and perhaps different groups. Itzamná and the bird deity Seven Macaw were revered as the highest of gods in the early days of Maya civilization, but later on Seven Macaw alone was worshipped in this way. Yet in the *Popol Vuh* of the Quiché Maya, Seven Macaw is no more than a boastful fraud and the Quiché acclaim the one-legged fire god Tohil as the supreme divinity.

A variant Aztec creation legend tells the story of how a multiplicity of gods was born. A primeval goddess gave birth to a *técpatl* or sacrificial knife, which fell on to the northern plains that were the land of origin of the Aztecs' Chichimec ancestors. As it hit the hard ground in that inhospitable desert place, gods beyond number were born and spread out to fill the earth.

Left: A Zapotec gold pendant depicts (top to bottom) the ball game; the sun; a knife representing the moon and an early form of Tlaltecuhtli, the Earth Monster of Aztec myth.

Right: Scholars often identify this basalt deity as Ometéotl, the Aztec 'Lord of Duality'.

THE BLOOD OF MANY

One of the most important religious ceremonies of the year in Tenochtitlán was Panquetzalíztli, held to honour Huitzilopochtli, the divine leader of the Aztec state and unique to the Méxica. Panquetzalíztli was held after the harvest, when the nation readied itself for war.

BATHED SLAVES

Many captive warriors of subject peoples were put to the knife before the shrine of Huitzilopochtli. Other victims were so-called 'bathed slaves', who had been purchased at market by successful merchants and offered for sacrifice in the hope of winning divine blessing. The slaves were often picked for their good looks and musical or dancing ability, for in the build-up to the festival they had to entertain guests at magnificent feasts thrown by the merchant for senior traders and noblemen. Nine days before Panquetzalíztli, the slaves were washed in a spring sacred to Huitzilopochtli and began religious preparation for their own sacrifice. On the day of the festival, the slaves were led four times around the Great Temple then, in the company of the merchant-donor, they climbed the temple's steep steps to the shrine of Huitzilopochtli at the top. There, a priest dressed as Huitzilopochtli dispatched them. They were spreadeagled across the sacrificial stone, the chest was sliced open and the heart torn from its cavity. The merchant was awarded the bodies, and afterwards he would take them back to his house to be consumed with maize in a cannibalistic banquet.

Below: A tzompantli *or skull rack for displaying victims' heads stood atop the Great Pyramid in Tenochtitlán.*

VICTIMS BECOME GODS

Each of the Aztec months was sacred to a particular deity and, at the end of each month, victims dressed as the god in question were respectfully slaughtered. The victims, known as *ixiptla* ('in the god's image'), became the gods they honoured and were treated with the greatest reverence and ceremony. They were said to hold the fire of the god in their bodies, and when they were slaughtered this divine flame was set free to take residence in the body of a victim marked for sacrifice in a year's time.

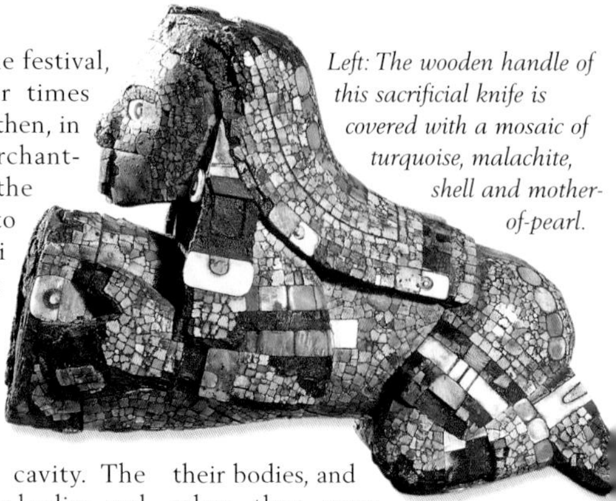

Left: The wooden handle of this sacrificial knife is covered with a mosaic of turquoise, malachite, shell and mother-of-pearl.

Perhaps the most remarkable of these ceremonies was that held to honour Tezcatlipoca. Each year, at the close of the month holy to Tezcatlipoca, a young man of intelligence and good looks was selected to represent the god and for a year was treated as his embodiment. By day, he lived in the god's temple, where he learned to play the flute and dance steps sacred to the 'Lord of the Smoking Mirror'. By night, he was sent out into the city, accompanied by a guard of eight warriors. In every quarter he visited he played evocative tunes on his flute, shaking the rattles tied to his legs and arms as he danced to signal his coming. The people of Tenochtitlán would nod reverently and sometimes carry out sick children to be blessed and cured by the passing god.

As the year drew to an end, the preparations for the sacrifice intensified. The Emperor visited Tezcatlipoca's temple and dressed the young man in the costume sacred to the god.

The god-victim was given four young wives, embodiments of significant goddesses. With five days to go to the sacrifice, the *tlatoani* or ruler went into devout retreat and the people understood that Tezcatlipoca was governing the Aztec capital of Tenochtitlán.

Above: Worshippers gaze reverently up the pyramid's steep steps as a victim's warm heart is flung skywards to honour the gods.

On the final day of the month, the youth was led with full ritual to Tezcatlipoca's shrine on the Great Pyramid. There he said goodbye to his four divine consorts, was placed over the sacrificial stone and his heart was pulled from his body. His corpse was taken down the steps and a meal of his cooked flesh served to the *tlatoani* and most prominent of the city's nobility and military elite. One of those in the select company was the young man who had been chosen to carry Tezcatlipoca's sacred flame within his body for the following 20 Aztec months – and be slaughtered in the god's name on the same day the following year.

Solar eclipses were terrifying times for the Aztecs, suggesting the unnatural encroachment of night into day, and *tzitzimime*, vengeful female spirits associated with darkness, were believed to rise in power. They could send sickness epidemics and were expected to play a part in the destruction of the Fifth Sun at the end of the current age. At times of eclipse, Aztecs made offerings of their own blood to persuade the god to sustain the sun and life on Earth. People with fair complexions were said to be full of light and were sacrificed to strengthen the sun in its struggle against darkness.

The Aztecs also held frequent sacrifices in the name of the rain gods, the *tláloques*. The gods cruelly required the blood of young children. As they were led to their deaths, the children would weep and the onlookers understood the tears that fell would become the rain they prayed for.

Right: On a pre-Toltec stela carved at the Maya site of Santa Lucia, Guatemala, a priest holds a severed head that drips blood.

COMMUNION WITH THE DIVINE

Sacrificial victims were treated with the greatest reverence. When an Aztec warrior captured a prisoner who would be taken to a ritual death, he treated him with solemnity and respect, declaring, 'Here I find my well-loved son'. A prisoner taken in this way was also said to take a grim satisfaction in the event and to declare, 'Here I encounter my well-respected father.' The only honourable fate for a warrior was to kill or be killed in battle or, if captured alive, to be taken to the temple for ritual death.

TLAHUICOLE

The story of the Tlaxcaltec warrior named Tlahuicole graphically demonstrates this concept. So great was Tlahuicole's renown in battle that, when he was captured by Aztec warriors, the *tlatoani* decided to spare his life and give him command of the Aztec army in a campaign against the Tarascans. Tlahuicole took on the command as he was ordered, but when he returned from the field he asked to be put to ritual death, for he felt that living on in captivity shamed him, whereas his sacrifice would restore the honour he had laboured so hard to win.

Below: A Yaxchilán lintel shows Lady Xoc having an ecstatic encounter with the Vision Serpent after sacrificing her own blood.

Above: Sacrificial rituals presented a magnificent spectacle, with sacred music and extravagant costumes on display.

MESSENGERS TO THE GODS

Those killed in ritual sacrifice were seen as messengers to the gods or were sometimes understood to become the very gods in whose honour they were put to death. Both priests and victims sometimes dressed as the gods they honoured and, among the Aztecs, victims were sometimes declared to be *ixiptla* ('in the god's image'). In this sense, the sacrificial ritual was a way of honouring and renewing the divine presence on Earth. The gods entered and united with the bodies of the victims and so were made manifest before the watching crowds.

The sacrifices presented a magnificent spectacle. Priests were bedecked in splendid costumes and feather headdresses and flowers adorned the temples. Musicians performed on conch-shell trumpets, flutes made from bones or reeds, drums and rattles. Dancers wore gold and silver bells that made a high ringing sound and blood flowed in a bright river from the steep temple steps to the bodies of the slain piled high at the temple front.

CANNIBALISM

Among the Aztecs it was common practice for the warriors who captured prisoners in battle to feed and care for them in captivity before the sacrifice. After the ritual, the bodies were decapitated and the heads put on display on the skull rack. The cannibalistic rite in which the victorious warriors would eat the bodies particularly shocked the Spanish conquistadors. However, if we understand that the Aztecs saw the victims as touched by or even embodying the gods, then we can see the act of cannibalism as a religious ritual, an act of communion with the divine. By eating the flesh of the victim, the warriors were able to share in the offering made to Huitzilopochtli at the summit of the temple-pyramid.

RELIGIOUS ECSTASY

Maya bloodletting was sometimes seen as a mystical act, an attempt to enter an ecstatic state in which a worshipper could communicate with ancestors or gods. Celebrated carvings in the Maya city of Yaxchilán show Lady Xoc, wife of King Shield Jaguar, in a bloodletting ritual.

In the first carving, Lady Xoc is shown drawing her own blood by pulling a thorned cord across her tongue, while her husband holds a flaming torch above her head. The second carving shows that her devotions deliver her to a visionary state. The blood she has produced has been collected on a piece of bark paper and set alight, producing a swirl of smoke in whose coils she can see the awesome Vision Serpent who commands the gateway through which the supernatural becomes visible in the natural realm.

The serpent has two jaws through which ancestors or deities can make themselves known in the world of men. From one peers the head of the war god, while from the other emerges the founder of the great Yaxchilán dynasty, Yat Balam ('Jaguar Penis'). Lady Xoc is asking for the help of Jaguar Penis and the war god in a military campaign which her husband, Jaguar Shield, is preparing. The inscription alongside the carvings dates the events shown to *c.* AD724–726.

Religious sacrificial ritual was not intended to bring the divine from another place into the physical world. The universe was filled with spiritual presence and the many gods, with their defined powers and roles, were everywhere. The sacrificial ritual celebrated this ever-present divine power in magnificent and devout spectacle.

Below: Masked dancers, priests and musicians congregate for a sacrificial ceremony in the Maya city of Bonampak.

REACHING FOR THE SKY

To Mesoamericans, the sky was a sacred place. The rising of Venus or of the sun and the movements of the stars played out the events of mythology and the deeds of the gods. The holiest places were those such as mountain peaks or the tops of temple pyramids that were nearest to the sky. At the climax of religious festivals, reverent processions would make the steep climb to the top of the pyramids to honour the gods high above the earth.

Many Aztec pyramids had temples at many levels, with the shrines of the most revered deities situated in the holiest of places at the top. The Great Temple at Tenochtitlán, which was inaugurated with such fervour by Emperor Ahuítzotl, had twin shrines to Huitzilopochtli (decorated with white and red symbols of war) and to Tláloc (coloured with white and blue symbols of water and rain) on its summit. There were areas sacred to other deities lower down the temple.

Above: The eastern stairs on the Pyramid of the Magician at the Maya site of Uxmal climb directly from ground to sanctuary.

Below: Cortés struck a blow to Aztec hearts when his men captured and wrecked the sacred arena on top of the Great Pyramid.

HUMILIATING AZTEC DEFEAT

At the time of the Conquest, this temple-top area, the most sacred place in the entire Aztec realm, was effectively appropriated for Spain and for Christianity by Hernán Cortés in an act of astonishing bravado and symbolic weight.

After the Spaniards had taken Moctezuma captive, when the Aztec leader was still nominally in control of his empire, Cortés demanded that a place of Christian worship be established on the highest level of the Great Temple. Moctezuma, fearful for his life and playing for time in case he could effect an escape, had no choice but to agree.

A Christian cross and an image of the Virgin Mary were placed at the summit of the temple, which could be viewed from all over Tenochtitlán and could even be seen from the shores of Lake Texcoco. Beneath these sacred icons, Cortés and the most prominent of the Spanish party held a Christian Mass, while the Aztecs looked on in dismay and rising fury.

In the wake of this event, the Aztec warriors and nobility attacked the Spaniards in the Europeans' compound. Subsequently, Cortés and his conquistadors added insult to injury by storming and destroying the upper levels of the Great Temple, throwing down and burning Tláloc's and Huitzilopochtli's shrines.

Above: *The main pyramid at Cobá rises to 42m (138ft). A sacred way (*sacbé*) runs from its base towards Chichén Itzá.*

MAN-MADE MOUNTAINS

Throughout Mesoamerica, mountains were important religious symbols and sometimes also the settings for sacred rites. The Maya believed that the souls of their dead ancestors found a dwelling place in the rocky heights of mountains.

The Maya living in lowland regions erected their own peaks in the form of the steep-sided temples that dominate the magnificent ruins of Maya cities. Some of these man-made mountains were royal mausoleums as well as temples; like the pyramids of ancient Egypt, they were built primarily to house the tombs of great kings. The Aztec peoples of the Triple Alliance built shrines and celebrated important religious fertility festivals on the hills of Huixachtlán and Tetzcotzingo and on Mount Tláloc. Like the Maya, they viewed their pyramid temples as sacred peaks.

Huixachtlán ('Place of the Thorn Trees') is an extinct volcano that stands between Lakes Xochimilco and Texcoco. It was a sacred place long before the Méxica made their way into the Valley of Mexico in the 13th century. On a temple platform high on Huixachtlán, the Aztecs celebrated the human sacrifice that was the central event in the New Fire rites that marked the end of one 52-year cycle and the beginning of the next.

Right: This clay temple was probably sacred to Quetzalcóatl-Ehecatl and may have been used as a household shrine.

Mount Tláloc, the highest peak on the eastern rim of the Valley of Mexico, rises well above 4,000m (13,000ft) and commands awe-inspiring views of the volcanoes Popocatépetl and Ixtaccíhuatl. It, too, was a sacred spot from ancient times. The Méxica and their allies in the Triple Alliance maintained a temple on the mountain-top where they celebrated an annual fertility rite. The rulers of Tenochtitlán, Texcoco, Tlacopán and Xochimilco made a pilgrimage to the mountain-top at the high point of the dry season to make offerings to Tláloc the rain god and usher in the rainy season. On Tetzcotzingo, a lower peak that lies in the foothills of Mount Tláloc, were several shrines to earth and maize deities. Netzahualcóyotl, the ruler of Texcoco, rebuilt and redeveloped many of these temples and shrines.

THE GREATEST OF AZTEC TEMPLES

In 1487, Emperor Ahuítzotl inaugurated El Templo Mayor, the Great Temple in Tenochtitlán, with an immense ritual sacrifice described by the chronicler Fernando de Alva Ixtlilxóchitl as, 'butchery ... without equal in human history'.

Work on the Great Temple had begun many years earlier under Moctezuma I (1440–68). To the warrior leader Ahuítzotl fell the task of dedicating a temple worthy of the gods who had delivered such a great empire to the Aztecs.

Ahuítzotl had become emperor only the previous year, in 1486, and had spent the first year of his reign in military campaigns against rebel provinces. They must have furnished many prisoners of war. Back in Tenochtitlán, the festival in honour of the Great Temple lasted for four days. According to some sources, as many as 80,000 victims were sacrificed during the festival. From all points of the compass, seemingly endless lines of captives were led towards the temple and up its steep sides to their deaths. In the sacred area at the top, Ahuítzotl stood waiting, attended by the rulers of his imperial allies Texcoco and Tlacopán. Ahuítzotl himself made the first sacrifice, plunging his obsidian knife into the chest of the victim on the sacrifical stone, then holding the heart up to the sacred sky before making obeisances to the new shrine of Huitzilopochtli. An army of priests was ready to take over in the emperor's wake. Bodies almost beyond counting were flung down the temple steps, staining them with the blood that the Aztecs understood to be the water of life, the offering sweetest to their gods.

SPIRIT JAGUARS: SHAMANS

The religious life of Mesoamericans went beyond the public rites of sacrifice conducted by the emperor, the warrior elite and the priests in temples. The people had a strong and enduring belief in shamans. These were people gifted with visionary and religious powers who were capable of making journeys of collective psychic discovery on behalf of the tribe, who could conjure the powers of the spirit world and influence the destiny of individuals and of the city-state itself.

Above: According to myth, the Maya god Itzamná built the great Pyramid of the Magician, Uxmal, in a single night.

JAGUAR IMAGERY

Belief in shamans in the region of Mexico and Guatemala dates back at least to the Olmec civilization of *c.*1500–400BC and probably much earlier still, into the Siberian past of Mesoamerican peoples. Shamans are still active among certain Siberian and Arctic peoples, the descendants of contemporaries of the first nomads who made the trek across the Bering landmass to North America as long as 23,000 years ago.

Jaguar imagery used by Olmec craftsmen is thought to honour the shape-shifting shamans. The jaguar's furtive behaviour and deadly capacity to hunt in the hours of darkness made it one of the key allies of the shaman in his demanding spirit-journeys. Shamans were said to be able to transform themselves into these majestic creatures during their trances.

The jaguar later became the principal animal form of the god Tezcatlipoca, the patron deity of shamans and the god of night among many other things. According to the Franciscan friar Diego Durán, a polished obsidian statue of Tezcatlipoca stood in the temple dedicated to the god on the Great Pyramid at Tenochtitlán. The god Tezcatlipoca's image held a gold mirror, indicating that he saw everything that happened. The builders of Teotihuacán almost certainly practised shamanism like their forebears of the Olmec civilization and their cultural descendants among the Aztecs. A carving of a jaguar or other feline emerging from a doorway decorated with starfish and zigzag markings symbolic of light was found in excavations at Teotihuacán in 2001.

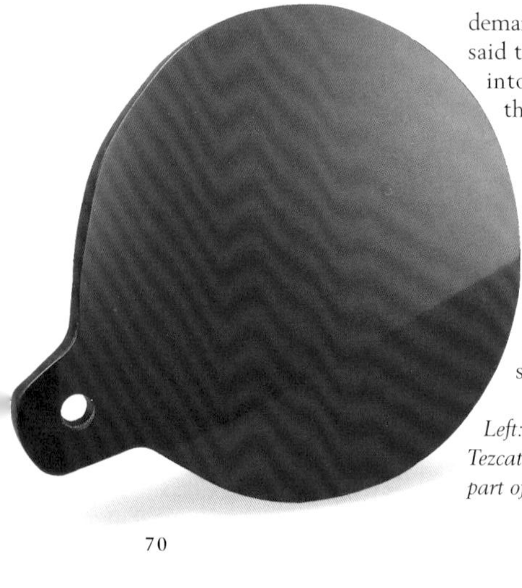

Left: This obsidian mirror sacred to Tezcatlipoca, god of shamans, was probably part of the treasure Cortés sent to Europe.

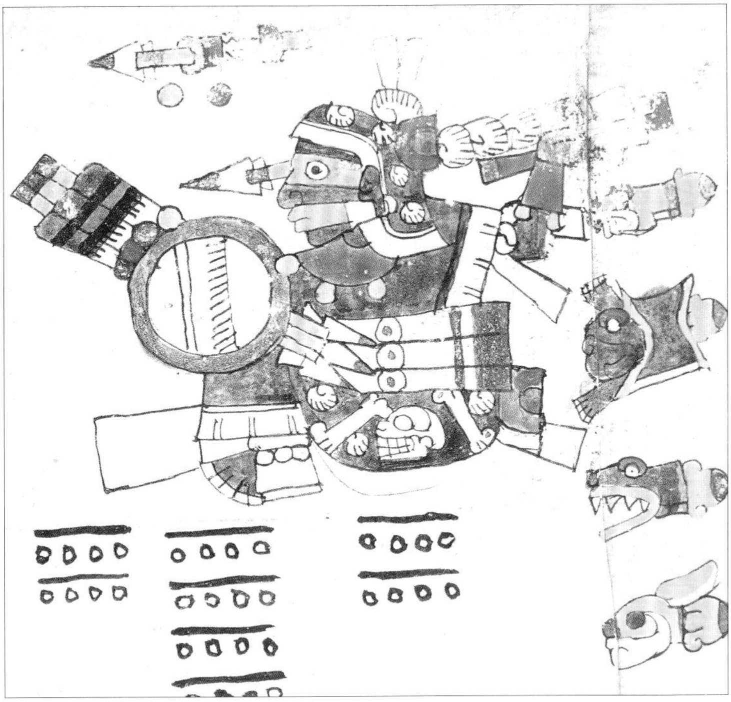

Right: An image from the Codex Cospi *(c.1350–1500) depicts the 'black aspect' of Tezcatlipoca, associated with sorcery.*

The carving is thought to represent the shaman-jaguar emerging from the spirit world on his return to the world of men after a journey. It was uncovered in the ruins that scholars believe were once a large palace, just north of the Pyramid of the Sun.

ANIMAL DOUBLES

Many Aztec gods had the capacity to appear in animal, human or other form. Tezcatlipoca, the deceiver and sower of discord, was said to appear as a coyote, a monkey or a skunk in addition to his more princely jaguar form. Moreover, Mesoamericans believed animal doubles were not the sole preserve of the gods. Each person had an animal form, a kind of animal familiar, which functioned as a protector. In the Aztecs' Nahuatl language, the animal form was called *tonal*. The word *nahual* was used to refer to the secret ability to shift shape and to the shamans who could practise it.

TRANCES AND VISIONS

From far back in Mesoamerican history, shamans took hallucinogenic substances to induce trances and visions. They made narcotic substances for ritual use from the toxin that toads make and store in small bumps on their head, as well as from the seeds of morning glory, from the peyote cactus and from various hallucinogenic mushrooms.

Some shamans were also temple priests, while others were not part of the traditional religious hierarchy. A shaman played an important role within the temple functions among the Maya. Known as a *chilam*, he was a man believed to be gifted with visionary powers. He would enter a visionary trance, after ritual bloodletting from his cheeks, earlobes or penis, and in the trance would receive and transmit messages from the gods. Other priests gathered round to translate his divinely inspired speech.

Some shamans offered to cure sickness using herbs and healing plants or native rites of magic. Others practised black magic and were deeply feared. One group of magicians known as 'sleep throwers' claimed that, through spells involving the arm of a woman who had died in child-birth, they could ensure that victims would be asleep so that a passer-by could steal from them. Other unscrupulous lay-priests promised to bring harm to enemies by burning tiny effigies of them.

THE SERPENT'S DOUBLE

Among the Aztecs, the god Xólotl's ability to change shape made him a patron of magicians and sorcerers.

In one version of the Aztec myth of the birth of the sun and moon, the assembled gods chose to sacrifice themselves in order to make these celestial bodies begin their cycle of movements across the sky. But one god, Xólotl, refused to give himself up. In his attempts to escape he transformed himself into a double ear of maize, a double maguey plant and a fish before he was caught and the gods' collective will was carried out.

Xólotl was god of monsters and of twins and other dual manifestations. He was associated with dogs, especially with the hairless dogs known as *xoloitzcuintli* by the Aztecs. Xólotl was celebrated also as the dog-double of the Plumed Serpent Quetzalcóatl and in this guise travelled with Quetzalcóatl into the underworld, Mictlán, where they succeeded in collecting the bones of past generations of humans. They later used the bones to create a human race for the new age of the world. Quetzalcóatl, of many attributes, was associated with the planet Venus and, in his form as Xólotl, was Venus rising as the evening star. Scholars believe that Xólotl was originally an independent Mesoamerican god of monsters who became associated with Quetzalcóatl in the Postclassic Period.

READING THE FUTURE

Mesoamericans believed that time was sacred, part of the substance of the gods themselves, and that those skilled in sacred rites could read the events of the future. One of the priest's key roles among both Maya and Aztecs was as a diviner of what was to come. This mystical activity had its full complement of practical applications on the level both of the city-state and of the humble farmer or merchant.

Such was the demand for information about the future that, as well as trusting in their priests, Mesoamericans also turned to a range of lay figures who offered access to arcane knowledge. Some claimed to be able to decipher patterns of future events in the shifting of light on an obsidian mirror or on water in a pot. Others could see what was to come in the lines made by a handful of maize grains when they were flung down on a cloak.

Right: A priest makes an offering. This Classic Maya stone disc (c.AD600–700) was found at Tonina in Chiapas, Mexico.

SACRED BUNDLES

Some aspects of religious life in Mesoamerica were distinctly different from the public ritual of major human sacrifices. One example is the Aztec and Maya practice of worshipping bundles that contained objects holy to a god or ancestor. This tradition may have dated back to the ancient days of migration, when nomads packed up their gods when they raised camp to move on. According to the *Popol Vuh*, the Quiché Maya brought a holy parcel with them on their migrations and worshipped it in honour of a revered ancestor, and the Méxica and other Chichimec groups are also known to have carried sacred bundles held holy to forebears. Among the Méxica, sacred bundles were carried by special priests named 'god-bearers'. The bundles were said to contain the mantles of the gods, which were left at the dawn of this era when the deities sacrificed themselves to give motion to the sun and moon, as well as jaguar skins, pieces of jade, jewels and other precious items. Maya of all social ranks kept life-sized clay idols for use in religious rites in the home.

RITUALS OF ATONEMENT

The need to propitiate and satisfy the gods could go beyond ritual sacrifice, whether of humans, animals or the worshippers' own blood. There were several established rituals among Mesoamericans for atonement, confession or mortification of the self. The Aztecs allowed men to make amends for sexual wrongdoing by

AFTER THE CONQUEST

The shapeshifting gods of Mesoamerica lived on after the conquistadors imposed Christian culture and doctrines.

The Mesoamericans were quick to take to the new faith of Christianity. They appear to have seen in the worship of Jesus Christ a similarity to the cult of the Plumed Serpent Quetzalcóatl. Jesus's teachings on brotherly love were in harmony with Topiltzin-Quetzalcóatl's pious and peaceful government, while the Christian idea of the second coming clearly resonated with the ancient Mesoamerican myth of Quetzalcóatl's departure and promised return. In an unlikely marriage of faiths, the Plumed Serpent became closely associated with Christ.

The Mesoamericans also adapted Roman Catholic Christian practices to the old faiths and continued to follow aspects of the old religion under the noses of the Christian monks. Among both Maya and Aztecs, for example, old gods were linked to Christian saints: Tláloc the rain god was revered under the guise of St John the Baptist. At the same time, traditional practices were aligned with Christian festivals: the yearly visit to the graves of the ancestors was carried out on All Souls' Day. In 1531, a peasant named Juan Diego had a vision of a dark-skinned Virgin Mary near a temple to the ancient Earth goddess Tonantzin. Under the name of the Black Virgin of Guadelupe, this hybrid Mesoamerican-Christian deity became Mexico's patron saint.

The way in which Aztecs and Maya accepted Christian practices while also maintaining the ways of the old faith is typical of Mesoamericans' approach to religion. They were generally willing to accept that new gods and new practices were an extension of what they already knew, rather than a completely new departure, and built upon existing practices and pantheons rather than replacing them.

Above: The Aztecs made regular devotions at household shrines containing clay temples and models of the gods and goddesses.

abasement before Tlazoltéotl, a fertility goddess associated with filth, excrement and sex. The individual would take his confession to a priest dressed as Tlazoltéotl and would be allowed freedom from his past deeds in return for faithful performance of penitential acts.

The Zapotecs made the rite of ritual bloodletting an occasion for confession. After making cuts in their cheeks and arms, they would let the blood flow on to husks of maize while they made a solemn statement of their evildoing.

The Maya had a scapegoat tradition, in which an individual took on the punishment for a whole community's wrongdoing. The villagers would choose one person, often an elderly woman, who would listen as each person recounted how they had shamed themselves or the group. The scapegoat would then be put to death by stoning.

Right: Fertility goddess Tlazoltéotl had the power to wipe away sexual wrongdoing. Her image is from the Codex Rios *(c.1570–95).*

DEATH AND THE AFTERLIFE

Mesoamericans had a highly developed awareness of death and its proximity. Life expectancy was low, child mortality was high, wars were frequent, if not almost continuous, and religion called for a steady stream of human victims for sacrificial rituals. Death, its rituals and speculation about a human's fate after this life inspired intriguing narratives in both Aztec and Maya mythology. Ancient Mesoamerican beliefs associated with death, sacrifice and the afterlife are as profound as those of other major civilizations. Their investigation of the human spirit's destiny after death ranks alongside the ancient Egyptian and Tibetan Books of the Dead.

Below: These solid clay figurines of elegantly attired members of the Maya nobility were left in graves on Jaina Island.

COSMOLOGY

The cosmology of both Aztec and Maya envisaged a many-layered universe, with thirteen tiers of heaven rising above the Earth and nine levels of Mictlán, a sinister underworld beneath. To the Aztecs, the underworld was a place of darkness and fear, of endless misfortune. Its rulers were the skeleton god Mictlantecuhtli, Lord of the Dead, and his serpent-skirted spouse Mictecacíhuatl.

According to the Aztecs, a select few were bound for the happy realms above. What was decisive was not how individuals lived but how they died. Those who died a natural death were bound for the underworld, but warriors killed in battle, women who died in childbirth and even those who took their own lives were spared the lower realms. Warriors who died on the battlefield became *cuauhteca* ('Eagle Companions') and could enter the eastern paradise Tonatiuhichán. They were destined to join the entourage of the great sun himself in the form of hummingbirds or butterflies.

Above: Among the Aztecs, the corpse was tied in a squatting pose prior to cremation or, for richer people, burial with grave goods.

One tradition told that the souls of these great men were responsible for the daily miracle of the sun's return. At dawn and throughout the morning hours, the spirits of warriors slain on the battlefield hauled the sun up from its nightly residence in the underworld to its position at its zenith in the sky. Those who died by water or in storms – for example, by drowning or by lightning – were said to be destined for Tlalocán, a paradise presided over by the great rain god Tláloc, where life-giving waters fell in a constant light drizzle and flowers, fruit and delectable foods grew abundantly without need for the human labour of irrigation, digging and planting.

The Maya also believed that some would progress to a life of heavenly ease. Shaded by the strong boughs of the world's first tree, they would enjoy their leisure drinking chocolate. However, the great majority were destined for the dark and dangerous realms of the underworld. The Maya called this dread place Xibalba ('Realm of Fright'). Here the dead would have to undergo many trials at the hands of foul and sadistic divinities.

FUNERARY RITES

Both rich and poor were buried with supplies to help them on this afterlife voyage. Poorer Maya were laid beneath the floors of their house. People were buried with the tools of the trade they followed. For example, hunters would be interred with their spears and fishermen with their harpoons and nets. The dead were also supplied with pottery containers of water and food supplies. Most would also have a little ground maize placed in their mouth and a handful of jade beads for use as money in the world after death. After an entire generation of burials, the house would no longer be used for daily living and would be kept as an ancestral shrine.

Below: A tomb in the Maya city of Uxmal marks the spot at which the deceased noble began his journey to the underworld.

Nobles, royalty and the priestly elite were buried in splendid tombs with generous supplies and even helpers. A Maya nobleman buried at Tikal was surrounded by fine ceramic vessels that contained maize stew and chocolate drink. He was accompanied by the bodies of nine servants who had been sacrificed at his death. Many took worldly wealth with them on their journey, presumably in the hope of using it during their underworld ordeals. A priest buried at Chichén Itzá was adorned with a splendid necklace of pearls that may have been brought from as far away as Venezuela by traders. The rulers and nobility were buried in the great plazas of the Maya cities. The Maya understood that the voyage to the underworld began by water, and nobles were often depicted travelling to the lands below by canoe. The great plazas were seen as symbolic lakes that gave access to the land of the dead below.

In Yucatán, some members of the nobility were cremated. Their ashes were placed in pottery or wooden urns carved with the dead person's features. Sometimes portrait statues were commissioned. These were left with a hollow space in the back of the head in which to place the ashes.

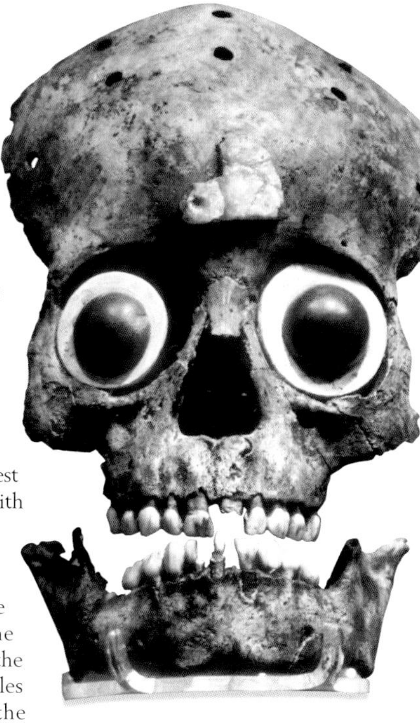

Above: To the Aztecs, death was a frequent visitor. This decorated child's skull was offered to Mictlantecuhtli, god of the dead.

Most Aztecs were cremated. The corpse was dressed in his or her best clothes, then tied in a squatting pose and wrapped in cloth before being set alight. Interment in stone vaults was reserved for prominent members of the nobility and rulers. As among the Maya, a notable man might have a number of servants and even wives killed on his death so that they could accompany him to the underworld.

Among both Aztecs and Maya, a dead man was sometimes buried with his dog to provide a companion and protector-guide on his journey. The custom had religious and mythological resonance, for the revered deity Quetzalcóatl was accompanied by his dog-twin Xólotl on his journey to the underworld.

CHAPTER FOUR

WARFARE AND MILITARY LIFE

War was a way of life for Mesoamericans. The Aztecs waged war for practical gain to secure resources, raw materials and slave labour. They also understood that to wage war was to be intimately connected with the religious duty to return energy to the cosmos and to make devotions to the gods through offerings of lifeblood. Military might was an instrument of empire, used to conquer territory and deter rebellion, and also a means of capturing victims for the sacrificial knife. Some Aztec campaigns were conducted for this purpose above all others. It was not markedly different among the Maya. Classic-Period inscriptions and surviving texts suggest rival Maya city-states were almost constantly in conflict. Like the Aztecs, the Maya were hungry for live prisoners; ordinary folk were earmarked as slave labourers and the nobles among the captives were destined for sacrifice on the temple pyramids.

War was therefore understood as a natural condition by both the Aztecs and the Maya. The great god Huitzilopochtli leapt from his mother Coatlícue's body fully armed and immediately began to wield his weapons, slaughtering his sister Coyolxauhqui, the moon goddess, and hundreds of his brothers in the first moments of his life. The Aztecs saw their male offspring in Huitzilopochtli's image, envisaging them as warriors from the day of their birth, or even before. Women who died in childbirth were understood to have perished at the hands of their unborn offspring.

Left: Toltec stone warriors at Tula stand 4.6m (15ft) tall. Ready for battle, each carries an atlatl *spear-thrower.*

THE FLOWER WARS

Some Aztec military campaigns were planned in advance and carried out with the agreement of both sides as a testing ground on which warriors could capture prisoners for religious sacrifice. Such a battle was known as *xochiyaóyotl* ('war of flowers') in reference to the magnificently dressed warriors rounded up and carried home like a garland of blooms.

Some scholars believe that the practice originated in the distant Mesoamerican past, but no examples have yet been found of Toltec or earlier wars conducted solely to capture live prisoners. Among the earliest known instances of *xochiyaóyotl* is the war between the Méxica/Tepanecs and the Chalca, which began in 1376 and which is believed to have started as a 'flower war'.

Above: Images of soldiers at Bonampak show that fighting was at close quarters using spears.

BUYING FOOD AT MARKET

In the 1400s, the city-states of the Triple Alliance conducted regular campaigns of this kind against Atlixco, Huexotzingo and other cities. Tlacaélel, brother of Moctezuma I Ilhuicamina (1440–1468), likened the gathering of victims through war to buying food at market. Discussing plans for the inauguration of the Great Temple in Tenochtitlán and the constant need for a plentiful supply of sacrificial victims, Tlacaélel declared that there was no actual need for their war god Huitzilopochtli to wait for an insult, diplomatic quarrel or some other conventional reason to start a war: he should simply find and enter a convenient 'market' for the food he needed. At this market, Tlacaélel said, Huitzilopochtli and his army could gather victims like so many tortillas. The market should be nearby, because the flesh of distant peoples might not be to his liking.

Rather than fight in such distant realms as the lands of the Huastecs, the army should take their war to the conveniently situated cities of Atlixco, Tecoac, Cholula, Huexotzingo, Tlaxcala and Tliluhquitepec. The war against local enemies should not be decisive. Fighting must always continue or be easily renewed, so that Huitzilopochtli would have the victims for whom he hungered within easy reach. Huitzilopochtli would feed on them with pleasure, as a man enjoys a tortilla warm from the oven.

Right: A Totonac carving from east-central Mexico shows a prisoner of war bound hand and foot.

ESCAPE TO VICTORY

On the night of 30 June 1520, canoe-borne Aztec warriors swarmed around Spanish conquistadors as the Europeans attempted to flee Tenochtitlán along one of the many causeways that connected the city to the mainland. The Aztecs had the Spaniards at their mercy, but they did not finish them off. Instead, they allowed the surviving conquistadors to proceed on to Tlaxcalán and once there prepare for a renewed assault on Tenochtitlán.

In the darkness of the *Noche Triste* ('sad night') on 30 June, the Aztecs were in familiar surroundings while the invaders were panicking on the narrow causeway in driving rain. The defenders of Tenochtitlán had the chance to exterminate the Spaniards. Instead, they directed their attention to seizing booty and capturing prisoners. Their decision would lead to the collapse of their empire, the end of their Mesoamerican world.

Above: Battling for honour and to feed the gods, Aztec soldiers round up prisoners destined for sacrifice in Tenochtitlán.

A WAR GAME?

Some scholars suggest that the flower wars of the Aztecs might have had their origins in a kind of war game, a substitute for full conflict in which the contestants would put their fates in the hands of the gods. Historians have compared the practice to the ball game. This distinctive sport, which was practised throughout the Mesoamerican region, was seen, among other things, as a ritual enactment of cosmic struggles between good and evil or light and darkness; a kind of mythic encounter between Quetzalcóatl and his dark brother Tezcatlipoca and also between the Hero Twins and the lords of Xibalba.

Given the demand for sacrificial victims, the war game of the flower wars might have grown into a major military event, regularly conducted and leading to the deaths of thousands of warriors. Other experts suggest that the flower wars had a political and a religious dimension and were an important instrument of government. According to this theory, the wars maintained control over enemies by capturing and eliminating the leading warriors and nobles in the enemy group. It might be that in some flower wars, military and strategic aims existed alongside religious and ritual ones. Certainly, the demonstration of the Triple Alliance's military might can only have helped to discourage rebellion among subject peoples.

The flower wars took place alongside other more conventional types of conflict. The Triple Alliance regularly used its military might to extend the territory of the empire by winning land, enforcing alliances and also ensuring tribute payments were made. The religious and ritual elements so evident in the flower wars informed the Aztec approach to all types of conflict. Some historians have even suggested that the Mesoamerican understanding that ritual triumph was more important than all-out victory, was a major reason why the Aztecs were ultimately undone by Cortés's small force of conquistadors.

Below: Prisoners of the flower wars knew they had no chance of escape, but they were treated with respect. The illustration is from the Florentine Codex *(1575–77).*

CHAIN OF COMMAND: THE AZTEC ARMY

The *tlatoani* or ruler was the chief army commander. He was expected to demonstrate his own battlefield prowess by leading a military campaign as part of his coronation celebrations. His chief adviser on military matters was the *cihuacoatl* ('female serpent'). This was a position of supreme importance. Tlacaélel, the brother of Moctezuma I Ilhuicamina – who made such an eloquent statement of the values lying behind the flower wars – was *cihuacoatl* to five successive rulers of Tenochtitlán: Itzcóatl, Moctezuma I Ilhuicamina, Axayácatl, Tizoc and Ahuítzotl.

Next in command was a council of four noblemen: the *tlacochcalcatl*, the *tlaccatecatl*, the *tillancalqui* and the *etzhuanhuanco*. They were usually brothers or near relatives of the *tlatoani* himself. Top-ranking warriors reported directly to the council members.

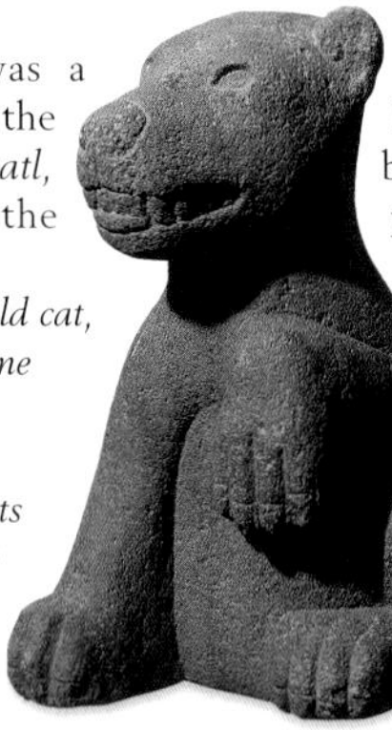

Right: The ocelot, a native wild cat, was the symbol adopted by one group of Aztec warriors.

Below: In a violent phase of its cycle, the planet Venus shoots an ocelot-warrior. This detail is from a Mixtec document, the Codex Cospi.

MILITARY ORDERS

The military was the prime promoter of social mobility among the Aztecs. A warrior from the common ranks could rise to all but the very highest army positions by dint of bravery and success in battle. The two supreme orders of warriors were the *cuauhchique* ('Shaved Ones') and the *otontin* ('Otomies'). To be admitted, a warrior must have carried out 20 or more deeds of remarkable bravery and, naturally, also have brought home a great number of prisoners for sacrifice. The elite groups of the jaguar-warriors and the eagle-warriors were members of these top-ranking groups. These elites made the most of their right to wear the feathers, jewellery and cloaks that were emblems of their high standing. In Tenochtitlán, the eagle- and jaguar-warriors had

EAGLE-WARRIORS AND JAGUAR-WARRIORS

One of the many versions of the myth explaining the creation of the Sun and Moon accounts for the appearance of the eagle and jaguar in whose honour the elite warriors were named.

On the plain before Teotihuacán the twin gods Tecciztécatl and Nanahuatzin stood before the sacred fire. Would they throw themselves into the flames in order to light the world?

Tecciztécatl, haughty and boastful and dressed in magnificent robes, went forward four times to sacrifice himself, yet each time pulled back, afraid. However, his twin Nanahuatzin, humble and weak, an insignificant figure in paper clothes made from tree-bark, flung himself fearlessly into the blaze, creating the Sun. Then Tecciztécatl, inspired by the other's bravery, finally leapt into the flames, becoming the Moon.

Nanahuatzin, the twin who turned out to be the brave one despite his feeble appearance, became the patron deity of twins.

The eagle was the first creature to follow the gods Tecciztécatl and Nanahuatzin into the blaze. Forever afterwards his beautiful feathers were blackened. The jaguar followed the eagle into the fire. His burning gave his coat black spots that sometimes form a line along his back.

These brave creatures, first into the holy flames that had frightened Tecciztécatl, were worthy exemplars for the elite groups of the eagle- and jaguar-warriors of the Aztec army. If warriors proved that they knew no fear, then they were permitted to adorn themselves to accentuate their likeness to their animal forebears.

meeting houses within the temple precincts. Here, young boys were initiated into the military way of life from an early age. While still at school, the boys were taught how to handle their weapons, march on campaign and manoeuvre in battle. They learned the importance of discipline and obedience to the military hierarchy and practised using the clubs, shields, darts and spears that were used on the battlefield. The impressively dressed elite warriors mingled with them, sharing tales of their exploits on campaign and cementing the boys' love of army life. Later the boys would compete for the chance to carry equipment and other loads into battle for the elite warriors.

DUTY TO THE EMPIRE

The Aztecs had no standing army; the military hierarchy called up warriors for campaigns as necessary. Each *capultin* – a town or area of a city, based on old tribal clans – was required to provide a unit of around 400 men. They were commanded by a local leader and marched under their own standard, but were also grouped in larger divisions of around 8,000 warriors. As many as 25 divisions would be sent on longer campaigns, making a total of 200,000 fighting men.

Right: An Aztec terracotta statue shows an eagle-warrior ready for combat. Eagle-warriors were dedicated to 'feeding' the sun with the blood of prisoners.

Before a campaign began, the supreme council dispatched orders for supplies to be collected. Tribute-paying areas had to provide beans, salt, pumpkin seeds, maize meal and maize cakes to feed the army. Army porters carried these supplies.

ON CAMPAIGN

The army would march in a long, ordered procession along the narrow roads of the Aztec empire on its campaigns. Leading the way were the army's barelegged scouts, identifiable by their simple loincloths and shirts of white cotton, faces painted with yellow ochre and long hair tied with red ribbons. They were armed with spears and carried conch-shell trumpets, which they used when they needed to send messages to the main ranks of the army behind. With them marched the warrior-priests carrying images of Huitzilopochtli, the martial god in whose name the empire's wars were waged. They were followed by the top warriors and members of the military elite. This group would include the *tlatoani* himself, if he were leading the campaign, together with members of the supreme council.

The army units from Tenochtitlán came next in the train, followed by troops from Tlatelolco, Texcoco and Tlacopán and any other currently allied cities. In the rearguard, many miles down the road from the beginning of the procession, came the troops provided by subject cities of the empire as part of their tribute payment. So narrow were the tracks the army followed that an army unit of 8,000 men might stretch out for as much as 25km (15 miles), according to leading historians.

Left: An illustration from the Codex Mendoza *(c.1541) represents six triumphs in the career of a successful warrior.*

INTO BATTLE

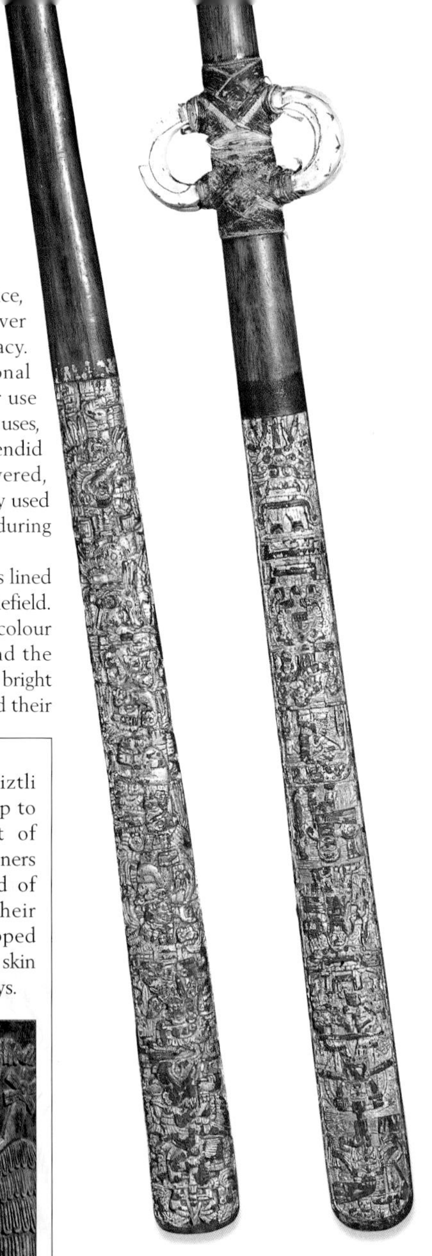

Ordinary members of the Aztec army wore a simple wrapping around their thighs and loins and were given a mantle or overgarment of maguey cloth. Some went barefoot into battle adorned with body paint.

HOW THEY FOUGHT

Aztec warriors fought hand-to-hand with stabbing javelins and clubs fitted with blades of the volcanic glass obsidian, protecting themselves with leather-fringed shields. Some of the older or elite warriors wore wooden helmets carved with the symbols of the order to which they belonged. They also used the *atlatl* or spear-thrower, a spear carved with a holding place for a dart. With practice, a warrior could send these darts over great distances with deadly accuracy. The *atlatl* was usually a functional object, made from plain wood for use in battle. But it also had ceremonial uses, and archaeologists have found splendid carved and painted, even gold-covered, spear-throwers. These were probably used by priests impersonating the gods during religious ceremonies.

In a typical battle, the two armies lined up opposite one another on the battlefield. There would have been a blaze of colour as the light caught on plumes and the spears waved by warriors dressed in bright animal skins. The men demonstrated their fearlessness by urging the enemy to do their worst or by dashing out from their own ranks to adopt a threatening or insulting pose. Excitement built as the men's voices rose to a steady roar. The blowing of the conch-shell trumpets

Above: These two magnificent examples of the Aztec warrior's atlatl, *or spear-thrower, are covered with gold and carved with scenes depicting ritual sacrifices.*

GLADIATORIAL SACRIFICE

A sacrificial ritual celebrating the power of the Aztec warrior was the climax of the festival of Tlacaxipehualiztli ('Flaying of men')held in honour of Xipe Totec, 'Our Lord, the Flayed One', god of spring and vegetation.

In the rite, which the Spanish called 'gladiatorial sacrifice', five prisoners of war were put to death by elite Aztec warriors in a staged conflict. The prisoners, treated as always among the Aztecs with the greatest respect and even reverence as divine offerings, were dressed in a costume that identified them as Xipe Totec and tied to a sacrificial stone. They were given a club covered with feathers with which to defend themselves. Five warriors – two eagle-warriors, two jaguar-warriors and a fifth of either order who was left-handed – were set loose upon them. The battle must have been short, for the warriors fought fiercely with *macáhuitl* (clubs with obsidian blades). The blood of the sacrificed prisoners fed the earth. The Tlacaxipehualiztli festival took place in the build-up to the rainy season. Also as part of Tlacaxipehualiztli, a group of prisoners were slain by the usual method of having their heart ripped from their chest. The bodies were then stripped of their skin. Priests wore the flayed skin in honour of Xipe Totec for 20 days.

Right: A detail from the delicate carving on an Aztec huehuetl, *or wooden drum, represents a jaguar-warrior in his finery.*

Right: Unlike Cortés and his men, the Aztecs did not have iron armour. A ceramic model gives a detailed impression of the protective jerkins worn by Aztec warriors.

spilled forth and the warriors burst forward, screeching and whooping with bloodlust. They hurled stones into the enemy ranks and let loose the darts from their spear-throwers, roaring as opposing warriors fell, clutching their heads or sides. When the two advancing forces met in hand-to-hand combat, warriors fought desperately with obsidian-bladed clubs which inflicted terrible slicing wounds.

REWARDS FOR VALOUR

An Aztec warrior could express his devotion to the gods through valour in battle, but there were also many worldly incentives to urge soldiers to high achievements. Those who impressed in war and won significant numbers of sacrificial captives were presented with suits of animal skin. These soldiers could win the right to drink the favourite Aztec alcoholic drink, *pulque*, in public places, to dine in the royal palaces and to keep concubines for their pleasure. Warriors who particularly distinguished themselves, by repeatedly proving their bravery or by taking captive many scores of prisoners, might be admitted to one of the elite companies of warriors such as the jaguar- or eagle-warriors. They had the right to wear sumptuous feather headdresses, leather bracelets, jewellery and cloaks adorned with feathers and were given their marks of rank at special presentation ceremonies, often in the presence of the *tlatoani* himself. The jaguar-warriors had the right to wear a jaguar skin over their cotton body armour, while eagle-warriors wore an eagle-head helmet.

Left: A detail from the Florentine Codex *(1575–7) shows a prisoner of war making a show of defiance when surrounded by four jaguar-warriors in a gladiatorial sacrifice.*

RUNNING THE AZTEC EMPIRE

The capture of the city of Azcapotzalco and the ritual slaughter of its ruler, Maxtla, in 1428, marked the end of the Tepanec empire and the establishment of the Triple Alliance of Tenochtitlán, Texcoco and Tlacopán that was the driving force behind Aztec expansion.

Below: This stone standard-bearer was found at the heart of the Aztec empire, the Great Pyramid in Tenochtitlán. He carried a banner outside a temple honouring Huitzilopochtli, Tláloc or another major Aztec deity.

These three independent city-states shared both in the military activity needed to conquer and control the lands of the Aztec empire and in the inflow of tribute that was its reward.

CONSOLIDATION

Following the defeat of Azcapotzalco, Itzcóatl, who was the *tlatoani* or ruler of Tenochtitlán, wasted no time in attempting to consolidate the position of his city-state and of the alliance. With the assistance of forces from Texcoco and Tlacopán, Itzcóatl led a campaign to conquer the agricultural settlements of Cuitlahuac, Culhuacán, Mixquic and Xochimilco on Lake Xochimilco to the south of Tenochtitlán.

Netzahualcóyotl, the exiled prince of Texcoco who had led the capture of Azcapotzalco, had then to attend to unfinished local business, for he was not yet established as ruler of his city-state. His father, Ixtlilxóchitl, had been ruler of that city, but in 1418 had been killed in the course of a failed war against the Tepanec warrior leader Tezozómoc. For some years Netzahualcóyotl, who had witnessed his father's death, lived in hiding, but in time he won the support of his uncle, the Méxica leader Itzcóatl, and played a major part in the war against Azcapotzalco. Now, with Itzcóatl's backing, he eliminated elements hostile to his position and re-established his family's rule in Texcoco.

EXPANSION

The armies of the Triple Alliance looked further afield and prepared for a major campaign to conquer the fertile Tlalhuica territories that lay beyond the Ajusco Mountains, well to the south of Lake Xochimilco. They raised a vast army that marched behind a company of scouts and priests across the forest-covered Ajusco range and down to the plain beyond. The tramping soldiers carried their weapons and battle-costumes, while companies of porters transported food and other supplies. They took their objective, Cuauhnahuac, the main town of the region, and returned in triumph, carrying booty and leading prisoners for sacrifice. The Tlalhuica lands had been a valuable possession of the Tepanecs, the previous imperial power. In taking them, the Triple Alliance widened its horizons, seeking to establish itself on an equal footing with the great Tepanec state established by Tezozómoc.

The Aztec empire was a network of dependencies paying tribute to the cities of the Triple Alliance but otherwise retaining a sense of their own independence. As they acquired new territories, it was the Aztecs' policy to leave the conquered rulers in place, as long as the arranged tribute was provided on time. The initial plan, formed in the reign of Itzcóatl, was to replace local rulers with centrally appointed ones. However, Netzahualcóyotl, who had first-hand experience of the intrigues and plotting of royal factions in Texcoco, argued that leaving rulers nominally in control of their domains would reduce ill-feeling and the likelihood of revolt. Itzcóatl saw the success of Netzahualcóyotl's policy in the lands controlled by Texcoco and adopted the practice himself.

SUCCESSION

Itzcóatl's successor, Moctezuma I Ilhuicamina, consolidated the gains that had been made before embarking, in 1458, on a series of military campaigns that greatly expanded the imperial possessions. He was succeeded by his grandson Axayácatl who, in a reign of 13 years (1469–81), further expanded the empire, conquering 37 towns

Above: A battle scene from the Codex Tlaxcala *shows conquistadors overcoming Aztec resistance in the region of Culhuacán.*

n the Toluca Valley, the Gulf Coast, he Puebla Valley, Guerrero and to the north of the Valley of Mexico. He was a skilled leader and soldier, who succeeded n putting down a rebellion by Tenochtitlán's neighbouring sister-city, Tlatelolco, in 1473.

SETBACKS

Axayácatl's reign was marred six years later by a major defeat, when the Tarascans of Michoacán humbled the imperial army. n two disastrous engagements near Taximaloyán (modern Charo), the 32,000-strong Aztec army was crushed. Only 200 Méxica warriors limped home o Tenochtitlán, accompanied by fewer han 2,000 comrades from Texcoco, Xochimilco and other imperial cities. Axayácatl put this defeat behind him and ed a successful campaign to put down ebellions on the Gulf Coast.

Axayácatl's brother, Tizoc, became ruler of Tenochtitlán in 1481, but his reign was a military disaster. A *tlatoani* had to lead a war as part of his coronation rites: the campaign was expected to be a triumphant procession, culminating in a magnificent sacrifice of legions of newly captured victims. In Tizoc's case, the coronation war was a near-defeat that produced only 40 prisoners. He failed to build on Axayácatl's expansionist triumphs, merely putting down revolts in already conquered parts of the empire. Rebellions became more frequent as his weakness became obvious and his reign was brought to a premature end, probably by poisoning, in 1486. Despite its military failure, Tizoc's reign produced a magnificent celebration in stone of the empire and its divine mandate.

Tizoc was succeeded by his brother Ahuítzotl. A natural leader and fearless warrior, he restored the pride of the imperial army. He led a renewed expansion, capturing 45 towns and adding great sweeps of territory to the empire, notably Oaxaca, rich in gold, painted cotton and cochineal. Under his rule, the empire stretched from the land of the Huastecs in the north to Xoconochco in the south-east and Itzapán in the south-west.

In 1502, Ahuítzotl was succeeded by Moctezuma II Xocoyotzin, the last independent ruler of the Aztec empire. Moctezuma II further expanded the empire and consolidated it by conquering territories and countries within the imperial boundaries that had not been subjugated by his predecessors. He fought wars against Tlaxcala and Huexotzingo without marked success but with the unfortunate effect of generating a profound hatred for the Aztecs in those cities. When Hernán Cortés arrived there he found willing and unexpected allies for a war against Tenochtitlán. Overall, however, his campaigns were successful. At the time of Cortés' arrival in 1519, the empire's influence covered almost 200,000sq km (77,000sq miles) and was still growing. Moctezuma believed himself to be 'master of the world'.

Below: Aztec military might was the key to enforcing the obedience and cooperation of fellow Mesoamericans within the empire.

TRIBUTE AND TRADE

Each of the three city-states of the Triple Alliance had its own tributary areas within the empire. When they fought together on joint campaigns, tribute was divided along agreed lines: 40 per cent each for Tenochtitlán and Texcoco and 20 per cent for Tlacopán. Usually, the entire tribute would be despatched to Tenochtitlán and then sorted for redistribution. On occasion, one city agreed to assign tribute from within its tributary area to another of the allies: for example, Texcoco arranged for tribute from Tepetlaoztoc, within the Texcocan region of dependency, to be paid to Tenochtitlán as a reward for military support during the Texcocan leader Netzahualcóyotl's rise to power.

Tribute was paid to individuals as well as to cities: a ruler would often reward his committed followers with the promise of tribute payments. The wealth of many prominent lords was boosted by deliveries of rare goods from distant territories.

Above: In an image from the Florentine Codex, *Moctezuma II watches serenely as tribute offerings are arrayed before him.*

Left: Scholars believe that this stone warrior once stood in a building celebrating the Aztecs' divinely ordained power.

TRIBUTE PAYMENTS

Once a city or chiefdom had accepted defeat in battle, its rulers were required to agree payment of set amounts of tribute to a fixed schedule. The Aztec conquerors would usually appoint a tribute collector to see that regular payment was made. The use or threat of violence kept tribute flowing for, if payment of tribute stopped, the armies of the Triple Alliance were mobilized to enforce the tribute agreement.

Tribute payments ranged from basic produce such as maize, beans, chillies and cotton clothing to rarer and more valuable items such as jaguar skins, gold or jade ornaments, cacao beans and brightly coloured feathers. Pages from the *Codex Mendoza* detail the tribute required of particular provinces and the schedule for its delivery. For example, Cuauhnahuac was required to send tribute of skirts, loincloths and cloaks every six months and war costumes and decorated shields once each year.

WEALTH OF THE EMPIRE

Diego Durán's 1581 work, *History of the Indies of New Spain*, lists the great variety of tribute paid to the lords of Tenochtitlán. This included feathers and decorated blankets, mats and seats, painted cotton clothes, and also parrots, eagles and geese.

Some tributary areas sent live lions and tigers in cages, while others sent deer, quails and rabbits. Some tributary areas sent insects, including spiders, scorpions and bees in their hives. From the coastal dependencies there came seashells, coloured stones, pearls and turtleshells, and from the city workshops came metalwork in the shape of cups and bowls and plates.

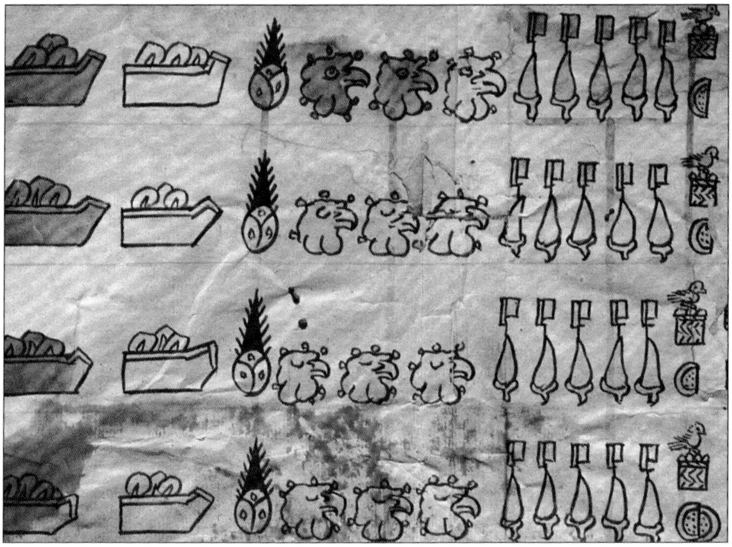

Left: Tribute exacted by the Aztec imperial power from villages within the empire included corn and trees.

The wives and courtesans of prominent Tenochtitláns benefited from tribute payments of women's blouses and elegant skirts decorated in coloured thread with designs of roses, eagles and feathers, while other tributes included the white cotton shifts worn by women who served in the temples and the plain clothing worn by servants. Forested areas, Durán wrote, were required to send in wood, charcoal and the bark of trees for use as fuel. Food tribute included maize, beans and chillies, potatoes, avocados, bananas, pineapples, plums and honey. Rose flowers and bushes were provided for the gardens of Tenochtitlán nobles. Some provinces paid tribute in war materials: padded cotton armour, wooden shields, bows and arrows, flint arrowheads, darts, slings and stones. Some areas sent building materials such as stone and lime, while the poorer provinces, which were not able to provide worthy tribute, sent women, girls and boys to be shared among the nobility as concubines and slaves.

THE FLOW OF TRIBUTE

Demand for tribute was meticulously planned to meet needs in the cities of the Triple Alliance. In the latter years of the empire, the amount of elite produce, such as jaguar skins or golden ornaments used in warrior or priestly costumes, rose as a proportion of total tribute, reflecting an increased number of far-flung provinces able to provide such goods and a growth in the nobility's taste for extravagant display.

The flow of tribute was essential to the great religious sacrifices held in cities of the Triple Alliance. Feathers and materials were used in costumes, and tributary provinces provided the building materials and labourers used to construct the temples of Tenochtitlán.

The movement of high-quality tribute goods took place alongside commercial trading by merchants. Some combined trade with information-gathering in the marketplaces of potentially rebellious cities, working as undercover spies. Merchants working on behalf of the emperor, seeking or selling elite goods, could gather important information or make significant friendships that might facilitate political alliances within the empire.

Some provinces were not required to pay tribute to a set schedule. Instead, these cities or chiefdoms, usually situated in strategic areas such as border regions or at important sites on trade routes, were engaged in alliances cemented by marriage or other ties of kinship. While their rulers remained nominally in power, some of their prominent relatives and allies were required to live at court in Tenochtitlán or Texcoco and pay homage to the *tlatoani* during state celebrations. Any goods they sent to Tenochtitlán or the other cities of the Triple Alliance were treated as gifts. Itzcóatl, Netzahualcóyotl and Moctezuma I built a series of alliances through negotiation and marriage.

Below: In Tenochtitlán towering architecture and imposing statues impressed on imperial subjects the invincibility and power of the Aztecs.

CAMPAIGNS OF MOCTEZUMA I

Moctezuma I Ilhuicamina is celebrated as the 'father of empire' who greatly expanded the Aztec lands. However, he did not begin significant campaigns of distant conquest until 18 years after his coronation in 1440. He spent those first years building and strengthening alliances within regions already conquered by Tenochtitlán and fighting a long, intermittent war against Chalco at the eastern end of Lake Chalco that ended in victory in the mid-1450s. He also faced a series of devastating famines in the years 1450–54. These ended, presumably thanks to the gods' blessing, following the New Fire Ceremony over which the emperor presided at the close of the 52-year cycle in 1454 and the rebuilding work he began on the Great Pyramid in Tenochtitlán.

THE TIZOC ABD SUN STONES

The carving known as the Stone of Tizoc, found in Tenochtitlán's ruins in 1790, projects the empire of the Triple Alliance as an enduring achievement heroically inspired by the *tlatoani* and supported by the gods of Sun and Earth.

The cylindrical stone is carved on its upper face with a sun-disc that sends rays to east, west, north and south and, at the rim, a string of all-seeing stars. On the cylinder's bottom rim four faces of the earth-goddess Tlaltecuhtli represent the land on which the Aztec army marches, balancing the upper sun image associated with Huitzilopochtli, in whose honour the armies conquer the enemy. Around the side of the stone, Aztec soldiers are represented holding prisoners from captured cities by the hair, proudly surveyed by the *tlatoani*, Tizoc, who is dressed in the regalia of the gods Huitzilopochtli and Tezcatlipoca.

Another great carved cylinder bearing an image of the sun god – known to scholars as the Sun Stone – was carved in the era of Moctezuma I and subsequently found close to the ruins of the Great Pyramid.

EARLY CAMPAIGNS

The ruler's first major campaign was into the Huastec region in the Gulf of Mexico, an area rich in natural resources. The army coped impressively with the logistical difficulties of the long march needed to take war to the northern coast and used canny tactics in pretending to retreat in order to lure local forces into a trap. After a triumphant return to Tenochtitlán, the next move was to the south-east to capture the trading centre of Coixtlahuaca in the forbidding mountain valleys of the Mixtec lands. The pretext for war was that Aztec merchants had reported being both insulted and attacked in Coixtlahuaca, although the main attraction was the tribute that might be exacted from an area celebrated for its manuscript work, weaving, gold- and metalwork, and ceramics. Following careful preparations, an army of some 200,000 troops left the city of Tenochtitlán and headed south, accompanied by 100,000 porters bearing supplies. In the rugged land around Coixtlahuaca, this great force came face to face with the Mixtecs and their Huexotzingan and Tlaxcalán allies. Hostilities began with taunts, then spear-throwers and slings were brought to bear before the two armies charged. The Aztecs broke the Mixtec line, and pursued them mercilessly through the streets of Coixtlahuaca. Eventually they reached the temple pyramid, which they climbed and torched to signal their triumph. Any Mixtec warriors who escaped fled in despair to the hills, while their brothers were rounded up.

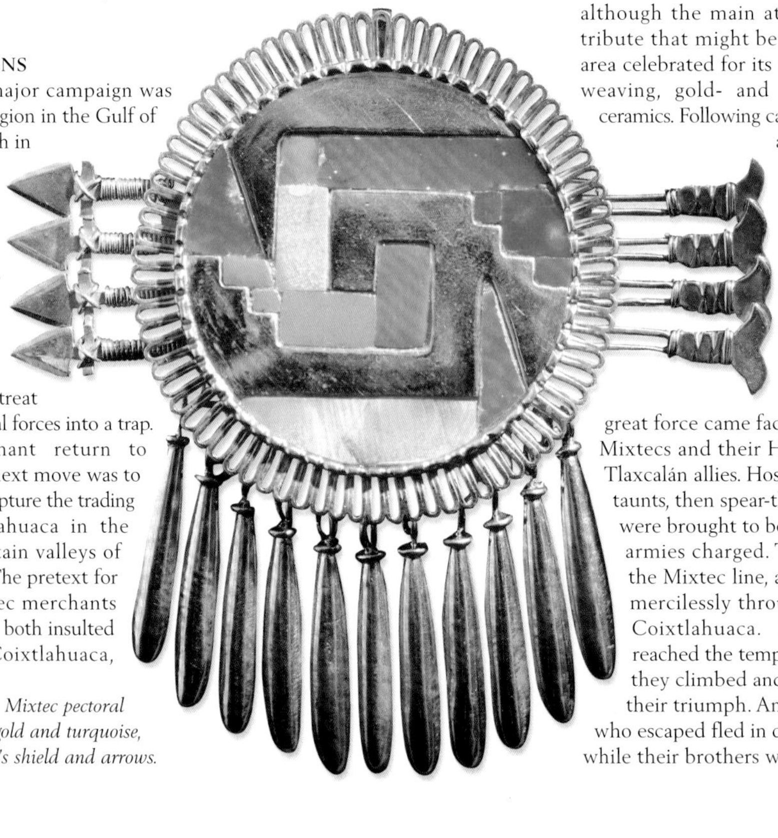

Right: This exquisite Mixtec pectoral ornament, made of gold and turquoise, represents a warrior's shield and arrows.

Right: The Mixtecs conquered by Moctezuma I's great army were celebrated for their metalworking. This Mixtec eagle's head, of solid gold, was intended to be worn as a lip ornament.

As the dust settled, a group of Mixtec chieftains agreed to pay tribute as a dependency of Tenochtitlán. Their ruler, Atonal, was strangled and his relatives were taken into slavery but, in the usual Aztec procedure, the other local chiefs were permitted to remain in power so long as tribute was forthcoming on the agreed schedule. The rewards for the Aztec victory included tribute of blankets, greenstone beads, feathers, gold dust, red dye, cotton, chillies and salt.

The conquerors also took home whatever they could plunder from the town, a long line of prisoners for sacrifice and religious statues from the sacked Mixtec temple. The worshippers of Huitzilopochtli would keep enemy idols 'captive' within the ceremonial area in the city of Tenochtitlán as one more sign of Aztec supremacy. Moctezuma's army returned in triumph to its homeland, its soldiers hailed as heroes by cheering crowds. The long lines of prisoners were led up the steep sides of the Great Pyramid to be dispatched in Huitzilopochtli's honour on the sacrificial stone.

Below: A detail from the Stone of Tizoc, carved during the rule of Tizoc (1469–81), shows Aztec victories over the Mixtecs.

EXTENDING THE EMPIRE

These were the first of many famous victories for Moctezuma I Ilhuicamina. The following year he sent the army eastwards to the town of Cosamaloapán, and afterwards to Ahuilzapán and Cuetlachtlán. Each time they returned in triumph, bearing tribute and plunder, having extended the might and influence of the empire and secured strategic settlements on trading routes.

When Moctezuma I Ilhuicamina's fruitful reign came to an end with the ruler's death in 1469, the Aztec lands stretched north-east to Xilotepec, east to Cosamaloapán and south to Oaxaca.

CITY-STATES IN CONSTANT CONFLICT

There was no Maya empire. Throughout the Classic Period (*c.*250BC–AD900), the city-states of the Maya lands were almost constantly at war, but no one central state emerged to establish rule over the others. Scholars liken the Maya cities to the city-states of ancient Greece: all shared a common language, religion and group of cultural assumptions, but all were strongly independent and often at each other's throats. To judge from surviving inscriptions, the dynastic ruler of a Maya state gained great prestige if he could capture a rival king, hold him captive, inflict punishing tortures on him and finally decapitate him. In the Classic Period at least, he appears not to have set much store by capturing land for himself or his subjects. The boundaries between the city-states remained largely unchanged over many years that were marked by great bloodshed.

It might be that some city-states were more powerful than others. In recent years, some scholars have suggested that the more powerful cities held the weaker ones in a client relationship that can be likened to the relationship between tribute-paying cities and the Triple Alliance in the Aztec empire. One of these powerful Maya cities was Calakmul. In the mid-6th century AD and afterwards it had control over Naranjo, Dos Pilas, El Perú and Cancuen. Calakmul had a great rival in Tikal and the two cities endured a long and bitter conflict.

There is also evidence that Maya cities built alliances by forging links through dynastic marriage in the same way as the Aztecs. The daughters of the nobility at Tikal, for example, appear to have made marriages with members of the ruling dynasty at Copán, Yaxchilán and Naranjo. The children of such marriages would have had strong links through their maternal family to Tikal. Scholars have demonstrated from surviving inscriptions that a noble bride from Tikal who married into the dynasty of Naranjo had a son known as Scroll Squirrel, who in turn made his wedding with a bride from Tikal, further strengthening the alliance.

Above: An image from a Maya codex depicts the disruption and misery of war. Two prisoners are marched into captivity.

Below: Facial paint and helmet feathers impress this Maya warrior's importance and aggressive intent on his enemies.

HOW AND WHY THEY FOUGHT

The high-ranking Maya warrior went into battle gloriously attired. He wore a wooden helmet with brightly coloured quetzal or parrot feathers that fell across his shoulders, and painted his face with war paint. Jade jewellery around his neck and on his wrists added to the dazzling image. Maya soldiers, like the Aztecs, wore quilted jackets of cotton body armour that had been soaked in salt water to make it tougher. The Spaniards were so impressed with the effectiveness of this body protector that they adopted it in place of their own steel armour.

The principal Maya tactic was to take the enemy by surprise. The Spaniards found that Maya tactics of ambush and raiding made them a troublesome enemy. Campaigns often began with a stealthy raid into the enemy lands to seize captives. Once battle was joined, fighting was fierce, accompanied by a musical cacophony produced by the beating of drums and the blowing of whistles and conch shells. The war leaders and priests carrying divine images would occupy the centre of the battle line and were flanked by groups of foot soldiers.

Like the Aztec soldier, the Maya warrior fought mainly with a war club fitted with obsidian blades and a spear-thrower that could send darts flying over great distances when handled with skill. He also used a sling and large stones. Some accounts report that the Maya attacked by throwing fire or the nests of hornets and other stinging insects into the enemy ranks. For close-quarters fighting, the Maya warrior also had distinctive weapons in the shape of a three-pronged knife made from shell and another knife with a broad flint blade.

As among the Aztecs, warriors fought less to inflict violence than to seize booty and capture prisoners. The top prize was the ruler of a rival city. If he were captured and his capture was made known, the battle was at an end. His warriors fled if they could escape. The king faced torture and sacrificial death.

Below: A lintel at Yaxchilán shows King Shield Jaguar receiving his war gear from his wife Lady Xoc prior to battle in AD*724.*

*Above: A Classic Maya vase (*AD*600–900) shows a well-equipped warrior preparing to use his spear-thrower.*

WHEN THEY FOUGHT

The fighting season was kept separate from the times of planting and harvest. Campaigns often took place in October. If they went on too long, they might well fail. There are reports of Maya campaigns fading away as the farmers fled the army to attend to their fields.

Although war was effectively continuous in that there were no prolonged periods of peace, campaigns did not need to be of particularly long duration. The Maya city-states were small and in stark contrast to the great distances covered by the army of the Triple Alliance, a Maya force often needed to march for no more than one day to reach its enemy.

The city-states of the Maya lowlands in the Classic Period were each ruled by a dynasty that claimed descent from a historical founder and – usually – also from the gods. Each dynasty was identified by its own emblem, which would be written in inscriptions after the personal name of the ruler and his consorts.

WAR BETWEEN MAYAPÁN AND CHICHÉN ITZÁ

According to Spanish and native accounts, in the 13th and 14th centuries Mayapán was the capital of a league of city-states in northern Yucatán that also included Chichén Itzá and Uxmal. The dominant city, Mayapán, was destroyed in the 20-year period 1441–61 at the close of a struggle between tribal dynasties that had begun 250 years earlier. The dating is that given in the *Books of Chilam Balam*, which identifies events according to the Maya Short Count. (This is a variant of the Maya Long Count. The Short Count places events in 20-year periods within a cycle of 256-¼ years.) The two dynasties that came head to head were members of the Itzá people.

Below: This unsettling face was created for an incense vase found at the Itzá city of Mayapán, home to the Cocom dynasty.

WHO WERE THE ITZÁ?

In the Maya chronicles, these incomers to Yucatán are described in contemptuous terms as 'lewd ones', 'tricksters' and 'those without mothers and fathers'. They clearly did not speak the local language, because the chroniclers also called them 'people who use our tongue brokenly'. Scholars believe that the Itzá were a group of Maya who came north from the Tabasco region between Yucatán and central Mexico. The chronicles describe how they lived in the city of Chakanputún (perhaps Champotón in the coastal area of Campeche), but were driven from that place by force *c.*AD1200 and made their way north into Yucatán. They settled the city of Chichén Itzá in the period 1224–44. The Itzá renamed the city, originally called *Uucil-abnal* ('Seven Bushes'). Its new name meant 'Openings of the Wells of Itzá'. They promoted the worship of the sacred well or *cenote* in the city, where offerings have been found by archaeologists. The Itzá also appear to have been devout worshippers of Ix Chel, consort of the supreme Maya deity Itzamná, in her guise as goddess of medicine.

Above: A stucco mural at Mayapán includes space for the insertion of the skull of a slaughtered prisoner of war.

The coming of the Itzá might have been the second settlement by Mexican incomers. Traditional histories suggest that Chichén Itzá was taken over by Toltec emigrants from Tula in AD967–987, perhaps even led by the historical prince Topiltzin who was associated with the god Quetzalcóatl. There is strong evidence of Toltec style at Chichén Itzá dating from this period. However, many archaeologists doubt whether this points to a Toltec invasion and argue that it simply represents the strength of Toltec religious and archaeological influence spread by trading contacts.

Above: The Group of the Thousand Columns was erected to surround the Temple of the Warriors at Chichén Itzá.

STRUGGLE FOR POWER

The Itzá founded Mayapán in 1263–83, leaving some of the tribe in charge at Chichén Itzá. In about 1283 the vicious quarrel between Itzá dynasties that would result in the city's downfall began. (An added complication of the dating given in the *Books of Chilam Balam* is that events are identified by their place within a 256¼-year cycle, but there is no information as to which 256¼-year period is meant. As a result, there is disagreement among scholars as to when the Itzá refounded Chichén Itzá. Some authorities believe that they settled Chichén Itzá and founded Mayapán within an earlier time cycle almost 300 years before, in AD967–87.)

The Cocom dynasty of the Itzá in Mayapán seized power from the Tutul Xiu dynasty in Chichén Itzá. The leader of the Cocom dynasty hired a mercenary army from Tabasco to enforce his will. These soldiers, who were perhaps Toltec emigrants, swept all before them with their superior weapons. They came armed with bows and arrows, perhaps bringing them for the first time into Yucatán. Their skill with the *atlatl* or spear-thrower was extraordinary and they fought fiercely at close quarters with the spear.

The capture of the city of Chichén Itzá by this Mexican force was depicted on frescoes in Chichén Itzá and in carvings on gold discs thrown as offerings into the *cenote*. There is a marked contrast between Mexican and Maya weapons and appearance in these images. The Cocom rebuilt Chichén Itzá. The Tutul Xiu princes were driven from their city, but they did not give up. They settled near the ruins of Uxmal and nursed their hatred in exile from generation to generation, awaiting their chance. The Cocoms finally met their end in the era 1441–61.

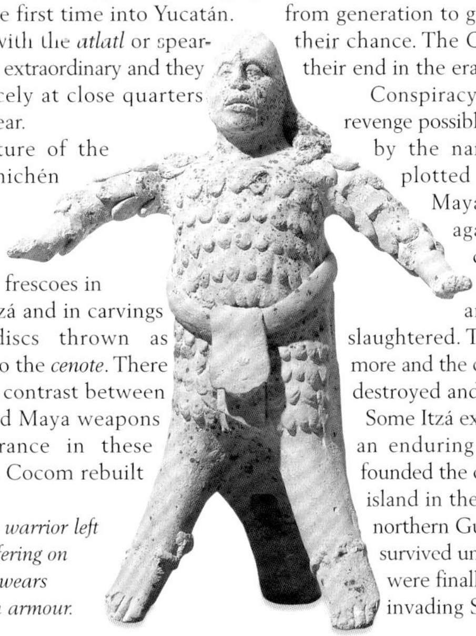

Right: A clay warrior left as a grave offering on Jaina Island wears quilted cotton armour.

Conspiracy made Tutul Xiu revenge possible. A Tutal Xiu chief by the name of Ah Xupán plotted with nobles in Mayapán to rise up against the Cocom chiefs. All of the Cocom princes and nobles were slaughtered. The dynasty was no more and the city of Mayapán was destroyed and left to decay.

Some Itzá exiles, however, made an enduring new home. They founded the city of Tayasal on an island in the Lake Petén Itzá in northern Guatemala. Here they survived until 1697, when they were finally conquered by the invading Spaniards.

THE MAYA COLLAPSE

In the 9th century AD, the cities of the Southern Maya Lowlands began to be abandoned. The jungle vegetation that the Maya farmers had tamed grew back and, in time, even swamped the great temples and plazas where priests and kings had celebrated royal power. Further to the north, in the Puuc Hills and towards the tip of the Yucatán peninsula, cities such as Mayapán, Uxmal, Labná and Chichén Itzá were thriving, making the decline of the lowland settlements all the more puzzling.

A HUGE HUMAN TRAGEDY

This was undoubtedly a human tragedy on a vast scale. Within four or five generations, a great civilization faded. Archaeologists and historians dubbed this remarkable development 'the Maya collapse' and for years speculated as to its causes. Why would a determined people abandon these great constructions of stone, which had been laboriously erected over many years in honour of their ancestors and gods?

THE END OF THE CLASSIC MAYA

In the years before they were left to the jungle, the Southern Lowland Maya cities one by one ended their established practice of erecting stone columns carved with the dates in the Maya Long Count of their ruling dynasties and their kings' battle victories and religious sacrifices. In archaeological terms, the Classic Period of ancient Maya civilization (*c.*AD250–900) is demarcated as the years during which the cities carved these stelae. The final Classic Period Maya inscription was cut in AD909.

In the cities of Yucatán in the north, meanwhile, craftsmen continued to carve inscriptions, but they did not celebrate dynastic achievements.

Above: This detail from a mural at Bonampak depicts the Maya warrior's jaguar-skin costume and feathered helmet.

Left: One of many figures of Maya warriors left in graves at Jaina Island appears serene before battle.

DIFFERING THEORIES

Archaeological evidence shows that the Maya population in the Southern Lowlands collapsed in the 9th century AD. Between AD830 and AD930, numbers fell by one third. Some writers suggested the Maya were undone by an epidemic of disease, a natural disaster such as an earthquake or hurricane, or even by an invasion.

One simplified theory is that the Maya people effectively wiped one another out in the lowlands. Centuries of almost incessant fighting between the city-states led to severe damage to the environment and greatly depleted the population. In time, the combination of falling numbers and inadequate food supply meant that the cities could not be maintained and so the cities were gradually abandoned.

The latest scholarly thinking is broadly in agreement with this picture, although it makes significant changes to the causal links of the argument. The consensus is that the trigger for the 'Maya collapse' was over- rather than under-population. The Classic Maya civilization was so successful that its population grew beyond

Above: Over-population followed by intensive farming seems to have been the cause of the southern Maya collapse.

Right: In a Bonampak mural the halach uinic *(lord) and lieutenants, standing, watch as prisoners have their nails torn out.*

the point at which the land could support it. The farmers turned to highly intensive methods of cultivation, which disturbed the ecological balance and in time this led to severe environmental damage. Disease may also have contributed. Now the population began to fall, as evidenced in the archaeological record. Rising levels of hunger and fear over future shortages fuelled ever-more violent exchanges between city-states, which competed for the fertile land available. Finally, the area was abandoned.

Throughout the previous centuries, when the Maya cities were locked in almost continuous conflict, there had been few changes in the boundaries of the city-states. Wars were conducted in large part in search of royal or noble captives for sacrifice and for common soldiers to be sold as slaves. But there is evidence from the last of the carved stelae (see box) that in the final years, lowland Maya cities were seeking to expand in an entirely new way, fighting for land more than for honour.

The modern scholarly argument therefore suggests that intensifying war between the city-states was a symptom rather than a cause of the collapse of the southern Maya region. The Maya fought themselves to a standstill as they competed for land – and perhaps also sought to capture armies of prisoners in order to mount lavish sacrifices that might be enough to bring back times of plenty.

CHAPTER FIVE

ROYAL POWER, LAW AND ORDER

In the Maya city of Palenque, in northern Chiapas, three temple-pyramids known to archaeologists as the Temple of the Cross, the Temple of the Foliated Cross and the Temple of the Sun contain stone panels carved with images and hieroglyphic inscriptions that establish an ancestral line for the dynasty of Palenque's most celebrated ruler, Lord Pacal. The images present the royal ruler as a link to the realm of the gods and ancestors, as the guarantor of fertility, rain and crops, and as a warrior, powerful in battle. These were the three key roles performed by the Maya ruler to justify his pre-eminent position.

The Aztec *tlatoani*, or ruler of each city-state, was understood to be both a promoter of fertility and a great warrior prince. His ritual names included *inan, ita altepetl* ('Mother and Father of the City') and he took the role of rainbringer in an important fertility ceremony conducted each year on Mount Tláloc. He was essentially the chief priest, conducting certain sacrificial rites himself, and was understood to assume divine power during his complex coronation rites. The power of the gods burned in him and was refreshed from time to time in ritual sacrifices. He was the living image of the warrior god Huitzilopochtli and the army's commander-in-chief. As part of the coronation rituals he had to conduct a military campaign to celebrate his divinely ordained election to the post.

Left: At Palenque, city of King Pacal, a wooded hill looms behind the raised Temple of the Foliated Cross (left).

STRUCTURES OF POWER

The rulers of Classic Period Maya states were dynastic leaders revered by their people as 'holy kings'. A man such as King Chan Muwan of Bonampak held sway, from a canopied throne protected by a curtain and sometimes covered with jaguar skins, over a large palace retinue that included his extended family, military staff, kitchen workers, dancers with a band of musicians and the *ak k'u hun* (chief scribe), himself in charge of a team of artists, sculptors and scribes. The important position of *sahal*, head of the military staff, was usually filled by a close relative of the king. A *sahal* could be dispatched to govern a provincial town.

The Spanish conquistadors encountered a similar situation in 16th-century Yucatán. Each state was governed by a ruler known as *halach uinic* ('true man'), who governed with the support of a council that was doubtless appointed from his blood relatives. He lived in great splendour in the state's main city at the head of an impressive retinue, receiving the highly prized cacao and other produce from the lands he governed and setting himself apart by the magnificence of his appearance and many layers of ritual. Like the Aztec *tlatoani*, the *halach uinic* was viewed in a paternal light; the Spaniards said he was 'father' and 'lord' of the city. He appointed officials known as batabs whose job was to govern provincial towns, with the support of a council. Batabs were magistrates and war leaders as well as administrators.

Left: One of the kings of Copán adorns the lid of a ceramic vase left as a mortuary offering c.AD650–800.

The Maya ruler took one legitimate wife, but also kept concubines. His wife was greatly revered and, on the evidence of the Bonampak murals, she cut a truly magnificent figure. She is depicted at Bonampak as wearing a necklace and earrings, with swirling hair tied up and a red stole on her arm, setting off the fine white dress that she wears.

Left: A cylindrical vessel left in a tomb in the Maya city of Tikal represents a splendidly attired lord receiving a visitor.

STONE RECORDS

In the Classic Period, the holy kings of Maya cities such as Piedras Negras, Tikal, Yaxchilán, Quiriguá and Palenque erected inscribed stelae, thrones, wall panels, door lintels and other monuments recording their accession and its major anniversaries, together with the duration and major military triumphs of their reign and significant ritual sacrifices. At Piedras Negras, for example, each king appears to have set up a monument celebrating his accession on its fifth anniversary. The inscriptions record the anniversary, the date the ruler came to the throne and an earlier date that scholars suggest may be his date of birth or the date on which he was named. The ruler then set up new monuments every five years for as long as his reign lasted. These monuments were carved with an 'accession motif', identified by Tatiana Proskouriakoff. It shows a figure seated on a throne at the top of a ladder, with footsteps visible on a mat over the ladder, indicating the ruler had climbed to his position of royal pre-eminence.

MODES OF SUCCESSION

In the Classic Period, royal power was almost always inherited from father to son, but there is evidence that the line could pass through the daughter in some instances. At Tikal, the daughter of King Kan Boar was given a remarkably rich burial that included valuable imported

oyster shell and the skeleton of a spider monkey. Kan Boar's daughter, who is known to archaeologists as 'the Lady of Tikal', is shown on a lintel standing at the right hand of her husband, who succeeded her father as king.

The evidence suggests that a woman could succeed her father in the royal palace only as a wife. Her husband would be 'adopted' by her father and become the rightful heir in her place. Their children would then inherit the throne. In some cases, the son of a royal marriage was not considered fit to rule and power might be passed to his brother, or, if no male member of the immediate family was available, to a more distant relative from the ruling council.

Among the Aztecs, succession was not hereditary. An election was held among the nobles of the highest ranks to determine who should succeed the *tlatoani* and the new ruler was then blessed, following complex coronation rites, by the high priest. However, the election was essentially token. The old ruler would nominate a successor and it would usually have been clear who this would be, for the ruler-in-waiting generally filled the role of *tlaccatecatl* on the elite military council. The appointment was then approved by the nobles' council, although sometimes the leaders of Texcoco and Tlacopán were asked for their input. The successor generally came from among the ruler's close blood relatives. At Tenochtitlán, three grandsons of Moctezuma I Ilhuicamina took power in turn; Axayácatl, Tizoc and Ahuítzotl. In Texcoco, sons usually succeeded fathers.

Above: This shell, delicately carved with the prominent nose and features of a Maya nobleman, was worn as a pendant.

Left: Moctezuma II prepares for coronation as tlatoani *in an illustration from the* Codex Durán *(1579–81).*

THE POWER OF APPEARANCE

Both Maya kings and Aztec rulers dressed in great splendour as a mark of status and to associate themselves with the gods whose authority they claimed.

THE COSTUME OF KINGS

Classic Period Maya kings wore racks on their backs to support large headdress frames that sometimes rose a metre or more above the brow. The rack and the headdress frame, both made of wood, were covered with elaborate decorative designs which used shells, carved jade, feathers and textiles. The long, bright-green plumes of the quetzal bird were the most highly prized. The headdress often contained the mask of the rain god Chac or the sun god Ahau Kin.

Some kings wore the stick bundles of the scribe in their headdress, indicating both the high status of the scribe and the fact that the king was literate. The king wore his hair long and wove jewellery and ornaments into it. He built his nose up into a great beak, using putty, wore large ornaments in the enlarged lobes of his ears and had his teeth filed and inlays of jade added.

The king dressed in specific and different costumes when performing his various roles as priest, war leader and civil ruler. In each case, the king carried a symbol of his authority. Along with leading nobles, the king wore a ceremonial version of the costume worn by players of the ball game. This must have been donned for rites associated with the game.

MAYA KINGSHIP

The magnificent appearance of the Young Maize God in ceramic and other imagery made him a fitting representative of Maya kingship.

The Young Maize God, mythical father of the Hero Twins Hunahpú and Xbalanqué, was patron deity of scribes, as well as a divine embodiment of Maya royalty. He is depicted with splendid jewellery, a royal headdress and a long, tonsured head whose shape represents that of an ear of maize. Sometimes, his fine headdress contains an image of a jester god. On ceramics, the Young Maize God is often shown twice or as one of a pair of twins, reflecting the fact that the father of the Hero Twins, One Hunahpú, descended to Xibalba with his twin brother Seven Hunahpú to play the ball game with the gods of that frightful place. Scholars can only speculate why the Young Maize God should be a patron of scribes. They point to the fact that the paper used for Maya books was made by soaking bark in the same way that maize was treated to make dough, usually using the same water that had been used for the maize.

Left: A late Classic Period terracotta figure of a Maya warrior has a deer headdress and facial tattoos.

Below: Scholars identify this figure from a Maya vase as a palace dignitary attendant on the king.

Above: The decoration on a cylindrical vase grave offering from Tikal depicts a noble with elongated earlobes and large earrings.

Maya kings also appear to have played the ball game, and carvings survive showing kings in the protective costumes worn for the game. A stone panel from La Amelia, Guatemala, depicts the King of Dos Pilas performing a dance of triumph or ritual importance in his game clothes, with a belt and kneepads.

SYMBOLS OF AUTHORITY

In Aztec lands, only the *tlatoani* was permitted to wear the *xicolli*, a decorated waistcoat, and Aztec rulers marked their status by wearing rich jewellery and ornaments made of rock-crystal and jade. The plumes of the quetzal were also used as a symbol of kingly authority. The quetzal was understood to be an important *nahualli* or animal form of the god Quetzalcóatl, the Plumed Serpent who was identified with the wise ruler and high priest of Tollán, Topiltzin. Aztec rulers wore green quetzal feathers or green stones as a mark of sovereignty. When Moctezuma II sent an offering of gifts to Hernán Cortés shortly after the Spaniards landed in April 1519, he included a headdress of green feathers. Cortés sent it on to his lord, Charles V, in a consignment of treasures from the New World, and it is now held by the Museum für Völkerkunde, Vienna. Scholars believe that this particular headdress, which contains 450 quetzal feathers, was worn by priests, possibly when representing Quetzalcóatl himself in temple rites.

Below: A late Classic Period figurine represents a Maya king as both a warrior, with a shield, and a ball player, with a padded protective belt. He is also associated with the rain god Chac.

CORONATION SPECTACLE

The power of the ruler in both Maya and Aztec realms was often expressed through public ceremony. The vast temple rituals that culminated in human sacrifices impressed not only the rulers' subjects but also outsiders, including both allies and enemies.

VISIBLE MIGHT

The Aztecs required the lords of some allied states to live in Tenochtitlán. Here they witnessed spectacular demonstrations of Aztec might and authority on the steps and at the summit of the Great Pyramid. Ahuítzotl's rededication of the Great Temple in 1487, in which as many as 80,000 victims may have been sacrificed, was a dramatic expression of his power as recently installed *tlatoani* and of the Aztecs' pre-eminence, as well as of his people's devotion to their gods.

Another public statement of the Aztec ruler's might was his complex coronation ceremony. In Tenochtitlán, the council's approval of the appointment of a new ruler was the start of a prolonged coronation ceremony, a powerful religious drama of several days' duration in which the whole state took part.

Left: The splendour of Maya royal ceremony is celebrated in this image on a polychrome vase buried at Uaxactún near Tikal.

RETREAT

The rites began with a sober period of retreat. Following the death of the previous *tlatoani*, his elected successor was publicly stripped of all finery and symbols of status. Before the Great Pyramid in the centre of Tenochtitlán, he stood before the silent crowd dressed only in a loincloth, before being led by the rulers of the allied cities Texcoco and Tlacopán up the steep side of the pyramid to the shrine of the god Huitzilopochtli. There he was given a robe of dark green marked with the image of skulls. He burned incense in honour of the god. Afterwards, he descended the pyramid with a company of nobles and began a retreat lasting four days and nights in the military headquarters (*tlacochcalco*) within the ceremonial precinct. Every 12 hours, at noon and midnight, he climbed once more to the shrine of Huitzilopochtli and made offerings of his own blood, pricked from his ears, lower legs or arms.

ROBING AND ENTHRONEMENT

Following the sombre retreat, the second stage, a magnificent robing and enthronement, was full of colour. The new ruler and the company of penitent nobles processed from the *tlacochcalco* to one of the city's great palaces. The *tlatoani* of Texcoco dressed the new ruler in a robe of shining fabric with a glistening waistband, solemnly placed a greenstone crown on his head and adorned him with fabulous jewellery, including emerald earrings and nosepiece, gold armbands and anklets, and jaguar-skin sandals. He led him to a splendid throne covered with jaguar skins and eagle feathers.

This enthronement was followed by a public ceremony. The new ruler was carried on a litter to the Great Pyramid, where, before the sacred shrine of Huitzilopochtli, he used jaguar claws to let his own blood for a sacrificial offering and made a sacrifice of quails. He was then taken to a place containing either a sunstone or an eagle vessel, according to differing accounts, to make further blood sacrifices in honour of the sun.

Next, the new ruler made a stately progress, still carried on his litter, to the *coateocalli*, the building within the ritual enclosure where the Aztecs kept the captured gods of conquered peoples, some of which were accepted into the Aztec pantheon. Here he made further offerings of his blood to signify his devotion to the religious calendar, before proceeding to an earth temple used in spring planting

Above: Elite warriors donned ceremonial finery including feathered helmets and decorated armour for the coronation.

and other agricultural festivals. He made offerings to the sacred earth, validating his succession as ruler of the land.

The public ceremonial of enthronement was concluded when the king returned to the palace in the company of leading nobles for a series of speeches. He was informed that he was now greater than his fellow men, for his sacred role as leader gave him the power to speak to the gods and made him the deities' embodiment on Earth. The divinities filled him and were within him, they were his eyes, his tongue, his ears; symbolically, they were his claws and his sharp jaguar teeth.

BLESSED BY THE GODS

The new ruler now called on his people to follow him to war, for the next stage of his coronation ceremony required that he lead a military campaign to prove that the gods blessed him in battle. When Moctezuma I Ilhuicamina's grandson Tizoc led a dismal failure of a coronation campaign to Metztitlán following his accession in 1481, the people saw his poor performance in the field as a very bad omen for the reign that he had been seeking to celebrate. However, the campaign was judged a success and a propitious omen when the new ruler returned laden with booty and leading ranks of prisoners for sacrifice. This was the judgement made of Tizoc's successor, his brother Ahuítzotl, upon his return from his coronation campaign.

CONFIRMATION

The final stage of the sequence of rituals was a great public celebration known as confirmation, in which allies and even enemy states were expected to send offerings of tribute and the new *tlatoani* gave feasts in Tenochtitlán. On the first day, the new ruler made public demonstration of the primacy of Tenochtitlán within the Triple Alliance, when he presented the leaders of Texcoco and Tlacopán with their symbols of status. Afterwards, the allied rulers led a 2,000-strong company of nobles and warriors in a stately dance.

The new ruler of Tenochtitlán then made a triumphant entrance wearing a magnificent costume adorned with quetzal feathers and laden with jewellery, and the dancing group made a circle around him. He made a formal presentation of the insignia of office to the gathered ranks of Aztec society, so that his authority and pre-eminent status were clear to all. The ceremony had a bloody ending in a vast public sacrifice of the prisoners brought back from the coronation campaign.

The ritual coronation was a means of reaffirming and celebrating the many aspects of the Aztec ruler's greatness as the chief figure of the leading city of the mighty Aztec empire.

Below: Members of the Aztec nobility and imperial bureaucracy received official recognition of their status from the new tlatoani *in a palace ceremony.*

SUN KING: THE GLORY OF KING PACAL

The greatness of King Pacal of Palenque can be judged from his magnificent funerary crypt, rich grave offerings and towering sepulchral monument, the Temple of the Inscriptions, which stands atop a 20m (65ft) stepped pyramid. His city-state, Palenque, stands in a striking position, beneath a line of hills thick with rainforest, at the edge of the Usumacinta River floodplain, looking toward the Gulf of Mexico.

SPLENDOUR IN DEATH

The crypt, accessed by a long stairway leading downwards from the Temple of the Inscriptions, lies some 24m (80ft) below the temple floor. Within the crypt, the king's body was laid in a sarcophagus of red-painted stone, wearing a collar of precious jade, a green headband, several jade necklaces and mother-of-pearl and jade earpieces. Over his face was a lifelike mask fashioned from jade, obsidian and shells. The outside of the sarcophagus was carved with images of the king's ancestors, while nine stucco figures around the walls of the crypt represented the main gods of the underworld. In the corridors of the Temple of the Inscriptions were stone slabs carved with lists of kings. From these, together with accompanying lists commissioned by Pacal's son Chan-Bahlum, scholars have been able to construct a succession of 12 rulers. Together with the list from Copán, these are among the most detailed and complete dynastic lists of any ruling family in the Maya realm.

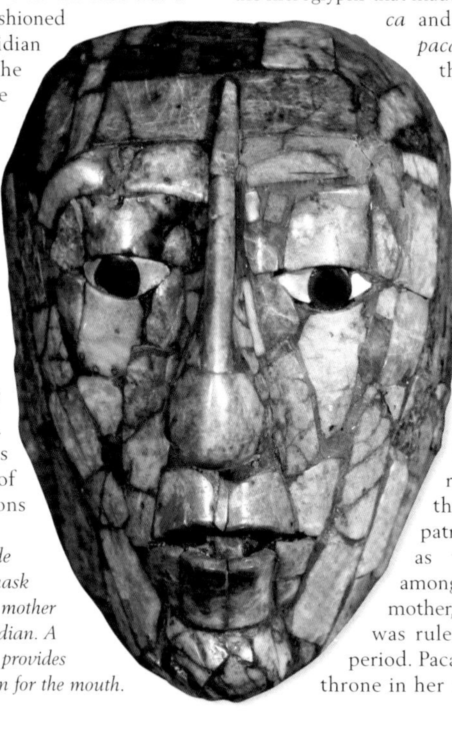

Right: Pacal's jade mosaic funeral mask has eyes of shell, mother of pearl and obsidian. A T-shaped amulet provides magical protection for the mouth.

WHO WAS HE?

The remarkable King Pacal reigned at Palenque for 68 years. From carvings in the temple and an inscription that runs along the edge of the lid of his sarcophagus, we know that he was born on 24 March in AD603, acceded to the throne on 27 July AD615 and died, aged 81, on 29 September AD684. Scholars have identified his name, which is written both with the image of a small warshield and the hieroglyphs that made the sounds *pa*, *ca* and *la* – spelling *pacal*, which was the word for 'shield'. His full name was K'inich Janaa' Pakal ('Lord Great Sun Shield').

King Pacal is also a most unusual ruler in that the king apparently inherited the throne through his mother's line rather than by the more usual patrilineal descent, as was expected among the Maya. His mother, Lady Zac-Kuk, was ruler herself for a period. Pacal inherited the throne in her name when he was 12, but she lived for a further 25 years and may have been the power behind the throne. Only after she died in AD640 did Pacal begin to have significant inscriptions carved to justify his rule.

Above: This Palenque relief depicts the ceremony transferring power from Lady Zac-Kuk to her 12-year-old son Pacal.

In Pacal's reign, Palenque became the dominant city in the region. As its ruler, Pacal controlled a large area: Palenque made marriage and other alliances with Tikal, Pomoná and Tortuguero. The city appears to have been at war with Toniná, for in the 8th century, a king of Toniná captured Kan Xul, one of Pacal's sons.

LEARNING FROM BURIAL RITES

The details of Pacal's burial rites show that both he and his subjects expected the deceased ruler to live on as a god after his death. When the great king was buried, five of his subjects were sacrificed so that they could accompany him on his journey to the underworld. The burial also shows that Pacal claimed authority

Above: Palenque's Temple of the Count pyramid (right) commands a view of the Temple of the Inscriptions (upper left).

for his dynasty by associating his ancestors and descendants with the sun god. The lid of his sarcophagus, which shows him descending the length of the world tree to the underworld, also depicts the sun moving between death and life. At his side within the sarcophagus was a jade figure of the sun god, suggesting that the king would rise again into the eastern sky after his underworld trials. The royal succession from Pacal to his descendants was symbolically blessed by the sun.

PASSING ON ROYAL POWER

Pacal's son, Chan-Bahlum, succeeded his father in AD684. He built the Temples of the Sun, the Cross and the Foliated Cross to celebrate his succession. The relation of this group to the main Temple of the Inscriptions confirms the sun god's approval. Once in every year, at sunset on the winter solstice, the Maya understood the sun to undergo a symbolic death. The setting sun would shine through a dip in the ridge behind the Temple of the Inscriptions and fall on the carved scenes in the Temple of the Cross that celebrate Pacal passing his royal power to Chan-Bahlum. As the sun set, its light would travel down the stair to King Pacal's tomb, symbolically entering the underworld with the king, prior to its rebirth the next morning.

Scholars believe that Pacal ordered the construction of the Temple of the Inscriptions as his own mortuary monument when he reached his seventies and understood that he was nearing the close of his long reign. The temple pyramid was completed after Pacal's death by Chan-Bahlum. The discovery of Pacal's tomb by Mexican archaeologist Albert Ruz in 1952 entirely changed the way that scholars view Maya temple pyramids, for it was the first evidence to emerge that some of these great constructions were essentially mortuary monuments.

Left: Pacal's final home, the Temple of the Inscriptions pyramid, has nine levels. Its stairway climbs to a five-bay sanctuary. The secret staircase to Pacal's crypt within the pyramid begins inside the sanctuary.

MOCTEZUMA II IN HIS POMP

Remembered primarily today as the last independent Aztec leader, Moctezuma II is the ruler who was ignominiously captured by the Spaniards and who apparently lost the confidence of his people; the man who lived to see the empire of the Triple Alliance swept away by a small band of invaders like a spider's web in the wind. However, at the time of the Spanish Conquest, the empire was still expanding and apparently healthy.

Below and far right: 17th-century Spanish artists Miguel and Juan Gonzalez show Cortés riding to meet Moctezuma II.

HIERARCHY AND ETIQUETTE

Moctezuma II ruled with great pomp and absolute authority over Tenochtitlán and the Aztec empire. One of his first endeavours, after his coronation war and the celebration of his confirmation rites, was to boost his own status and reinforce the standing of the nobility by introducing new court etiquette. He brought in laws on clothing and behaviour that set the *pipiltin* or nobility apart from the *macehuales* or commoners. For example, he stripped commoner-warriors who had excelled in battle of their much-valued privilege of wearing special clothes and insignia and insisted that they dress like the other members of their caste. He also introduced elaborate court ritual that underlined his own standing as an absolute ruler, the living image of the god Huitzilopochtli.

To further boost his authority, Moctezuma II brought his own men into government and the palace hierarchy. In the inner circle, he removed the officials

Above: This later portrait of Moctezuma II presents a Europeanized view of the last Aztec leader's magnificent appearance.

THE RAIN MAN

An annual ceremony held on Mount Tláloc cast the *tlatoani* in the role of rainmaker and illustrates how the cult of the Aztec ruler reflected his dual status as a warrior-leader and a fertility lord.

The ceremony was held in April or May, during the dry season, to draw the rain out from within the mountain. The rulers of Tenochtitlán, Texcoco, Tlacopán and Xochimilco made a pilgrimage to a temple high on Mount Tláloc. The temple was roofless, but built with high walls that cut off the view of the surrounding countryside. Within were rocks set out to echo the arrangement of peaks normally visible from the mountaintop, which included the divine mountains Popocatépetl and Ixtaccíhuatl.

The rulers carried gifts for the mountain-gods into the temple, then dressed the rock-idols in magnificent costumes. They left the temple but re-entered with offerings including food and the blood of a male infant. Afterwards, the rulers themselves feasted with their retinue on the open mountaintop.

Scholars interpret the ceremony as an act of fertilization, likening the rock temple to a cave, which the Aztecs understood to be a way into the spiritual world. This mountaintop cave was a place of opposites, where the earth met the sky and the spirit world met the physical world. The rulers' offering, like the large human sacrifices in city temples, was intended to recycle energy within the cosmos.

In the weeks after the ceremony, the dry season would come to an end. The first sign of the change would be rain clouds collecting around the summit of Mount Tláloc.

appointed by his predecessor, Ahuítzotl, and replaced them with his own close relatives and followers. (In some accounts, he ruthlessly had Ahuítzotl's men put to death.) He even removed the servants from the palaces of Tenochtitlán. In a canny move, he brought junior nobles from provincial cities of the empire and put them to work in the palaces. He calculated that the rulers of those cities would not consider revolt while their children were under his control in Tenochtitlán.

When Hernán Cortés and the Spaniards first encountered Moctezuma II at the entrance to Tenochtitlán, the Aztec leader emerged from the city borne on a litter by four noblemen and surrounded by a great number of slaves carrying goods to be offered to the gods. Moctezuma wore golden jewellery, a diadem encrusted with turquoise and the brilliant green feathers of the quetzal bird. He dismounted and walked forward supported by two nobles of the inner circle in a ceremonial manner of walking that showed great respect for the visitor. When Cortés approached to make a gift of Venetian pearls he was prevented from touching the Aztec ruler. After both had made speeches, Moctezuma led the visitors into a temple where he called on the god Huitzilopochtli, calling him his 'father', and received offerings from the rulers of Tacuba and Texcoco. At one point Moctezuma, the living embodiment of the Aztecs' principal god, lifted his clothes to show Cortés his arms and torso, saying, 'Look, I am only flesh and blood, like you'.

Moctezuma's quasi-divine standing played a significant part both in his own downfall and in that of the Aztec empire. His capture by the Spaniards was only possible because the Aztecs could not imagine that anyone would dare to manhandle this imperial figure and hold him to ransom. A Spanish delegation led by Cortés merely asked for an audience,

Above: Moctezuma II approaches his fateful first meeting with Cortés, carried out from Tenochtitlán in great style on a litter.

claiming that they wanted to complain of a supposed Aztec plan for a military action against the Spanish garrison at Veracruz. They were admitted and, finding no precautions to safeguard the emperor's person, seized him. Moctezuma had to cooperate, for his own survival. In captivity, and pleading for the Aztecs not to attack the Spanish compound, Moctezuma found that his authority was melting away.

On a larger scale, the Spaniards benefited from the fact that so much power was concentrated in one man. By eliminating him, they created a power vacuum that they were able to exploit to their advantage. The conquistadors certainly found that among the Maya, where there was no single figure to be eliminated at a stroke, conquest was a more difficult and challenging undertaking.

WISE GOVERNANCE, STRICT PUNISHMENT

The rulers of the Triple Alliance developed a legal code that defined the punishments for a range of misdemeanours and crimes, as well as set solutions for particular types of dispute. The code was used as a unifying factor and was strictly applied throughout the empire, without allowance for local differences or the details of a case.

THE BASIS OF THE LEGAL CODE

Scholars are unsure whether the code was based on ancient Mesoamerican tradition, as Netzahualcóyotl of Texcoco claimed, or whether it was developed specifically to deal with the difficulties of keeping law and order across the empire, with its many different terrains and complex mix of urban and rural peoples. The code was certainly a valued tool of central control, for it eliminated the risk of provincial lords undermining Aztec authority by developing their own legal system or list of punishments.

SON OF THE GODS

The Aztec legal system is said to have been devised by Netzahualcóyotl, the remarkable ruler of Texcoco who as a youth witnessed the killing of his father Ixtlilxóchitl and fled into exile before returning many years later to take power in the city of his birth.

Netzahualcóyotl was both a skilled politician and also a brilliant ruler who presided over his city for 41 years (1431–72) and won a glittering reputation for himself as a builder, poet, philosopher and legislator.

In part, perhaps, because of the dramatic events of his youth, an aura built around him and his life became enshrouded in myth. The story was told that he was son of the gods themselves, and that he would never taste death.

The chronicler Fernando de Alva Ixtlilxóchitl even suggested that Netzahualcóyotl had an understanding of divine reality that went far beyond that of his contemporaries, grasping the possibility of a single supreme creator deity rather than a multiplicity of many-faceted gods. He was the *tlatoani* who built a temple to an abstract god named Tloquenahuaque ('The One Who is Always Near').

Part of Netzahualcóyotl's brilliance may have lain in the fact that he constructed this godlike image for himself. He lent authority to the legal system he created by claiming to have revived the laws of Quetzalcóatl-Topiltzin, wise and fair ruler of Tula, in days of yore.

Aztecs were generally agreed as to what constituted good behaviour. According to Bernardino de Sahagún, author of *General History of the Things of New Spain*, virtuous Aztecs were obedient and honest, treating their fellows with respect and showing discretion in their dealings with others. Virtuous men and women worked hard, whether in the fields, at their sewing, preparing food, in an artisan's workshop, or in the marketplace. They brought energy to their work, without overindulging in sleep but rising early and labouring for long hours. They ate and drank in moderation; drunkenness was particularly frowned upon. They did not make a great noise when eating, thought carefully before speaking and were circumspect in what they said. They dressed and behaved with modesty. Children were raised to understand and follow this code.

Left: Although drunkenness was not encouraged, large amounts of pulque *were drunk during religious festivals.*

Below: A bronze image of Netzahualcóyotl seeks to capture his character as wise governor and deliverer of laws.

Above: A Florentine Codex *image shows judgement passed and punishment meted out under the Aztec law and order system.*

The *Codex Mendoza* contains a visual record of the trial and execution of the Mixtec leader of Coixtlahuaca, whose people attacked some Aztec merchants. This event was used by Moctezuma I Ilhuicamina as the pretext for a war that brought the Mixtecs to their knees and resulted in the payment of rich tribute into Aztec coffers. The codex image shows the merchants being killed and the arrival of Aztec emissaries to administer justice. They deliver a symbolic headdress, which indicates that the chief faces severe punishment. One of their number delivers a judgement on the ruler, who is put to death by strangulation while his child and principal wife are tied up roughly with slave collars around their necks.

The Mapa Quinatzin depicts legal process in Texcoco, whose ruler Netzahualcóyotl was famed as a legislator. A provincial chieftain who has had the temerity to rebel is warned, like the ruler of Coixtlahuaca, by being presented with a symbolic headdress. Then he is executed. Judges are depicted being put to death by strangulation because they have failed to follow required procedures and heard cases in their private lodgings.

PUNISHMENT

Punishments for wrongdoers included jailing and execution by strangulation, at the stake, or stoning. Theft was punished by strangulation. Drunks was strictly punished, with a sliding scale of penalties. The alcoholic drink *pulque* was only allowed for nobles, those who were sick and those aged over 52 years, although warriors could win the right to drink *pulque* as a reward for great bravery in battle. Those found drunk would have their heads shaved on the first occasion, on the second they would suffer the additional penalty of having their house knocked down. People found drunk on a third occasion would be put to death.

Right: Among the Aztecs, the rabbit was associated with the strong alcoholic drink pulque *and with drunkenness.*

THE MAYA LAW CODE

The Maya imposed severe penalties on those people who threatened social cohesion by committing crimes such as murder or adultery.

DIVINE PLAN

The Maya did not accept that bad things could happen by accident, for they viewed every event as the fulfilment of patterns that could be read in the stars and perhaps in the past, and which were set in motion by the gods. A hunter who killed another man by accident in the forest was just as guilty of murder as a man who killed another before witnesses in a quarrel over food. The unfortunate hunter must have been chosen by the gods to meet this end. Similarly, a person who lost or damaged someone else's belongings by accident was treated as if he or she had done it with intent and was required to compensate the unfortunate victim. Those who had no wealth of their own with which to pay compensation, nor wealthy relatives to provide help, faced slavery. They would be freed once they had worked off the money they owed to the victim.

Above: Punishments for adultery were very severe and the man was executed. This clay couple was found in a Jaina Island grave.

Left: The figure on this Maya vase appears to be giving instruction or delivering a judgement on a question of law.

PUNISHMENT

The punishment for murder was death. According to Bishop Diego de Landa, the murderer was placed in stocks and put to death by the relatives of the person he had killed. It appears that killing an animal for no reason was seen as akin to murder and the perpetrator might be severely disciplined for having brought shame on his patrilineal or matrilineal social group. Maya hunters were very serious about their responsibility to respect the animals on which they relied. They

Right: Royal anniversaries were a time of clemency. A king of Copán wears a headdress celebrating the rain god Chac.

would make ritual atonement after killing an animal by sprinkling blood drawn from the penis or tongue on to a part of the creature.

When couples were caught committing adultery, the man was punished with death. If the couple were caught *in flagrante*, the man would be taken from the bed and bound hand and foot, humiliated and dragged before the judges. After hearing the case and declaring his guilt, the victim would be handed to the husband, who was permitted to exact revenge by taking the other's life. The usual method of execution, or so Bishop de Landa reports, was to crush the adulterer's head by dropping a heavy rock on it from a height.

Theft was also considered a serious offence. The Maya did not add doors to their houses, so that there was no way of barring entry to passers-by; many people hung a bell-string in the doorway that would sound when someone entered and alert whoever was at home. A person caught stealing would be thrown into slavery. He would often be given a set period of time in which to work off the cost of his crime, after which he could return to free society. However, if the members of his patriarchal or matriarchal social group were wealthy, they would pay compensation to the person he stole from and he would be free to go.

The Maya did not put thieves, murderers or adulterers in jail. The only people they kept in captivity were the captives they brought home in triumph from war who were kept for sacrifice on festival days or at the celebration of a king's anniversary. These victims-in-waiting were treated with respect until the time for sacrifice came, when they might be subjected to severe physical indignities in the name of the ancestor-gods.

Below: Maya merchants traded near and far. This Preclassic vase (c.900–200BC) is from the Sula Valley, Honduras.

TRADE AND ENFORCEMENT

Maya merchants were a privileged class known as *ppolms*, some trading by sea in great fleets of canoes, others carrying goods along trails and roadways.

A merchant god, Ek Chuah, presided over the transactions of the land traders. It was a religious duty to act with honour, but such was the wealth involved in large transactions for precious cargoes of cacao or greenstones that sometimes greed got the better of individuals and sharp practice crept in.

Maya merchants did not make written deals. Instead, they would come to a verbal agreement, which was usually signalled by drinking a toast in public. These deals were then considered binding. If a merchant refused to honour the terms of a deal, his deceit might be considered justification enough to launch a war. The end result might be wealth far greater than that involved in the deal in the form of booty, slaves and tribute.

However, while sometimes a cause of war, Maya trade may have been a source of peace in one important respect. The success of Maya merchants may have saved their people from attack by the land-hungry armies of the Aztec empire. The Maya traded regularly with the peoples of the Triple Alliance, exchanging salt, cacao beans and the highly prized green plumes of the quetzal bird for ornaments and tools in copper. The success of these trading links perhaps served to deter the Aztecs from launching military campaigns in Yucatán.

CLANS AND POWER: MAYA SOCIAL GROUPS

Each Maya belonged to two blood groups: the matrilineal group, descended from the mother, and the patrilineal group, descended from the father. Each individual had both a name given by and inherited from the mother and another taken from the father.

PATRIMONY

Property could only be inherited from the father. Like the king's crown, belongings only passed down the patrilineal line. Members of a patrilineal group were expected to help one another in times of need. For example, they would buy out a relative who had been thrown into slavery because of debt or crime. The patrilineal group also held lands in common.

According to Bishop de Landa, each family among the common people was allocated 37sq m (400sq ft) of land to farm. This unit of land was known as a *hun uinic.* Scholars believe the matrilineal and patrilineal groupings were also used to control marriage between relatives. For example, a man might marry his mother's brother's daughter or his father's sister's daughter, but he would be barred from making other particular marriages.

CLASS DIVISIONS

Alongside and cutting across these blood groupings there were strong class divisions. It was extremely prestigious to be able to trace your lineage on both your mother's and father's side back across many generations to a noble family. Indeed, the word for a noble, *almehen*, translates as 'a man whose bloodline can be read on both sides'. Among members of the nobility were wealthy farmers who owned their own land, prosperous merchants, priests, leading warriors and priests. All those who held office within the political hierarchy, including councillors, judges and governors, were members of the nobility. The most important positions were filled by close members of the ruler's own blood group. The chiefs were carried in a litter decorated with plumes and borne on the shoulders of strong men.

Above: Members of the Maya nobility refashioned their looks by using clay to join the bridge of the nose to the forehead.

Below: The 'Nunnery' at Uxmal may have been occupied by members of one social class or worshippers of a particular god.

Scribes also occupied an elevated social position. They were leading members of the king's retinue. Most cities probably had a school for scribes, where royal and noble children such as the younger sons and daughters of the king or his children by secondary wives and concubines would learn the complex skills of reading and writing Maya hieroglyphs.

LITERACY AND CLASS

Literacy was probably not widespread among the general population. Scholars estimate that perhaps one in four of the Maya could read, and probably far fewer could write. Archaeologists have found attempts at writing by non-elite scribes at minor settlements or on the bricks that were fired at Comacalco, but these are not comprehensible because those responsible had clearly not mastered the difficult technique required. All they could manage was a crude imitation of the fine calligraphy found on carvings and ceramics produced by the elite scribes.

Beneath the nobility were the free workers, those who were allotted the *hun uinic* on which to grow their maize. They were liable to pay taxes in the form of crops to a tax collector. The priests who played such a vital role in reading the stars and patterns of history to determine the correct planting times were supported with crops from the field. The farmers probably saw the food sent to the temple as a gift to the gods, eaten by the priesthood on their behalf.

SLAVES

Some of the men worked the lands on behalf of the wealthy. There was also a large class of slaves. Many were men and women captured in war for, in general, only the more noble among the captives were sacrificed while the poorer prisoners were put into slavery. Others were individuals from Maya homelands who had been brought to slavery by wrongdoing or by poverty. Slaves were also traded across the vast network of routes that crisscrossed the Maya lands. For most, there was no way out of their condition and their children also would be slaves, although it was possible to buy individuals out of slavery.

Female slaves worked drawing water from wells, dyeing cloth and grinding maize. Male slaves were put to work as labourers, fishermen and carriers of cargo for merchants. The males were given an ill-kempt appearance, with ragged clothing and roughly cut short hair.

Maya architecture and city planning reflected and reinforced these class divisions. In general, the king, his retinue and the nobility lived close to the centre of the city. The Maya city was usually centred on the temple complex and its fine plazas. Around this were grouped the palaces and homes of the elite nobles, with the merchants and other professionals living in smaller dwellings beyond them and the humble homes of the working people more distant still.

Above: Maya rulers are regularly modelled or depicted on vases occupying the throne that symbolizes their power.

Left: In the Maya social pyramid, the king at the highest point was raised far above the workers of the land and slaves at the lowest level.

THE MANY LEVELS OF AZTEC SOCIETY

Aztec society was highly stratified. The most important division was between the *pipiltin*, or nobles, and the *macehuales* or commoners. These two social groups were essentially castes; there was no possibility of a man of humble birth rising to join the nobility. A boy's destiny was determined not just by his date of birth in the ritual calendar, but also by his caste. To be born on the date 1-Alligator was a good omen: the priests promised that a noble's son born on this day could expect to become a wealthy ruler of men. The best they could promise a farmer's son born on the same day, however, was that he might become a valiant warrior in the service of the city-state.

Below: An image from the Florentine Codex *shows an Aztec metalworker making objects of gold for the wealthiest of the nobility.*

Left: Gazing upwards, this life-size clay figure may represent a learned astronomer-priest.

THE NOBILITY

Nobles often received income from land holdings. They had access to prestigious positions in the priesthood and in the highest ranks of the army. Some served in the civil administration as provincial governors and judges, ambassadors and tax-collectors. Those of the highest rank were advisers to the *tlatoani*. Other nobles of lesser standing might become scribes and teachers. They had many privileges. The men were allowed to take several wives and build houses of two storeys. They sent their children to *calmecac* or priestly schools. Here they learned to read and write, and to study the ritual calendar and its meaning. They also learned battlefield strategy, history and mythology, and practised martial arts.

THE COMMONERS

Commoners were primarily farmers, fishermen and soldiers. Members of the tribal clan or *calpulli* held land in common and most farmers worked the land or water owned by their clan grouping. They were liable to pay tax to the *tlatoani* and could be called on to serve in the army or to work on construction projects. If a man neglected his area or died without having children, the clan would reassign that particular piece of land to another member of the blood grouping. Another type of farmer, known as *mayeque*, worked land owned by nobles.

Soldiers had the best chance of rising through the social ranks. There were many rewards for bravery in battle, including social privileges. But there was no way into the highest positions in the army, which were reserved for members of the nobility.

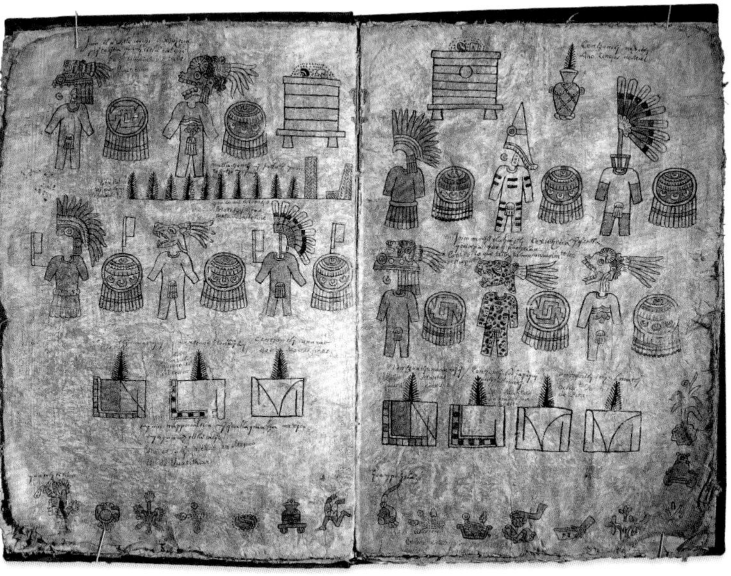

Above: Some of the many Aztec styles of clothing, headdresses and jewellery are detailed in the Codex Mendoza *(c.1541).*

Some men and women became slaves. People could volunteer for slavery if they were destitute and could become free again if circumstances improved; perhaps if clan members aided them. The children of slaves were not considered slaves.

ARTISANS

Some commoners achieved a measure of wealth by working as professional merchants (*pochteca*) or as artisans. Both groups lived in their own quarters in Aztec cities. Merchants were usually their own masters: they travelled widely throughout the empire, some trading on behalf of the ruler as well as carrying their own goods. They brought to the Aztec lands many of the raw materials such as precious metals and quetzal feathers needed by the artisans in their work. Some were secret agents, used to spy on allies and enemies and to listen out for whispers of impending revolts and other trouble. If prominent merchants were attacked or killed abroad, the *tlatoani* was quick to send the army to exact retribution. The Aztecs had a very high regard for the work of the skilled artisans who produced precious jewellery, feathered headdresses, fine costumes and stone ornaments. They honoured their craftsmen with the name *tolteca*, a reference to the ancient Toltecs whom the Aztecs revered. Some artisans were employed by individual nobles but others were free agents, producing artefacts as required. The more successful merchants and artisans became wealthy but they could never cross the caste line to become members of the nobility.

As the empire grew, divisions in Aztec society blurred and private ownership of land increased. When Tenochtitlán was founded, most land was held by tribal clans or *calpulli*. By the time of the Spanish Conquest, there were two types of landholding nobles. At the highest level stood a small group of nobles of ancient families directly related to the *tlatoani*, who owned territories that were worked on their behalf by farmers legally tied to the soil. At a lower level were warriors who had gained land as a reward for military achievement. These awards were normally for one generation, but in practice warriors tended to be allowed to leave land to their offspring. For this reason, Moctezuma II reinforced the distinction between nobility and commoners. He enforced strict laws on the dress code permitted for the castes and introduced ceremonial procedures that further set nobility apart.

Below: This illustration from the Codex Mendoza *(c.1541) presents the stages in the career of an Aztec imperial officer.*

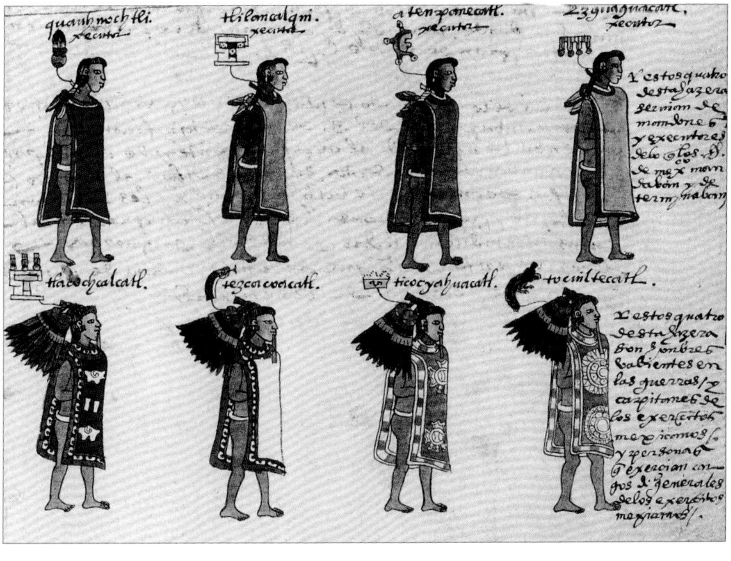

CHAPTER SIX

PAST, PRESENT AND FUTURE

Mesoamericans did not understand time to be an orderly procession from the past to the future, from the beginnings of the world to its end. For one thing, they believed time to be cyclical. The Aztecs, for example, believed that we live in the Fifth Sun or 'age' and that our age would be brought to a sudden end, as had its predecessors. They also believed that time was sacred, charged with the power of the gods. Its movements could be fluid and unpredictable as the gods chose. Mesoamerican deities could take many forms simultaneously and one of these forms was time itself. In any moment there were divine influences at work for good and bad and the people relied on priestly diviners to interpret time.

A 52-year time span was produced by the intersection of the two calendars used by the Aztecs and their Mesoamerican cousins. Mesoamericans separated by centuries and by miles – perhaps from as early as the Olmec civilization in the first millennium BC to the Maya and Aztecs at the time of the Conquest, and from the Teotihuacanos in the north to the inhabitants of Copán in the south-east – used a 365-day solar calendar to plot religious festivals alongside a 260-day calendar for divining the future. The first day of the 365-day calendar and the first day of the 260-day calendar intersected only once every 52 years. The Aztecs called this time span a 'bundle of years' while the Maya version is usually 'the Calendar Round'.

Left: Hunting god Mixcóatl slays a feline predator. In one Aztec creation myth, Mixcóatl hunted down earth goddess Cihuacóatl for love. Their union produced Quetzalcóatl, the great Plumed Serpent himself, bringer of winds and light.

STARTING FROM ZERO: MATHEMATICS

The Maya used a sophisticated mathematical notation that enabled them to write very large numbers in their carved inscriptions and in codices. They were among the first peoples – along with the ancient Babylonians, the Chinese and the Hindus of India – to develop the concept of zero and a symbol for it. Among the Maya, zero was represented not by an empty circle (0), but by a stylized image of a shell.

DOTS AND BARS

The Maya did not have the familiar decimal system, based on 10, but instead a count based on 20 (called a vigesimal system). Scholars suggest that the unit of 20 may have been used because it matches the number of fingers and toes in the human body. The Maya scribes and craftsmen wrote the numbers 1 to 4 with simple dots. One dot meant 1, two dots 2 and so on. The number 5 was written with a horizontal bar, and 6 was a single bar with a dot above it. They were able to write numbers up to 19 with a combination of horizontal bars and dots. For example, 17 was written with three bars, making 15, and two dots.

To write larger numbers they used these same symbols arranged in vertical columns. The bottom line showed units (1 to 19), the line above it numbers of twenties, the line above it numbers of 400s (20 units of 20), the line above that numbers of 8000s (20 units of 400) and so on. A single bar in the first line, with a dot in the line above, two bars in the line above and one bar in the line above would represent (1×5) plus (1×20) plus (10×400) plus (5×8000), which makes 5+20+4000+40,000=44,025.

The first breakthrough in deciphering the Maya bar and dot system was made in 1832 by Constantine Rafinesque (1783–1840), a brilliant naturalist and traveller-writer. Noticing the frequent use of bars and dots in the *Dresden Codex*, he surmised that these symbols were being used as numbers. He saw that the dots never appeared in groups of more than four and guessed that the bar stood for 5 and the dots for single units. Subsequently Ernst Förstemann, archivist at Dresden where the codex was kept, discovered the Maya scribes' use of the shell symbol to stand for 0.

This system was used primarily to mark and record dates. However, the Maya apparently also used this positional mathematics for practical calculation. According to Diego de Landa, Maya merchants negotiating a deal would use grains of maize or cacao beans spread out on the dry ground or a flat rock to reckon

Above: The Aztec bar and dot counting system can be read in this page from the Codex Cospi *(c.1350–1500). Tezcatlipoca, lord of night and fate, is in warrior garb and equipped with weapons. The images to his right are symbols for calendrical dates.*

Below: This detail from the Postclassic Madrid Codex *shows the bar and dot symbols used by the Maya in counting.*

Above: The profiles of gods' heads carved on this Yaxchilán lintel stand for numbers. The inscribed date is 11 February AD*526.*

even large numbers. The writers of codices generally used the simple bar-and-dot system for writing dates, but the craftsmen who carved the Classic Period stelae sometimes produced a more elaborate version. Each number from 0 to 19 had its own patron divinity and stonemasons began to carve heads or full images of these gods to represent particular numbers. This practice was particularly common among the sculptors who produced the elegant stelae at Quiriguá and Copán. A well-known example is found on the east side of Stela D at Quiriguá, where the god of the number 7 (Uuk) is carved in place of the number. Another example, on a lintel at Yaxchilán, is illustrated above – gods' heads representing numbers are combined with animal carvings standing for cycles of time.

AZTEC NUMBERS

The Aztecs also used the bar and dot system. Some scholars believe the system to have been an ancient part of the shared Mesoamerican culture, possibly dating as far back back as the Olmec era (c.1500–400BC). Like the Maya, the Aztecs seem to have been happy to use bars and dots to record dates in manuscripts and on monuments. However, because their growing empire drew in vast quantities of tribute from dependent territories, they also developed a system of number glyphs for use in accounting.

The newer system was still based on units of 20. A feather glyph meant 20, a flag glyph stood for 400 and a symbol representing a bag of incense was 8000 (20×400). A scribe who wanted to note receipt of 540 items of produce would draw one flag and seven feathers – 400 plus (7×20) = 540. He would generally draw a line alongside the glyphs to indicate they should be read in conjunction, then draw an image of the item received – say, a bag of cacao beans – and make a second line connecting the bag to the number. The readers of the tribute list would then understand that 540 bags of cacao beans had been received, counted and stored. Scholars would be able to decipher the system of number glyphs by examining the *Codex Mendoza* (c.1541). Part of this document comprises a detailed list of the tribute paid to Moctezuma II by subject towns and regions of the empire. It also has glosses in Spanish, written by an interpreter who understood the Nahuatl language and the Aztec system of numbers.

Above: The date carved on Lintel 26 at Yaxchilán marks the day on which King Shield Jaguar received his battle equipment from his wife: 9.14.12.6.12 in the Maya Long Count, or 12 February AD*724.*

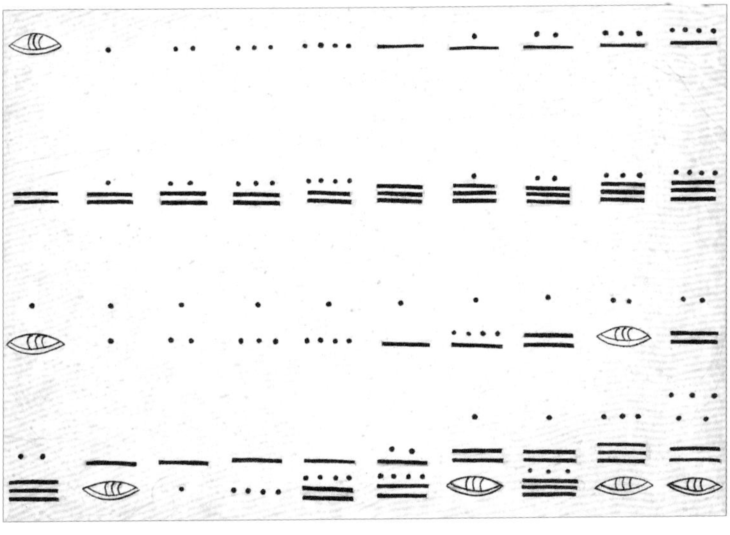

Right: Aztec numbers, from top left – 1, 2, 3, 4, 5, 6, 7, 8, 9, 10, 11, 12, 13, 14, 15, 16, 17, 18, 19, 20, 21, 22, 23, 24, 25, 29, 30, 40, 50, 55, 100, 101, 104, 114, 154, 600, 618, 1500 and 25,000.

THREE INTO ONE: INTERLOCKING CALENDARS

Above: This Aztec carving represents a 52-year cycle or 'bundle of years'. A bundle of sticks was burned to celebrate a new cycle.

The Aztec 365-day cycle contained 18 'months' of 20 days, plus five days at the year's end that were considered a time of ill omen. The 365-day count was called *xiuhpohualli* ('counting of the years') and was used for plotting religious festivals and for marking the seasons. The Aztec 260-day calendar combined the numbers 1–13 with 20 names of creatures, objects or forces such as crocodile, house, wind, flint knife, jaguar and reed. When the calendar was written down, each day name was denoted by a hieroglyph showing the object, animal or force, while each number was shown by dots. The cycle was called *tonalpohualli* ('the counting of the days'). It began with 1-Crocodile, 2-Wind and 3-House. The thirteenth and fourteenth names in the cycle were reed and jaguar, but there was no fourteen in the number sequence, so after 13-Reed the *tonalpohualli* proceeded to 1-Jaguar, and then carried on through the day names while prefixing the numbers 2, 3, 4 and so on. The cycle was therefore divided into 20 'weeks' of 13 days, which the Spanish called *trecena*.

Below: A Codex Borbonicus *image shows the deities Ometecuhtli and Omecihuatl creating the divinely ordained calendar.*

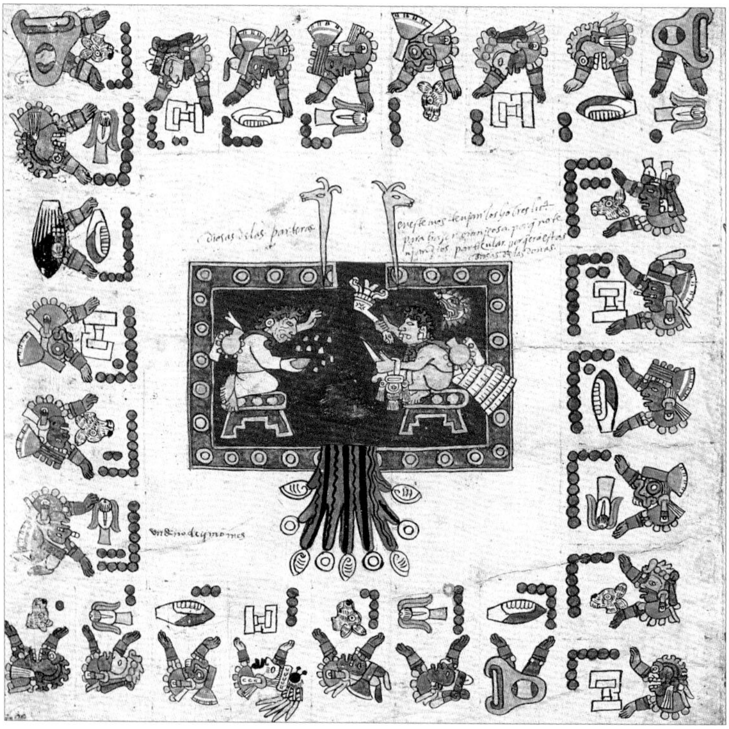

Together, the *tonalpohualli* or day count and the *xiuhpohualli* or year count produced 18,980 unique combinations before repeating the same intersection of days in the two calendars. This was the equivalent of 73 years in the *tonalpohualli* calendar or 52 years – the 'bundle of years' – in the *xiuhpohualli* calendar.

RELIGIOUS FESTIVALS

In the year calendar, each 20-day month was associated with a religious festival. Most were linked to the agricultural year and there were three principal kinds. One group honoured the sun, the land and maize. A second included offerings to mountains and sources of water, while a third paid homage to patron deities.

Some of the days of the calendar marked religious festivals, but priestly ceremonies were usually timed according to the year calendar. Priestly astronomers also looked to the heavens, in particular to the movements of the moon and Venus, when attempting to divine the events of the future.

Above: On the Aztec Sun Stone, the glyphs in the enclosed circle surrounding the sun god are those of the 20 days of the week.

The five-day period at year's end, the *nemontemi*, was a time of withdrawal. People did not carry out their normal activities. Fields were left untended and markets were deserted. Householders broke their plates and utensils, fasted and let their fires go out. They even refrained from talking. One ritual looked to the new beginning the Aztecs hoped would follow the New Fire rites: a pregnant woman was locked in a granary in the hope that her fertility would be transferred to the corn.

The patterns of intersection between the two calendars meant that a new year in the *xiuhpohualli* could only begin on one of four possible names from the *tonalpohualli*. These were rabbit, reed, flint knife and house. Each year took its name from the 'year bearer', whichever one of these four day-names fell on the first day of the new year. Within a 52-year cycle, the year bearers were numbered one to 13 in succession – 1-Rabbit, 2-Reed, 3-House, 4-Flint-knife, 5-Rabbit, 6-Reed, 7-House, 8-Flint-knife, 9-Rabbit, 10-Reed, 11-House, 12-Flint-knife, 13-Rabbit, 1-Reed, 2-House and so on.

Because there were 20 days in each month of the *xiuhpohualli* and a recurring pattern of 20 day-signs in the *tonalpohualli*, each month in the *tonalpohualli* began with the same day-sign as the year. That is, the year-bearer was also the 'month-bearer'. The year-bearer was also celebrated repeatedly throughout the year.

Among the Aztecs, the 52-year cycles were not differentiated from each other. The date system could specify that an event took place on a particular day in a particular year within a 52-year cycle, but not in which 52-year cycle it happened. This presented significant problems in long cycles of time. The problem was solved by the 'Long Count', which marked time from a year zero in the distant past. Scholars believe the Long Count was widely used in Mesoamerica in early times, but that it fell into disuse in all except Maya lands, where it was developed into a sophisticated system.

Below: The 20 Aztec day names are (from top left) flower, rain, flint knife, movement, vulture, eagle, jaguar, reed, grass, monkey, dog, water, rabbit, deer, death, serpent, lizard, house, wind and crocodile.

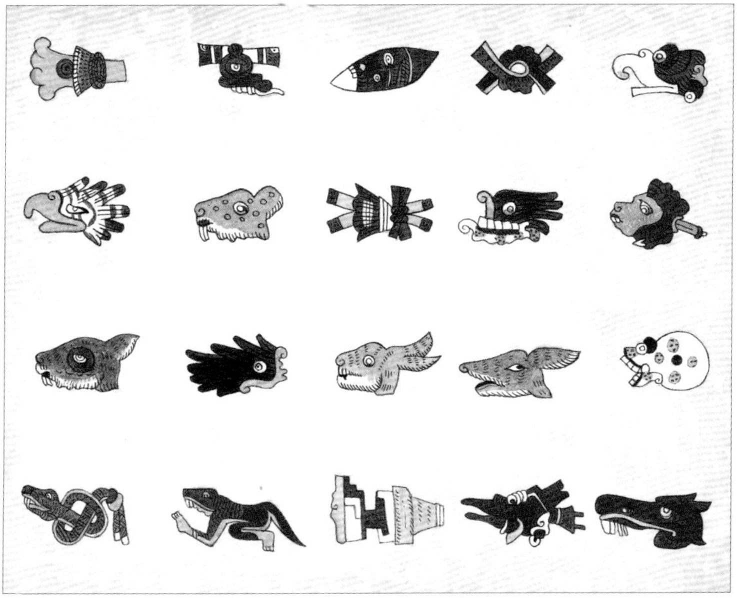

THE MAYA CALENDAR

The Maya used the same combination of a 260-day ritual count with 13 20-day cycles and a 365-day solar count with 18 20-day months and a five-day unlucky period at year's end. The Maya called the 260-day calendar the *tzolkin*, and the 365-day calendar the *haab*. Scholars sometimes call the 365-day measure the 'Vague Year' because Mesoamericans did not take account of the fact that a solar year lasts slightly more than 365 days and add an extra day every four years. Nor did they make any of the other sophisticated adjustments of the Gregorian calendar now widely used in the West. Over time, their solar year must have dragged behind the movements of the stars and sun.

Bishop Diego de Landa gave a detailed description of the Maya calendars and made careful note of the glyphs used by the Maya for day-signs and months. To give a day its full Maya calendrical date would require the *tzolkin* date and the *haab* date. For example, 13 Ahau 18 Cumku. This date would have been towards the close of the final month before the unlucky five-day period (*uayeb*) at the end of the year.

COUNTING THE DAYS

Scholars cannot agree why the early Mesoamericans first fixed on 260 days as a useful unit for measuring time. Some have argued that it was based on observation of the movements of Venus and of the sun in our skies. The 260-day period roughly corresponds to the gap between the appearance of Venus as the evening star and its emergence as the morning star. There is also an interval of 260 days between the sun's annual southward movement and its northward return when viewed from a latitude close to Copán. This celestial observation might have been used to time planting and harvest and over centuries it could have become a hallowed measurement strongly associated with divine rhythms underlying fertility.

Above: At El Tajin, Mexico, the Pyramid of the Niches has 365 niches, supposedly one for each day of the solar year.

HUMAN RHYTHMS

Most modern scholars argue that the 260-day cycle is based on human rhythms. Midwives may have used the measure, counting forward 260 days from the date of a woman's last menstrual period, to predict when a baby would be likely to be born, as do the modern Maya still living in the mountains of southern Guatemala. The 260-day calendar has proved a most enduring invention. It is still used among the Quiché inhabitants of the tropical mountains of southern Guatemala.

Left: The 20 Maya day names include Imix (top left), Akbal (centre top), Etznab (centre bottom) and Ahau (bottom right).

THE MAYA LONG COUNT

In addition to the twinned 260-day and 365-day calendars, the Maya people greatly refined a much longer-running measuring system, the 'Long Count', which is known to have been used in many parts of Mesoamerica at the start of the first millennium BC. During the Classic Period (*c.*AD250–900), the Maya dated their monuments using the Long Count to record births, deaths, royal accessions and anniversaries, the dates of ritual sacrifices and battle triumphs. This system counted forward from a zero date of 4 Ahua 8 Cumku, equivalent to 11 August 3114BC in the Gregorian calendar.

The Maya Long Count counted days in units of 20 and used a 'year' of 360 days. Its five units were the *baktun* (144,000 days), the *katun* (7,200 days), the *tun* (360 days), the *uinal* (20 days) and the *kin* (1 day). Dates were carved in this order, with units separated by full points. For example, the date 3.3.2.1.1 would be three *baktuns* (432,000 days), three *katuns* (21,600 days), 2 *tuns* (720 days), one *uinal* (20 days) and 1 *kin* (1 day), making a total of 454,341 days after the zero date of 11 August 3114BC.

The earliest Maya Long Count inscription is from El Baúl on the Pacific coast in the southern Maya or highland Maya region and dates to AD37.

A date carved on a stela gave the Long Count followed by the position in the Calendar Round (the combination of the *haab* calendar and the *tzolkin* calendar). Because there are so very many dates on stelae, early scholars thought that the Maya worshipped time itself. However, breakthroughs in understanding hieroglyphics enabled the successors of those scholars to grasp that the dates were provided to set in time the image carved beneath them of a king's accession or triumph over a rival ruler.

The Long Count date is usually only carved once on a stela: dates given later for the ruler's birth-date or accession are almost invariably given only in the *tzolkin* calendar because the larger context of the Long Count date has already been established. Dates on stelae also often provide information about the moon. Scholars call the Long Count and Calendar Round dates, which come first in inscriptions, the 'Initial Series' and the information on the moon cycle the 'Lunar Series'.

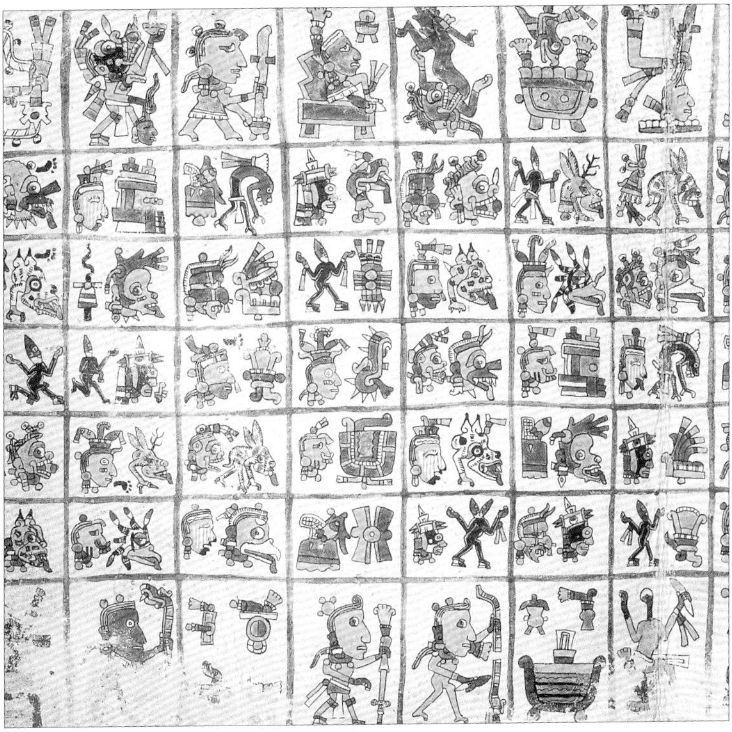

Above: The Mixtec Codex Cospi *(c.1350–1500) contains a ritual calendar and a detailed survey of the movements of Venus.*

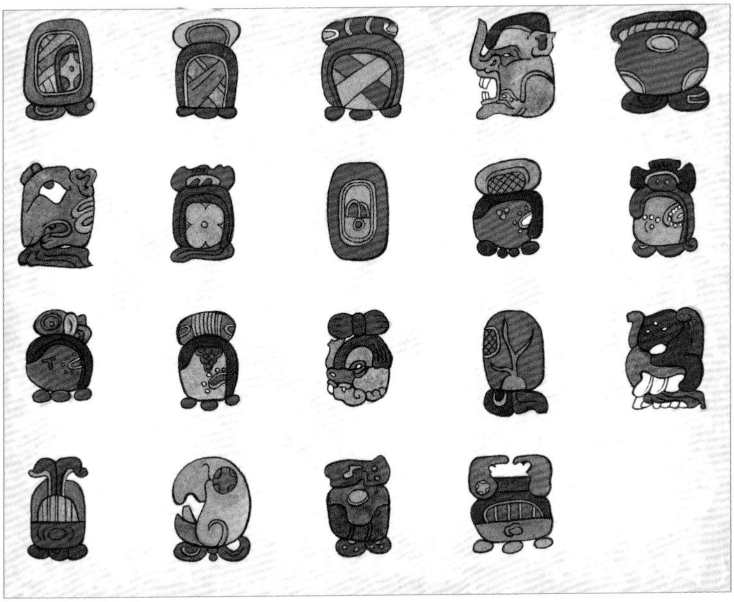

Left: The glyphs for the 19 Maya months include Pop (top left), Zotz (top, fourth from left), Pax (bottom left) and Uayeb (last).

MAJOR AZTEC FESTIVALS

AZTEC MONTH 1
Western dates 14 February–5 March
Festival name Atlcaualo (The Ending of Water), Cuauhitleua (The Lifting of Trees)
Gods/goddesses honoured Tláloc (rain and fertility god), Chalchiúhtlicue (goddess of springs, rivers and the sea), Chicomecóatl (maize goddess), Xilonen (maize goddess), Quetzalcóatl (storms, wind and rain god)
Rites Offerings to maize divinities, including the sacrifice of children; banners erected in homes and temples.

AZTEC MONTH 2
Western dates 6–25 March
Festival name Tlacaxipehualiztli (Skinning of the Men)
Gods/goddesses honoured Xipe Totec (god of vegetation and spring, patron of goldworkers)
Rites Victims slaughtered, priests wear their skin over their face and body; five prisoners of war killed in staged combat; *tlatoani* takes part in dance and military ritual.

AZTEC MONTH 3
Western dates 26 March–14 April
Festival name Tozoztontli (Minor Vigil), Xochimanaloya (Presentation of flowers)
Gods/goddesses honoured Tláloc (rain and fertility god), Chalchiúhtlicue (goddess of springs, rivers and the sea), Centéotl (maize god), Coatlícue (earth goddess)
Rites Ceremonial planting of seeds; donations of flowers to the festival deities; priests made offering of flayed skins.

AZTEC MONTH 4
Western dates 15 April–4 May (End of dry season)
Festival name Huey Tozoztli (Major Vigil)
Gods/goddesses honoured Tláloc (rain and fertility god), Chalchiúhtlicue (goddess of springs, rivers and the sea), Centéotl (maize god), Coatlícue (earth goddess), Chicomecóatl (maize goddess), Xilonen (maize goddess), Quetzalcóatl (storms, wind and rain god)
Rites Rulers of Tenochtitlán, Texcoco, Tlacopán and Xochimilco made sacrifices to the earth; a girl impersonating Chalchiúhtlicue was sacrificed and her blood poured on Lake Texcoco; priestesses of Chicomecóatl bless farmers' seed supplies.

AZTEC MONTH 5
Western dates 5–22 May
Festival name Tóxcatl (Drought)
Gods/goddesses honoured Tezcatlipoca (god of fate, kingship and other attributes), Huitzilopochtli (Méxica tribal god, also god of war and associated with the sun), Mixcóatl (hunt god), Camaxtli (hunt god)
Rites Youth who has impersonated Tezcatlipoca for a year sacrificed on the Great Pyramid in Tenochtitlán; impersonators of Huitzilopochtli, Mixcóatl and Camaxtli sacrificed separately.

AZTEC MONTH 6
Western dates 23 May–13 June (Start of rainy season)
Festival name Etzalcualiztli (Meal of Maize and Beans)
Gods/goddesses honoured Tláloc (rain and fertility god), Chalchiúhtlicue (goddess of waters), Quetzalcóatl (wind and rain god)
Rites Priests held vigils and fasts, praying for a cloudburst; noblemen danced with maize stalks; new reeds harvested on the lake; meals of maize and beans served.

AZTEC MONTH 7
Western dates 14 June–3 July
Festival name Tecuilhuitontli (Minor Festival of the Lords)
Gods/goddesses honoured Xochipilli (god of flowers, song and dance), Huixtocíhuatl (goddess of salt)
Rites *Tlatoani* dance in public and hand out gifts to the people; nobility hold feasts open to commoners; sacrifices made to salt goddess and to Xochipilli.

AZTEC MONTH 8
Western dates 4–23 July
Festival name Huey Tecuilhuitl (Major Festival of the Lords)
Gods/goddesses honoured Xilonen (maize goddess), Cihuacóatl (fertility goddess)
Rites *Tlatoani* dance and hand out gifts; nobility hold feasts for commoners to celebrate the appearance of the first maize shoots; offerings made to a girl who is impersonating Xilonen.

AZTEC MONTH 9
Western dates 24 July–12 August
Festival name Miccailhuitontli (Minor Festival of the Dead), Tlaxochimaco (Emergence of Flowers)
Gods/goddesses honoured Tezcatlipoca (god of fate, kingship, darkness, masculinity and many other attributes), Huitzilopochtli (Méxica tribal god, also god of war and associated with the sun), ancestor gods
Rites Sacrifices to Huitzilopochtli in his guise as the ancestral leader of the migrating Méxica; offerings made to the dead; feasts and dances held in their honour.

AZTEC MONTH 10
Western dates 13 August–1 September
Festival name Huey Miccailhuitl (Major Festival of the Dead), Xocotlhuetzi (Ripening of the Xocotl fruit)
Gods/goddesses honoured Huehuetéotl (old fire god), Xiuhtecuhtli (fire god), Yacatecuhtli (trader's god)
Rites Fire sacrifices; offerings made to ancestors.

AZTEC MONTH 11
Western dates 2–21 September (Start of harvest)
Festival name Ochpaniztli (Clearing)
Gods/goddesses honoured Toci (earth goddess), Tlazoltéotl (goddess of love and filth), Teteoinnan (earth goddess), Coatlicue (earth goddess), Cinteotl (maize goddess), Chicomecóatl (maize goddess)
Rites Female sacrificial victim beheaded and flayed by priestess of Xilonen-Chicomecóatl, who then wore her skin; corn seeds thrown to the people; cleaning and repairs carried out. Preparations for the approaching season of war included military manoeuvres; *tlatoani* gives insignia to soldiers. Priests started a major fast that ran until the Festival of Panquetzalitzli.

AZTEC MONTH 12
Western dates 22 September–11 October (Harvest)
Festival name Teotleco (Coming of the Gods and Goddesses)
Gods/goddesses honoured All
Rites General festivities included dancing and feasting; footprint made at midnight in a bowl of maize flour in the temple signified the coming of the gods and the goddesses.

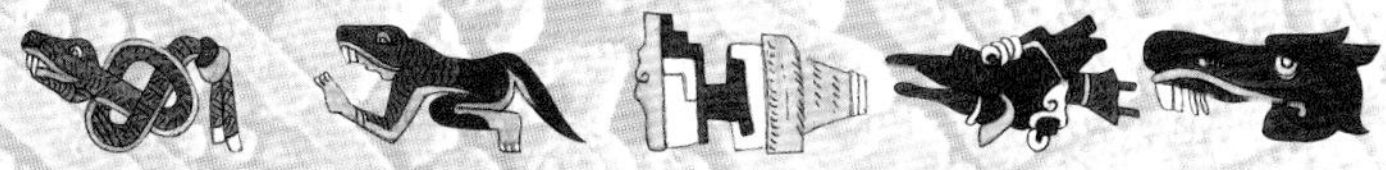

AZTEC MONTH 13
Western dates 12–31 October
Festival name Tepeilhuitl (Festival of the Mountains)
Gods/goddesses honoured Tláloc (rain god), *Tlaloque* (rain god's assistants), Tepictoton (rain god), Octli (deities of *pulque* drink), Xochiquetzal (flower goddess) and divine mountains Popocatépetl, Ixtaccíhuatl (Mount) Tlaloc and Matlalcueye
Rites Ritual offerings made at mountain sanctuaries.

AZTEC MONTH 14
Western dates 1–20 November
Festival name Quecholli (Treasured Feather)
Gods/goddesses honoured Mixcóatl (hunt god), Camaxtli (hunt god)
Rites Hunting competitions held; prisoners dressed as deer sacrificed in honour of the hunt gods; soldiers fast in preparation for war; weapons made for battle and hunting.

AZTEC MONTH 15
Western dates 21 November–10 December
Festival name Panquetzalitzi (Lifting of the Banners)
Gods/goddesses honoured Tezcatlipoca (god of fate, kingship, darkness, masculinity and many other attributes), Huitzilopochtli (Méxica tribal god, also god of war and associated with the sun)
Rites Major sacrifices of prisoners of war, including sacrifice of the 'bathed slaves'; sacred procession from the Great Pyramid to Tlatelolco, Chapultepec and Coyoacan, then back to the sacred precinct at Tenochtitlán; paper banners hung on houses and in fruit trees.

AZTEC MONTH 16
Western dates 11–30 December
Festival name Atemoztli (Coming Down of Waters)
Gods/goddesses honoured Tláloque (rain god's assistants) and divine mountains Popocatépetl, Ixtaccihuatl (Mount) Tláloc and Matlalcueye
Rites Ceremonies held in honour of the mountains.

AZTEC MONTH 17
Western dates 31 December–19 January
Festival name Tititl (Stretching)
Gods/goddesses honoured Cihuacóatl (fertility goddess), Ilamatecuhtli (ancient mother goddess), Tonantzin (mother goddess), Yacatecuhtli (god of traders and travellers)
Rites Merchants offer slave sacrifices to Yacatecuhtli; weavers made offerings to Ilamatecuhtli; public dancing involving priests, nobility and the *tlatoani*.

AZTEC MONTH 18
Western dates 20 January–8 February
Festival name Izcalli (Growing)
Gods/goddesses honoured Xiuhtecuhtli (fire god), Tláloc (rain god), Chalchiúhtlicue (water goddess)
Rites Animal sacrifices to the fire god; corn toasted and tamales served with greens; dough effigies of Xiuhtecuhtli made.

The five days at the end of the year (9–13 February) were a time for doing as little as possible to avoid ill fortune. People stayed at home and did not do any business.

DIVINING THE FUTURE

Priests used the ritual calendar to divine the future. Aztec priests consulted long screenfold books called *tonalamatl*. In these books, which were made from bark paper coated with a white mineral paste, scribes recorded the calendar and the many meanings of its cycles.

ARCANE MEANINGS

The calendars contained a rich blend of arcane meanings. Each number in the *tonalpohualli* was under a divine influence. Each of the 13 lords of the day was associated with a butterfly or bird. Each of the day-names also had its associated deity (see chart). A further cycle of nine lords of the night cast its influence over the calendar. The influences that were in place at the start of each 13-day period remained a powerful force throughout.

Below: A priest on this pre-Toltec stela from Santa Lucia Cotzumalhuapa uses a staff to help make an astronomical observation.

AZTEC DAY GODS IN THE *TONALPOHUALLI*

Day	Symbol	God
1	Crocodile (cipactli)	Tonacatecuhtli (Creator god)
2	Wind (éhecatl)	Quetzalcóatl (Storm/wind god among many other attributes)
3	House (calli)	Tepeyolohtli (God of regeneration)
4	Lizard (cuetzpallin)	Huehuecóyotl (Old Old Coyote, a trickster god)
5	Serpent (cóatl)	Chalchiúhtlicue (Water goddess)
6	Death (miquiztli)	Tecciztécatl (Moon god)
7	Deer (mázatl)	Tláloc (Rain god)
8	Rabbit (tochtli)	Mayáhuel (Maguey plant goddess)
9	Water (atl)	Xiuhtecuhtli (Fire god)
10	Dog (izcuintli)	Mictlantecuhtli (Lord of the underworld)
11	Monkey (ozomatli)	Xochipilli (God of flowers, song and dance)
12	Grass (malinalli)	Patécatl (Medicine god)
13	Reed (ácatl)	Tezcatlipoca (God of night and destiny, among many other attributes)
14	Jaguar (océlotl)	Tlazoltéotl (Goddess of filth and love)
15	Eagle (cuauhtli)	Xipe Totec (Vegetation god)
16	Vulture (cozcacuauhtli)	Itzapapálotl (A form of Coatlícue, an earth goddess)
17	Motion (ollin)	Xólotl (double of Quetzalcóatl)
18	Flint (técpatl)	Tezcatlipoca
19	Rain (quiáhuitl)	Chantico (Hearth goddess)
20	Flower (xóchitl)	Xochiquetzal (Flower goddess)

The Maya understood that the last day of each solar month fell under the influence of the month that was about to begin. The 20th day of Zotz, for example, was influenced by the next month, Tzec, and was said to be 'the seating of Tzec'. The following day was 1-Tzec. A baby's destiny might be read in the influences prevalent on its birthday. Parents whose child was born on an ill-omened day could improve his or her chances by holding a naming ceremony on a day that carried positive associations.

Priests consulted the movements of celestial bodies. Priest-astrologer-diviners would plot the best days for planting, harvesting and other daily activities. For example, Maya planting books instructed farmers on which days to plant during the months of Chen and Yax.

Below: Priests determined the auspicious date for ceremonies. This marker from the Maya city of Chinkultic says that the ball court was dedicated on 21 May AD591.

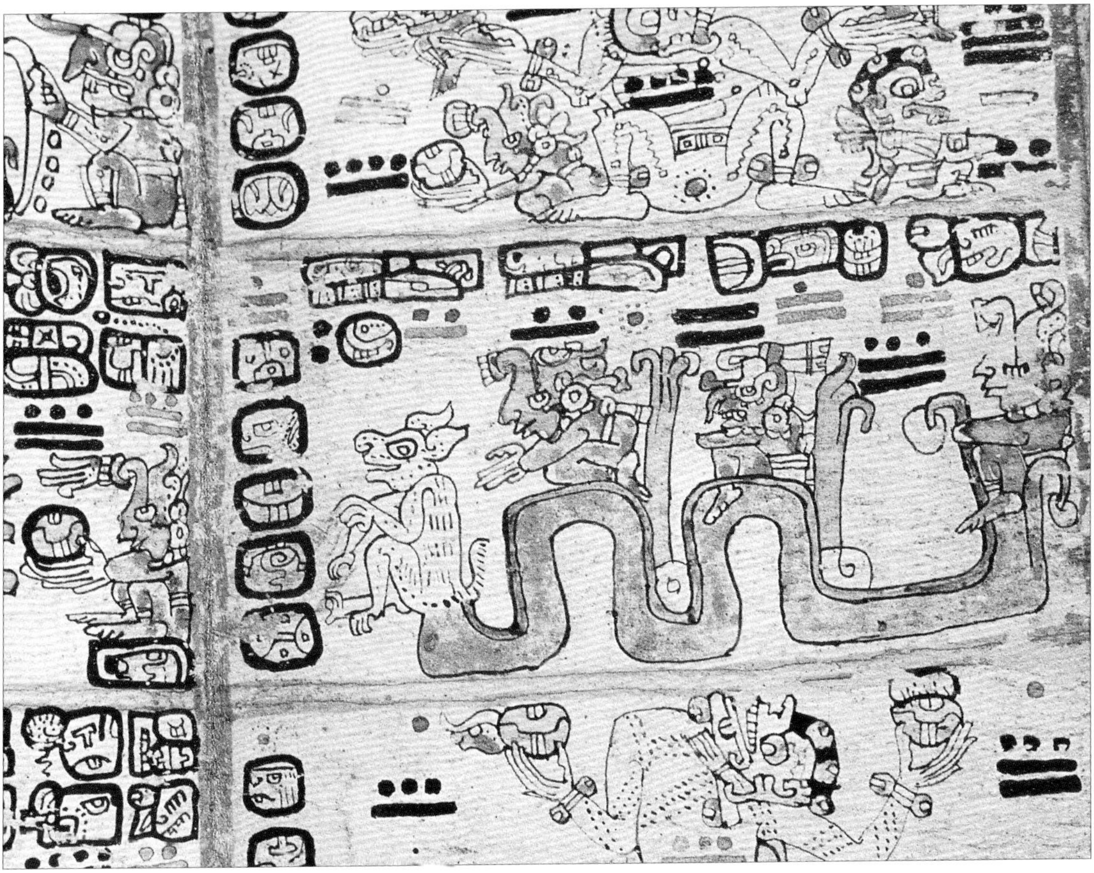

Above: The Madrid Codex *contains almanacs used by priests for timing religious rites and plotting astronomical movements.*

Merchants would take diviners' advice when planning their departure and return dates for journeys. In the Maya realms, rulers would visit the astronomer-priests to check on celestial movements: they often launched attacks to coincide with the rising of the malign planet Venus. Fittingly, the Maya hieroglyph for war consists of the logograph for Venus (one image representing the whole word) combined with another sign.

Among the Aztecs, the *tlatoani* himself and his advisers would take account of the meanings of the calendars and the heavens when plotting military campaigns. Indeed, it was one of the *tlatoani*'s duties to scan the heavens for guidance.

DAYKEEPERS AND MODERN DIVINING

Anthropologists have discovered modern diviners at work using the 260-day calendar in Guatemala.

Shaman-priests who are known as 'daykeepers' work among the Quiché people of Momostenango in Guatemala, using the ritual calendar to divine solutions for people's problems. Burning copal incense, they take a handful of coral seeds and count them out in piles of four. The number left over at the end provides information about the problem. The priest then counts the number of piles and counts back the same number of days through the 260-day round to give an indication of when the problem began. He or she may feel a 'lightning' in the blood when counting past a particular day, which gives further information to be interpreted. At this moment, the priest's body becomes an image of the universe in microcosm. The sensations he or she feels have meaning in a larger context. The priest makes use of the many associations of each day-sign to intuit the arrangements of cosmic energy around the individual and his or her difficulty, and so work out a possible response to the problem.

The Momostenango Quiché have safeguarded many traditional Maya religious practices. They hold a celebrated religious festival in which new daykeepers are initiated on the day 8-Monkey in the 260-day calendar.

READING THE STARS

In Mesoamerican societies, priests were guardians of time. As well as computing the calendar and keeping track of festivals and necessary religious ceremonies, they watched the movements of the stars and planets for bad omens or propitious dates. By interpreting the movements of the celestial bodies, priests could gain knowledge of the divinely inspired future. Among the Maya, the priest was known as Ah Kin ('Servant of the Sun'), making clear his connection to both astronomy and the calendar. As timekeeper, the Maya priest-scribe was also in charge of the genealogies of the city-state.

UNIVERSAL FORCES

Just as the priests understood the pattern of days and weeks in the ritual and solar calendars to be full of divine energy and meaning, so they saw the orbits and phases of the planets and the movements of stars to be a manifestation of universal forces that impacted upon the lives of men. The movements of the planet Venus were considered of great importance. In Mesoamerican latitudes, Venus shines brilliantly in the morning sky, as large as a tennis ball. The planet assumed an important role in religion and mythology.

Venus follows a near-circular orbit around the sun: one orbit takes 225 days. Like the moon, Venus goes through a number of phases: one cycle of phases takes 584 days. The Mesoamerican astronomers knew about this because they had measured it from observatory-towers such as the ones in the Maya cities of Mayapán and Chichén Itzá. They knew that Venus goes through four phases. It rises first in the morning sky and is visible as the morning star for 236 days. Thereafter it disappears into the light of the sun and is lost to sight for 90 days. At the end of this period it rises in the evening sky and is visible as the evening star for 250 days. In its fourth phase, it is invisible for eight days before reappearing as the morning star.

Left: The standing figure on this terracotta incense burner from Palenque may be the Maya sun god.

Below: The circular Venus observatory in Chichén Itzá was built to let astronomers observe the four phases of the planet Venus.

PHASES OF VENUS

The Maya associated the 'invisible phases' of Venus, when the planet disappears from view, with voyages to the spirit realm of the underworld. Quetzalcóatl's descent to the underworld to claim the bones of fish-men, the 'people' of a previous world-age, was understood to take place during the eight-day phase when Venus is invisible. When Quetzalcóatl returned successfully from his task, he rose into the heavens as the morning star. Every Maya ruler was thought to travel to the underworld after death and, if he passed successfully through the trials he encountered there, would rise into the skies as Venus.

In another tradition Quetzalcóatl-Topiltzin, overcome with shame after being outwitted by his dark double Tezcatlipoca and brought to sleep with his sister, takes his own life on a blazing pyre. From the flames his heart rises as Venus the morning star.

The appearance of Venus as the morning star would appear to be a reminder of the king's immortality and a celebration of the victory of Quetzalcóatl over the lords of the spirit realm and over death. Yet Venus did not generally have positive

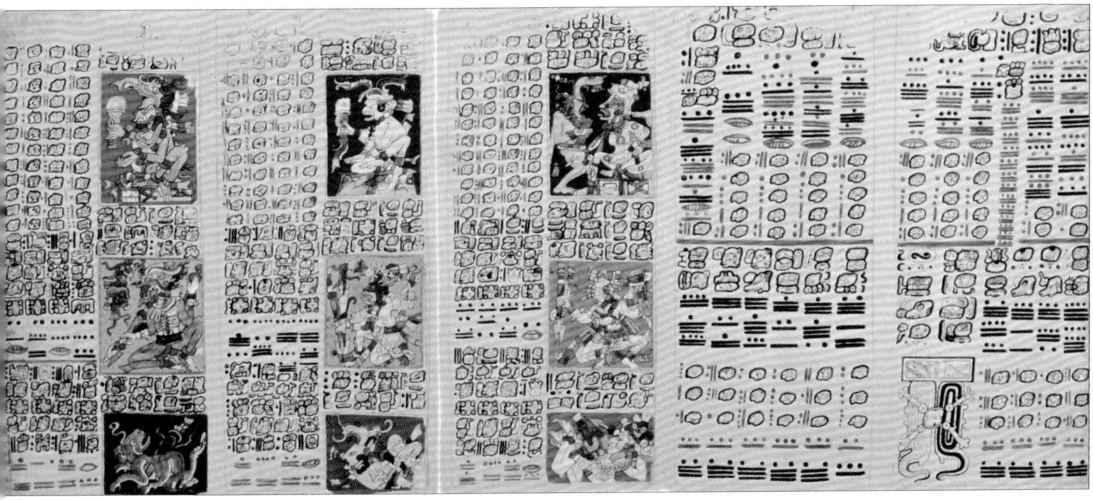

Above: Priests used the information in these pages from the Dresden Codex *to calculate the future cycles of the planet Venus.*

associations in the Mesoamerican mind. The planet was believed to have a negative influence on earthly affairs.

MAYA OBSERVATORIES

Maya star-watchers, who had no specialized astronomical equipment, predicted the rising of Venus as morning star and evening star with astonishing accuracy; to within one day in 6,000 years. The tower-observatory in the Maya city of Chichén Itzá tells of the dedication with which Maya priests plotted celestial movements. The tower is known in modern times as the Caracol, from the Spanish for snail, because it has spiral passageways. It was built for observation of Venus. Three passages leaving the Caracol line up precisely with the spots in the western sky where Venus can be seen as the evening star, among them the most northerly and southerly point at which it sets. At Palenque, the square tower that rises above the palace is decorated with a Venus glyph and appears to have been used as an observatory for plotting the planet's movements, while at Uxmal, the Governor's Palace must have been used for astronomical observation. It is aligned with a mound above which Venus would have risen at the most southerly point in its cycle.

Priests also relied on books to plot celestial movements. The *Grolier Codex* of *c.*1230 consists of around half of a table for predicting the Venus cycle over 104 years. The *Dresden Codex*, which dates to just before the Spanish Conquest, contains tables for plotting the Venus and Mars cycles and solar eclipses, as well as details of rites and deities associated with the 260-day calendar. Both these books contain eight-year Venus tables which show that the Maya understood how, after five 584-day Venus cycles and eight 365-day solar cycles, the two met (5×584 = 2920 days = 8×365).

GODS AND ANIMALS: THE MAYA ZODIAC

There is disagreement among scholars over whether the Maya had a zodiac of star-signs like that developed by Western astrologers.

Some authors believe that there is evidence for a Maya zodiac on a badly damaged page of the *Paris Codex*, which shows animals hanging from a band thought to represent the heavens. The *Paris Codex* animals are a scorpion, a turtle and a rattlesnake. We know that the Maya saw a constellation in the night sky by the name of *tzab* ('rattlesnake rattle') where in the western tradition we see the Pleiades.

It is likely that a Maya zodiac would contain the turtle, because that creature plays an important role in Maya creation stories. In some accounts, the world was said to be lying atop a giant turtle; there is also an image on a surviving Maya pot of the maize god rising from the broken earth, which is represented by a broken turtle shell.

Scholars believe that the Maya may have associated the stars of our constellation Orion with a turtle. In one of the murals at Bonampak a turtle is shown with the three stars from Orion's belt adorning its shell.

Among the Aztecs, most of the gods had equivalents among the stars. Tezcatlipoca was associated with the Great Bear. The jaguar skin that he was often shown wearing was an Aztec image for the night sky itself. Aztecs believed that the Great Bear's descent into the waters of the ocean was a re-enactment of the myth in which Tezcatlipoca loses his foot while he is fighting the Earth Monster. Quetzalcóatl was Venus as the morning star and the same planet as the evening star was Quetzalcóatl's double, Xólotl, who travelled with the Plumed Serpent to the underworld when he went to outwit the underworld lords and launch the current world-age.

WRITTEN RECORDS

The Olmec peoples who flourished on the Gulf Coast of Mexico *c.*1500–400 BC are accorded the honour of being the first Mesoamerican people to develop a written script by some scholars. On one end of a basalt column from the Olmec site at La Venta, a craftsman carved the relief of a walking man with a beard and beside the man's head cut three signs that look like hieroglyphs. Experts have been unable to decipher the signs, but suggest that one of the glyph-like images, which looks like a bird's head, probably represents the man's name.

Below: A scribe incised Maya glyphs into this jade pendant in the 5th century AD. Added red colour makes reading easier.

Other examples of Olmec hieroglyph-like images are found on pots and celts of jade and serpentine. But most scholars now argue that while the Olmec certainly used symbols to communicate meaning, their carvings cannot be called writing because the symbols do not refer to the sounds of a language. They are symbols purely and simply. Like road signs, they carry meaning, but do not represent sounds or words.

FIRST BOOKS

Intriguingly, it appears that the Olmec might already have been using screenfold books made from *amate* bark. A ceramic bowl that might be dated as early as 1200BC is carved with two objects that resemble this kind of book. The Olmec appear to have had a working system of written communication even if it was not writing as we define it.

Following the collapse of Olmec culture, the Zapotec craftsmen of Monte Albán in *c.*600–200BC were the next to develop the art of writing in Mesoamerica. They carved images of male figures in the Temple of the Danzantes at Monte Albán alongside hieroglyphic signs that appear to represent the figures' names.

The men depicted were once thought to be dancers (*danzantes*) but are now believed to be sacrificed war captives. Later Zapotec monuments bear longer texts that include dates in the Calendar Round, cut with year signs, glyphs for days and months and bar-and-dot numbers. As with the Olmec inscriptions, scholars have been unable to decipher these carvings, apart from the dates. The earliest example of Zapotec writing is probably the stone called Monument 3 from San José Mogote in the Oaxaca Valley. It depicts a slain captive with

Above: The top section of this carving shows Aztec rulers Tizoc and Ahuitzotl. Beneath are the glyphs representing the date 8-Reed.

blood pouring from his chest and gives the Calendar date 1-Earthquake – perhaps his day-name. It has been dated to *c.*600 BC.

Some scholars claim this as the earliest example of Mesoamerican writing and argue that other forms derived from the Zapotec, but other authorities suggest that this was just one of several scripts that the inventive Mesoamericans developed independently in the years after the decline of the Olmec. Two monuments carved with Long Count dates survive from *c.*30 BC, one in Chiapas and one in Veracruz. Neither has an accompanying hieroglyphic text, so it is impossible to judge the development of writing locally at that stage.

THE ISTHMIAN SCRIPT

A writing system known as the 'Isthmian script' appears to have been used in southern Veracruz in the 2nd century AD.

Only four objects carved with this script survive. The most important are a jade figure known as the Tuxtla statuette, now in the Smithsonian Institution, Washington, DC, and a basalt stela found in 1986 at La Mojarra in Veracruz. The script used only 150 signs, so scholars argue these signs probably represented whole words rather than phonetic elements (the distinctive sounds of a language). Some of the signs used bear superficial resemblance to later Maya signs, but experts believe the Isthmian script was not a close relative of early Maya writing. Maya writing was read in double columns from left to right and also top to bottom. However, the Isthmian script does not link its columns in twos and may not have been read left to right, for the glyphs appear to face towards a standing figure in the centre of the carving.

Below: This stone calendar, inscribed with glyphs, was carved by a craftsman of the Huastec culture in north-eastern Mexico.

Carving found on a stone stela at Kaminaljuyú (near modern Guatemala City) from around the same time appears to have a much greater similarity to Maya scripts. The inscription does use paired columns as in Maya writing, and it may contain some of the same glyphs. Indeed, the carving may even be in Maya writing, but is too fragmentary to provide definitive evidence.

The earliest surviving piece definitely identified in the Maya writing system is the Hauberg stela of AD199. The stela shows a king wearing the mask of the rain god Chac and the two-headed serpent that indicates royal standing. The dating inscription does not include a Long Count date, but the scholar Linda Schele has interpreted the given date to be AD199. The inscription uses the emblem glyph, which is commonly found in Maya inscriptions. The emblem glyph generally identifies the ruler as *k'ul ahaw* ('holy king') of a particular city, in this case, puzzlingly, the 'holy king of Fire'.

Above: In the intriguing Zapotec carvings that depict war sacrifices at Monte Albán, a number of early glyphs are believed to give the victims' names.

ROYAL SCRIBES AND CODICES

Scribes were members of the Maya elite. They were usually the sons and daughters of nobles or even royalty. A late Classic Period vase thought to have been made at Naranjo was signed by the artist Ah Maxam, who wrote that he was the son of a king of Naranjo and a princess from Yaxhá. Many kings appear to have been scribes. They are shown on vases wearing a bundle of pens in their hair, which was an accepted mark of high-ranking scribal office. Royal sons and daughters were doubtless educated in scribal schools.

The most important scribe in the Classic Period Maya city state was the *ak k'u hun* ('guardian of the sacred books').

Below: A skilled Maya stonecutter incised 32 hieroglyphs on this lintel at Yaxchilán. The work is dated AD*534.*

Above: Maya scribes also cut glyphs in wood, but little of their work has survived. This is a lintel from Temple IV at Tikal.

THE DUTIES OF SCRIBES

From the evidence of images on Maya vases in murals, the chief scribe or *ak k'u hun* had many courtly jobs in addition to artistic endeavours. He or she was expected to arrange royal ceremonies, was a negotiator of royal marriages and a record-keeper responsible for recording offerings of tribute from client states or allies and keeping royal genealogical lists. He or she may also have taught in scribal schools.

The Maya scribe probably painted the images that accompanied his words. Both calligraphers and painters were given the title *ah ts'ib* ('he of the writing'). Those who produced hieroglyphic inscriptions and images in stone were accorded the honour of being named *yuxul* ('sculptor'). Both women and men – although probably more men than women – were scribes. The titles *ah ts'ib* and *ak k'u hun* were given to women and men.

Students at scribe schools must have followed long and demanding courses of study, for reading and writing Maya hieroglyphs required great knowledge and skill. A scribe had many choices when writing. He or she could write the same phrase in a number of ways. Some logographs (images representing whole words) could also be used as phonetic signs (symbols representing spoken sounds). Scribes sometimes used both the logograph for a name or word and the phonetic signs that would spell out that name. An example often given by Maya experts is that the word *balam* ('jaguar'), could be written with a single logograph representing the head of a jaguar, with the logograph and

GODS OF THE SCRIBES

One 8th-century AD Maya vase depicts a rabbit deity writing in a screenfold book. The creature is one of the large number of gods who are associated with Maya scribes.

Itzamná, the supreme Maya god, was believed to be the creator of writing, and is shown as a scribe in the *Madrid Codex*. Itzamná's animal form was a bearded dragon: carvings at Copán show scribes emerging from the mouth of this creature. Another high-ranking Maya god, Pawahtún, was often shown in images of scribes and on one vase is seen teaching novice scribes in an elite school. The Monkey-men, half-brothers of the Hero Twins in the *Popol Vuh* cycle, are often portrayed with writing implements or working at codices. Both the Hero Twins' father, the Young Maize God, and Hunahpú, one of the Twins, were associated with kingship and writing. They, too, were often shown with quill pens working at calligraphy. The rabbit deity was linked to the moon goddess. Mesoamericans thought they saw a rabbit in the face of the moon whereas in Western tradition we think we see a man's figure or a man's face.

some phonetic signs, and also with the three phonetic signs that spelled *ba*, *la* and *ma*.

Some signs were both logographs and phonetic signs. To help readers know in which way a sign was being used, scribes often used additional phonetic signs alongside the logographs.

On most Classic Period Maya monuments, the hieroglyphs are written to be read in paired columns from left to right and also from top to bottom: you read the first line/first column, first line/second column, then second line/first

Right: A terracotta figure left as an offering on Jaina Island represents a noble or perhaps princely scribe at work.

column, second line/second column etc. Some shorter pieces of writing on monuments and on ceramic objects and carved bones or shells were arranged differently; sometimes as horizontal lines, sometimes as vertical lines. An intriguing variation, found on the markers of ball courts and on some altars, was for the text to be arranged in a circle; the reader would know by a marker in the text (usually a date) where to begin reading. At Quiriguá and Copán, hieroglyphs are sometimes written on monuments in a complex criss-cross pattern to resemble a woven mat. In a very few cases – for example, Lintel 25 at Yaxchilán and on four pages of the *Paris Codex* – the hieroglyphs were inscribed to be read from right to left.

MAYA WRITING

Surviving Maya writing is of various kinds. The stelae of Classic Period Maya cities such as Yaxchilán, Tikal and Copán celebrate the achievements of holy kings and the dynasties to which they belonged. However, the northern Maya cities such as Uxmal and Chichén Itzá that continued to thrive after the 'Maya Collapse' in the lowlands left few stelae from this Postclassic Period. Surviving inscriptions tend to be on stone lintels and wall panels. They do not portray great kings and tell their life histories. Instead, they use few pictures and celebrate fire rites and the dedication of buildings. It seems there was not any dynasty to celebrate. These inscriptions refer to shared rule by a council of up to four people.

The writing in the four surviving Maya codices mainly concerns priestly rituals and tables for calculating astronomical events. Writing on carved bones and jade and on the pots and other ceramic goods left with deceased royals and nobles in their graves mostly gives the name and titles of the deceased and sometimes also contains dedications to the gods. Some also name the artist who drew them.

Below: Maya stonecut glyphs from stele M at Copán. It honours the city's 15th king, Smoke Shell, who completed Copán's Hieroglyphic Stairway. The stair has 2,500 glyphs listing the kings of the ruling dynasty.

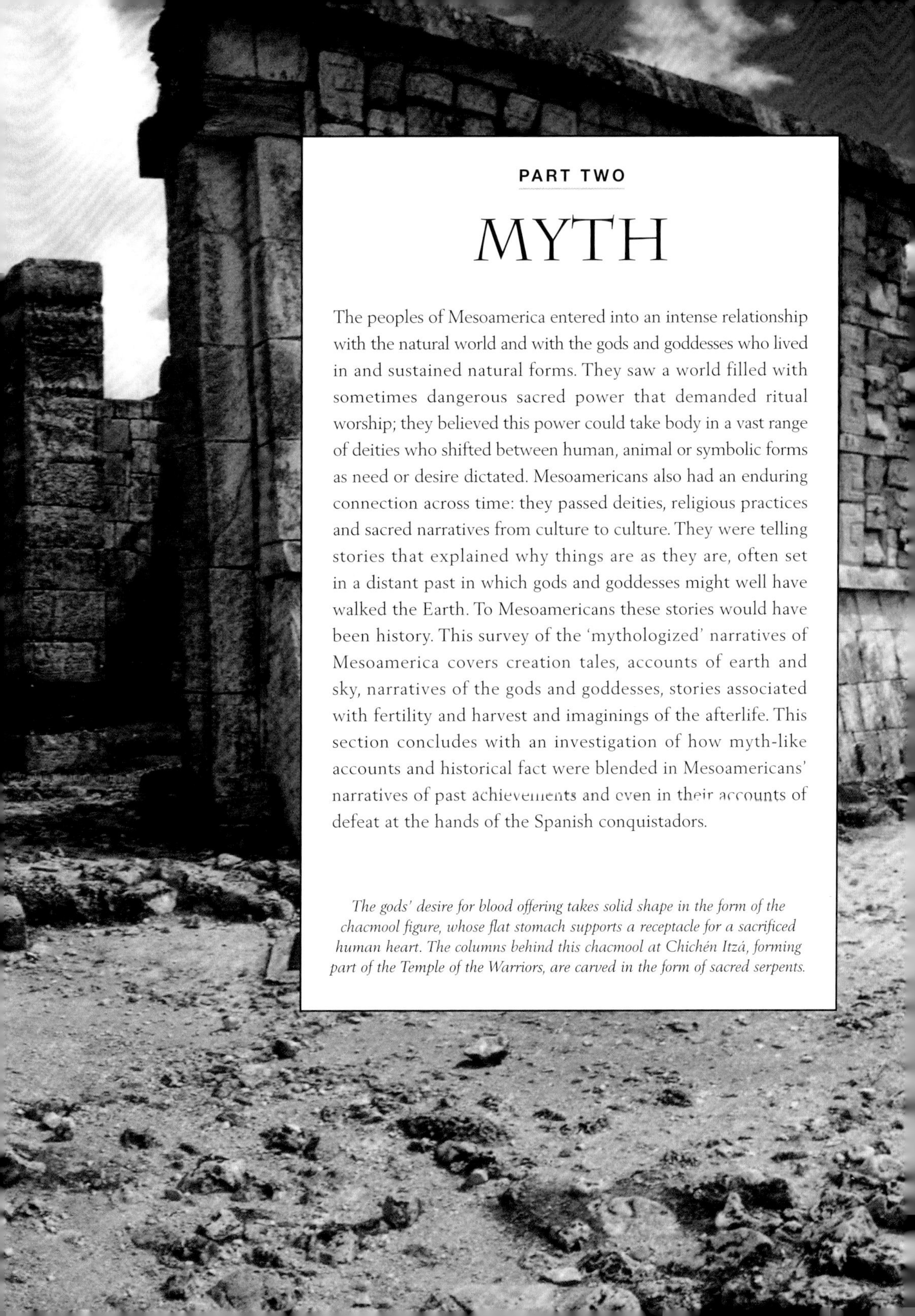

PART TWO

MYTH

The peoples of Mesoamerica entered into an intense relationship with the natural world and with the gods and goddesses who lived in and sustained natural forms. They saw a world filled with sometimes dangerous sacred power that demanded ritual worship; they believed this power could take body in a vast range of deities who shifted between human, animal or symbolic forms as need or desire dictated. Mesoamericans also had an enduring connection across time: they passed deities, religious practices and sacred narratives from culture to culture. They were telling stories that explained why things are as they are, often set in a distant past in which gods and goddesses might well have walked the Earth. To Mesoamericans these stories would have been history. This survey of the 'mythologized' narratives of Mesoamerica covers creation tales, accounts of earth and sky, narratives of the gods and goddesses, stories associated with fertility and harvest and imaginings of the afterlife. This section concludes with an investigation of how myth-like accounts and historical fact were blended in Mesoamericans' narratives of past achievements and even in their accounts of defeat at the hands of the Spanish conquistadors.

The gods' desire for blood offering takes solid shape in the form of the chacmool figure, whose flat stomach supports a receptacle for a sacrificed human heart. The columns behind this chacmool at Chichén Itzá, forming part of the Temple of the Warriors, are carved in the form of sacred serpents.

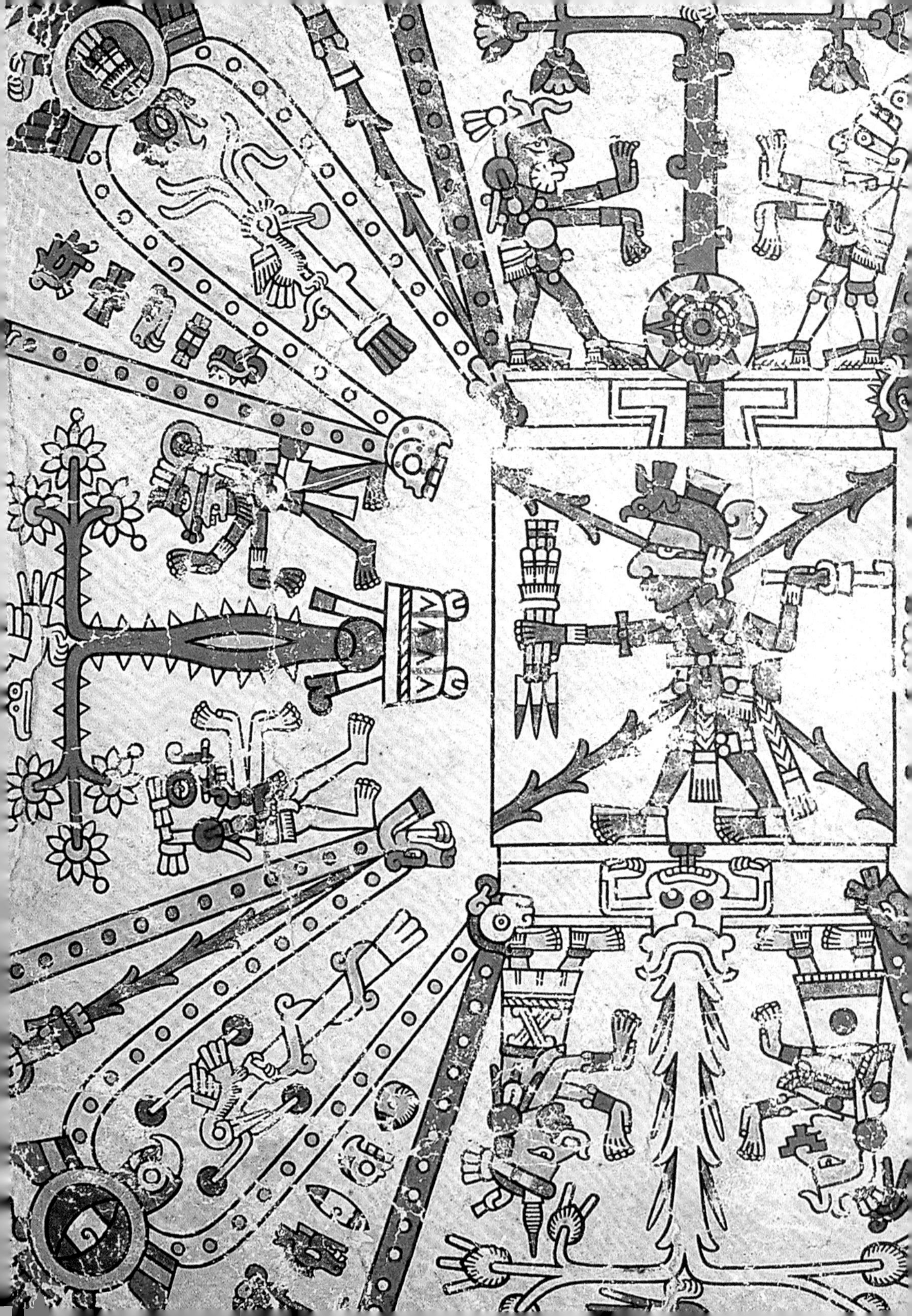

CHAPTER SEVEN

CREATION AND THE FIRST PEOPLES

The Aztecs understood both time and space in terms of four cardinal directions and a central anchoring point. They believed that the Great Pyramid in Tenochtitlán was the centre of the Earth, which spread in a vast flat expanse to east and west and north and south. Four gods and their directions were also associated with the four 'suns' or ages that had preceded the current era on Earth. The first age was associated with Tezcatlipoca and with the north. The second was under the control of Quetzalcóatl, and linked to the west, while the third was governed by the rain god Tláloc and connected to the south. The fourth age was presided over by Tláloc's consort Chalchiúhtlicue and connected to the east. The fifth 'sun' or contemporary age was linked to the centre because the number of the centre is five; it was under the control of the fire god Xiuhtecuhtli.

According to Aztec cosmology, above the flat Earth rose thirteen layers of heaven, where Ometeotl, the supreme creator, dwelt. Beneath the earth were nine levels of the underworld or Mictlán, presided over by Mictlantecuhtli, god of that realm, with his consort Mictecacíhuatl. In some accounts, waters encircled the Earth at the farthest reaches of north, south, east and west and curved up above the land to make the sky. If the gods decreed, the sky waters could fall to wipe out men and all their achievements in one cataclysmic flood.

Left: An illustration from the Mixtec-Aztec Codex Fejérváry-Mayer *depicts the fire god Xiuhtecuhtli at the centre of the universe with four directions emanating outwards.*

THE POWER IN THE CENTRE: COSMOLOGY

At north, south, east and west of the Mesoamerican universe stood four pillars, or trees, that both supported and connected the three levels of the cosmos. In the centre was a fifth tree, whose roots were in the underworld but whose topmost branches touched the very highest of the celestial planes. The four other trees at the points of the compass were in fact outgrowths of the main cosmic tree. The trees stood on hollow hills and were themselves hollow, and within them the power of the underworld and of the heavens was always flowing, powering the repeating movements of time, of the seasons, of the sun, moon, stars and planets and of the energy recycled in acts of blood sacrifice. Only after the creation of the four trees of north, south, east and west could time be measured and sacred events honoured through use of the ritual calendar.

THE FOUR GODS

In one Aztec myth, four gods were born, sometimes known as the four Tezcatlipocas after the god of night and destiny, the sons of the supreme creator Ometeotl in his dual male-female forms Ometecuhtli and Omecíhuatl. According to this tradition, all was chaos in the first days until the four sons agreed to separate heaven and earth and take the form of the four world trees at the four cardinal points. Their act of separation created a space in which the new world could be made.

Right: This stela, carved in c.1250, shows the Earth Monster Tlaltecuhtli, ravenous for human heart blood.

A developed iconography was associated with these myths. Each of the four points of the compass was associated with a god, a glyph, at least one colour and a plant. For example, the glyph for north – the direction of Tezcatlipoca – represented a *técpatl*, the knife used for sacrificing victims; its colours were yellow and black. North was associated with the xerophyte tree, which naturally grew in northern regions of Mesoamerica. Death and cold were linked to the region, which was known as Mictlampa (the land of death). Dampness was associated with the south, where Huitzilopochtli held sway. The glyph for south represented the rabbit; the region was linked to the colour blue. The west was governed by Quetzalcóatl. Its glyph represented a house and its colour was white. The east was associated with Xipe Totec and its glyph showed a reed. Its colour was red.

Sometimes the Aztecs likened the Earth to a flower with four petals, one for each quadrant. One interpretation of the myth of the four suns or ages is that in each successive age one of the four quadrants and its tree or pillar was created and that in the fifth (current) age, the centre – that is, the Templo Mayor at the Great Pyramid in Tenochtitlán – came into being.

THE WORLD TREE

This basic cosmology was common in Mesoamerica. The Maya also told of a vast flat earth, with thirteen levels of heaven rising above and nine layers of underworld beneath. The Quiché Maya told in the *Popol Vuh* how, in the first hours of creation, the earth and sky emerged following a 'fourfold cornering [and] measuring', a process analogous to the one used by Maya farmers to plot their fields. The Maya also understood that in each of the four corners of creation grew a tree, supporting the sky in that place, and that in the centre rose a greater world tree, which connected the realms of earth, heaven and the underworld. The Maya king Pacal, ruler of Palenque, is depicted on the lid of his magnificent sarcophagus travelling down to the underworld along the trunk of this great cosmic tree.

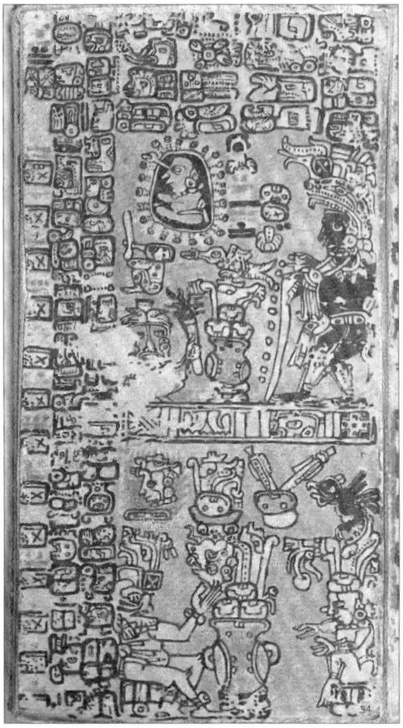

Above: A Maya priest ceremonially plants corn. Maintaining the Earth's fertility was a focus of Mesoamerican religious life.

In some accounts of Maya cosmography, the four supporting structures are not trees but giants called bacabs who, curiously, were patrons of beekeepers. A depiction of the bacabs survives on an 8th–9th

Right: A mural from a residential building in Teotihuacán represents the Earth Mother (centre) supporting a great cosmic tree.

century building at Chichén Itzá that was called the *Iglesia* ('church') by the Spaniards. Their names were Mulac (associated with the north and with white), Kan (linked to the east and yellow), Ix (connected to the west and to black) and Cauac (associated with the south and red). Like the Aztecs, the Maya linked colours to the four directions, but the associations of particular colours was different in the two traditions. For example, white was the colour of the west for the Aztecs but of the north for the Maya. According to the *Books of Chilam Balam*, which contain the legends of the Maya of Yucatán, the four trees at the four corners of the Earth were created in the first moments of each new age.

Below: Xipe Totec (left), god of the east, confronts western deity Quetzalcóatl in an image from the Aztec Codex Borbonicus.

Below: The ancient rain god worshipped by the Maya as Chac was sometimes said to have power over the cardinal directions.

THE MAKING OF THE EARTH

The Mixtec people who made their home in former Zapotec lands in the Oaxaca Valley left a distinctive creation mythology in the images and words of their codices. They told that life began in the union of a nameless couple who lived before time. In the darkness of the unborn world, this pair of gods gave birth to another divine couple named Lord One Deer and Lady One Deer, and they in turn produced many children. Two of Lord and Lady One Deer's offspring pleased their parents by creating a sweet-smelling garden retreat, where flowers bloomed in the gentle shade of magical trees. The first of the Mixtec race climbed from a hole in the trunk of one these remarkable trees. In another account, the Mixtecs were born in a tree that grew in Mexico in Apoala, where a river fed an oasis that kept the desert at bay. The men and women went from this place to the four corners of the flat earth, establishing settlements in which to grow crops, raise children and worship the gods. The tree must be a representation of the world tree that Mesoamericans believed linked the spirit realms of the underworld and the many-layered heaven to the earth. It may suggest the family tree of many generations of revered ancestors.

Another version of Mixtec creation mythology told of a primordial era when earth and sky were not separated in complementary opposition as they are now, but were mixed in wetness and darkness. The earth was no more than waterlogged, muddy slime.

Left: This cedar-wood fertility goddess was still receiving offerings when it was discovered in Veracruz in the 19th century.

Then a creator god named Lord Nine Wind arose from the dark and separated the waters from the earth, raising the waters up to form the sky. Mist engulfed the earth, but from the shadowy half-light a divine couple emerged: they were Lord One Deer Jaguar-Serpent and Lady One Deer Jaguar-Serpent. As the sky perfectly complements the earth, so this god and goddess matched one another. They were two separate beings but also at the same time were one divinity encompassing male and female. Their union was fruitful: they created all the other gods of the Mixtec pantheon and built a palace on earth near Apoala. Apoala is well known, but the palace has never been found. It is said that if a mortal man could find this palace, he would discover that on its roof was set a great axe of copper, its blade facing up to and supporting the overarching sky.

Below: In this Codex Fejérváry-Mayer *image, Tezcatlipoca loses his right foot to the ravening Earth Monster Tlaltecuhtli.*

CONNECTING STORIES

Lord Nine Wind is a version of the Plumed Serpent god worshipped by the Aztecs as Quetzalcóatl and by the Maya as Kukulcán. In the Quiché Maya creation myth, this same deity is a god of the sea, Sovereign Plumed Serpent, who joins with a sky god to create the unity of sky and earth.

Quetzalcóatl is also a creator-protagonist in the ancient Mexican myth of the Earth Monster Tlaltecuhtli. The Aztecs told the myth, which they had inherited from earlier cultures in the Mexican region, to glorify the gods Quetzalcóatl and Tezcatlipoca. These normally

Above: Ancestors of the Mixtecs depicted in these codex images believed they were born from a tree trunk in a garden paradise.

implacable foes decided to join forces to curb Tlaltecuhtli's power when they saw her spreading terror as she walked on the sea. The Earth Monster, like many Mesoamerican deities, was sometimes described as male and sometimes as female; she had a gaping mouth not only on her face but also at her knees, elbows and other joints.

Quetzalcóatl and Tezcatlipoca approached in the form of great, slithering serpents, muscles rippling in their strong shoulders and thighs, their eyes flashing, their long tongues darting from their mouths. Their power was wild as they seized Tlaltecuhtli. One took her left arm and right foot, the other took her right arm and left foot and together they tore her into two great pieces. The first they hurled upwards to make the sky. The second they laid out in four directions to make the flat expanse of the earth. In some accounts Tezcatlipoca fought the Earth Monster in his usual form rather than as a serpent and in the course of the great battle lost one of his feet, explaining his one-legged appearance.

The other gods were not pleased to see this violence done to their sister Tlaltecuhtli. Angrily they addressed Quetzalcóatl and Tezcatlipoca, declaring that although she had been torn in pieces, her earthly part would form the basis of future life. They made herbs, flowers and trees grow from her hair, while grasses and sweet-smelling flowers issued from her skin. The life-giving waters of springs and wells were made from her eyes; her mouth made rivers and larger caverns. Her nose gave rise to tall snow-capped mountains and the deep valleys of the sierras where the air is thin. Men and women have grown used to walking on the body of Tlaltecuhtli.

Right: Quetzalcóatl is born from the Earth as Venus the morning star in this carving from a Santa Lucia Cotzumalhuapa stela.

ORDER FROM CHAOS: MAYA CREATION STORIES

The Quiché Maya give a detailed account of the creation of the world, and also of the gods' efforts to make the first humans, in their sacred book the *Popol Vuh* ('Book of Advice').

CONVERSATION OF THE GODS

The book tells how the earth was born from the conversation of the gods. Before time began, the waters stretched out endlessly in all directions beneath a blank sky and nothing existed in all the universe except these gathered waters and the sky above. There were no animals or fish, no birds or plants, no rocks and no people. There was not even the potential for life hidden in the waters or the half-darkness of the sky, waiting to be brought to life. Yet the waters did contain the sea god, Gucumatz or 'Sovereign Plumed Serpent', and so despite the near-darkness there was a stirring in the sea, a glittering like blue-green quetzal feathers. His presence was echoed and balanced high above by the sky god Huracán or Heart of Sky.

Huracán came down to meet the sea god and these two divinities, who were deep thinkers and possessed of profound knowledge, started a conversation. Their words brought life into being. The discussion was not easy. They were troubled because they could not at first be sure of the right way to proceed. However, in the course of their debate they created a vision of how life should be in the world, how the trees and bushes should grow and how the people should walk among them. As they talked, it was like the time just before dawn. They discussed how the 'sowing' and the 'dawning' should be brought about. First they decided that the waters should be cleared so that the earth could rise up, and then life could be sown in the earth and in the sky. But they knew that people were needed for this world. The sky and sea gods wanted praise for their work, and they understood that they would not receive this until they created a people capable of keeping track of time and expressing wonder and worship on the appointed days.

The words they used in their discussion had concrete effect. The waters fell away and the earth rose up, just as they said. Mountains appeared and wide forests of pine and cypress trees covered their sides. Waters collected in great lakes and ran on the mountainsides in streams. The gods were pleased. Gucumatz said to Huracán that it was a good thing that the sky god had come down to the sea and that they had begun their conversation. He had seen from the beginning of their work that it would turn out well. Now they turned to creating animals and people to inhabit the good world.

Above: Gods above and below – the god depicted on the lower half of this Maya vessel appears to be Chac-Xib-Chac, known for his power to raise hurricanes.

Left: This Classic Maya stone carving represents the Plumed Serpent god feared and worshipped across eras and cultures by Mesoamericans under such names as Quetzalcóatl, Kukulcán and Gucumatz.

The *Popol Vuh* account of creation is dense and highly allusive. The scholar and translator of the *Popol Vuh*, Dennis Tedlock, provides many helpful explanations gleaned from his training as a 'daykeeper' or shaman-priest among the contemporary Maya in the region of Momostenango in Guatemala. He states that the 'sowing and dawning' discussed by Huracán and Gucumatz can be understood in terms of the planting and growing of plants, the life cycle of humans and the movements of the planets in the sky. Plant seeds are sown in the earth and 'dawn' by emerging from the ground as

Above: Tezcatlipoca, unpredictable Aztec god, had counterparts among storm deities elsewhere in Mesoamerica.

crops. Similarly, humans are 'sown' in the womb during sexual relations, then 'dawn' nine months later when they emerge screaming into the world. They are also 'sown' in the earth when they are buried after the body's death, but 'dawn' again as spirits after death, taking the form of celestial lights or stars in the sky. The sun, the moon, Venus and other planets disappear in their own form of 'sowing' when they appear to sink into the earth at the horizon, but they rise again at the appointed time of their dawning.

Left: This powerful but simple Maya mask was fashioned from jade to be worn as an ornament on the chest or a belt.

LORDS OF CREATION

The creator gods are versions of major Mesoamerican deities. Hurakán's name can be understood as 'one-leg' and he is associated with the Classic Period Maya deity Tahil ('Obsidian Mirror' or 'Torch Mirror'), a one-legged god who was honoured in carving at the city of Palenque. Through this connection, Hurakán can be identified with the Aztec god Tezcatlipoca ('Lord of the Smoking Mirror') who, among many attributes, was a divinity of hurricanes, wore an obsidian mirror and was said to be one-legged (in some accounts, because he lost a leg while fighting the Earth Monster Tlaltecuhtli).

Tezcatlipoca was also a god of rains and Huracán's name is linked linguistically with the words used by the Quiché Maya to describe the very large raindrops that come before and after thunderstorms. Sovereign Plumed Serpent or Gucumatz is more obviously a version of the feathered serpent deity Quetzalcóatl, and is also known as Kukulcán by the Yucatec-speaking Maya.

Above: This Classic Maya terracotta vase (c.AD650–950) bears the face of a sky god, perhaps the sun god Ah Kin Chil.

The *Popol Vuh* creation story describes these creator gods both as individuals and as members of a group. The group of sky gods includes Newborn Thunderbolt, Raw Thunderbolt and Heart of Earth. The collection of sea gods includes Heart of the Sea and Heart of the Lake, as well as gods named Begetter, Modeller, Bearer and Maker. This willingness to allow seemingly contradictory things to be true, in this case to allow each creator god to be both individual and also a group of many, is typical of Mesoamerican thought and mythology.

BOTH ONE AND TWO: AZTEC CREATION STORIES

The Plumed Serpent god played an important role in creation mythology of the Aztecs. He was not the Aztecs' primal or original creator, but he was one of the active deities who carried out the work of creation. According to the peoples of the Valley of Mexico, the supreme creator was Ometeotl, a god of duality who existed in both male and female forms as Ometecuhtli and Omecíhuatl, twin gods who were also known as Tonacatecuhtli ('Lord of our Sustaining') and Tonacacíhuatl ('Lady of our Sustaining'). They lived in the thirteenth and highest level of the Aztec heaven, called Omeyocán.

Below: This Aztec wooden mask depicts either rain god Tláloc or Quetzalcóatl as Éhecatl, lord of the winds.

Right: A terracotta image from Veracruz (c.AD500) represents a gruesome rite in honour of Xipe Totec, 'Our Flayed Lord'.

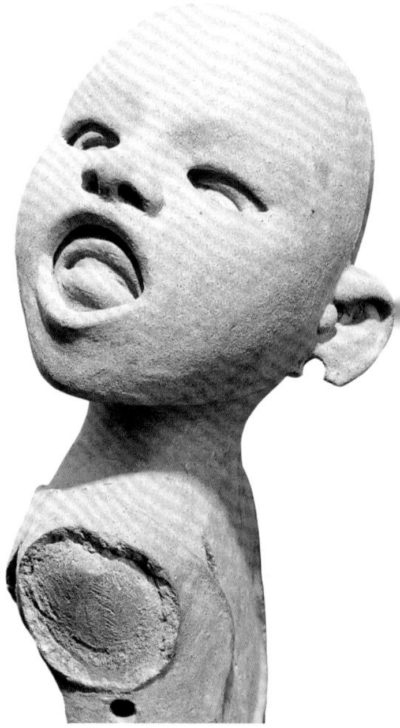

BIRTH OF THE GODS

In one account, Tonacatecuhtli used his divine breath to bring life to a universe that was bathed in darkness. From his breath Quetzalcóatl was born, the Plumed Serpent as associated with the wind, particularly in his guise as Éhecatl. In another version, Omecíhuatl gave birth to all the gods and goddesses. In still another myth, the primal couple Ometecuhtli and Omecíhuatl gave birth to four gods, who they charged with the job of creating other deities, the world and the human race. They were the four Tezcatlipocas, each associated with a direction and a colour and some later identified with other gods.

Red Tezcatlipoca, connected to the east, was later identified as Xipe Totec, the god of vegetation and new life. Black Tezcatlipoca, associated with the night sky and the north, was later known simply as Tezcatlipoca. White Tezcatlipoca, associated with the west, was later known as Quetzalcóatl, while Blue Tezcatlipoca, linked to the south, was later Huitzilopochtli, the Aztec tribal god.

For six hundred years the four Tezcatlipocas delayed, then at last two of the gods, White Tezcatlipoca (Quetzalcóatl) and Blue Tezcatlipoca (Huitzilopochtli), began the ordained work of creation. First they created fire and raised a forerunner of our sun in the sky. After this, they created the first human couple, Oxomoco and Cipactonal. They made the earth from a primal crocodile, the same creature later

Right: Chalchiúhtlicue, river goddess and consort of the rain god Tláloc, was praised for her power over the waters of spring.

Right: This intricately finished ornament, thought to represent an early version of the Mesoamerican sun god, was found at the Zapotec site of Monte Albán.

identified as the Earth Monster Tlaltecuhtli. From the crocodile's body they also fashioned the rain god Tláloc and his female counterpart Chalchiúhtlicue and they must also have made the underworld region of Mictlán, for the myth says they gave life to Mictlantecuhtli and Mictecacíhuatl, the god and goddess of the underworld. At this time they fixed the sacred calendar of the 260-day count. They also created Xochiquetzal ('Flower Feather'), goddess of flowers and the earth and of dance and love.

THE FIRST HUMANS AS GODS

Oxomoco and Cipactonal gave birth to a son named Piltzintecuhtli. He was the first human to enjoy the pleasures and duties of marriage, for he took as his wife a beautiful American maiden created by the great gods from the hair of Xochiquetzal. The first human husband is sometimes identified as a god, and his consort is seen by some as a human incarnation of Xochiquetzal. After this creation, the gods began the four ages or 'suns' of the Earth's history.

Below: Images of Quetzalcóatl as the wind god Éhecatl characteristically have a bird-like mask on the lower face.

Oxomoco and Cipactonal, the first humans, are similarly often viewed as gods. They played an important role in the myth that details the discovery and spread of the Mesoamericans' staple maize plant. According to this myth, the red ants had hidden maize deep inside Mount Tonacatépetl but Quetzalcóatl, bringer of so many good things to the human race, intuited that the ants' mountain store contained something of great value and transformed himself into a black ant to investigate. On the mountainside he tried out the limitations of his new body, clambering over rocks and into crevices, then followed the line of red ants along narrow paths within the mountain to their hidden store. He found great piles of cereal there and carried some back to his brother gods. They tasted it and found it good, so they ground it up to make meal and placed some in the mouths of human babies. The babies thrived on this new food and the gods decreed that the maize should be shared with humans across the lands of Mesoamerica. But how would they free it from its hiding place? First Quetzalcóatl tied a great rope around the mountain and attempted to split the hard rock. But even the Plumed Serpent was not strong enough to bring down the mountain. The gods then turned to Oxomoco and Cipactonal for advice. The divine human couple consulted with one another and at last declared that the task should be entrusted to Nanahuatzin, the unappealing god who had become the Fifth Sun. He split the mountain and the rain god spirits or *tláloques* spread the maize far and wide.

THE ANGER OF THE GODS

The *Popol Vuh* of the Quiché Maya begins the tale of creation by describing the establishment of the fertile lands of the Earth, the gathering of the lakes and rivers that feed the soil and the springing to life of forests and life-giving plants. The account continues with the decision by the creator gods Huracán and Gucumatz to fill the Earth with animals and the first people.

They made animals to inhabit the mountains and forests, including deer and jaguars, snakes, pumas and birds. They appointed the creatures to their rightful places in the world, telling the deer to live in canyons along the banks of rivers and to roam freely in the fields and forests, while telling the birds to nest in the branches of trees and the safety of thick bushes. Then the creators called on the animals to speak to them and honour the gods who had given life to the forests and mountains. There were many names to choose from: Heart of Sky, Raw Thunderbolt, Hurricane, Plumed Serpent, Begetter, Maker, Modeller. But the animals could not speak a single name; all they could utter were wild cries, screeching and squawking. The gods were not pleased, for what they wanted was a creature who was capable of keeping count of days and offering praise and sacrifices. They told the animals and birds that they would become food for each other and for the people whom the gods hoped to create.

Above: This image of the Plumed Serpent god dates from 1300–1500. He was held in awe for his power to unleash floods.

Below: The toad was among the creatures created before the first people. This Classic Period Maya offering vessel dates from AD250–600.

MAN OF MUD?

Next the creators tried to make a human being from mud. However, try as they might, they could not make the body hold together: it kept sliding apart and dissolving into a watery mess. Its face was not pleasing, because it had a lopsided look and although the creature could speak, its words made no sense. The gods agreed to let the body dissolve. The man of mud was a false start and they decided to let it be a thought that led nowhere. However, they were determined to keep trying to create a human being. They decided next to consult an ancient pair of deities, divine equivalents of the 'daykeepers' or shaman-diviners of the Quiché Maya. The couple were called Xpiyacoc and Xmucané. Huracán and Gucumatz addressed the couple as grandfather-grandmother, matchmaker-midwife, makers of jewellery and incense, carpenters and craftsmen.

MAN OF WOOD?

Huracán and Gucumatz asked the diviners whether human beings could be made from wood. The grandfather and grandmother performed a divination using kernels of corn and coral seeds and declared that wood was a suitable material for making people. They also warned Huracán against trying to trick Gucumatz. This aside perhaps reflects the gods' associations with forms of the Aztec deities Tezcatlipoca, linked to Huracán and always connected with deception and trickery, and Quetzalcóatl, linked to Gucumatz and in many myths the victim of Tezcatlipoca's plotting. Dennis Tedlock, the translator of the *Popol Vuh* and an initiated diviner, points out that Maya priests expect some trickery from the gods and will sometimes warn them in this way not to give a false answer during a divination.

Huracán and Gucumatz listened to the grandparents' reply and decided at once to fill the Earth with wooden people. 'Let it be so', they said, and their words were enough to make it happen; wooden people spread across the lands of America, the men made from the wood of the coral tree and the women made from the core of bulrushes. The people formed families and multiplied, but although they could speak, their hearts and minds were empty. They did not remember their creators or count the days and honour the gods at the appropriate times. Moreover, although the people could walk and behave much like human beings, their skin was dry and flaky because they had no sweat, and their bodies warped in the heat because they had no blood to keep them moist.

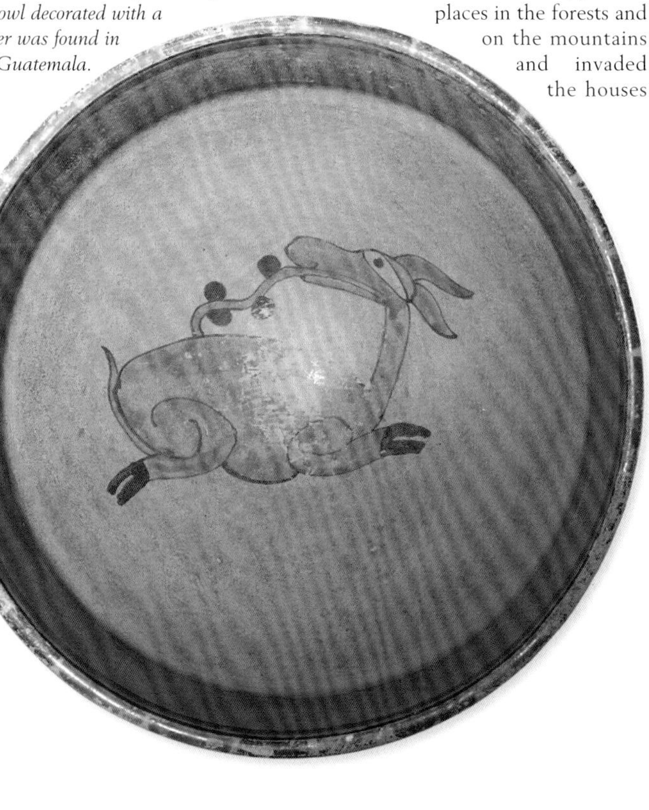

Below: This late Classic Maya Period painted ceramic bowl decorated with a resting deer was found in El Petén, Guatemala.

AN UNMAKING

The gods determined to do away with this race of wooden people. Huracán sent powerful rainstorms that produced a vast flood and many people were drowned. To deal with the survivors, Huracán sent terrifying monsters, including Gouger of Faces, who carved out eyeballs, and Sudden Bloodletter, who pulled off their heads. The natural order the gods had established unravelled. Animals left their appointed places in the forests and on the mountains and invaded the houses of the people. The grinding stones, tortilla griddles and cooking pots rose up in violence and smashed the faces of the terrified people. The dogs they had kept attacked them. Even the hearthstones in the family fireplaces leapt out and set about the people's heads.

Above: Images of the Maya creator god Itzamná were often shown with crossed eyes.

MONKEYS

The few survivors of the failed creation of the wooden people had battered heads and faces, but still looked a little like human beings. They were allowed to live on in the world in the form of monkeys. For this reason, the monkeys and apes of the forest resemble people. They are a reminder of a less than perfect creation. If humans forget their duty to mark the days, offer praise to the gods and seek the divine patterns in their lives, then they have become little better than the wooden people whose hearts and minds were empty.

Huracán and Gucumatz had now made three failed attempts to create a being capable of marking sacred days with a calendar and offering praise to the creators. They were still determined to keep trying, and their next attempt was destined to succeed.

THE HERO TWINS AND SEVEN MACAW

The *Popol Vuh* account digresses from the creation attempts of Huracán and Gucumatz in order to describe the valiant work of the divine Hero Twins in making earth and sky safe places. These events took place during the era of the wooden people.

Below: Mesoamericans revered the tobacco plant and shredded its leaves to smoke in pipes such as this ceramic parrot.

A BID FOR POWER

In those days there was no day or night as we know it now, but only a long, unchanging twilight. Then a vain and boastful god called Seven Macaw tried to set himself up as supreme deity. He was a macaw and lived in a tree nest high above the earth of the wooden people. He had eyes of metal and teeth encrusted with turquoise and jewels, a great shiny nose and a nest of metal. Preening high in his tree, he declared that the light reflecting off his teeth was the blue of the sky while his nose could shine as brightly as the moon. He was also the sun, he said. When he came out in front of his shiny nest he gave light to the people below and his face shone far into the distance. The diviner-narrators of the *Popol Vuh* comment that, in truth Seven Macaw was none of these things, for as yet there was no sun or moon and the whole of creation existed in a half-light.

Below: An earthenware vase from Teotihuacán shows a quetzal bird in a cacao tree.

HERO TWINS

The young twin gods known as the Hero Twins, Hunahpú and Xbalanqué, discussed the behaviour of Seven Macaw and agreed that it was unacceptable for this vainglorious bird to puff himself up and claim to be greater than Gucumatz and Huracán, the wise modellers and makers who had created the world by the power of their spoken word. The twins were the children of the god Hun Hunahpú and Blood Moon, a maiden of the underworld. Both the twins were skilled hunters and went far and wide shooting birds and animals with their blowpipes. They decided to use their hunting skills to puncture Seven Macaw's pride.

One morning the twins lay in wait for Seven Macaw beneath a tree where the bird came each day to feed. Hunahpú waited until the macaw was busy eating, then used his blowpipe to deliver an accurate shot that broke Seven Macaw's jaw. The bird fell from the tree and Hunahpú ran across the ground to seize it but, just as he arrived, Seven Macaw caught hold of his arm and wrenched it from its socket. Hunahpú was left in agony, with blood pouring from his wound, while Seven Macaw went slowly home, ruminating over the damage to his jaw. His wife Chimalmat greeted him, expressing surprise at his appearance, and he described the sudden attack that had broken his jaw and given him an almighty toothache. However, he had a trophy from the conflict, he said, and held up Hunahpú's arm. He hung the arm above his fire and declared that the trickster twins could come and get it if they wanted it.

PUNCTURED PRIDE

Hunahpú and Xbalanqué now devised a plan for outwitting Seven Macaw. They approached Great White Peccary and Great White Tapir, a wise grandfather and grandmother, for help. The twins proposed that the old couple should approach the boastful macaw pretending to be travelling medics and offer to ease his pain. Hunahpú and Xbalanqué would travel with them in the guise of their grandchildren. The bird would probably beg for help and then, once his guard was down, the elderly couple and the twins could strip him of his finery and retrieve

Above: This detail of a clay vase dating from c.AD200–400 shows Seven Macaw wearing a necklace that denotes his power.

Hunahpú's arm. Great White Peccary and Great White Tapir agreed to the deception and they went, with the twins in tow, to Seven Macaw's splendid home.

The plan worked exactly as the twins had hoped. The grandparents persuaded Seven Macaw his toothache was caused by worms gnawing in his mouth and that it would ease if he let them extract his jewel-entrusted teeth and replace them with new ones of the finest ground bone. But the 'teeth' they put in his mouth were just corn kernels. Next, while he was still under their control, they removed the precious metal from around his eyes.

The battle was now won. Seven Macaw grew weaker and weaker as his finery was stripped from him and at last he died. His wife Chimalmat, who was seemingly weakened by his decline, expired at his side. It was a simple task for Great White Peccary and Great White Tapir and the Hero Twins to retrieve Hunahpú's arm from Seven Macaw's fireplace. The aged couple then proved that they did have genuine medical skill by putting Hunahpú's arm back in place so that it was perfectly healed.

Seven Macaw's likeness can still be seen on Earth in the scarlet macaw, which has a strangely shaped beak with a larger upper part and smaller lower part, suggesting the image of the dislocated jaw. It also has featherless patches around the eyes, which resemble the bare region surrounding the god's eyes after his face had been stripped of its shining metals.

Left: A late Classic Period Maya censer, sanctified by the face of the sun god, from the Temple of the Cross, Palenque.

THE TRIUMPH OF THE HERO TWINS

Seven Macaw had two sons, boys who were as self-deceiving and boastful as their father. One, Zipacná, named himself 'Maker of Mountains' and claimed to have raised the great peaks of the early world that had in fact been created by Huracán and Gucumatz. The second son, Earthquake, said he could unseat the foundations of the world and bring everything crashing down in an avalanche of earth. The Hero Twins, having dealt with Seven Macaw, decided to rid the world of his arrogant offspring too.

ZIPACNÁ'S DOWNFALL

The Hero Twins made their move against Zipacná at a time when the Maker of Mountains had not eaten for several days. In normal times, Zipacná's favourite diet was crabs and fish and he spent his hours trawling the waters and lifting huge rocks – even mountains – to see if any crabs were underneath. The Twins built a mechanical crab from flowers and a rock and placed it in a crevice beneath a great mountain, then casually approached Zipacná on the beach. When he complained of his hunger, they mentioned that they had seen the biggest of crabs in the crevice nearby. He followed them and went eagerly into the crevice in search of his next meal. However, try as he might he could not reach the crab until he turned over on to his back. At this point, with the mechanical crab on his chest, he suddenly expired and his body turned to stone. For all his bravado and undoubted strength, the genius of the Hero Twins had brought him low.

EARTHQUAKE'S UNDOING

Next, the sky god Huracán talked to the Hero Twins, asking them to deal with Zipacná's brother Earthquake. When

GODS OF DRUNKENNESS

Before the Hero Twins turned their attention to Zipacná, the 'Maker of Mountains' had a bruising encounter with the Four Hundred Boys, the gods of a strong alcoholic drink called *quii* by the Quiché Maya.

The Four Hundred Boys met Zipacná on the seashore as they were dragging along a huge log which they had cut to use as a doorpost for their house. Zipacná offered to help and lifted the great trunk on his own, carrying it all the way to the house. The Four Hundred Boys asked him to stay with them to help them the next day, but secretly they plotted to kill him, for they were frightened by his enormous strength and guessed that they could not trust him.

The Four Hundred Boys dug a deep hole and enticed Zipacná into it. When he was at the bottom, they dropped a log on top of him. They thought they had killed him and rejoiced, planning a great celebration with the *quii* drink. They would wait, they said, for two days. When ants swarmed in the hole and carried parts of Zipacná's body to the surface they would know for certain that he was dead and they would have their party.

However, Zipacná had scrambled out of the way of the log and lay at the bottom of the hole listening to their every word. Two days later, when the ants came to investigate, Zipacná handed them tufts of his hair and pieces of his nails and told them to carry them to the surface. The Four Hundred Boys saw the ants and whooped for joy. They went into their new house and toasted their own bravery, jeering at Zipacná. Soon they all became very drunk and unruly. Zipacná crept from the hole and knocked the house down around the drunkards. Every one of the Four Hundred Boys was killed and Zipacná had his revenge.

The Four Hundred Boys, who were revered as the gods of drunkenness, rose into the sky and became the constellation of the Pleiades.

Below: A Maya polychrome vase depicts the Hero Twin Hunahpú with stern expression, magnificent headdress and regal bearing.

Above: Scholars believe that this stone carving of a macaw's head was used as a ball court marker. It is from Xochicalco.

mountains rose up by the word of Huracán and Gucumatz, Earthquake had the power to bring them down again. He tapped his foot on the ground and even the greatest of mountains came tumbling down. Huracán said that this was not right; the Twins should lure him into lying down in a grave in the east, where he could cause no more trouble in the creation.

The Twins approached Earthquake on a forest path and told him of a vast new mountain they had seen in the east. They told him that they had heard he boasted of destroying mountains, but that he must have missed this one. Earthquake asked to go with them to see the mountain. He would show them his powers, opening up the foundations of the land and making the mountain collapse. So they went eastward in single file along the narrow track, Earthquake walking between the twins. He was impressed by their skill with the blowpipe, for they brought birds down from the trees to left and to right. After a while, the travellers halted to cook some of the birds. Now the Twins used a sacred spell in their cooking that was to be the undoing of Earthquake. They coated one of the birds in plaster made from rocks and told one another that as their companion ate this, so his body would end up in a rocky grave.

Earthquake was hungry and ate the bird enthusiastically. The threesome went on their way to the east, but when they came to the foot of the new mountain Earthquake found that his strength was gone from him. The magic of the Twins' spell had worked. He fell helpless to the ground at their feet and died.

Hunahpú and Xbalanqué bound him, tying his hands behind his back and his ankles to his wrists, and then they cast him into a grave as Huracán had demanded. In this way, the Hero Twins saved the world in its early days from the threat presented by the false-talking and vainglorious trio of Seven Macaw, Zipacná and Earthquake. They brought Earthquake to his rightful place, in the earth, where his strength holds up the mountains rather than destroying them. From time to time, though, he shifts and it is at these times that the surface of the earth moves dangerously.

Above: The Hero Twins were a popular choice for decorations on Maya ceramics. This vase dates from C.AD*600–700.*

Below: These Plumed Serpent carvings overlook the ball court at Chichén Itzá.

THE PEOPLE OF CORN

The Quiché Maya account of creation in the *Popol Vuh* concludes with the sky and sea gods' third and finally successful attempt to make the first human beings. Huracán and Gucumatz were not happy with their attempts to make people from mud or wood, but when they tried using the maize plant they found it was the right material for fashioning a human.

Left: The Plumed Serpent god was associated with the Sun among both Aztec and Maya.

MAN OF MAIZE

The world was still laid out beneath half-light. Animals and birds followed their paths through the forests and valleys, in the thin air above the high peaks. The gods knew that the dawn was coming soon, when the sun, moon and stars would appear in the sky. They knew that one piece was still missing from the creation: a human capable of offering praise and keeping track of time.

The creators were alerted to the presence of maize by four animals, which came to them with news of a spot in the mountains named Bitter Water Place, where they had found an abundance of growing things, including cacao beans and many fruits as well as the yellow and white corn. The animals – a crow, a parrot, a fox and a coyote – all became known as corn-eaters. They knew that what they had found was good and brought some ears of maize to the creators. Huracán and Gucumatz then gave the maize to Xmucané, the grandmother goddess and sage who had performed a divination rite to determine whether the creators should try making humans from wood. Xmucané washed her hands in cold, bright spring water and ground the ears nine times. She mixed the flour with the water in which she had washed her hands and made a paste. Huracán and Gucumatz used the paste to make the living, breathing flesh of human beings and with the remaining water they made the blood that flows in our veins. The process was like modelling in clay.

THE GRANDFATHERS

The creators made four males, who became the founding fathers of the principal Quiché Maya lineages. Their names were Jaguar Quitze, Jaguar Night, Mahucutah and True Jaguar. At last the creators had made men capable of pleasing them. They could talk clearly, walk smoothly over the uneven land and work hard with their hands. Their hearing was sharp and they could see far and wide, even into the hidden meanings of things. The creators addressed them, asking, 'Isn't this good, the power we have given you to see and walk and work hard? Try out your gifts.' The first men gave thanks to Huracán and Gucumatz, calling them grandfather-grandmother, and also acknowledging that humankind had been perfectly made. The men reported that they could see everything, even the hidden structures and meanings of the universe, and that they understood it all perfectly.

The creators were unsettled by this and decided that they had given their creatures too many powers; the first men were in all respects the equals of the sky god and the sea god. Therefore Huracán and Gucumatz took away the clear vision of the early humans. This process was exactly like breathing on a mirror. The gods clouded men's vision so that the human forefathers could only see what was near at hand.

THE GRANDMOTHERS

Afterwards the gods made four women as wives for the grandfathers. Jaguar Quitze had Celebrated Seahorse as his spouse; Jaguar Night wed Prawn House,

Below: The bird's head on this Maya bowl suggests the all-seeing gaze of the first people in the Quiché Maya creation tale.

Above: In the top two panels of this codex image, rain god Tláloc blesses the corn, which is represented as his consort Chalchiúhtlicue (right), while Xipe Totec (left) brings his power to bear.

Mahucutah settled with Hummingbird House and True Jaguar married Macaw House. These maidens were as intelligent, lithe and fine-looking as their husbands and brought great joy to the men. They were the grandmothers of the great Quiché lineages.

The creation was now complete: all was now ready for the dawn of the very first sun. The first Quiché embarked on many wanderings as they awaited the first light.

There were a number of variant Mesoamerican myths explaining the creation of early humans. In the Mixtec tradition, the first people were sometimes said to have climbed from a great tree in a desert oasis. In Aztec mythology the first men were created by the Plumed Serpent Quetzalcóatl and his double Xólotl at the beginning of the fifth 'sun', the current world age, from the bones of a previous race he had rescued from the underworld realm. In some Aztec accounts the divine couple Oxomoco and Cipactonal were the first humans and were ancestors of the common people or *macehuatlin*.

Right: Quetzalcóatl had malign influence in his guise as a form of the planet Venus.

CHAPTER EIGHT

EARTH AND SKY

Mesoamericans believed that the age we live in was not the first in the history of the world. Just as the Quiché Maya told that there had been other, failed creations before the making of the first people by the sky god Huracán and the sea god Gucumatz, so the Aztecs held that there had been previous world ages before our own. The current age, in the Aztec view, was the fifth.

Each of these five eras had its own sun, was associated with one of the elements and was presided over by a different god. The celebrated Aztec Sun Stone, discovered in the late 18th century beneath Mexico City's central plaza, depicts each of the five 'suns'. Its main face, 3.6m (almost 12ft) in diameter, has a head in the centre, representing either the ancient sun god Tonatiuh or the Earth Monster Tlaltecuhtli. Around this face in the central circle are four images in square frames. The one to the upper right represents the first sun, that of the jaguar, while the one to the upper left shows the second sun, that of the wind. The one to the lower left is for the third sun, of rain, and the one to the lower right refers to the fourth sun, of water. The central face celebrates the current sun or world age in which the Aztecs had risen to such glory. Scholars also link the four suns to the four directions of Aztec cosmology. According to this theory, the Fifth Sun represents the centre.

Left: The Sun Stone was probably carved during the rule of Axayácatl (1469–81), with the aim of validating Aztec rule. The 'people of the sun' were divinely sanctioned to govern.

LIFE UNDER THE FOUR SUNS

In the primordial era, Black Tezcatlipoca decided to set himself up as the sun. This god was one of the 'four Tezcatlipocas' associated with the primal creation, each of whom was linked to a god in the Aztec pantheon. He was linked to the god of night and destiny later worshipped as Tezcatlipoca. His age, or sun, began after the time of the initial creation, when White Tezcatlipoca (Quetzalcóatl) and Blue Tezcatlipoca (Huitzilopochtli) made fire, the first human couple and several of the other gods.

Above: A detail from an Aztec stone column depicts the head of Tláloc, rain god and creator of the third sun.

THE JAGUAR SUN

Black Tezcatlipoca rose into the sky. His era was associated with the element of earth. There were no humans; instead the lands of Mesoamerica were filled by a race of giants. These towering creatures were so strong they could rip trees from the rocky mountain ground and hurl them through the air down on to the dusty plain below. But they were not bloodthirsty and lived on a vegetarian diet of acorns. Black Tezcatlipoca's era lasted 676 years. It ended in a cataclysm when Quetzalcóatl grew displeased at seeing Tezcatlipoca in the height of the sacred sky. He used his staff to knock his rival down into the seas that lay at the farthest extremes of the flat earth.

In his anger, Black Tezcatlipoca rose from the salt waters in the form of a powerful jaguar. The sun was down and darkness covered the land. Tezcatlipoca, god of night, raced on to the plains and mountains of Mesoamerica and suddenly jaguars were running everywhere. A plague of the fierce night predators howled for blood. The jaguars hunted down the giants and killed every one. According to the Aztecs' complex calendar, this carnage occurred on the day 4-Jaguar in the year 1-Reed.

Because jaguars brought the age or sun to an end, it is usually named the 'Jaguar Sun' (*Nahui Ocelotl*); it is also sometimes called the '4-Jaguar Sun' after the day on which it ended. All the four suns would end in a cataclysm of violence and death and each one was named after the terrible event that brought it to an end. Tezcatlipoca himself leapt into the sky, still in his jaguar form, and there made the constellation of the Great Bear.

THE WIND SUN

Quetzalcóatl created the second sun, which provided light for the next age of the world.

This era was associated with the air and Quetzalcóatl took his form as the wind god Éhecatl to perform the creation. The inhabitants of Mesoamerica in this age were more like modern humans than their primitive predecessors. They also followed a vegetarian diet, eating the seeds of the mesquite tree. The second age lasted 364 years. Tezcatlipoca revenged himself on his great cosmic rival by bringing this age to an end. He used his dark power to overwhelm the wind god by launching a great hurricane that swept the sun from the sky and the people from the earth. Darkness fell once more on the lands of Mesoamerica and after the hurricane everything was suddenly still. The survivors clambered up into the branches of the few trees that were still standing after the storm. They were no longer people but had become monkeys and they chattered and called in the echoing dark. The era ended on the day 4-Wind in the year 1-Flint. The sun or world age is known as the 'Wind Sun' (*Nahui Éhecatl*) or 'Sun 4-Wind'. The

Aztec myth parallels the account of the Quiché Maya in the *Popol Vuh*, in which the survivors of a failed creation, the wooden people, were the ancestors of the monkeys of the forest.

THE RAIN SUN

After the hurricane, the fertility and rain god Tláloc took charge of creation. His era was associated with the element of fire. In some accounts, the people of this age made one of the great breakthroughs in human history by discovering the skills of agriculture and began to cultivate a form of maize. In other versions, however, the people lived entirely on a wild water-based plant like the water lily. Then they were transformed from human form into turkeys, dogs and butterflies.

Tláloc's era lasted 312 years before Quetzalcóatl again turned destroyer. This time, he sent a rain of fire that poured destruction on the earth for a whole day. The inferno of flame swept the sun from the sky. The inhabitants were burned up, but some must have hidden from the fire, for their descendants are the dogs, butterflies and turkeys of today. The destruction came on the day 4-Rain in the year 1-Flint. This sun or age is called 'Rain Sun' (*Nahui Quiahuitl*) or 'Sun 4-Rain', but is also sometimes called the 'Fire Sun' because this era of creation ended in a firestorm. The coming of fire from the sky was an appropriate ending for Tláloc's era, for this god, in addition to being the deity of rain, was associated with lightning – a form of celestial fire.

Right: A wooden inlaid mask honours Chalchiúhtlicue, creator of the fourth world age.

Left: Images of the rain god Tláloc are usually identifiable from their 'goggle' eyes and fang-like teeth.

THE WATER SUN

Tláloc's consort Chalchiúhtlicue, goddess of lakes, oceans, streams and rivers, created a new sun. The people of the age of water lived on the seeds of a wild plant. Chalchiúhtlicue's era lasted 676 years; as long as the previous two eras combined, and was the first of the world ages in which the presiding deity herself brought creation to an end.

The Aztecs believed that the waters of the oceans enclosed the lands on all four sides and also rose up into the sky above. In one account, Chalchiúhtlicue made these sky waters break so that they crashed down and obliterated life on earth. In another version, she made the underground waters rise up, gushing from natural wells and bursting from solid rock. Either way, a great flood covered the land. The people adapted, turning into fish, whales and other inhabitants of the deep.

The flood lasted for an entire 'bundle' of 52 years. Even the mountains were swept away, as water covered the entire creation. The flood came on the day 4-Water in the year 1-House. The era was therefore called 'Water Sun' (*Nahui Atl*) or 'Sun 4-Water'.

There is some disagreement in different sources over the order in which the suns or ages occurred. The sequence given here of Jaguar, Wind, Rain and Water is that depicted in the carvings on the Aztec Sun Stone, a 3.6m- (almost 12ft-) wide carved stone found in Mexico City in the 18th century. Some other sources report that the Water Sun came first and that the other three followed in the sequence Jaguar, Rain, Wind. The end of the fourth sun was the occasion for the creation of the current world age, the fifth sun, the time in which the Aztecs, their revered Toltec ancestors and modern Mexicans all live.

The Quiché Maya account of creation also included the notion that previous creations had their own suns that lapsed when the creation failed. For example, the vain bird Seven Macaw who was outwitted and defeated by the Hero Twins Hunahpú and Xbalanqué was the Sun in the era of the wooden people.

DAWN OF THE FIFTH SUN

Following the end of the fourth sun or age in a great earthquake, Tezcatlipoca and Quetzalcóatl had to fashion the Earth anew. They encountered the Earth Monster Tlaltecuhtli swimming in the waters of the great flood and by tearing apart her body they made a new sky and a new earth.

A period of 26 years passed between the creation of a new world for the fifth sun and the creation of the sun and moon that ushered in the age in which we live.

Below: The ancient fire god Xiuhtecuhtli was generally depicted without eyes, seated with arms crossed on his knees.

Like the four previous ages, the fifth era was named after the cataclysm that would bring it to an end. The Aztecs believed that the current age would end in earthquakes; they also said that the current sun began moving on the day 4-Ollin (4-Earthquake or 4-Movement), and that the world would end on the day 4-Earthquake. On that fateful day the god Tezcatlipoca would once more fulfil his dark destiny as a destroyer, sending earthquakes that would bring the mountains low and cause a famine in which all creatures would die. The Aztecs named the age in which we live after this day of destruction, 4-Ollin.

CREATION OF THE SUN AND THE MOON

The Aztec myth of the creation of the sun and moon tells how the gods gathered in darkness at Teotihuacán. There was no light on the earth, for the fourth sun had been destroyed in the watery cataclysm that brought an end to Chalchiúhtlicue's era. The gods were voices in the blank darkness. They agreed that what was most necessary for the creation was a new sun and a moon to provide light when the sun did not.

The god Tecuciztécatl ('He of the Sea Stone') stepped forward and volunteered to be the sun. But a second deity also volunteered. This was the small and humble god Nanahuatzin, whose face was disfigured by pimples and sores. These two began to prepare themselves for the honour of lighting the world with rites of penitence and self-discipline like those of a new Aztec *tlatoani* or ruler before he took power. Nanahuatzin and Tecuciztécatl prepared for four days and nights. When they were finished, they saw that the other gods had lit a vast pyre on the hard ground at Teotihuacán. The orange flames threw unsettling shadows all around that holy place.

Above: Some scholars identify this Aztec stone carving as an image of a priest in the service of the fire god Xiuhtecuhtli.

Nanahuatzin and Tecuciztécatl made offerings: the self-regarding Tecuciztécatl, dressed in splendid robes, offered fine goods such as quetzal feathers, stone flints and coral incense, while the humble and self-effacing Nanahuatzin laid out simple reeds, cactus thorns he had used to make an offering of his own blood and, instead of incense, the scabs from his pimples. They approached the sacred fire. Tecuciztécatl went first, but was driven back by the heat. He tried again, and a second time did not have the courage or resolve to carry through his intention of entering the flames. In all, he approached

the fire and turned back four times. Then Nanahuatzin stepped forward. He shut his eyes and steadied his nerves with deep breaths, then went fearlessly into the flames. The other gods watched in awe as his body caught, crackled and burned fast. At last, inspired by his rival, Tecuciztécatl rushed into the flames. An eagle and a jaguar followed the two gods into the flames, so gaining their distinctive markings and their reputation for fearlessness and power.

A NEW AGE

The sacrifice was complete. The other gods waited for the first day of the new age to begin. In one account, the proud but fearful Tecuciztécatl rose first into the sky in the form of the moon, shining very brilliantly. He was followed by Nanahuatzin, the new sun. In another version, the new sun and moon rose together. In both accounts the light of the moon was too bright and cancelled out that of the sun. One of the gods on the ground threw a rabbit up at the moon's face, giving the moon its distinctive markings, in which Mesoamericans saw the shape of a rabbit.

The sun and moon hung in the sky, motionless and lifeless. This was not as it should be. How could time progress and the seasons be measured if there were no movements in the heavens? Nanahuatzin made an announcement from his position at his zenith in the sky. He would consent to follow the required daily motions of the sun, but only if the other gods offered their hearts and lifeblood in sacrifice, as he had made an offering of his earthly body. At first the gods on the ground were outraged and one, the morning star, attacked Nanahuatzin, but then they agreed to make the first of the many blood sacrifices that maintained the flow of life-energy in the Mesoamerican cosmos. They cut their own bodies and offered their hearts to the sun. The sun began to move and the moon sank behind the Earth's horizon.

Left: All life came from the gods' initial sacrifice. This sacrificial knife, made of wood and flint, dates from c.*1500.*

Below: The Cerro Gordo peak behind gives Teotihuacán's Pyramid of the Moon the look of a natural formation.

THE CELESTIAL WEAVING GIRL

Other Mesoamerican myths explain how the sky and earth were separated and the moon and sun were brought into being. A Mixtec tale recounted that Lord Nine Wind, a god associated with the Aztec deity Quetzalcóatl, separated the waters and the Earth, using the waters to make a sky that would arch over and contain the land.

PARALLELS

Quiché Maya mythology in the *Popol Vuh* tells that water and sky were always already separate: the sky god and the sea god cooperated to make the earth after a fruitful discussion of what would be right. In the Quiché tradition, the sun and moon were created later, when the Hero Twins Hunahpú and Xbalanqué rose up into the heavens after their successful mission to the underworld. The Quiché Maya and Aztec creation myths therefore both put some time between the creation of the Earth in its current age and the rising of the sun and moon to give light.

Below: Mesoamerican myths told that the sun, here honoured on a Maya pyramid, first rose above a well-established Earth.

Right: This terracotta mask may represent the ancient Maya counterpart to the Aztec fire god.

THE EARTH MONSTER'S BODY

In the Aztec myth, Quetzalcóatl and Tezcatlipoca made the Earth from the Earth Monster's body and Quetzalcóatl made the first people some time before the sun and moon were made by the gods' sacrifice at Teotihuacán. In one version of the Aztec myth there were 26 years between the creation of the Earth and the first appearance of the sun.

This myth explains that the waters of the heavens fell, unleashing the great flood that swept away the fourth sun in the year 1-Toctli (1-Rabbit), which was associated with the south. Quetzalcóatl and Tezcatlipoca made the Earth and then Tezcatlipoca assumed a new identity as Mixcóatl, an ancient hunt god sometimes said to be god of the north. This happened in the year (2-Ácatl) 2-Reed. In the diviners' calendar, the day named 2-Reed was sacred to Tezcatlipoca. The next period began on the year 1-Ácatl (1-Reed). It was sacred to Quetzalcóatl, one of whose attributes was as god of the east. The gods made the sun 13 years

Above: *The Zapotecs, makers of the enigmatic figures thought to be slain war captives at Monte Albán, taught that there were separate creators of animals (made by Cozaana) and men (made by Huichaana).*

afterwards, in 13-Ácatl (13-Reed). This sequence suggests how Mesoamerican myths are intimately connected to the day-names, year-names and other timings of the sacred calendar, as well as to the movements of the stars and planets.

A LOVE STORY

A different Maya tradition explained the relationship between the sun and moon and their ascension to the sky in terms of an earthly love story and explains thereby the origins of human sexual relations. At one time, according to this story, the sun and moon lived on Earth: Sun was a sturdy young hunter and Moon a fair maiden who earned her corn bread by working as a weaver. Sun fell for the pale, luminous beauty of Moon the moment he first saw her and he was drawn back to her grandfather's house again and again to try to catch a glimpse of her peaceful face. Every morning Sun arrived at the house, carrying a vast deer carcass on his shoulders in an attempt to impress the maiden with his strength and hunting prowess. But although Moon was pleased by the attention and began to have feelings for the hunter, her grandfather was against the relationship and did all he could to prevent it flowering into love.

Now Sun had magical powers as well as virile strength and he transformed himself into a hummingbird. In this shape he could come and go as he pleased without the maiden's grandfather seeing, and he loved to haunt the garden behind the old man's house, where tobacco plants grew. The maiden, either displeased by the attentions of the hummingbird or guessing its true identity, had her grandfather shoot the swift-winged bird in flight. In the moment he was shot, the hummingbird reverted back into human form. The moon-maiden then nursed Sun back to health, keeping his identity secret from her grandfather. When Sun was well again, she fled with him.

Left: Mixtecs, proud of their creative skills, believed that from the beginning their gods were blessed with genius in fine arts, metalworking and other crafts.

PREVENTING AN ELOPEMENT

Now other gods joined in to try and prevent the elopement. Spying them in a canoe on the river far below, the rain god hurled a thunderbolt at the pair. Sun changed himself into a turtle and Moon transformed herself into a crab, but for Moon it was too late. She was broken into many pieces and died.

Grieving, Sun collected the remains of his love and, with the help of a band of dragonflies, stored them in thirteen hollow logs. He waited for thirteen days, then opened the logs. The first twelve logs were filled with poisonous snakes and angry insects, which fled into the world and have been an unpleasant and sometimes deadly presence ever since. But in the thirteenth log, by a thoroughly breathtaking miracle, he found the Moon maiden, restored to life. Now a deer was passing and stamped on the moon through the log, creating the very first female sexual organ. Sun and Moon then had sexual relations. This was the first time male and female had combined in this perfect complementarity.

Once again the lovers were united. They lived for many more years on Earth but Sun discovered that he could not trust his love, who had a carnal nature. She took many lovers when his attention was elsewhere and in his anger and desperate, continuing love he took her with him into exile in the sky. In one tradition, his anger and fear of her sexual happiness made him attack her, blinding her in one eye. For this reason the light given by the moon is weaker by far than that given by the sun.

MYTHS OF THE NIGHT SKY

Above: One face of the Aztec altar of the nocturnal animals shows an owl. The other sides depict a bat, a scorpion and a spider.

The gods and heroes of Mesoamerican mythology were visible in the night sky. The movements of the stars and planets gave solid form to the repeating cycles of the myths. The stories of many deities ended with their ascension to the night sky to take the form of this or that group of stars, and the rising, falling and other movements of the constellations were a regular reminder of the truth of the myths and of the divine transactions that sustained life.

ASTRONOMY AND THE GODS

The movements of the stars were also connected to farmers' cycles of planting and reaping, for astronomical phenomena were used to time the agricultural cycle. For example, in the Quiché Maya *Popol Vuh* cycle, the early humans known as the Four Hundred Boys were killed by Zipacná, son of the boastful solar deity Seven Macaw. At their death they rose into the sky to become the Pleiades constellation. In Quiché lore, the Pleiades were associated with a handful of seeds. Dennis Tedlock, translator of the *Popol Vuh*, points out that the period in March when high-altitude farmers plant maize is marked by the setting of the Pleiades in the evening. When the lower altitude maize is planted in May, the Pleiades are completely invisible. The disappearance of the Four Hundred Boys of the Pleiades marks the time when the maize seeds 'disappear' into the earth and later the constellation is visible again as the seeds 'dawn' in the form of plants.

Seven Macaw became the seven stars that make up the Plough or Big Dipper. In the latitude of the Quiché Maya, the seasonal disappearance of this constellation appears to usher in the rainy storms of the hurricane season. In mid-July, at the start of the hurricane season, the Plough can be seen descending at twilight and afterwards disappears for much of the night. In mid-October the reappearance of all seven stars of the constellation before dawn marks the end of the hurricanes and the start of the dry season. In the myth, the god's fall from the tree when he is shot by Hunahpú occurs just before the great flood that is sent against the wooden people. In the same way, the descent of Seven Macaw's constellation brings the waters of the rainy hurricane season.

CYCLICAL MOVEMENTS

The *Popol Vuh* cycle is entirely built on the cyclical movements of the stars and planets – especially the Venus cycle – and on the sacred calendar that is derived from them. Before the Hero Twins are born, their father and uncle One and Seven Hunahpú are summoned to the underworld because their playing of the Mesoamerican ball game makes such a racket that it annoys the underworld lords. This corresponds to a day named Hunahpú in the calendar and to the rising of Venus as the morning star in the eastern sky. One and Seven Hunahpú then descend to the underworld, where they play ball against the underworld

Below: This vast Aztec stone head is of the moon goddess Coyolxauhqui, with her characteristic lunar nose pendant.

Above: Quetzalcóatl descends to Earth in his most familiar guise, as the Plumed Serpent.

lords. This corresponds to the time in the Venus cycle when the planet is not visible. When One Hunahpú is killed, this equates to the reappearance of Venus as the evening star. When an underworld maiden, Blood Woman, becomes pregnant with One Hunahpú's sons (the Hero Twins) and climbs to the Earth's surface, she convinces One Hunahpú's mother, Xmucané, that she has come from the underworld pregnant with the sons of One Hunahpú. This corresponds to the new rising of Venus as the morning star. In addition, One Monkey and One Artisan, the half-brothers of the Hero Twins, correspond to the planet Mars. Their names are both associated with the day in the diviners' calendar when Mars becomes visible.

Aztec myths were similarly tied into astronomical movements. Tezcatlipoca brought the first sun or world age to an end by unleashing the rage of the night predator, the jaguar. He then rose in the sky in the form of a great celestial jaguar and became the Great Bear constellation. When the Great Bear dips into the sea, Aztec stargazers understood it to mark the moment in the cosmic myth of the world's creation when Tezcatlipoca lost a foot in his struggle with the Earth Monster, Tlaltecuhtli.

Quetzalcóatl's myth closely parallels the Venus cycle. In one tradition, after being outwitted by the followers of Tezcatlipoca in Tollán and subsequently disgraced, he sacrificed himself on a pyre and his soul rose as Venus. In this guise he was known as Ce Ácatl and Tlahuizcalpantecuhtli (Dawn), and understood to be an enemy of the sun. When Quetzalcóatl made a voyage to the underworld to collect the bones of the fish-men of the fourth world age, he was Venus during its invisible phase and when he returned in triumph with the bones to make a new race of men he was Venus rising again as the morning star.

Right: This small clay idol may be Xólotl, Quetzalcóatl's form as Venus the evening star.

MANY FACES OF THE SUN GOD

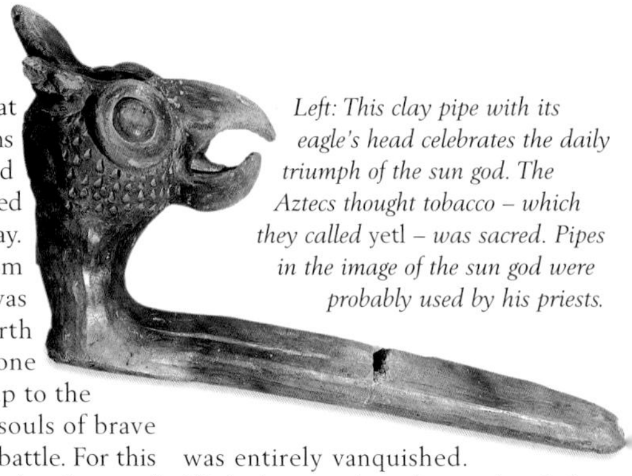

Left: This clay pipe with its eagle's head celebrates the daily triumph of the sun god. The Aztecs thought tobacco – which they called yetl *– was sacred. Pipes in the image of the sun god were probably used by his priests.*

The Aztecs thought of themselves as the people of the sun. At Teotihuacán, the gods had performed the first blood sacrifice to set the sun and moon in motion in the sky, but the ritual did not prove sufficient to feed the blood-hungry sun. Fortunately, the Aztec people and their neighbours were able to take on the task of feeding the sun and maintaining its daily movements through war and blood sacrifice.

AZTEC DAWN

Each dawn was a time of trepidation. The moment of transition between dark and light might be the world's last, for if the sun refused to move across the sky then there would be no day, no time and no seasons to mark with the calendar. To ensure that the sun was sufficiently nourished, Aztec priests had to follow the religious calendar with the utmost devotion and make all the appropriate sacrifices at the right time.

The Aztecs believed that the sun took different forms at different times of day and night. An ancient god named Tonatiuh was the sun by day. Each dawn, as he rose from the eastern horizon, he was born anew of the earth goddess Coatlícue. In one tradition he was hauled up to the zenith of the sky by the souls of brave warriors who had died in battle. For this honour the souls took the form of hummingbirds. The Aztecs saw Tonatiuh as a strong, vibrant young man with an ochre and yellow-painted face and a red-painted body. He was guided across the sky by a great fire-serpent called the *xiuhcóatl.*

Some accounts reveal that at its zenith, when the sun is most powerful, it changed from Tonatiuh to the Aztec tribal god Huitzilopochtli. At noon, beneath the brilliance of Huitzilopochtli, darkness was entirely vanquished. With the sun directly overhead there were not even any shadows to remind men of the encroaching coldness and the many demons of night.

After noon, as the sun descended towards his nightly disappearance at dusk, he was pulled down the length of sky by the *cilhuateteo*, the souls of women who had died in childbirth, slain by unborn warriors in the womb. At dusk, as he sank beyond the horizon, he was understood to be devoured by the Earth Monster Tlaltecuhtli.

A JAGUAR BY NIGHT

By night, the sun travelled through the dread realms of the underworld, Mictlán. During these hours, Tonatiuh took the shape of Tepeyolohtli, a jaguar named 'Heart of the Hard Mountain'. The roaring of this great beast, who was caged within the mountain, could be heard in the thundering of avalanches and the noisy eruption of volcanic lava.

The jaguar was a night predator, capable of striking suddenly and fatally in the blackness of the wild countryside and so the jaguar was naturally associated with the night and with the dark underworld. In some traditions, the sun defeated his enemies in the underworld each night with the *xiuhcóatl* or fire-serpent.

Left: An Aztec codex depicts preparations for a sacrifice in the sun god's honour at the pyramid-top temple halfway to the sky.

Right: The Maya sun god Kinich Ahau was the husband of the moon goddess Ix Chel. At night, as he travelled through the underworld, it was believed that he turned into a jaguar.

The Classic Period Maya also believed that the sun became a jaguar by night. By day they thought the life-giving star was a male god named Kinich Ahau ('Sun-faced Lord'), a fresh-faced young man at dawn who aged during the long day and who, by dusk, had an old man's face and beard. In carvings and pictures, he is depicted with a fierce face and a single front tooth. On his forehead is often carved the four-petalled glyph for *kin*, which means 'day' or 'sun'. A fine stucco mask of the god survives among the remains of the main pyramid at the Maya site of Kohunlich in the Mexican state of Quintana Roo.

After dusk, the Maya sun god was reborn in the first moments of night as a jaguar who travelled through the underworld, where he had to do battle – like the Hero Twins and the souls of the dead – with the lords of Xibalba. Some images of Kinich Ahau prefigure this night-time transformation by depicting the day-sun god with the characteristics or features of a jaguar. A number of representations of the jaguar god of the underworld show him with the *kin* glyph ('sun' or 'day') on his sleek stomach.

DARKNESS AND LIGHT

Night was also a time to be feared. The Aztecs believed that Tezcatlipoca was at large in the hours of darkness, sometimes taking the form of a headless demon called Night Axe, sometimes of a wandering demon who approached travellers at the crossroads. It was also the time and the realm of the demons called *tzitimime*, female spirits who sparkled with malevolence like stars in the blue darkness. They were responsible for unleashing many of the ills that afflicted humankind, such as the epidemics that swept through the Valley of Mexico after the Spanish Conquest. Their power was at its height when night encroached upon day in the form of a solar eclipse. At these times the Aztecs made sacrifices of fair-skinned victims to fortify Tonatiuh in his weakness.

The opposition between darkness and light was central to Mesoamerican mythology. Whereas Tezcatlipoca was associated with dark, his eternal rival and counterpart Quetzalcóatl was linked to dawn. Quetzalcóatl was associated with the east and, in his aspect as Tlahuizcalpantecuhtli, with Venus as the morning star that heralded the sunrise. His rising symbolized resurrection while the darkness of Tezcatlipoca stood for death. The ball game played throughout Mesoamerica may have been seen as a re-enactment of the struggles between Tezcatlipoca and Quetzalcóatl that were such an important part of the myth of the four suns before our own; of struggles in the Aztecs' lives between darkness and light, between death and life. The balance between light and dark also corresponded to the opposition between dryness and dampness, height and smallness and, in some instances, between masculinity and femininity.

Below: An image from the Codex Borbonicus *shows the sun god (left) in the form he assumed by night.*

BRINGERS OF RAIN

One version of the Aztec myth of the creation of the sun and moon gave a vital role to Éhecatl, the wind god who was an aspect of Quetzalcóatl. After the gods Nanahuatzin and Tecuciztécatl had thrown themselves on to the sacrificial pyre and ascended into the sky as sun and moon, they hung motionless above the Earth. In this tradition, it was Éhecatl who initiated their movements. He blew on them with all the strength of his breath. At first, only the sun moved and the moon remained stationary, but when the sun set at last in the west the moon was drawn into his proper cycle, which complements that of the sun.

Below: At Chichén Itzá, the ruined tower of the Caracol – perhaps a temple to wind god Kukulcán as well as an astronomical observatory – contained a spiral corridor.

In contrast to other gods, who were generally associated with a particular point of the compass, Éhecatl was linked to all four directions because the wind blows from the north, south, east and west. Temples built to honour the god were partly circular in form. A circular temple to Éhecatl-Quetzalcóatl reputedly stood opposite the great temple of the Aztecs in Tenochtitlán. Éhecatl was associated with, and at times represented as, a spider monkey, a duck, a spider and a snail. Statues of him often wear a half-mask with the appearance of a duck's bill, open to allow the tongue to show.

Left: This stone carving of Éhecatl-Quetzalcóatl has obsidian eyes. The god blew through his beak to make the winds.

Scholars believe the Aztecs associated the spider monkey with the wind because of its great speed and agility when swinging through the trees. Another connection is that, at the end of the fourth age, humans were destroyed by a great wind and turned into monkeys. Quetzalcóatl in the guise of Éhecatl was patron of the second day in the Aztecs' day-count calendar.

Above: *This dancing monkey honours the power of the wind god Éhecatl-Quetzalcóatl. The snake suggests the whirlwinds with which Éhecatl ushered in the rainy season.*

THE BREATH OF LIFE

The wind unleashed by Éhecatl-Quetzalcóatl was the breath of life itself for, without the setting and rising of the sun, there would be no seasons, no cycles of planting and harvesting, no crops and no life in Mesoamerica. The god blew the damp winds that carried rain clouds to the grateful farmers at the start of the rainy season. He also unleashed whirlwinds that cleared the skies for the clouds. For this reason the Aztecs called him 'the *tláloques*' road-sweeper' – a reference to the little rain gods who were assistants to the main rain deity, Tláloc.

An illustration in the *Vienna Codex* shows Éhecatl connecting earth and sky and supporting the clouds above. An Aztec sculpture also depicts Quetzalcóatl rising, serpentine, from the earth-mother to connect with the rain god Tláloc above. It was all part of the Aztecs' cosmological view that the rains were present in the sky above because the sea that lay at the far extremes of the earth curved up to join over it.

The connection provided between the earth and the sky by Éhecatl-Quetzalcóatl was necessary to provide a conduit or pathway by which the waters could return to the earth in the form of windblown rainclouds.

KUKULCÁN-QUETZALCÓATL

The wind god was worshipped as Kukulcán by the central and northern Maya, while the southern Maya knew him as Gucumatz. The wind god was associated with the rain god Chac as bringer of fertility.

Some scholars believe that the circular Caracol at Chichén Itzá, while certainly an astronomical observatory, may also have served as a temple to the god Kukulcán-Quetzalcóatl. Its circular shape means that the building was probably sacred to the wind god aspect of the Plumed Serpent.

Like Quetzalcóatl, Kukulcán had many other attributes as a creator, a god of new life and as a cultural hero who taught the ancestors skills such as farming in ancient times. In the Maya realms, his cult appears to have been an aristocratic one and he was particularly associated with lords and nobles. The cult of Kukulcán-Quetzalcóatl was very strong under the Toltecs, but temples in his honour were built much earlier at Teotihuacán and Tikal.

According to the Quiché Maya, the sky god was one of the two primal creators. He was associated with wind and rain, thunder and storms. The many names and identities he could adopt included Hurricane, Raw Thunderbolt and Newborn Thunderbolt. This associated him with the Aztec god Tezcatlipoca, who was also linked to hurricanes and rainstorms. The Aztec thunder god was Tláloc, bringer of rains.

Left: Éhecatl-Quetzalcóatl's breath brought the rains that fed the plants. Here the god carries five maize cobs on his back.

DELUGE: THE UNIVERSAL FLOOD

In both Aztec and Maya traditions there are myths of terrible destruction wrought by a great flood. According to the Quiché Maya, the failed creation of the wooden people was swept away by a universal flood sent by Huracán, who is associated with Tezcatlipoca. The Aztecs told that the fourth sun or world age was ended by a destructive flood sent by its ruling deity Chalchiúhtlicue, the goddess of oceans, lakes, rivers and streams.

THE WATERS UNLEASHED

In the version found in the late 16th-century *Codex Chimalpopoca*, one woman and one man were given the chance to survive the cataclysm in a story that is strikingly similar in some ways to the biblical narrative of Noah.

As the era reached its end, a man and woman named Nata and Nena were forewarned by the god Tezcatlipoca, who came to them and called them away from their activities. Nata was making the strong alcoholic drink *pulque*, but the god told him to put it aside and to go quickly to cut and hollow out a great cypress tree. In this makeshift boat Nata was to build a covered cabin in which to shelter from water, for at the end of the month of Tozoztli the waters that rise over the earth in the arc of the sky were going to be unleashed. The earth would be swamped. Just before this time, Nata and Nena should clamber into the cypress boat and wait. They should take with them just one ear of corn each and eat no more than that.

The couple did what they were told and they were thankful for, when the waters came, the flood submerged even the highest mountains in a single day. Death was everywhere, because there was no escaping from the water's awesome power.

Left: This intriguing stone lizard was carved by a Totonac craftsman in the period 1200–1300.

Below: This image of a beast in floodwater was carved on a stone box that held the ashes of the Aztec tlatoani *Ahuítzotl.*

However, the two human survivors were soon hungry, for their corn was quickly gone. They clambered on to the roof of their makeshift cabin and looked around them. They realized that the great population of Mesoamerica had not been entirely wiped out for the people that Nata and Nena left behind had turned into fish, dolphins, whales and other sea creatures. The water was thick with marine life.

DISOBEDIENCE

Nata cried happily to his wife that they need not go hungry: the waters were teeming. They had a few sticks laid by in the cabin and with one of these Nata began to fish, while with some others Nena made a fire. Soon the smoke was rising in the sky and four meaty fish were roasting on the sticks above the fire. The sole human survivors ate them greedily, crying with joy that they had banished their hunger pains.

They did not look up to see that the smoke from their fire was rising to the thirteen layers of the heavens. Two gods – named in this source as Citlalícue and Citlatona – were angered by the smell and complained to Tezcatlipoca. He went quickly down to confront Nata and Nena, who had disobeyed his command that they should eat no more than one ear of corn each. He punished them for their greed. He took the fish Nata had caught and fashioned a long nose for their heads, with lithe legs and a tail for their hindquarters. The fish were transformed into dogs, which barked at the sky. They had no more escaped the flood than their fellows who had been transformed into fish. The flood lasted for a total of 52 years before the creation of the new world by Tezcatlipoca and his divine ally-rival the Plumed Serpent.

FISH, FLOODS AND FERTILITY

The Aztecs associated fish and waters with fertility. Fish were linked with the deities Chalchiúhtlicue, Xochiquetzal, Xochipilli, Mayáhuel, Quetzalcóatl and Cipactli. Fish from the lakes of Mexico were a staple food for the Aztecs. The majority of the offerings that have been found at the Great Pyramid in Tenochtitlán contained fish, but curiously there are few surviving representations of fish in Aztec art.

Below: Images of Tláloc's consort Chalchiúhtlicue often show her kneeling and wearing long ear tassels.

In view of its watery setting, the lake-city of Tenochtitlán must always have been vulnerable to flooding. The Spanish chronicler Diego Durán describes in his *History of the Indies of New Spain* describes how the *tlatoani* Ahuítzotl, his priests and people would perform obsequious offerings to the water goddess Chalchiúhtlicue in order to drive back a flood.

Left: The Aztecs removed masks such as this from Teotihuacán and used them as offerings at the Great Pyramid. This ritual mask may once have formed part of an incense burner used in religious ceremonies.

THE UNIVERSAL FLOOD: A RACE MEMORY?

Myths of a destructive universal flood are common in the traditions of diverse peoples across the world. In the Judaeo-Christian tradition there is the familiar tale of Noah, in which God sends a flood but saves Noah and his ark of animals and that of Gilgamesh in ancient Sumer.

Hindu religious mythology describes cycles of destruction and new life and tells how the universal waters cover the earth at the end of each age, before a new creation begins.

In Australia, the Worora aboriginals said that ancestral spirits once sent a vast flood to make space for the current world.

At the other end of the Earth, in the Arctic, the Inuit report that a previous world age knew no death, so that the world became dangerously overcrowded until a great flood swept the majority of people away, leaving a sustainable number, who were thereafter subject to death.

The myths are so common that some scholars have speculated there may once have been a great flood that brought near-universal destruction and that the memory of this cataclysm, buried deep in our subconscious, has inspired strikingly similar tales in cultures that have had no contact with one another.

However, in all likelihood the stories arose because flooding – whether by rivers and lakes or by the sea breaking through dykes and defensive walls – was common in so many places. Floodwaters brought death but also fertility. In the mythological imagination of early peoples, they became associated with the end of eras and the commencement of a new creation.

CHAPTER NINE

TALES OF THE GODS

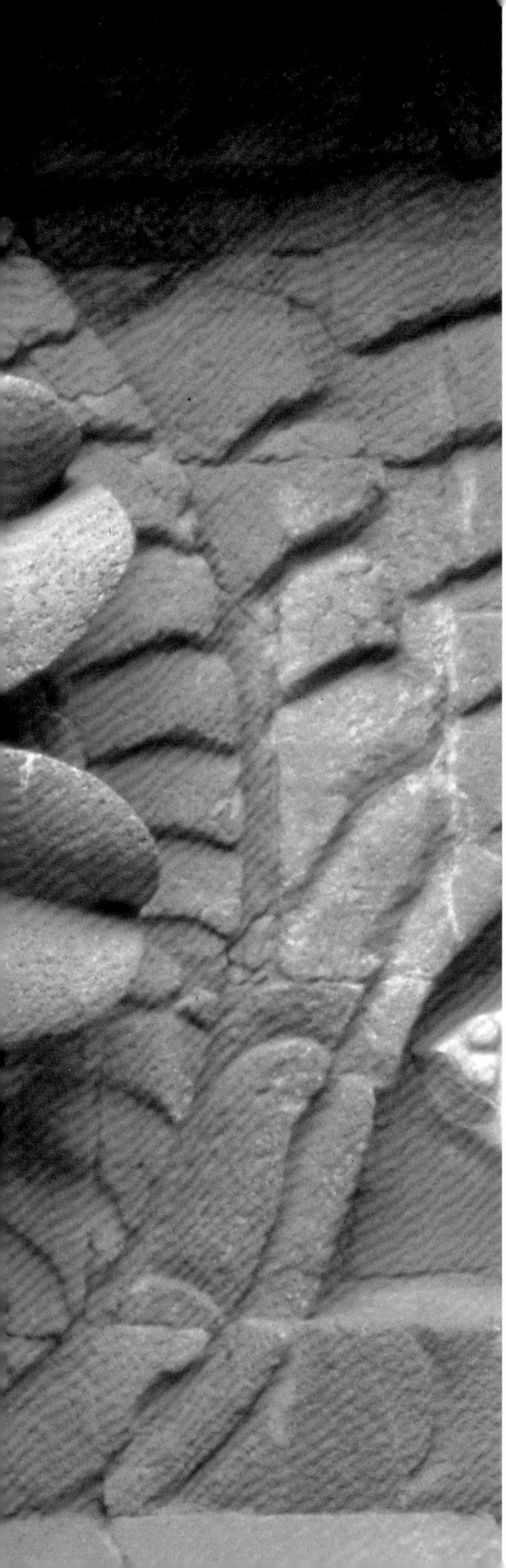

In considering their gods, Mesoamericans were happy to combine the concepts of 'many' and 'one'. The Quiché Maya creators Huracán and Gucumatz were each both an individual and also a group of cooperating gods. The Aztecs simultaneously believed in many gods and one god. They knew of Ometeotl, the primeval god and first cause of creation. The god was both male and female, taking the forms Ometecuhtli and Omecihuatl. They were mother and father deities, seen as the creative essence of the primeval god.

In general the primeval deity was inactive in his own guise: other gods issued from Ometeotl through Ometecuhtli and Omecihuatl and were engaged in action. One story tells that Omecihuatl was wandering above the dry plains of the north, and felt a movement within her like the turning of a child in a woman's womb. She squatted there to give birth: a sacrificial knife of obsidian emerged from her, fell to the plain below and gave issue to 1,600 gods and goddesses. The number 1,600 is intended to mean 'beyond counting' – and suggests the myth confirms both the primacy of sacrifice and of the multiplicity of the gods. And just as the gods coexisted as 'one' and 'many', so each individual deity could take many forms without losing his or her essential identity. The ancient god Quetzalcóatl, for instance, could be known as the celebrated Plumed Serpent, the princely priest Topiltzin, the wind god Éhecatl and the planet Venus, among many other forms.

Left: A temple to the Plumed Serpent stood in the revered city of Teotihuacán. This image of the god greeted worshippers.

A CROWDED PANTHEON

The Aztecs' primeval deity, Ometeotl, does not appear to have been carved or otherwise represented: although one surviving Aztec sculpture *c.*1350 showing a seated god has been identified by some scholars as an image of the primeval god, other historians consider it to be Quetzalcóatl or the old god Huehuetéotl. The Aztecs did produce images of Ometeotl's constituent parts, Ometecuhtli/Tonacatecuhtli and Omecihuatl/Tonacacihuatl. They were often given rich clothes, perhaps intended to associate them with light.

GOD OF TWO FACES

Artists and craftsman also made more abstract attempts to represent the primeval deities. As early as the 8th century BC Mesoamericans produced intriguing two-faced or twin-headed figures thought by historians to represent the force of duality that was strongly present in the culture. The idea of duality, which holds opposites such as life/death or wet/dry in equilibrium, takes solid form in mythology in two-as-one deities such as Ometecuhtli/Omecihuatl. Two-faced statues dating to this era have been found at Tlatilco. Scholars cite an Aztec mask that is half bare and half covered in skin as another representation of the same concept.

The Maya also believed in a creator deity, called Itzamná or Hunab Ku. In one version of the creation, Hunab Ku made the world three times: the first world contained dwarfs; the second contained a mysterious race called 'the offenders'; the third was the world of our era, inhabited by the Maya and their Aztec neighbours. Each of the first two creations was wiped out by a deluge and our own third age, too, was destined to end in the destruction of a universal flood. Sometimes Hunab Ku was seen, like Ometeotl, to be largely inactive in his own guise – but at the same time he was understood to be the father of Itzamná, who was moon god and bringer of culture to the people.

Right: This Zapotec idol is of the goddess of the thirteen serpents, perhaps a version of the Aztec fertility goddess Cihuacóatl.

SERPENT IMAGERY

Itzamná taught the Maya how to write and use the sacred calendar, and he brought them knowledge of the maize and cacao plants.

As bringer of writing, Itzamná was the patron of scribes and priests. He is shown as a scribe in several illustrations to the *Madrid Codex*. He is usually shown as an old man seated on a throne, with a lined forehead and hollow cheeks, and because he was the moon god his headdress or forehead carries the glyph for night. He was also connected with new life, and linked to the snail – which was associated with childbirth. But his principal animal form was the serpent or dragon. A carved bone discovered in a tomb at Tikal shows a scribe's hand emerging from the mouth of a dragon that represents Itzamná.

Itzamná's consort was Ix Chel, the moon goddess. They were the parents of the bacabs, the giants who supported the heavens, separating earth and sky, in the four corners of creation.

Left: Carved snakes' heads guarded the steps of the pyramid temples at Tenochtitlán.

The prevalence of serpent imagery among the attributes and associations of quite different gods is suggestive of the fact that many of the deities were very closely connected, almost interchangeable. Mesoamericans believed that the divine essence was fluid and that it could take many associated forms. For the Classic-era Maya, Itzamná was linked to the serpent, and his consort Ix Chel was often shown with a snake hair-band. Itzamná was considered to be a creator, as was the sea god Sovereign Plumed Serpent by the Quiché Maya of the *Popol Vuh*.

The snake was also associated with spirit journeys and religious experience. The Maya developed the notion of the vision serpent, along whose coils the individual could travel to the spirit world or within which humans could encounter the gods. In Aztec carvings and art the open mouth of the serpent represents the cave Mesoamericans widely understood to be an entrance to the spirit world or to the underworld Mictlán.

Below: The Maya god Ix Chel was often depicted as a clawed goddess with a writhing serpent on her head and embroidered crossbones on her skirt.

Above: This large carved head at the Maya city of Copán is thought to represent the god Itzamná, culture-giver and scribes' patron.

The Aztecs (and the Toltecs before them) worshipped the snake in the form of the bird-serpent Quetzalcóatl, but the Aztecs also considered the earth goddess Coatlícue to have snake petticoats. The earth and sky were made from the dismembered body of a serpentine monster: sometimes the top layer of the earth was said to be composed of a carpet of interconnected serpents from which men, plants and animals had grown; the double-headed serpent represented in Aztec jewellery and art stood for the sky. One version of the myth of Topiltzin-Quetzalcóatl told how the god departed Mexico on a raft made of serpents.

Huitzilopochtli, sun deity and the Aztecs' tribal god, wielded a weapon called the *xiuhcóatl* or fire-snake to kill his countless brothers in the moments after his birth. In his form as Tonatiuh, the sun was led across the sky by the *xiuhcóatl* and by night fought in the underworld using the fire-snake as a weapon.

In one celebrated carving of Coatlícue, snakes represent the flow of blood from her cut arms and head. A sacrificial stone found in the Gulf of Mexico coastal region in the 19th century was carved in the shape of a two-headed snake, with a raised back on which the victim was pressed down while his heart was carved from his chest. Carvings of snakes-heads are known to have decorated the stairs on the Great Pyramid in Tenochtitlán.

Tláloc the rain and thunder god had a snake mask and was often depicted carrying a snake sceptre – driving rain was sometimes seen as a storm of water-snakes. In both Mesoamerican mythology and religion, the serpent was associated with the sun's rays, with rain, fertility and the earth, skill and power, the waters of the sea, human sexuality and rebirth.

LORD OF THE SMOKING MIRROR

Tezcatlipoca, the god of fate and bringer of discord and vice, was likened by Bernardino de Sahagún to the Christian devil. Tezcatlipoca had great powers and creative aspects but often put them to negative use, just like the angel Lucifer in the Christian tradition. Tezcatlipoca was a creator deity and shared the credit with Quetzalcóatl for the creation of the world from the body of the Earth Monster. However, whereas Quetzalcóatl was a civilizing cultural hero who introduced mankind to maize, Tezcatlipoca was a god of war who brought men into a cycle of destruction and new creation.

THE CULT OF TEZCATLIPOCA

Tezcatlipoca's cult went back at least as far as the Toltecs. They told a tale of a mirror of dark obsidian glass that could predict famine. At a time of great need, when people were starving in the land, Tezcatlipoca found and hid this mirror in order to prolong the people's suffering.

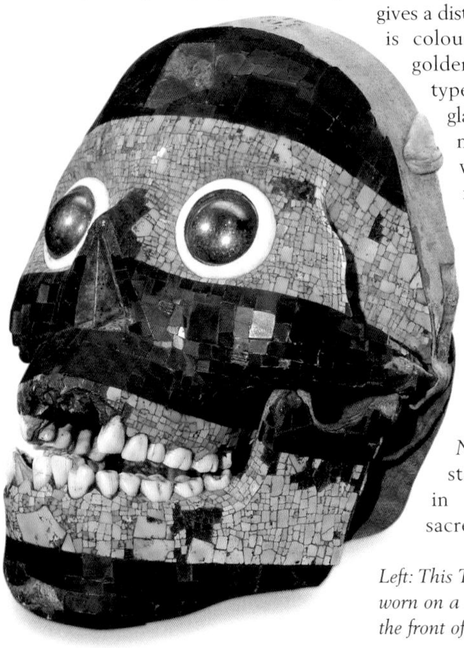

Left: This Tezcatlipoca mask was probably worn on a priest's waist. It was made from the front of a human skull.

The 'Lord of the Smoking Mirror', Tezcatlipoca, was believed to wear a mirror of the volcanic glass obsidian in the back of his head. Sometimes he was also said to have a mirror in place of one of his feet. Traditions vary as to whether Tezcatlipoca lost his foot when he and Quetzalcóatl were fighting the Earth Monster in order to create the earth and sky, or when he was flung out of the thirteenth heaven as punishment for misusing his dark power to seduce a fair goddess. Often he was depicted simply with a missing foot, his leg ending in the shinbone.

The glass he wore was said to be a 'smoking mirror' because it was made of obsidian, which characteristically gives a distorted reflection that is coloured green, grey or golden depending on the type used. Sometimes the glass was said to reflect the night even in full day; obsidian was linked in the Aztec imagination with cold and with the night, as was Tezcatlipoca himself. It was also associated with death and with the rain of windblown knives that travellers to the underworld of Mictlán had to pass through. According to the Franciscan friar Diego Durán, the author of *The History of the Indies of New Spain*, there was a religious statue made wholly of obsidian in the Templo Mayor or the sacred precinct in Tenochtitlán.

Above: An Aztec potter-artist painted his clay pot to make a wild eyed likeness of all-seeing Tezcatlipoca.

The statue held a golden mirror. Using his shadowy mirror, Tezcatlipoca could see the patterns of the future and the private imaginings of people's hearts.

REFLECTING THE DARK SIDE

As the god of night, Tezcatlipoca was patron of hidden nocturnal activities, often shameful or wicked ones such as adultery and stealing. Sometimes he was depicted carrying a *tlachialoni*, a sceptre concealing a hole through which he could see the hidden side of people and their motives. The smoking mirror gave him access to the dark side, not only of people but also of the wider creation. He had within his control the forces of destruction as well as those of creation.

Above: The jaguar, a fierce aspect of Tezcatlipoca, was viewed with religious awe in Mesoamerica. These ravening cats are part of a mural from Teotihuacán.

DEATH EVERYWHERE

Tezcatlipoca was everywhere, invisible yet ubiquitous. Like the cold night sky, he was found in the north, south, east and west, although north was his particular direction. He resided in all the levels of the universe at once, even the underworld. He was also a god of the air, and of violent tempests, particularly hurricanes: he was associated with the Maya god Tahil.

Tezcatlipoca was also the coming destruction, for he would unleash the inevitable cataclysm destined to wipe away the current creation.

Tezcatlipoca was said to carry a sacrificial knife made of obsidian that symbolized a black wind devoid of life. Sacrificial knives were found in many of the offerings uncovered by archaeologists at the Templo Mayor in Tenochtitlán. In many, the knives are inserted into the nose or mouth of a skull mask. This symbolized the black wind that delivers death by stopping the flow of air, in contrast to the bright wind that is the breath of life.

LIFE AFTER CONQUEST

Obsidian, the volcanic glass associated so widely with Tezcatlipoca, was used by Spanish priests in a way that may have given Aztec onlookers secret amusement or satisfaction.

Archaeologists and historians have uncovered a number of obsidian blocks set in wood dating from the post-Conquest colonial period. Some are carved with Christian symbolism. Although some were doubtless used as mirrors, scholars believe that others were put to use as portable altars by travelling priests. To an Aztec, the 'smoking glass' obsidian would at once have suggested Tezcatlipoca. The god's association with shamanism, sorcery and treachery made his glass an unlikely material for priests to use for celebrating Mass. The great majority of the priests were probably ignorant of this powerful hidden association.

THE ORIGINATOR OF WAR

Alongside Huitzilopochtli, Tezcatlipoca was one of the Aztecs' principal warrior gods. A round shield called the *chimalli*, which was a symbol for battle conflict, was one of his accoutrements. In his human form, Tezcatlipoca was as youthful, virile and energetic as any eagle or jaguar warrior. The sacrifice of young victims at the year's end granted the god eternal youthfulness. In this guise Tezcatlipoca was sometimes known as Telpochtli ('Young Warrior') and worshipped by a band of young devotees called the *telpochtiliztli*. A splendid funerary urn probably containing the ashes of a great warrior was found in the Templo Mayor in Tenochtitlán during excavations in 1978–82. It depicts Tezcatlipoca as a young warrior, carrying spears and an *atálatl* spear-thrower, wearing an eagle-feather headdress and spearhead nose-ring. In the Aztec codices he is also usually depicted as a soldier, carrying an *atlatl*, shield and darts and wearing two heron feathers in his hair to signify his status among the most elite groups of knights. His body is often painted black.

Below: The Maya also worshipped the underworld jaguar god. This image is from the Temple of the Jaguar at Tikal.

Above: In this image from the Codex Cospi *(c.1350–1500), Tezcatlipoca is in his black aspect, linked to the north and to death.*

YÁOTL, THE ENEMY

Tezcatlipoca was the bringer of war, always at work stirring up conflict. In this guise, he was known as Yáotl ('the Enemy'). His presence was felt on the battlefield, although not as a protector. He presided over the give and take of war and decided when warriors should succeed and when they should fall. On his jacket were the skull and crossbones.

Tezcatlipoca loved and desired conflict for its own sake, but there was a positive side-effect to his stirring of wars, for on the battlefield the Aztecs gathered prisoners to carry home for sacrifice in the sacred precinct in Tenochtitlán. In this sense, his promotion of war was less a malign activity and more a valuable contribution to the religious cycle of sacrifice.

Above: This codex image depicts the dark lord Tezcatlipoca as a virile warrior, equipped with shield and weapon.

Above: An image from Bernardino de Sahagún's Florentine Codex *(1575–7) shows a sacrifice in honour of Tezcatlipoca.*

ANIMAL FORMS

All Aztec gods had one or more animal forms. Tezcatlipoca was associated particularly with the jaguar, which was like the god in that it was fierce, unpredictable and favoured the night.

The Lord of the Smoking Mirror was believed to roam the earth in the dark hours, sometimes in the form of this stealthy, keen-visioned predator. As the jaguar, Tezcatlipoca was associated with the sun during its night-time passage through the dangerous regions of the underworld. In one version of the myth describing the end of the current creation, it is told how, in that era, Tezcatlipoca would steal the sun, so bringing the world, gods and men to black nothingness.

Among his other animal forms were the deceitful skunk, the mischievous monkey and the sly coyote. Aztecs thought the coyote had particular sexual potency and Tezcatlipoca's association with him was located in the god's aspect as a deity of masculinity.

NEGATIVE AND POSITIVE POWER

Tezcatlipoca had many other attributes, always combining negative and positive aspects. His connection to the night and to the jaguar made him god of sorcerer-shamans. He was said to be 'the Left-handed One', suggesting that he was never to be trusted and that he would come at men unexpectedly. He was understood to be mocking mankind, binding them with evil. If a man or woman endured great humiliation it was understood by all to be the work of Tezcatlipoca.

Tezcatlipoca was also associated with rulers and kingly qualities; the coronation preparations of the Aztec *tlatoani* included rites in Tezcatlipoca's honour. According to one tradition, it was Tezcatlipoca, alongside Huitzilopochtli, who guided the Méxica/Aztecs on their journey to find a place to settle. He is said to have inspired the travelling tribe by recounting the marvellous vision of their future riches and dominance that he could see in his shadow-mirror.

Some of the priests of Tenochtitlán painted their bodies black in honour of Tezcatlipoca, using a dark paste made from ground mushrooms, snake skin and tobacco. Tezcatlipoca helped the Aztecs in their divinely ordained mission to provide blood nourishment for the gods. The religious festival of Tóxcatl in May, when a youthful representative of Tezcatlipoca was sacrificed in the dark lord's honour, was one of the major festivals of the Aztec year. As the youth was led to sacrifice up the temple steps, the earthly form of Tezcatlipoca would play mournfully on a thin flute that was carved in the likeness of a flower at its end.

Tezcatlipoca's feast day was 1-Death in the sixth thirteen-day 'month' of the 260-day calendar. At the festival of Teotleco (Coming of the Gods and Goddesses), a bowl of maize flour was laid in the temple and a night vigil was kept until a footprint in the bowl was hailed as the sign that the gods had come. According to some accounts, this footprint was understood to be that of Tezcatlipoca, leading the main group of gods and goddesses. He was not the first to arrive, however. This was always the youngest and fastest god, Tlamatzincatl.

DARK CHALLENGER BY NIGHT

Tezcatlipoca was a constant danger by night. A man out alone on night roads might expect to be challenged by the dark god, who was believed to roam the country looking for victims. If Tezcatlipoca met a traveller, he would challenge him to a bout of wrestling. A mortal who defeated the god could ask for anything he pleased and know that it would be granted. In this guise, Tezcatlipoca was associated with the night wind. Stone benches were built alongside the more important roadways to provide a resting place for this most unpredictable of gods; unfortunately he often used these as sites for his ambushes. Some nights he sent thieves to do his work for him.

Above: An unknown deity emerges from the mouth of the divine jaguar in a terracotta piece from the Zapotec city of Monte Albán.

Below: Tezcatlipoca's reputation for virility associated him with the coyote, believed by Aztecs to be sexually powerful.

DANGEROUS ENERGY

A body of myths recounted how Tezcatlipoca's dangerous energy caused havoc among the Toltec people of Tollán at the time when the priest Topiltzin-Quetzalcóatl was at the height of his powers there. Tezcatlipoca travelled there to cause trouble, scantily clad with his almost naked body painted green, posing as a salesman of green paint. He knew that Huemac, who served Quetzalcóatl by governing Tollán, had a daughter whose beauty was the talk of the whole Valley of Mexico, for her appearance was more wonderful even than that of Mount Ixtaccíhuatl. Many Toltecs longed to marry her. Tezcatlipoca made sure that he passed close to her bedchamber for he hoped to arouse strong desires in her soul. His plan worked, as he knew it would.

The princess saw the vigorous body and bright flashing eyes of the wandering salesman and fell deeply in love. She took to her bed, pining for love, and her father became worried. When he asked her handmaidens what the matter was, they explained that a passing stranger had undone his daughter, arousing passions in her that would give her no rest. Huemac summoned the

Below: An enigmatic Aztec figure (c.1200–1500) combines the features of the living (right) and the fleshless dead (left).

stranger to his court and asked him his business. Tezcatlipoca was casual. He explained that he went almost naked because it was the custom where he came from and said that his life was not of great importance to him. The king could kill him, if he pleased, to punish him for stealing his daughter's heart. However, Huemac knew that if he sacrificed the young man it would be the death of his lovelorn daughter, so instead he commanded the handsome stranger to marry the beautiful princess.

This caused great upset among the people of Tollán, but the king launched a war in order to distract them.

Tezcatlipoca went unannounced among the troops, but some soldiers recognized him as the stranger who had stolen the princess from them. They tricked him into occupying a vulnerable position on the battle field, where they hoped he would be slain. When the moment came, however, he fought with the greatest valour and won a fine reputation.

A DEADLY DANCE

Back in Tollán, Tezcatlipoca was the toast of the city. He could do no wrong and was cheered wherever he went, attired in warrior's garb, with his beautiful wife on his arm. Now he unleashed the full force of his power on the unsuspecting people. He announced that there would be a public feast and celebration and at the appointed time the Toltecs crowded enthusiastically into the main plaza. Then he began to sing and made the people dance to his song. Faster he sang, and faster, and the people had to fling themselves into the steps to stay ahead of the music. Faster still and faster he sang, until the dance was unbearable for the assembled crowd.

The people could no longer keep their footing, and they fell helplessly into a ravine that the god had made in the solid earth. They tumbled down the steep sides like so many rocks. It was over – they were dead.

A GOD AVENGES HIS OWN DEATH

Another tale told how Tezcatlipoca invited all the people of Tollán to meet him in the city's fair flower gardens. He hid himself in the shade, then leapt out on his victims, killing many with a simple hoe, while others fled in panic, trampling one another. Many hundreds of innocents died.

Another story told how Tezcatlipoca punished the Toltecs for his own death. He was again entertaining the people in the main plaza, this time by displaying a child dancing in his hand, who was in truth, the warlike Aztec deity Huitzilopochtli. By using fantastic magic Tezcatlipoca made the child appear to dance on his outstretched palm. The people crowded urgently around, creating such a crush that many people were killed. This unleashed the fury of the survivors and they turned on the gods Tezcatlipoca and Huitzilopochtli, pummelling them until they died.

The gods' death was not the end of the affair. Their corpses began to leak a hideous-smelling liquid and gave off a gas so foul that any who smelled it died instantly. A few came in masks to drag the pestilential corpses away, but they found that the divine bodies were far too heavy to shift. They tied them up with strong cords and gathered a huge crowd to pull, but the ropes broke and the people tumbled in a great heap, one suffocating the next. In the end the entire population died.

Left: This elaborate funerary urn was found in Teotihuacán, revered by the Aztecs as perhaps the site of the Tollán of myth.

THE PLUMED SERPENT

Above: This magnificent double-headed serpent pectoral may have been part of the treasure sent to Cortés by Moctezuma II.

Quetzalcóatl's name has two meanings. In itself, it comprises two Nahuatl words, each of which also has two meanings. *Quetzal* can mean 'green feather' or 'precious' and *cóatl* can mean 'serpent' or 'twin'. The elements of the name taken together can therefore mean 'Plumed Serpent' or 'Precious Twin'. Each name evokes an aspect or role played by Quetzalcóatl in the Mesoamerican pantheon. Such dual meaning also demonstrates the concept of duality so characteristic of Mesoamerican deities and religion in general.

Below: A 4th-century homage to the Plumed Serpent is suggestive of the god's possible origins in an ancient dragon deity.

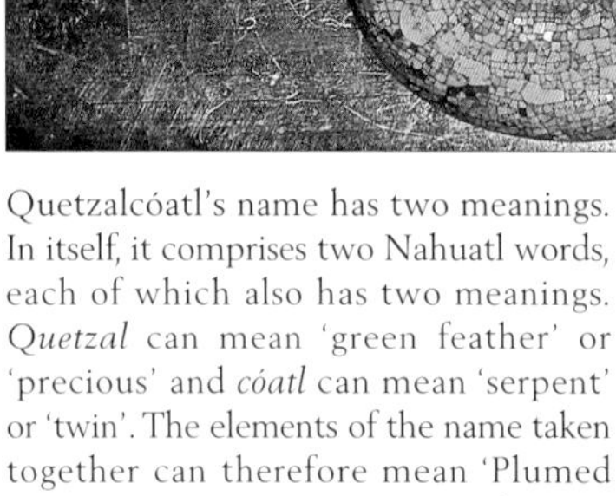

A HUMAN AVATAR

Quetzalcóatl was the only one of the Aztec gods to have had a human avatar in the person of Topiltzin, the priestly ruler of Tollán. In addition, because of his association with wise governance and kingly qualities, many earthly rulers took his name and wore the green feathers of his animal familiar, the quetzal bird. These rulers may have been understood to be representatives of the god on Earth. Quetzalcóatl was a protector of rulers and their families. He was also a great cultural hero, inventor of the ritual calendar, teacher of farming skills and protector of craftsmen. In the form of an ant, he was responsible for bringing the maize plant to humans.

TWIN FORMS

God and man, man and serpent, the 'Precious Twin' was a god of duality; of twin forms. His cult goes far back into Mesoamerican history. The oldest surviving image of Quetzalcóatl, found at Tlatilco, dates to *c.*800BC, while a pyramid temple to the god was built at Teotihuacán in the 3rd century AD. His cult probably grew from that of an ancient Mesoamerican sky god, a dragon who was also worshipped as a fertility and agricultural deity because of his ability to deliver fresh winds and life-giving rains. However, he was also seen as a god of land-level waters – in the *Popol Vuh* the Plumed Serpent is the sea god – and among his myriad attributes he had the power to unleash floods. When the Spanish conquistadors came to Cholula, the priests there tried to provoke the anger of Quetzalcóatl as god of the waters. They encouraged the invaders to desecrate the temple of the Plumed Serpent in the hope that the god would send a flood to drive the Europeans back. However, the plan misfired because Quetzalcóatl did not respond to their insults.

CONNECTIONS TO FERTILITY

The Plumed Serpent's connections to fertility were made clear in one Aztec myth of his conception and birth. According to this tale, Quetzalcóatl was the daughter of Cihuacóatl, a fertility and earth goddess whose name means 'Woman Serpent'. Cihuacóatl often took the shape of a deer. In early times, long before the Méxica travelled south from the northern steppes in which they originated, she roamed the earth as a two-headed deer. In this form she attracted the attention of the hunting god Mixcóatl ('Cloud Serpent'), who pursued her through steep valleys and across wide plains, and all along the shores of the lakes, until he had her in his sights. With one well-aimed dart he brought her low. However, in that same instant he also lost her, for before his eyes the beast transformed into a woman of surpassing beauty. Now the hunt was on again. Mixcóatl pursued this maiden across the landscape until he caught her. Then they had sexual relations. The fruit of their lovemaking was the Plumed Serpent Quetzalcóatl.

Quetzalcóatl was also associated with a range of attributes and natural states that were in opposition to those of his ancient rival and foe Tezcatlipoca. Tezcatlipoca was associated with night, deception and cycles of violence, whereas Quetzalcóatl was linked to daylight, clear thinking and a good life. Both gods were associated with the winds, but while Tezcatlipoca was the god of night winds and hurricanes, Quetzalcóatl-Éhecatl was lord of the morning winds that bring light to the fields. Some scholars understand the ancient image of the sky serpent – often represented with its tail in its mouth – as a homage to the sun, and Quetzalcóatl had some connection to the Earth's star. Indeed, many Aztec gods had solar aspects.

Priests of Quetzalcóatl wore a conch shell whose patterning represented the movement of the wind and honoured the god in his guise as the wind god Éhecatl. Quetzalcóatl was particularly associated with the priesthood and he was regarded as the protector of the priestly school in Tenochtitlán. The two foremost members of the priestly hierarchy were called 'Quetzalcóatl' as part of their title, despite the fact that they presided over the worship of other gods.

In his guise as a priestly patron, Quetzalcóatl was represented as a man with skin painted black and a long beard. In this role and in his form as the wind god, Éhecatl, Quetzalcóatl is often shown wearing a conical hat. The Maya of Yucatán worshipped the Plumed Serpent as Kukulcán, god of wind, light and waters with some solar characteristics. Among the Maya he was particularly revered as a thunder god.

Left: Some 14cm (6in) tall, this shell-mosaic piece dates from the Toltec period and may once have graced a palace in Tula.

Above: Another view of the shell-mosaic piece of Quetzalcóatl, in human form. Bursting forth from the jaws of a coyote, he represents life springing from the Earth.

QUETZALCÓATL AND THE RAFT OF SNAKES

Many myths tell of Quetzalcóatl's enduring conflict with the dark lord Tezcatlipoca. In his guise as the historical-mythical Toltec ruler Topiltzin, Quetzalcóatl was decisively defeated by his opponent and forced to leave the city of Tollán. So ended a golden era of peace and wonderful artistic achievement. There are various versions of his downfall, but according to one, the formerly pure-minded priest-king was tricked by Tezcatlipoca into becoming drunk on the strong liquor known as *pulque* and disgraced himself by seducing his own sister. He left in shame.

Topiltzin-Quetzalcóatl determined to sacrifice himself as a mark of his penitence. He dressed himself in his purest finery, including the kingly mask of turquoise, and built a pyre of great tree-trunks. Then he stepped on to the bonfire and lit it himself. He did not flinch at the touch of fire, just as the god Nanahuatzin, who became the sun, went unflinching into the flames. The flames roared. In an instant, all the king's finery and his royal body were ash. His soul became a spark that rose to the sky and settled in the form of Venus, the morning star. In this guise, Quetzalcóatl was known as Ce Ácatl or Tlahuizcalpantecuhtli: he was a malign force, the enemy of the sun. He was also feared and revered – in the form of Xólotl – as Venus the evening star.

Below: A figurine from Teotihuacán shows Quetzalcóatl in human form but with a serpent's divided tongue.

Above: This turquoise and shell mask has holes in the eyes to allow the wearer to see and was probably worn by a priest.

THE END OF TOLLÁN

Another version of the myth describes how Topiltzin-Quetzalcóatl left the city, made a penitential procession to the seacoast and departed on a raft made of snakes, bound for the land of Tlapallán, whence he had originally come. First he burned the splendid buildings of Tollán, then buried the great treasures and artworks for which his reign was famous in the deep mountain valleys nearby. He transformed the cacao trees that had grown in the city into mesquites and commanded the beautiful bird that had graced Tollán to depart a great distance. Tollán was bereft of its leader and of its beauty. An era had ended.

Topiltzin-Quetzalcóatl departed, with a troop of palace assistants and pages following in his footsteps. After some hours of walking and exhausted by grief, he stopped at a place called Quauhtitlán. He asked his assistant to hand him a mirror and, examining his reflection, sighed deeply. 'I am old,' he said quietly, and handed the mirror back to his assistant. The pages were weeping, because of the king's inexplicable wrongdoing and because they understood that, in this time-bound physical world, what is perfect and true, like the era of Topiltzin-Quetzalcóatl's rule in Tollán, cannot endure for ever. The dark shadow of Tezcatlipoca is behind every beam of light. The place was ever afterwards known as Huehuequauhtitlán ('Old Quauhtitlán') because the king saw his aged face there and was saddened. They went on then, with one of the palace musicians playing a mournful air on the flute like the victim who impersonated Tezcatlipoca in the festival of Tóxcatl. When Topiltzin-Quetzalcóatl was too tired to go further, he sat on a roadside

rock, again sighing deeply. The god-prince left the mark of his hands in this stone, and the place was afterwards known as Temacpalco ('The Imprint of Hands').

They went on again when Topiltzin-Quetzalcóatl was rested. At Coaapán they met a group of Aztec deities who asked the god-prince where he was going and for what reason. He replied that he was going back to his place of origin, Tlapallán, because his father the sun had called him home. The gods allowed him to pass, but demanded that Quetzalcóatl deliver the secrets of his divine magic; the supreme spells that lay behind the creation of the wonders of his rule in Tollán. Topiltzin-Quetzalcóatl refused and threw all his spells into the fountain named Cozcaapa.

The procession of penitents came to a high pass close to a volcano in the Sierra Nevada mountains. It was too cold in this forlorn spot for mere mortals and all of the palace followers died, leaving Topiltzin-Quetzalcóatl to mourn them with singing and flute-playing of the most exquisite beauty. He climbed to the peak of Mount Poyauhtécatl, then went down to the far side by sliding. He came at last, and alone, to the shore of the Eastern Sea (which today is known as the Gulf of Mexico) and here summoned the snakes of the entire coastal region. From them he made a raft and then he threw the magical vessel made of snakes on to the waters. He departed for Tlapallán on his snake raft. Those who await his return know that he will come back in the same way, by sea, to found anew the glorious kingdom of Tollán.

It has often been suggested that Moctezuma believed Hernán Cortés to be the returning divinity Topiltzin-Quetzalcóatl and that it was for this reason he treated the Spanish conquistadors with reverence rather than the suspicion they merited. It was a happy coincidence for the Spanish invaders that they arrived in the year 1-Reed, which had been prophesied as the year in which the god would return, and that the first encounter between Cortés and Moctezuma took place on Quetzalcóatl's name day. The *tlatoani* received a gift of wine and biscuits from Cortés, but refused them and sent them to be buried in the temple of Quetzalcóatl at Tollán in honour of the god 'whose sons have arrived'. According to Bernardino de Sahagún, when Moctezuma greeted Cortés with a splendid speech at the gates of Tenochtitlán, he declared that the arriving leader had come from the 'unknown…a place of mystery'.

Above: This powerful statue of Quetzalcóatl in his guise as Éhecatl, lord of the winds, was found in Calixtlahuaca, Mexico.

Below: A 3rd-century BC bas-relief celebrates the life-giving force and regal power of the ancient Plumed Serpent.

THE TRIBAL WAR GOD

The Aztecs' patron god, deity of war and of the sun, was a fierce warrior from the first moment of his life. According to the myth of his birth, Huitzilopochtli came from his mother's womb fully armed. His mother was the earth goddess Coatlícue, who in one account also mothered Quetzalcóatl. Coatlícue was priestess of a shrine high on the mountain at Coatepec, near the Toltec capital of Tollán or Tula. One day, as she was cleaning the shrine, she saw a ball of brightly coloured feathers descend on to her breast. She thought little of it, but rather than discard the feathers she placed them in her belt. However, when she next looked she found out that the ball had disappeared and soon afterwards she discovered the feathers had miraculously made her pregnant.

A PROTECTIVE SON

Coatlícue's existing children included one daughter, the moon goddess Coyolxauhqui, and sons almost beyond counting, the Centzonhuitznahuac ('The Four Hundred Southerners'). When they saw their mother was pregnant they were angry, for they were suspicious of her claim that the pregnancy was a miracle and suspected that she had been promiscuous. The children gathered at the foot of the mountain and Coyolxauhqui convinced her brothers to punish their mother by putting her to death. High above in her mountain shrine, Coatlícue heard their raised voices and knew what they were planning. She shivered with fear, but then heard a voice issuing from her womb: she must not be afraid, the voice said, for her new child would protect her.

When Coyolxauhqui and the Four Hundred Southerners arrived to launch their attack, Huitzilopochtli emerged to repel them. His skin was painted blue and he wore the body armour that would later be adopted by Aztec warriors. The bright feathers of the hummingbird – the same feathers that had fallen in a ball on to the chest of Coatlícue – covered his left leg. This justified his name of 'Hummingbird of the Left'. With the *xiuhcóatl* or fire-serpent he held in his hand, he cut Coyolxauhqui into many pieces. These fell down the mountainside and landed, all jumbled up, on the plain below. Then he killed his brothers, left and right, allowing a few bedraggled survivors to escape to the south.

Above: Huitzilopochtli's mother Coatlícue represents the surface of the Earth and its power to bring life from the death of winter.

Below: The xiuhcóatl *or fire-serpent brandished by Huitzilopochtli forms the motif on this mosaic disc from Chichén Itzá.*

VICTORY FOR THE SUN

The myth proclaims the primacy of the sun, represented by Huitzilopochtli, over his moon sister Coyolxauhqui. The weapon the sun god used was the fire-serpent which was believed to guide the sun across the sky by day. His mother is the serpent-skirted earth from which the sun appears to issue each dawn, and the Four Hundred Southerners are the southern stars of the night sky that are routed every morning as the light of the sun spreads far and wide.

This victory was commemorated in a celebrated sculpture of Coyolxauhqui's dismembered body that lay at the foot of the steps of the Great Pyramid in Tenochtitlán, where the bodies of sacrificial victims landed. The tale of sun and moon deities Huizilopochtli and Coyolxauhqui is therefore a variation on the myth of the creation of the sun and

Below: This sculpture of Coyolxauhqui's massacred body received the blood of many victims that poured off the Great Pyramid.

The heart was termed 'eagle cactus fruit' and the gaping body of the victim was called the 'eagle man'. The 'Eagle' was considered an appropriate title for brave Aztec warriors because the bird was sacred to the war god.

A surviving Aztec hymn to Huitzilopochtli praises him as a young warrior dressed in yellow feathers who makes the sun appear. It praises the god for moving the sun across the heavens and associates him with the god Nanahuatzin when it declares, 'Here he comes forward, one well dressed in paper, who lives in the place that burns.'

Below: The fire serpent is celebrated in this Aztec sculpture at Tenayuca.

Above: Made from stone, with shell eyes and obsidian for the eyeballs, this arresting mask evokes qualities of youthful vigour.

moon at Teotihuacán and of the enmity born there between the sun, Nanahuatzin and the moon, Tecuciztécatl. The story of Huitzilopochtli's birth also celebrates and establishes the Aztec tradition of martial vigour, conflict and bloodletting.

Spanish chroniclers have likened Huitzilopochtli to Hercules, the mythical Greek hero who performed twelve wondrous 'labours' or feats of strength and bravery. Huitzilopochtli was usually depicted wearing a plume of humming-bird feathers on his head, with his face, arms and legs painted with blue stripes. He carried four spears in one hand and a reed shield bearing five tufts of eagle's down on his other arm. The spears had eagle's down rather than the usual hard flint at their tips.

EAGLE IMAGERY

The eagle was principal among the creatures associated with the war and sun god, and eagle imagery played a major part in acts of ritual human sacrifice performed in Huitzilopochtli's honour in which the human heart was torn out. When the priest removed the heart from the victim's flayed chest, he held it up to the sun in triumphant dedication, then flung it into one of the *cuauhxicalli* ('eagle vessels') placed nearby.

HUMMINGBIRD OF THE LEFT

Huitzilopochtli, the Aztecs' war and sun god, had no antecedents among the deities of earlier Mesoamerican peoples. According to their own origin myths, Huitzilopochtli travelled south with the Méxica or Aztecs when they entered the Valley of Mexico from the less hospitable lands to the north. In some accounts he led the tribe on its migration, in others his idol was carried by a group of four priests and made several divine prophecies of their coming greatness.

DUALITY OF LIFE AND DEATH

The Aztecs took care to establish their god's standing alongside older Mesoamerican deities. At the top of the Great Pyramid in Tenochtitlán, a shrine to Huitzilopochtli stood alongside one to the rain god Tláloc, one of the oldest gods of the region. In Huitzilopochtli's temple a sacred flame burned that had to be kept alight at all costs. The Aztecs understood that if it were allowed to die then their power and ascendancy over the other peoples of the region would abruptly come to an end. Twin temples to a rain god and a war god symbolized the duality of life and death. It also symbolized the incompatible opposition of water and fire, which the Aztecs used as an image for war. The Great Pyramid in the sacred complex at Tenochtitlán was intended as a recreation in stone of the hill of Coatepec ('Serpent Mountain'), where the tribal god was born, and of Mount Tonacatépetl, where the staple food maize was discovered, as well as of Mount Tláloc, the peak sacred to the rain god, on which important fertility and rain festivals were held.

Huitzilopochtli's own standing was further bolstered by the god's identification with south, the sacred direction of Blue Tezcatlipoca, one of the four creator-sons of the lord of duality Ometeotl.

Right: The god Huitzilopochtli's mother, Coatlicue, was believed to take the bodies of the dead.

HUMMINGBIRDS

Huitzilopochtli's name means 'Hummingbird of the Left'. Left was used in the Aztecs' Nahuatl tongue to refer to south, the region with which hummingbirds were associated. Hummingbirds were connected to blood sacrifice, for the blood let by the priest from his own body or that of a sacrificial victim was compared to the nectar drawn by a hummingbird from a flower. The birds also became connected to war. The souls of warriors killed in battle were said to take the form of hummingbirds and to accompany the sun in its climb each morning from the dawn horizon to its zenith.

Huitzilopochtli occupied a primary position in Aztec religious life. The festival of Panquetzalíztli ('Lifting of the Banners'), which was held in November and December in Huitzilopochtli's honour, was one of the most important of the Aztec year. Although none survives, we know from documentary evidence that major statues of Huitzilopochtli stood in the sacred precinct of Tenochtitlán and in the main religious areas of Texcoco and Tlatelolco.

Above: Some authorities identify this highly polished obsidian mask as an image of Ixtilton, Huitzilopochtli's lieutenant.

LADY OF DISCORD

Huitzilopochtli was thirsty for human blood and many thousands of human victims were slain in his honour by the Aztecs. The majority were prisoners of the wars that the god promoted, but on occasion he demanded other victims.

A tale recounted by Fray Diego Durán in *The History of the Indies of New Spain* paints a vivid picture of the personal horror associated with these religious rites. Before they reached Tenochtitlán, the Méxica/Aztecs were living near Culhuacán. Durán reports that Huitzilopochtli wanted to foster discord, so he declared that he required the princess of Culhuacán to serve him. Her honouring of the god would provoke unrest between the Aztecs and the uolhua and she would become known as 'Lady of Discord'.

The Aztecs went faithfully to the ruler of Culhuacán, Achitometl, and declared that his daughter had been chosen by the Aztecs' ruling deity to be his bride, to rule as a living goddess. Achitometl agreed, because he was dazzled by the prospect of having a goddess as a daughter. The Aztecs then took the princess to their temple, where, following Huitzilopochtli's urging, they sacrificed her. They flayed her, then dressed one of the priests in her skin and arrayed her in royal garments. They then asked Achitometl to come to see his daughter in her guise as a living goddess. The king was proud and came with many of the leading men and women of Culhuacán to see his daughter and make sacrifices to her.

He went gladly into the temple and made many sacrifices before the altar. The atmosphere was gloomy and the king could not see far beyond his hands, which were busy preparing quails for sacrifice. But when he threw incense into the fire, the flames flared up suddenly and he saw a truly horrific sight: his daughter's skin ripped from her body and worn as a cloak by a priest who was sitting just a few feet away beside the altar. Achitometl ran from the temple, maddened with grief, and calling on his kinsmen to avenge the cruel slaughter of his daughter. They drove the Aztecs out. The travellers continued their search for a permanent home.

Above: The Codex Tudela *(c.1550) graphically illustrates a priest tearing open a victim's chest and wrenching out his heart as blood flows down the temple steps.*

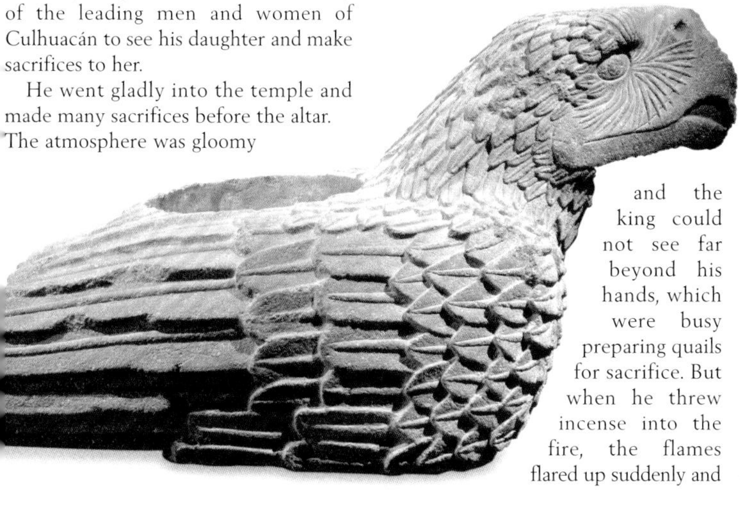

Left: Symbol of the sun and of a warrior elite, the eagle received the blood of sacrifice. Stone eagle vessels were used to store victims' hearts and blood.

DIVINE CREATURES

Animals were revered as manifestations of divine power from the first days of Mesoamerican civilization. From the time of the Olmecs in *c.*1500BC the fearsome jaguar was a cult object and its features were carved on sacred sculptures. The unknown builders of Teotihuacán in *c.*100BC decorated a temple with jaguar images. In the Classic Maya Period the jaguar had divine and regal associations and many Maya kings took the name jaguar as part of their title.

ANIMALS AND GODS

Mesoamerican deities took several guises simultaneously and many had more than one animal form. The Plumed Serpent Quetzalcóatl could be a brilliantly feathered quetzal bird or a serpent, but equally he was associated with the dog in his form as Xólotl, the god of monsters and twin forms; Tezcatlipoca could roam the earth as a jaguar and he was often depicted wearing a spotted jaguar skin, but he was also at times the coyote, an animal associated by the Aztecs with sexual potency – the 'Lord of the Smoking Mirror' assumed this form in his guise as a patron god of males. Moreover, just as a god could take the form of more than one animal, so an animal could be associated with more than one god. The coyote was also Huehuecóyotl ('Old Old Coyote'): men prayed to this deity to be granted health and virility and to enjoy a long life.

Below: Deer and jaguar were among the first creatures made in the Popol Vuh. *A Maya deer pot was found in El Petén.*

Below: The knotted form of this Aztec stone snake (c.1500) is suggestive of vitality.

For the Aztecs the serpent was a profoundly important religious symbol: of fertility and life-giving waters, of sacrificial blood, of skill and cunning. The Maya held the turtle in high regard: some creation myths told that the earth floated on the back of a great turtle and in some images from painted vases the turtle represents the earth.

The Aztecs worshipped and feared rabbit gods as the patrons of drunkenness. According to Aztec myth, a rabbit discovered the intoxicating secrets of the alcoholic drink *pulque* when it bit into the maguey cactus from which the liquor was made. A god known by the date name 2-rabbit was one of the patrons of *pulque*, while the members of the group known as the 'Four Hundred Rabbits' were the gods of drunkenness. In the *Popol Vuh* of the Quiché Maya these same deities were not rabbits, but an early form of humans: known as the Four Hundred Boys, they were defeated and killed by Zipacná, Maker of Mountains, then rose to become the Pleiades constellation.

The Quiché Maya envisaged One Monkey and One Artisan, the divine half-brothers of the Hero Twins Hunahpú and Xbalanqué, as monkeys. When the Hero Twins were first born, One Monkey and One Artisan treated their new brothers cruelly, but the new arrivals got their revenge by tricking their older siblings into climbing a tree, marooning them there and turning them into monkeys. One Monkey and One Artisan were linked to the arts and sedentary pursuits while the Hero Twins – expert hunters with their blowpipes – were keen outdoorsmen. Classic-Period Maya vases and codices often represent deities with human bodies and monkey heads, who are regularly shown writing in or reading from codices; they have been identified as patron gods not only of the Maya scribes, but also of other artists such as musicians, dancers and painters.

The power of the great predator cats is attributed to the Hero Twins – it is fitting that such celebrated hunters should be honoured for having the attributes of the animals they had to mimic in order to understand and kill. Maya vases generally show Hunahpú with spotted skin and Xbalanqué with patches of jaguar pelt on his skin.

Other animal deities depicted on Classic Maya vases and in codices were the vulture god and the fox god. The vulture god seems to have been a patron deity of Maya rulers and scribes – his head is used in inscriptions as a substitute for the word 'king', while in several codex illustrations scribes with the vulture god's face are depicted at work on bark books or holding pens. The fox god might have been a divine guide for those making pots and related wares – he is shown with implements suitable for carving in clay protruding from his headdress where scribes normally kept their pens. Curiously a rabbit god also appears to have been associated with scribes and book-making and in this Maya context had none of the animal's associations with drunkenness found elsewhere in Mesoamerica. The Mesoamericans believed they saw a rabbit in the markings on the face of the Moon and the animal was often depicted with the Maya moon goddess Ix Chel – a carving from Copán shows the goddess holding a crouching rabbit deity in her arms.

BIRDS

The hummingbird and eagle were both forms of Huitzilopochtli and other birds had powerful divine associations. The Aztecs associated owls with Tezcatlipoca, with night and sorcery; among the Maya the owl was also a bird of ill omen and was sometimes a guise of the god of death.

The quetzal was a form of the Plumed Serpent, and was associated with regal bearing and wise rulership. The bird's highly prized feathers were worn by many rulers. The loud macaw reminded the Maya of the boastful sun god who was brought down to earth by the Hero Twins in the *Popol Vuh*. The falcon was associated with Hunahpú.

Above: These Aztec images of a dog (left) and a monkey are taken from a codex illustration of the days of the month.

BATS AND THE UNDERWORLD

The Maya associated bats with the frightful scenes of the underworld. When One and Seven Hunahpú and later on the Hero Twins, Hunahpú and Xbalanqué, descend to the underworld of Xibalba in the *Popol Vuh*, they have to pass through a series of tests – one of which is entering the bat house, a dwelling dark and empty of anything save bats flying hither and thither, filling the air with their terrible shrieks. The Hero Twins spend the night in the company of the bats, waiting for dawn: and one of the shrieking bats rips off Hunahpú's head, which rolls on to the underworld ballcourt. These terrible creatures were often represented on Maya funerary vases of the Classic Period.

FISH

Among favourite offerings in Aztec religious rituals were fish and representations of fish. Their symbolic power derived from their association with the lakes and seas, which were presided over by Chalchiúhtlicue. Death by drowning or by diseases associated with water could carry the deceased directly to the heaven ruled by rain god Tláloc.

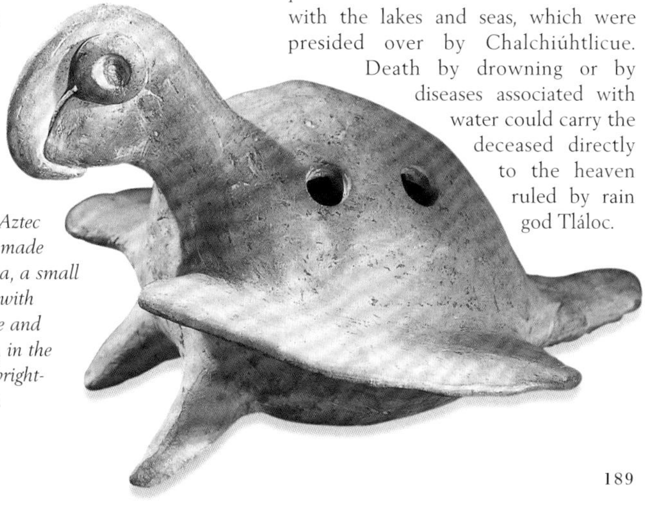

Right: An Aztec craftsman made this ocarina, a small wind-pipe with mouthpiece and fingerholes, in the form of a bright-eyed turtle.

CHAPTER TEN

WATERS, FERTILITY AND HARVEST

In ancient times, long before the Aztecs worshipped their hummingbird war god Huitzilopochtli, Mesoamerican farmers made regular offerings to fertility and water gods hoping to secure frequent rains and a bumper harvest. Major gods of the Aztec period, such as the Plumed Serpent, Quetzalcóatl, and Lord of the Smoking Mirror, Tezcatlipoca, developed from primordial deities whose powers were primarily over rain, waters and the fertility of the land – sky gods with the power to deliver wet winds, storms, lightning and thunderbolts. The cult of the Aztec rain god Tláloc and the Maya rain god Chac can be traced back to the Olmec civilization at La Venta in 800BC.

In the Aztec era, worshippers at the *Templo Mayor* within the sacred precinct in Tenochtitlán brought varied offerings to many gods, especially Huitzilopochtli and Tláloc, whose temples had the prime positions at the top of the pyramid, closest to the sacred sky. But while the two gods shared centre stage in the imperial capital, in most areas – particularly in agricultural communities – worshippers felt more attached to the older cult of the rain god and his associated fertility deities than to the worship of Huitzilopochtli, patron of the war-driven Aztec state and empire.

Left: The Aztec cult of Xochiquetzal – goddess of beauty, love, flowers and the domestic arts – was one of many that grew from ancient Mesoamerican worship of fertility goddesses. This image of Xochiquetzal is from the Codex Vaticanus.

THE SACRIFICE OF BLOOD AND WATER

The cult of the rain god was crucial to Mesoamerican religion. In the *Codex Borgia*, for example, the Aztec universe is represented with five figures of Tláloc, Aztec god of rains; one stands in the east, one in the north, one in the south and one in the west, with a fifth in the centre. This cosmic map is comparable to other similar representations of the Earth divided into four quarters and a centre. In other versions of the map, each place is associated with a different god and also with a different one of the five suns or world ages. In the Borgia version, each of the Tláloc figures is standing on an image of the earth goddess suggesting that, in every place and in every age, the relationship between the fields and the clouds, the land and the sky, the earth and the rain, is of prime importance.

Below: The temples of the ancient god Tláloc and the Aztec tribal deity Huitzilopochtli stand side by side at the Templo Mayor *in Tenochtitlán, in this fanciful print by Fumagalli.*

FERTILITY FOR THE EARTH

Even the demand for sacrificial human blood by Huitzilopochtli and other deities was driven by the desire to guarantee the fertility of the earth. The Aztecs equated blood and water: human blood was the precious liquid that sustained life as water was to the earth. This religious understanding was given symbolic form in sacrifices to the Aztec spring and vegetation god Xipe Totec, whose victims were often shot with arrows rather than despatched by another method of sacrifice. They were tied to frames and as the blood flowed from their wounds it dripped on to a stone that symbolically stood for the thirsty earth, just as the rains fed new growth each spring for Xipe Totec. Similarly, the reclining *chacmool* figures on which priests placed the hearts of sacrificial victims were representations of Tláloc. The mask visible over the eyes and mouth on the *chacmools* identifies them as images of the rain god.

Above: A priestly coat of shells must have made as much an audible impression as a visual impact during religious ceremonies.

THE ENDING OF WATER

Tláloc was honoured with human blood sacrifice in the festival of Atlcahualo ('The Ending of Water'), which took place in the first month of the Aztec year (14 February–5 March in the Western calendar). Children and young people were sacrificed in his honour and that of his consort Chalchiúhtlicue. The rain god's cult was strongly associated with the fertility of the land. The importance of rain to farmers meant that priests of

Above: Water goddess Chalchiúhtlicue is missing her face and hands because she was deliberately damaged by zealous Spaniards.

Tláloc played a crucial role in agricultural and fertility festivals such as Ochpaniztli ('Clearing'), which took place in September. The priests would make obeisances before Tláloc's image while wearing an elaborate costume. This included a Tláloc serpent mask and a one-shaped headdress decorated with bark paper strips, a snake sceptre and a bag of copal.

Tláloc's name derives from Nahuatl *tlalli* ('the earth') and *oc*, used as a suffix to denote something settling above or on the surface of an object. At the start of the rainy season clouds collected above the surface of the earth, rising from the canyons and floating up to jostle one another in the thin air around the mountain peaks. At shrines to Tláloc and Chalchiúhtlicue, piles of boulders represented the deities, who were associated with the mountaintops that appeared to summon the long-awaited rain-clouds.

ANNUAL PILGRIMAGE FOR WATER

One of the peaks visible from Tenochtitlán was named in Tláloc's honour and the rulers of the Valley's principal cities made an annual pilgrimage to a shrine on the mountain in the dry season of April and May. Offerings to Tláloc and Chalchiúhtlicue were regularly made in sacred caves high on the mountainsides. For example, a figure of Tláloc fashioned from sticks and covered in resin and copal was found in a cavern on the volcano Ixtaccíhuatl. Scholars believe that figures such as this would normally have been burned at the ends of the rituals and worshippers might have believed that the dark, holy smoke made by the resin and copal had the power to 'blacken' the clouds, turning windblown white travellers into dark clouds laden with rain.

NECESSARY EQUILIBRIUM

Tláloc did not always hold droughts at bay. The forces of dryness and wetness, rains and drought were balanced in a proper equilibrium. Blood sacrifices were necessary, not to propitiate the rain god or ease his anger, but to maintain this equilibrium. An intriguing greenstone figure discovered at Tlatilco and dating to *c.*1500 appears to be a three-dimensional representation of this concept. The figure's face is divided in two down the middle: one half wears the distinctive 'goggles' of Tláloc and has that god's snake-fang mouth, while the other suggests a smooth-faced young man, thought to represent drought. Together the two halves suggest the proper balance of the seasons in the Mesoamerican farming year. So long as the balance of the seasons held, all was well. If calamity struck it was not because part of the year was dry but because the drought did not end; because the equilibrium had been disturbed. Sacrifice was needed to maintain the flow of divine energy in the cosmos.

Above: Images of Xipe Totec, the god presiding over the germination of seeds, often show him with a crenellated headdress.

Right: Chacmool figures are sacred to Tláloc. The goggle eyes and mouth ornament link them to the rain god.

ANCIENT LIFEGIVERS

Worship of the rain god probably went back to the dawn of Mesoamerican civilization. From the earliest settlements, farmers feared the long and harsh droughts that periodically afflicted the region, bringing humankind's best efforts to nothing. They fervently worshipped the rain god to bring the end of drought and to provide lush crops. He was revered under various names by different peoples and in different periods. To the Maya he was Chac; to the Zapotecs he was Cocijo; to the Totonacs he was Tajín and to the Aztecs he was Tláloc. He was generally regarded as chief of the fertility gods, with dominion over lesser deities of the fields, flowers and crops, including maize.

FOUR GREAT JARS

Like many Aztec gods, Tláloc had a dual nature, bringing both good and bad. He could deliver drought and frosts as well as fertilizing downpours and brought welcome and unwelcome forms of rain – the gentler rains that fed the land and the torrential storms that made the lands flood and spoiled the crops where they stood in the fields. He governed lightning strikes and could also send disease. The Aztecs believed that Tláloc had four great jars, one for each of the four cardinal points. From the jar of the east he brought fruitful rains to Mesoamerica but from the others he unleashed disease, freezing conditions and drought.

The Aztecs also believed that Tláloc stored rainwater in the mountains that towered over the Valley of Mexico and that he was the god of running waters in the mountains. One myth tells how he sends his helpers, the *tláloques*, to collect water from the mountains in sacred vessels. With their way cleared by the wind god Éhecatl-Quetzalcóatl, they carry the water to the vault of the sky where it forms into rain-bearing clouds.

The *tláloques* could bring five types of rain. In addition to life-giving rain to nourish the crops, they also brought unwanted storms whose winds and lashing rains flattened plants, fungal rain that caused diseases in the maize, flint rain (probably hail or hard driving rain) that pummelled plants, and fire rain, which probably referred to the rain that accompanies lightning storms or to the absence of rain in times of drought.

The serpent imagery, so important in Mesoamerica, was powerfully connected to fertility and was central to the cult of Tláloc. The god's face was often depicted made of snakes, with two curled serpents representing the eyes and joining in the centre as the nose and a snake 'moustache' above the mouth. Two large serpent fangs usually appeared from his mouth. He always wore outsize ear ornaments and usually had a hat with several points that stood for the mountains in which he stored water.

Above: This figure of the Aztec rain god Tláloc wears the very large ear decorations usually associated with the god.

CHAC, THE MAYA RAIN GOD

The Maya rain god Chac shared many characteristics with the Aztec Tláloc. It is thought the 'two' gods had a common ancestor in Olmec religion and even earlier worship.

Right: A figurine of the Maya rain god Chac has the god's characteristic prominent nose.

Left: Stylized forms of toads flank an abstract image of the rain god Chac on a terracotta plate found at Tikal.

Like Tláloc, Chac was god of lightning nd mountain streams as well as of rains, nd had helpers (called the *chacs* by the /laya) to assist him in his work. Chac was hown with a long nose, like a spout for ouring rainwater over the thirsty earth. He often had T-shaped eyes, representing ain falling from the sky. A remarkable omage to Chac was carved at Kabah near Uxmal), where the building known s the Temple of the Masks is covered along its 50m- (150ft-) length with long-snouted faces of the rain god. The worship of the rain god was popular everywhere among the Maya. At Chichén Itzá, many offerings thrown into the sacred well (*cenote*) were made to Chac. The god is probably the most frequently represented in the Maya pantheon. Kings often wore the rain-god's mask in the Classic Period. The Hauberg stela of AD199, the earliest surviving artefact to bear writing in the Maya system, depicts a king wearing the mask of Chac.

THE RAIN GOD'S HELPERS

The rain god's helpers, the *chacs*, were assigned one to each of the four cardinal points. They are often depicted in Maya codices pouring out the waters of life from heavy vessels. Among the Yucatec Maya *chacs* were considered to be old men.

The *chacs* were also gods of thunder and stone axes were believed to be their thunderbolts. As among the Aztecs, worshippers burned copal resin incense – called *pom* by the Maya – to create black clouds of smoke that they believed had the power to call forth the larger rain-bearing black clouds in the sky.

Right: Tláloc images characteristically have protruding fangs. This squat green stone vessel dates from c.AD200.

RAIN SUN AND WATER SUN

In one version of the Aztec creation story, the rain god Tláloc and his consort Chalchiúhtlicue were created by White Tezcatlipoca (Quetzalcóatl) and by Blue Tezcatlipoca (Huitzilopochtli) from parts of the body of the Earth Monster. Other parts were used to create the sky and earth. Tláloc then presided over the third sun or world age, the 'Rain Sun' (*Nahui Quiahuitl*). Chalchiúhtlicue was in charge of the fourth age, the 'Water Sun' (*Nahui Atl*). Tláloc also presided over one of the Aztec heavens: Tlalocán, a place of bliss where drought was not known, where waters and foods were plentiful and cocoa drinks could be made and enjoyed at leisure.

GODDESS OF THE WATERS

The goddess Chalchiúhtlicue was the deity of lakes, the ocean, rivers and streams. She was often represented wearing green or blue-and-white clothes and a hairband or crown of blue reeds. She was usually said to be Tláloc's wife, but was sometimes identified as his daughter or sister.

Chalchiúhtlicue was hailed as 'Mistress of the Jade Skirt' and 'Lady of the Lakes and Ocean' and sometimes wore seashells on her blue dresses. A necklace made of precious stones – usually jade beads – adorned her neck and she often wore either a delicate mosaic of turquoise over her ears or circular earrings. She also often wore a turquoise nose-ring. The Aztecs associated turquoise with the sky and the ocean and so held it particularly sacred to Tláloc and Chalchiúhtlicue. Members of the Aztec *pipiltin* (nobility) wore turquoise ornaments to signal their devotion to Tláloc and his consort.

Chalchiúhtlicue's connection to the expanses of water made her the patron goddess of fishermen and of water-carriers. Many Aztec images of Tláloc were carved of green jadeite, which the Aztecs called *chalchiuitl.*

Images of Chalchiúhtlicue sometimes represent her as a frog, a creature sacred to and specially protected by Tláloc. On the rain god's festival day, priests would leap into Lake Texcoco, calling and kicking like frogs.

More commonly, Tláloc's impersonator-priests would wear his easily recognizable mask, with goggle eyes, an upper lip ornament and fanged mouth, and sport a fine headdress of heron feathers.

Left: This Tláloc pot was deposited as an offering to the rain god facing his temple in Tenochtitlán.

They would carry a stalk of corn or a rod to symbolize the lightning that the rain god also controlled. In the mountains where he was known to store his rain-waters, he could be seen in the form of tall-standing boulders. Tláloc's helpers, the *tláloques*, were sometimes said to be the rain god's children by his emerald consort. After Tláloc and the *tláloques* had done their work in the rainy season, the streams controlled by the water goddess rose. Precious water rushed between narrow banks in torrents that made the bare river beds of the dry season a distant memory. Chalchiúhtlicue was also associated with racing streams and whirlpools and was sometimes called 'The Foaming One'. She was represented sitting on a regal throne with water gushing forth about her.

SACRIFICE OF FROGS

In some accounts, Chalchiúhtlicue also had power over strong winds. Out of a clear sky she could summon hurricanes and whirlwinds with a destructive power to equal that of any flash flood. Like Tláloc, the goddess was associated with the fertility of the land, which was facilitated by the waters she controlled. She was also one of the goddesses of the maize plant. In her honour, a frog was sacrificed during the festival of the maize goddess Chicomecóatl. Th

Left: This vast statue of water goddess Chalchiúhtlicue dates from c. AD*150–450, the era of Teotihuacán.*

creature was cooked and placed with a cornstalk and some ground maize before images of the maize goddess to represent the free-flowing waters that were so necessary if the maize was to flourish.

Chalchiúhtlicue's shrines were built alongside streams, rivers and lakes. Her most important place of worship was at Pantitlán, a spot in the middle of Lake Texcoco marked by banners, where a young woman or girl impersonating the goddess was sacrificed during the festival of Huey Tozoztli ('Major Vigil') in the fourth Aztec month (15 April–4 May). The goddess's links to fertility are made clear by this celebration. A tree named Tota ('Father') was carried to Pantitlán on a raft and set up at that spot to symbolize new life and regeneration in the fields surrounding the lake. The 'precious water' of the sacrificial victim's blood was then poured on to the surface of the lake, which the Aztecs hailed as Tonanhuegatl ('Mother Vast Water').

Below: The bulk of this Tláloc statue, found in Mexico City, is suggestive of the awesome power of the storms he controls.

Above: In an image from the Codex Borbonicus, *Tláloc unleashes the rainwaters that the farmers long for.*

Chalchiúhtlicue was envisaged as a beautiful young woman, symbolizing the purity of the water in springs and fast-flowing streams or rivers. Her priestess took the central role in rites that early Spanish missionaries likened to Christian baptism for, among the Aztecs, new parents would take their baby to the priestess of Chalchiúhtlicue, who sprinkled the infant with spring water and dedicated him or her to the goddess.

SACRED ANIMALS

According to some accounts, during the celebration of the festival of Atlcahualo ('The Ending of Water') Tláloc's priests leapt into the waters of Lake Texcoco imitating the movements and calls of the frog, a creature sacred to Tláloc and Chalchiúhtlicue.

The duck was also a holy form of Tláloc. Like Tláloc, it can fly, swim and walk on land, is at home in the air (where Tláloc has power over rains and winds), in the water (where the rain god controls streams, rivers, lakes and oceans through his female counterpart Chalchiúhtlicue) and in the earth (where the rain god's fertilizing waters awaken the life held in the seeds of plants and make possible the germination of life).

Nappatecuhtli was a god associated with Tláloc and Chalchiúhtlicue. He was lord and patron of the respected craftsmen who made mats and thrones from reeds. Nappatecuhtli was depicted wearing a tall headdress decorated with quetzal feathers and strips of bark paper. He was shown holding a reed stick in one hand and a snake sceptre in the other.

THE FLAYED LORD

Like Tláloc, the Aztec god of vegetation and seeds, Xipe Totec, was an ancient deity whose worship was inherited by the Aztecs from earlier Mesoamericans. He was revered by the Zapotec builders of Monte Albán, where images of 'The Flayed Lord' have been found in tombs, and was also worshipped at Teotihuacán.

In Aztec belief, Xipe Totec was one of the four primary gods who were born from the union of Ometecuhtli and Omecíhuatl before the dawn of time. He was the oldest of the four, revered as Red Tezcatlipoca and associated with the east, where the new sun rises. He was the god of new shoots in spring and of the first growth of the maize plant.

Above: Moctezuma receives ambassadors under the watchful eye of a Xipe Totec priest wearing a victim's flayed skin.

FLAYING OF THE MEN

Xipe Totec was honoured with some distinctive and gruesome rites during the Tlacaxipehualiztli festival ('Flaying of the Men'), which was held in the second month of the Aztec year (6–25 March). This marked the start of the agricultural season, when seeds were germinating.

Sacrificial victims to Xipe Totec were shot to death with arrows so that the flow of their blood could symbolically represent the flow of rain on to the fields to nourish the seeds. At the festival's beginning, prisoners of war dressed as Xipe Totec were tied to a sacrificial stone and forced to defend themselves with mock weapons against fully armed warriors. After their death, the victims were flayed from head to toe. Priests then wore the skins over their own bodies for the entire month. Many sculptures of Xipe Totec show him wearing a flayed skin, drawn over his face and body and stitched up at the back. The mask of skin over the face usually allows the mouth and eyes of the wearer to show through.

This gruesome practice was a symbolic celebration of the splitting of seeds in the earth, which is a necessary part of their germination. The essence of plant life within the seed was likened to the essence of Xipe Totec in the sacrificial skin. The rite offered life to the gods to celebrate the renewal of life. Flaying may also have been practised on animals, for archaeologists have found statues of a coyote and a jaguar with their skin flayed along the backbone.

At the end of the festival, the priests divested themselves of the skins and stored them in a chamber within the sacred precinct in Tenochtitlán. For this purpose they used fired-clay bowls decorated with bobbles to suggest the puckered appearance of flayed skin. The bowls had tight-fitting lids to contain the smell of the rotting flesh.

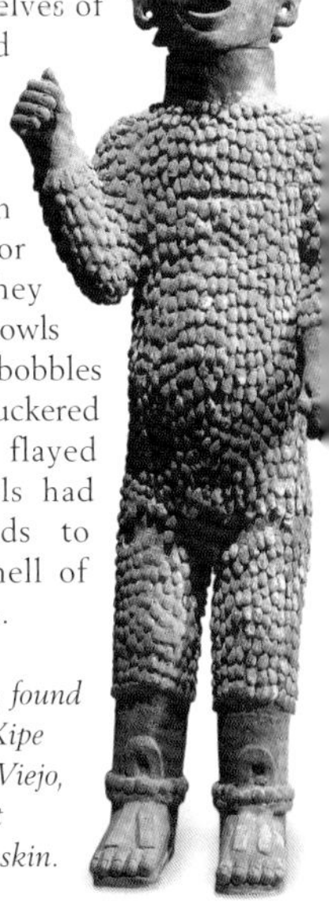

Right: This image, found in an offering to Xipe Totec at Tepeji el Viejo, represents a priest wearing a flayed skin.

Above: *In some accounts, the god of vegetation is said to have invented the arts of war by which the Aztecs thrived.*

A chamber within the temple complex was sacred to Xipe Totec. Called Yopico, it was a man-made cave that had been built to resemble the natural caverns that Mesoamericans understood to be openings to the spirit world and in which they had left religious offerings since time immemorial. Offerings to Xipe Totec were left in Yopico, particularly during the Tlacaxipehualiztli festival. A newly elected *tlatoani* would visit the Yopico temple as part of his coronation rites.

Xipe Totec was often represented holding a *chicahuaztli*, a pointed, hollow staff containing seeds. The staff represented the rays of the sun as they descended from the wide sky to the earth to promote the growth of maize plants. The *chicahuaztli* was also carried by Tláloc's consort Chalchiúhtlicue and by the flower goddess Xochiquetzal, who were both linked to fertility and germination. According to some accounts, sky gods such as Quetzalcóatl and Huitzilopochtli also carried the staff. In bringing maize and other plants to harvest, Xipe Totec had to work in tandem with deities of water such as Chalchiúhtlicue and with sun gods such as Huitzilopochtli.

Mesoamerican gods always had more than one aspect. Just as Tláloc brought both life-giving rain and its opposite, drought, so Xipe Totec gave people the maize crops but also brought diseases such as blindness or the plague.

LOST-WAX GOLD CASTING

Xipe Totec was also the patron god of goldsmiths. Gold objects were often made using the lost-wax casting method and the details of the method explain the god's connection to the craft. First the craftsman made a clay core in the desired shape, then he covered the core with wax before laying another layer of clay on top of the wax. Once the clay was set, two holes were made in the outer clay layer and the molten gold was poured in. As it filled the space between the two layers of clay, it forced the wax out through the other hole. The outer and inner clay layers were then destroyed and the object was revealed.

Scholars believe that this method was associated in the Aztec mind with the layers of earth, then shoots, then taller plants, then full-grown plants that they observed in the maize fields and therefore that Xipe Totec was an appropriate patron for the goldsmiths. Mesoamericans did not view gold as the most precious of all substances as people generally do in the Western tradition, for in their eyes such gold ornaments were no more valuable than the feathers of the quetzal bird or objects made from greenstone, both of which were important symbols of water and life.

Below: A priest wears a sacrificial victim's skin to honour Xipe Totec in the festival of Tlacaxipehualiztli. The hands dangle at the wrists where the priest's arms protrude.

MOTHER EARTH AND HER FLOWERS

Mesoamericans worshipped the fertile earth from the time of their first farming settlements in 7000–5000BC. The earth goddess, provider of food crops, cotton clothes and building materials, was also associated with death, decay and regeneration. She had many names.

Tonantzin was worshipped as a mother of all and associated with the moon. After the Spanish Conquest her cult appears to have been merged with that of the Blessed Virgin Mary. Tonantzin was also known as 'Our Lady' and 'Our Holy Mother'. Indeed, many historians argue that in Mexico's patron saint, the 'Black Virgin of Guadelupe', Tonantzin has survived into the 21st century. Following the peasant Juan Diego's vision of a dark-skinned divinity in 1531 near Mexico City, the Basilica de Guadelupe was built on the very spot where Tonantzin's shrine once stood.

Left: Ancient Mesoamerican religious life was founded in the cult of fertility. This fertility icon was carved by a skilled craftsman of the Huastec culture.

NAMES OF THE MOTHER

The mother goddess was also known under the name Teteoinnan-Toci ('Mother of the Gods and Goddesses' – 'Our Grandmother'). She was depicted with a calm and serene expression and a plaited cotton headdress. She was one of the main deities honoured in the festival of Ochpaniztli ('Clearing') at the start of the harvest season. Ochpaniztli also included the gruesome sacrifice of a young woman to maize goddesses Xilonen and Chicomecóatl.

Another aspect of the earth-mother goddess was Coatlícue ('Serpent-skirted'), who was particularly honoured by the Aztecs as the mother of their tribal god Huitzilopochtli and of the moon goddess Coyolxauhqui. In this form, the goddess made a regular connection with the sky realm since she was believed to give birth each morning to the sun on the eastern horizon in a blaze of red light.

RAPE IN THE UNDERWORLD

The fertility goddess was also the beautiful flower princess Xochiquetzal, who in some accounts was the twin sister of the god of flowers, Xochipilli. She was associated with love and lovemaking and with games, dancing and art as well as the fair flowers of the field. She was the patron of weavers, silversmiths, painters, sculptors and embroiderers, and she was also associated with sexuality, prostitutes, pregnancy and childbirth.

Above: Flower goddess Xochiquetzal was celebrated for her fresh-faced beauty and her patronage of the fine arts.

In another account the goddess Xochiquetzal was married to Tláloc, the god of rains. The divine couple lived in great happiness in the Aztec heavens of Tamoanchán, where Xochiquetzal was mistress, and in Tlalocán, where her husband presided over life after death. However, the shadow god Tezcatlipoca, sower of wicked deeds and lord of the night, was taken with her delicate good looks, the freshness of her appearance in the first light, her innocence and charm. He tried to dazzle her with his dark good looks, but Xochiquetzal only turned lightly away to look for her husband. Then Tezcatlipoca seized the goddess and carried her off to the underworld. The awful skeletal rulers of that realm, Mictlantecuhtli and Mictecacíhuatl, turned a blind eye when, in a wicked hour, Tezcatlipoca forced himself on the flower goddess. Afterwards he was weakened by his lust and Xochiquetzal was able to escape her captor to return

Above: Xochiquetzal was goddess of sexual beauty and lovemaking as well as being the princess of the Aztec heaven Tamoanchán.

to her abodes in the earth and sky above. Scholars suggest that the ravishing of Xochiquetzal in the underworld is a narrative representation of the seeming death of plants and flowers in winter that is followed by new life in the spring.

Although Xochiquetzal was said to be mistress of Tamoanchán, she was still subject to higher authority in the form of the supreme lord Ometeotl. One story tells that Xochiquetzal was banished from heaven when she broke an interdiction against touching a flowering tree in the midst of that realm. After that sad event she was sent to earth and known as Ixnextli ('Ash Eyes').

GODDESS OF FILTH AND PURIFICATION

The goddess Tlazoltéotl embodied unsettling dual aspects of the fertility-mother goddess. She was both the goddess of filth and the patron deity of childbirth, an all-encompassing mother figure and sponsor of sexual excess, associated not only with lustful degradation but also with purification. A celebrated statuette (*c.*1300–1500) depicts her in the act of giving birth, the pain and exhilaration of the experience making an ecstatic mask of her face as the baby appears between her legs.

Tlazoltéotl struck men and women with the diseases associated with sexual promiscuity, yet the goddess was also associated with purification and with new beginnings. Her priestess would hear the confessions of penitents and prescribe rites of self-sacrifice and self-abnegation to guarantee forgiveness and a new beginning.

In some accounts, Tlazoltéotl was the mother of the flower goddess Xochiquetzal and of the maize god Centéotl. This aspect of the mother goddess was imported to Aztec territories: Tlazoltéotl was originally the mother goddess of the Huastec people from the lands bordering the Gulf of Mexico.

In the form of Yohualtecuhtli, the mother goddess was patron of sweatbaths. These were tiny buildings built alongside a cold pool. Users would dash water scented with herbs on to hot stones, creating a sweet-smelling steam. After sweating for a while and also performing ritual incantations, they would leave the building and take a cold plunge in the pool.

Below: Xochipilli, the flower prince, is depicted fishing for a jewel in this image from the Codex Vaticanus.

THE GODS OF MAIZE

The 'Young Maize God', a youthful figure with an elongated head in the shape of an ear of maize, makes frequent appearances on Classic Period Maya vases, usually in the company of an identical twin. These gods have been identified as Classic Period equivalents of One Hunahpú and Seven Hunahpú, the father and uncle respectively of the Hero Twins of the *Popol Vuh*.

RAISING THE WORLD TREE

Among the Maya, the maize god was a deity of supreme importance, sometimes perhaps even the creator. Scholars who have attempted to piece together Classic Period Maya creation narratives from finds at Tikal, Izapa, Palenque and Quirigua suggest that in these myths the maize god descended to the underworld and was reborn as the creator of the current world age. He rose into the sky and raised the world tree that holds the centre of the earth and anchors the four directions. In this guise he is probably the god referred to at Quirigua as Wak-Chan Ahaw ('Lord of the Lifted-up Sky'), for Palenque inscriptions call the World Tree Wakah Chan ('Lifted-up Sky'). At times the Maya envisaged the world tree itself as a maize plant. The carvings at Palenque show both the world tree and a second tree, the tree of the foliated cross, which has images of the maize god's head in its branches.

Below: Yum Caax, or the 'Master of the Fields in Harvest' was the Maya god of the maize.

Left: A brazier, that was found in Tlatelolco honours Xilonen, goddess of maize.

THE STUFF OF LIFE

The Maya maize god was also known as Yum Caax, 'Master of the Fields in Harvest'. A magnificent and floridly carved stone head found at Copán represents either Yum Caax or a king dressed in his guise. At Palenque he was referred to as Hun-Nal-Ye ('One Revealed Sprouting'). He was patron of the number 8 and of the day Kan.

Maize was the Maya's staple food and the very stuff of life. In the *Popol Vuh*, the perfect ancestors of modern humans, who could see and understand all things, were made from maize.

The attributes of the Young Maize God and his twin indicate that they were among the patrons of writing as well as of corn. The twins are often represented at work on codices and with pens and other scribal equipment in their headgear. Scholars suggest that there is an association linking the maize god to writing and that it developed because the bark paper used by scribes was made by soaking bark fibres in just the same way that maize kernels were soaked before being made into dough.

Above: A celebrated image from the Codex Fejérváry-Mayer *depicts four trees, at the four points of the compass, and a fifth in the centre. Each point is associated with a deity. The south is the realm of the vegetation god Xipe Totec; the fire god holds the centre.*

DEITIES FOR DIFFERENT STAGES

The Aztecs worshipped a number of maize deities, some linked to different stages of the maize plant's development. Xilonen ('Young Ear of Maize') was goddess of the tender first shoots of corn, while Chicomecóatl ('Seven Snake') was linked to the two ends of the sowing and harvesting process; the carefully stored seeds and the joyously harvested plants.

A fine statue of Xilonen found at Teloluapan (in modern Guerrero state in Mexico) shows the goddess as a young woman dressed in a cotton headdress and holding two corn-cobs in each hand. In Chicomecóatl's temple in Tenochtitlán, the statue of the goddess shows her as an adolescent girl with arms wide open. Other images show her wearing a vast rectangular headdress or *amacalli* ('paper house') made from twigs and bark paper or holding a *chicahuaztli*, a staff filled with seeds, which celebrated the power of the sun, water and vegetation deities to bring life to maize seeds. This seed-filled *chicahuaztli* doubled as a musical instrument during fertility rites.

*Below: This ceramic whistle (*c.AD*300–900) represents a dancer taking part in a ceremony in honour of the maize deities.*

FLOWER GODS AND GODDESSES

Both Xilonen and Chicomecóatl were associated with the flowers that bloom at the start of the rainy season. Chicomecóatl was honoured in the festival of Huey Tozoztli ('Major Vigil') held in the fourth Aztec month (15 April–4 May). The Aztecs decorated their domestic altars with ears of corn for the festival and the goddess's priests blessed supplies of maize seeds in the temples.

Another maize deity was the god Centéotl, represented as a young man bearing maize in his headgear, his appearance usually dominated by the colour yellow. According to one story, maize, cotton, the sweet potato and other useful plants sprang forth from his buried body. Centéotl was closely linked to Xochipilli, god of plants and flowers, who was also associated with the joyful celebration of life in dance and song. Alongside Xipe Totec, Xochipilli was a divine embodiment of nature's powerful forces of regeneration, the drive that forces green shoots upwards to defeat winter each spring.

A celebrated statue of Xochipilli, found at Tlamanalco on the lower slopes of the great volcano Ixtaccíhuatl, shows him seated cross-legged on a flower-throne with four flowers emanating in the four directions of the universe. Like the Maya maize god, he is depicted holding the centre, embodying the flowering of life in the universe.

Another god who was linked to maize was Xólotl, god of monsters and twins and a twin manifestation of Quetzalcóatl. When the gods elected to sacrifice themselves to bring movement to the newly created sun, Xólotl tried to escape and disguised himself as a double ear of corn.

THE GIFT OF *PULQUE*

Below: The bowl bears the wind serpent symbol. The pulque *cups have the Earth Monster's eye.*

The Four Hundred Boys who were defeated and killed by the Hero Twins in the tale told in the *Popol Vuh* had their counterpart among the Aztecs in the Centzóntotochtin (Four Hundred Rabbits). Both groups were makers and lovers of strong alcoholic drink, were worshipped as gods of drunkenness and they were associated with celestial phenomena. Among the Maya, the Four Hundred Boys were connected to the Pleiades constellation, while the Aztecs linked the Four Hundred Rabbits to the southern stars of the night sky.

In the ritual calendar, the eighth day, *tochtli* ('rabbit'), had associations with drunkenness. The leader of the Four Hundred Rabbits was Ome Tochtli (2-Rabbit) and was known as a god of drunkenness. Other gods among his troupe were Techalotl, Patécatl and Tezcatzontécatl. The deities of drunkenness were particularly associated with the strong alcoholic drink *pulque*, which was made from the fermented sap of the maguey cactus and the root of a bush called 'pulque wood' (or 'wood of the evil one'). Images of *pulque* gods characteristically show them wearing a *yacameztli* ('nose moon'); a nose-ring in the shape of a half-moon that is connected to Tlazoltéotl, the goddess of filth and of sexual lust. They were associated thereby with promiscuous behaviour driven by drunkenness – and associated with rabbits – and also with the lunar cycles of woman's fertility.

Below: The connection of uncontrollable rabbits to the wildness of drunken behaviour is easy to comprehend.

RABBIT IN THE MOON

Rabbits were widely linked to the moon in Mesoamerican culture. The markings on the moon's face were thought to resemble a rabbit. One story of how the rabbit came to live on the moon tells that the moon god Tecuciztécatl shone too brightly in the first nights after the creation of the sun and moon and that the gods threw a rabbit up at his face to prevent him outshining the new sun. According to another version, the gods felt that Tecuciztécatl deserved to be punished, for when the time came for him to sacrifice himself and so create the sun he was fearful and refused three times to enter the fire. In the end, the unappealing god Nanahuatzin performed the sacrifice and became the sun, while Tecuciztécatl was relegated to the role of the moon. The other gods therefore punished Tecuciztécatl by casting a rabbit shadow across his face to dim the glory of his light by night.

THE ORIGINS OF SACRED *PULQUE*

Pulque was highly prized for its use as a sacred intoxicant in religious ritual. Its consumption in everyday life was strictly controlled and public drunkenness was fiercely punished. The patron deity of the *tochtli* day and of the maguey cactus that was used to make *pulque* was the goddess Mayáhuel.

A myth explains the origin of *pulque*. In the first days of the current world age, the great Plumed Serpent Quetzalcóatl watched men and women going about their daily tasks and saw that once the working day was done they did not dance or sing. This great god, who gave humankind so many good things, determined to provide people with a stimulating fermented drink that would quicken their spirits for dancing and joyful celebrations.

In the thirteen tall heavens Quetzalcóatl encountered Mayáhuel, a goddess of enchanting beauty who was

the granddaughter of one of the wicked *tzitzimime* night-demons. The pair fell quickly in love and Quetzalcóatl led Mayáhuel to Mesoamerica, where the two deities expressed their deep mutual devotion by making themselves into a great two-forked tree. However, Mayáhuel's grandmother was burning with anger and followed the couple to earth with a full complement of her fellow *tzitzimime* demons, bringers of sickness and woe. The night-demons swept into the blue sky like a sudden storm and travelled faster than light, following paths of darkness laid down by Tezcatlipoca. At long last they found the bodies of Quetzalcóatl and Mayáhuel entwined in a tree at the heart of a lush oasis. As they swooped down upon the tree it split into its two constituent halves. The sky was yawning wide as the *tzitzimime* poured down to get their revenge. Mayáhuel was torn to pieces by her grandmother and the *tzitzimime* gorged themselves on her flesh. Then, as quickly as they had come, they were gone.

Left: This exquisitely carved image of the Plumed Serpent is made from the fine-grained volcanic rock andesite.

Sorrowfully, Quetzalcóatl gathered the few remains of the goddess he had briefly loved and buried her far beyond the oasis. As he walked, he wept tears of grief that fed the earth. In time, the remnants of the beautiful Mayáhuel grew from the ground in the form of the maguey cactus. Many years passed and men and women learned to make the wonderful *pulque* drink from its sap. And in this way Quetzalcóatl's original purpose was fulfilled.

Below: This Codex Vaticanus *image depicts Mayáhuel (right), goddess of the maguey cactus from which* pulque *was made.*

HOW MAIZE WAS TAMED

One of the many interpretations of the Quiché Maya *Popol Vuh* narrative is that it is a mythical representation of the domestication of maize and the planting of corn in the agricultural cycle. The twin maize gods, One Hunahpú and Seven Hunahpú, went down under the ground into the underworld like seeds of maize.

DIVINE GARDENERS

Another sequence of the cycle tells how the Hero Twins Hunahpú and Xbalanqué became the first inhabitants of Earth to tend the land and raise plants. The episode occurred after the Hero Twins turned their elder brothers One Monkey and One Artisan into monkeys, and these two swung away screeching into the trees. Then Hunahpú and Xbalanqué told their grandmother that they were off to tend the garden. They took their gardening tools with them, and asked their grandmother to bring food for them to eat at lunchtime. Such was their stature as divine ground-breakers that they did not have to sweat and labour over the land as humans later did. They simply stuck their hoes into the ground and their axes into the tree trunks and sat back: the tools set to work, clearing great swathes of forest, levelling mounds of earth, and creating workable fields from the raw jungle.

Left: This Huastec statue depicts Chicomecóatl, the goddess of maize.

The Twins relied on their magic to clear a great plot of land while they spent their time practising their shooting, using the blowpipes they had employed to strike down the boastful Seven Macaw. However, they did not want their grandmother to discover that they were not really labouring over the land, for then she might refuse to give them their food. They asked a dove to call out when it saw the old woman coming.

When the dove uttered its mournful call, the Twins dropped their pipes and picked up their agricultural implements. One took the hoe and rubbed dirt on his face and hands; the other took the axe and liberally sprinkled his hair with woodchips. When the old woman arrived, she suspected nothing and gave them a hearty meal to eat. When she left they dropped their work implements and returned to shooting with their blowpipes.

That evening when they returned home the Twins made a great fuss, complaining of aching limbs and blistered hands and regaling their grandmother with extravagant accounts of how hard they had had to work to clear the land. However, the joke was shortly to rebound on the Twins.

Left: An image of the rain god adorns this colourfully painted vessel of the early Classic Period.

When they returned to their little farm plot the next day they found that the jungle had grown back in a single night and thick vegetation covered their carefully cut and terraced mountainside fields. So they set their tools to work again and cleared a new plot – and that night lay in wait to see what magic had caused the plants to grow so fast.

They discovered that the animals of the place were calling up new jungle growth like a thick cloth to cover the nakedness of the earth. The puma, the jaguar, the rabbit, the deer, the fox, the coyote, the peccary and the rat were responsible for the trick. They sang in the night, 'Rise up and grow tall, trees and bushes, cover the land.'

The Twins tried to catch the creatures. The puma and the jaguar were far too fast and they escaped in a flash. In awe Hunahpú and Xbalanqué watched them go by moonlight. Next came the deer and the rabbit. The Twins did manage to catch these two by the tail for a moment but

Above: An illustration from Bernardino de Sahagún's Florentine Codex *shows an Aztec planting the staple food maize.*

the animals were strong and broke away, each leaving part of its tail in the Twins' hands. For this reason those creatures have little or no tail. The only creature the boys did manage to corner was the rat. They caught him in a net and burned him over a fire to make him talk; ever afterwards the rat had no hairs on its tail.

The rat told the Twins that the field-clearing and farming techniques they had pioneered were not for them to develop and that they had a different destiny. They must follow the twin maize gods One Hunahpú and Seven Hunahpú to the underworld and tame the lords of that dark place. Some scholars believe this narrative to be a dramatization of the necessary move from a purely hunting lifestyle to a form of subsistence that relied both on hunting and domesticated food plants grown in laboriously cleared jungle fields.

CENTÉOTL AND DOMESTICATED MAIZE

The Aztecs had two main versions of the myth that described the discovery and first use of the domesticated maize plant. In one account the Plumed Serpent, Quetzalcóatl, transformed himself into an ant and brought the foodstuff back from the heart of 'food mountain', but in the variant myth the maize god Centéotl was the source of the staple food. The myth described how in the first years of the current world age Piltzintecuhtli, the son of the original human couple Oxomoco and Cipactonal, lived in great happiness with his beautiful wife Xochiquetzal. They had a son, who was named Centéotl. He was of earthy complexion and had ruddy good looks, full of the energy of the land. But despite his apparent good health Centéotl died suddenly and inexplicably – just as winter shrouds the land in lifeless cold. Then Piltzintecuhtli found no comfort in the beauty of his wife Xochiquetzal. He mourned his son long and loudly.

The gods themselves came down from the thirteen heavens and visited the grave of this fine young man. By their great goodness they caused his body to give issue to foods and useful plants, as the earth pushes up plants in spring: maize came from his fingernails and the sweet potato from his fingers, while cotton grew from his hair and other plants of great usefulness sprang from his body. And afterwards Centéotl was one of the many gods of maize revered by the Aztecs. In some versions of the myth Centéotl was the son of the Mesoamerican earth mother. She was known by the names of Teteoinnan or Tocitzin. In yet another account, he and flower goddess Xochiquetzal were the two children of Tlazoltéotl, goddess of childbirth, lust and dirt. Centéotl was also linked to Xochipilli, the flower god; both were strong young men with an abundance of creative energy.

Left: A Zapotec funerary urn, found at Monte Albán, honours the maize god.

SEX, PREGNANCY AND BIRTH

The flower goddess Xochiquetzal was patron of love and lovemaking, and she was also strongly associated with pregnancy and childbirth. According to one myth, she performed the first act of sexual congress, and in another account she was the first woman to give birth to twins.

Xochiquetzal was the archetype of youthful femininity, a young woman of great beauty and voluptuousness, with plentiful sexual allure. Her followers took the form of birds and butterflies. She was also embodied on earth in the first woman, who was fashioned from her hair in order to marry Piltzintecuhtli, the son of the primal couple Oxomoco and Cipactonal. The first woman took the goddess's name and had a son with Piltzintecuhtli named Centéotl, who after his death gave issue to the maize plant and was honoured as the maize god.

Xochiquetzal was the patron goddess of prostitutes. She protected the *ahuianime*, the city prostitutes, and the *maqui*, the priestess-prostitutes who attended to young single warriors and accompanied the soldiers on to the battlefield, where they willingly gave their lives. In some accounts, Xochiquetzal was the first woman to be sacrificed in battle. Her image in the *Codex Cospi* shows her in battle array, carrying a shield and arrows and wearing a warband as well as a garland of corn flowers.

The beautiful goddess enriched the world of men and women by giving flowers to grow on the side of the roadway and the steep mountain paths. These flowers were made from her vulva. In one myth she was wife to Quetzalcóatl or the Plumed Serpent. One day as he was washing himself he allowed his hands to move over his penis and the seeds that spilled forth became the first bat. The gods sent this creature to visit the bountiful Xochiquetzal. It bit the goddess in her vulva and carried a piece of flesh away to the other gods. They made roses from the bat's gift, but these flowers did not smell good. The bat repeated his visit to Xochiquetzal and this time took the flesh to Mictlantecuhtli, the lord of the underworld. This time the roses were as sweet-smelling and beautiful as anyone could wish. These marvellous flowers were the gift of the goddess Xochiquetzal to the peoples of the world.

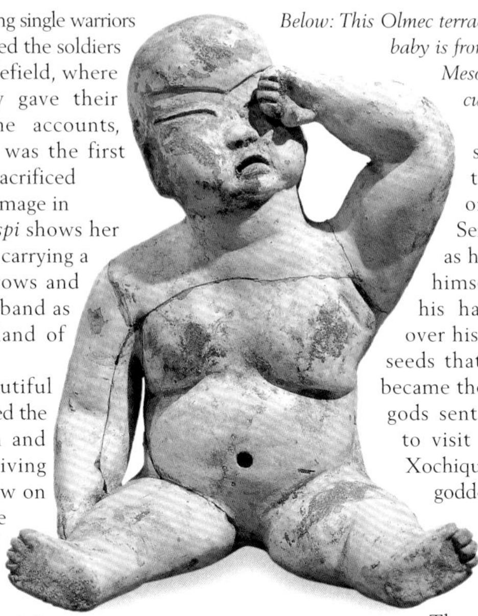

Below: This Olmec terracotta figure of a baby is from the dawn of Mesoamerican culture.

TLAZOLTÉOTL

The form of the mother-fertility goddess most powerfully connected to childbirth was Tlazoltéotl, the goddess of filth, excrement and sexual lust. She was often depicted squatting in the position that Mesoamerican women usually adopted for childbirth. Tlazoltéotl was associated with penitential rites, including the

Left: Tlazoltéotl, squatting in the typical Mesoamerican childbirth position, is a goddess of opposites, associated both with the noise of lust and the quiet of penitence. The image is from the Codex Vaticanus.

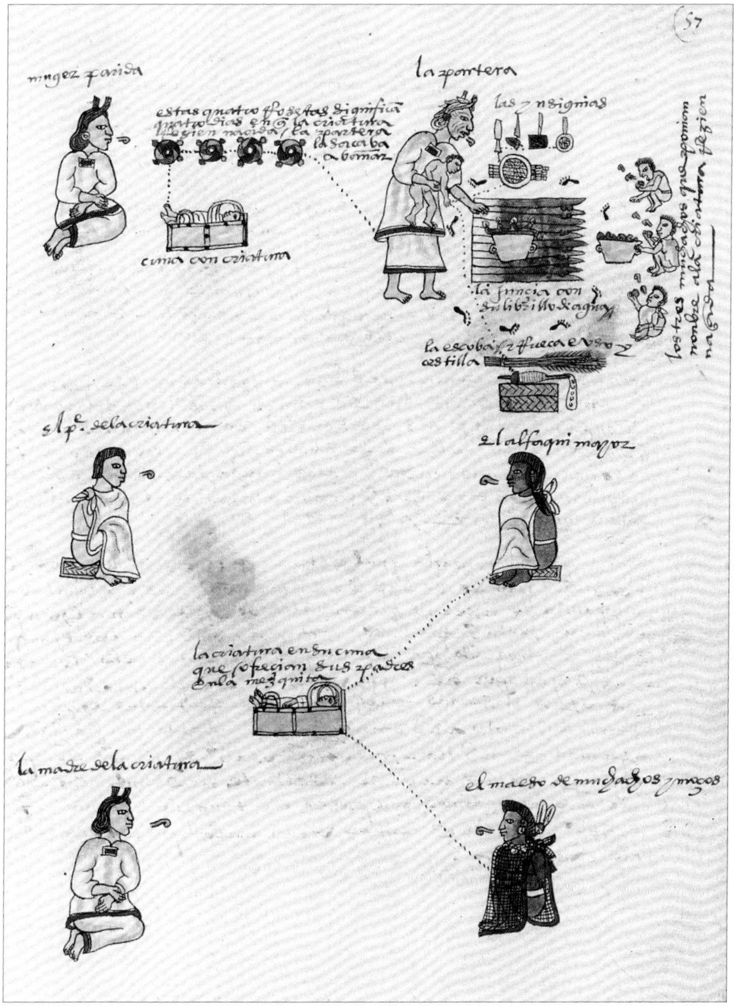

confession of sins. In one myth she was also a great temptress, who used her sexual power to unpick the virtue of a pious man.

This man was determined to win the gods' favour and took himself away from family life to settle on a rocky promontory in the northern desert. The gods wanted to probe the man's commitment, so they despatched the demon Yáotl ('The Enemy'), a much-feared manifestation of Tezcatlipoca, to test him. Yáotl the seducer brought forth a parade of the world's most beautiful women who called up to the pilgrim and tried to tempt him down, if only for a short break from his demanding religious observance. Backwards and forwards they went on the rocky ground, calling up to him and seductively singing the latest songs from the brothels of Tenochtitlán. However, the man refused to look at them and turned back to his sacred rites.

Viewing this from afar, Tlazoltéotl was determined to join in. She came to that inhospitable windswept place dressed in her finest and most seductive outfit and called up sweetly to the man, asking to be allowed to climb the rock for a conversation: perhaps she could learn something from him? Such was her appeal that he agreed to allow her to climb up. When she arrived there beside him she was to him as a breeze to a soldier in the desert, like a sweet and suddenly attainable dream to a man cursed by insomnia, and he succumbed to temptation.

Yáotl then appeared beside the couple and turned the man into a scorpion. Afterwards he fetched the man's wife and brought her to the place, told her the full story of her husband's disgrace and turned her into a scorpion too. They lived on in the desert under a rock and produced many generations of scorpions.

Another Aztec goddess associated with childbirth was Chalchiúhtlicue, wife of Tláloc. She was a patron of newly born children and was believed to protect virtuous married couples and honourable loves. Among the Maya, the goddess Ix Chel, consort of the supreme god Itzamná, was considered to be a protectress of women in childbirth.

Below: Tlazoltéotl rides the snake of sexuality and a broom with which she sweeps away the sins of the sorrowful.

Above: A page from the Codex Mendoza *illustrates the rites and experiences that fill the first months of an Aztec baby's life.*

CHAPTER ELEVEN

AFTER DEATH

From his place at the summit of the thirteen Aztec heavens, the primeval being Ometeotl, lord of duality, sent forth the souls of human babies about to be born. Ometeotl lived in his dual forms as Ometecuhtli and Omecíhuatl in the twelfth and thirteenth layers of heaven, in a place called Omeyocán. Here also lived the souls of babies who had died before their time and without cause, and those who had died inexplicably in their sleep. They expected a new life in a world freshly made after the cataclysmic end of the fifth sun or world age in a great earthquake. In Omeyocán a fork of the cosmic tree provided sweet milk for the nourishment of these babies' souls and the spirits newly made by Ometeotl.

The duality embodied by Ometeotl informed every particle of the sacred Mesoamerican universe. For the Aztecs and Maya, darkness was everywhere balanced by its opposite, light, night by day, dampness by dryness, feminine by masculine, death by life, the shadowy underworld by the bright heavens. The cosmic tree that held the centre grew both in heaven and on the earth, both on the earth and in the underworld. The level of the flat earth or Tlalticpac was the first plane of the nine underworld realms and also the first plane of the thirteen celestial realms. It was both celestial and terrestrial and also both terrestrial and infernal. Everywhere, two was also one: so darkness and light were both one and differentiated. Nothing was purely good or bad, for the good lay within the bad and vice versa; the gods possessed duality and had positive and negative attributes.

Left: The nine levels of the Temple of the Inscriptions at Palenque symbolize the nine levels of the underworld.

THE PARADISE OF THE FLOWER GODDESS

Tamoanchán, the level of the thirteen Aztec heavens presided over by the beautiful flower goddess Xochiquetzal, was imagined as an earthly paradise. There the branches of the cosmic tree were heavily laden with blossoms and fruit and released sweet perfume into the sunlit air. In some accounts, Tamoanchán was literally an earthly place, hidden near the holy peak of a mythical mountain in the far, far south, the region of Huitzilopochtli, where the air was thin and delightfully cool and the rocks rose almost to the moon herself. However, it was usually said to be high above the earth where the heavens climbed to a different sphere of reality.

RAW MATERIAL FOR HUMAN CREATION

Quetzalcóatl and Xólotl brought the bones they rescued from the underworld to Tamoanchán at the start of the fifth world age. In this fertile paradise they presented the raw material for a new human creation to the other gods. The deities gathered in the sweet air of the flower goddess's paradise to provide blood to mix with the ground bones and so make a paste with which to form the first boy and girl. These first humans were nurtured in Tamoanchán, but the human race would never be permitted to return to that place. It was an abode of the gods.

Below: An Aztec relief carving shows four-toothed Tláloc with the skulls of people whose death has given them access to his heaven.

FALL OF THE GODDESS

Meanwhile in Tamoanchán, Xochiquetzal passed her time weaving wonderful textiles in inspirational colours and patterns. She had many loyal maidens to keep her company and from time to time they would pause in their work to laugh at the antics of entertainers. Tamoanchán was a happy home for the goddess but, according to one of the myths, Xochiquetzal was thrown out of the restful paradise and made to spend the full expanse of time on the Earth.

According to this tale, the fruits and blossom on the tree that perfumed Tamoanchán were sweet and tempting to anyone curious, whether divine or human. The creator lord Ometeotl had decreed that this tree should not be touched. It was permitted, however, for the birds of Tamoanchán to alight on its branches and fill them with sweet song and for other animals to scamper up the trunk and leap hither and thither, but the gods and goddesses must not taste the fruits or pick the flowers.

Left: Heavenly flower goddess Xochiquetzal was associated with nose-rings shaped like a butterfly.

Xochiquetzal was captivated by the tree's beauty, which balanced and mirrored her own. Temptation got the better of her on a day when heady delight drove her from her sense of what is right. She picked a garland of flowers for her perfumed hair and stole and tasted one of the ripe red fruits of the tree. She thought that no one would know. What could be the harm, when the tree had so many blossoms, fruits and flowers on its heavy branches? However, in the instant that she violated the supreme lord's command, the tree began to shudder and then cracked and fell into two great pieces, just like the tree made from the entwined bodies of Quetzalcóatl and Mayáhuel in another place. Blood oozed from the spot where she had plucked the fruit and from the place where the two halves had split.

Restrained in his anger but determined to uphold the sanctity of his commands, Ometeotl told Xochiquetzal of her fate. She would be sent down to the mountains and dry plains of earth and live in that place, mourning her loss. She would weep as she passed and touched the flowers and blossoms and she would henceforth be known as Ixnextli ('Ash Eyes'). Xochiquetzal's enjoyment of beauty, of the flowers that she gave to men and women, would be limited because her vision would be blurred by ever-flowing tears.

Left: Xochipilli and Xochiquetzal are usually considered brother and sister. Xochiquetzal is often shown with quetzal feathers in her headdress.

PASSAGE TO THE HEAVENS

According to the Aztecs, only the souls of those who died in particular ways found passage to the heavens. The spirits of warriors who died in the heat of battle – a dart piercing their neck, their last breath escaping in desperation – would wake in the heaven presided over by Tonatiuh, an aspect of the sun god. They were joined in this blessed place by the souls of women who died during or after desperate labours, their infant warrior-sons having – like Huitzilopochtli – delivered death at the beginning of life. Tonatiuh's heaven was called Ilhuicatl Tonatiuh ('Sun Heaven') or Tonatiuichan. The souls of sacrificial victims also passed after death to Tonatiuh's heaven.

The souls of those who drowned in a sudden flood or when a canoe capsized, the souls of unfortunates who had been stricken by illnesses associated with water, and the souls of people caught in a violent storm or struck by lightning would find themselves in Tláloc's heaven, Tlalocán. This was a realm blessed with the utmost fertility, a land where water gently touched the brow in a light, warm drizzle that pleased the plants and encouraged them to deliver cacao beans and the finest fruits in abundance.

Below: This wall painting at Teotihuacán may represent inhabitants of Tlalocán, the paradise of the rain god.

THE BACABS AND THE COSMIC TREE

Like the Aztecs, the Maya also believed that in the centre of the universe the world tree linked the heavens, the earth and the underworld. According to one tradition of Maya cosmology, four giants named the bacabs, the sons of the supreme lord Itzamná and his goddess Ix Chel, upheld the four corners of the world in the north, south, east and west. The splendid sarcophagus of King Pacal at Palenque depicts the king's spirit making the journey downwards from the terrestrial level to the underworld along the length of the world tree.

ACCESS TO SPIRIT REALMS

The world tree could also serve as a conduit for spirits to access the realms above and below during this life. It delivered worshippers to a paradise of ecstatic spiritual experience through shamanistic voyaging. In this guise, the tree might be associated with the Vision Serpent. The Maya summoned the Vision Serpent during the solemn rites of autosacrifice in which worshippers cut themselves and offered the blood of their own wounds to the gods. The intricate carvings of Lady Xoc, wife of Shield Jaguar, at Yaxchilán, show her gaining access to a heightened state brought on by rites of bloodletting to the Vision Serpent. Through the jaws of the Serpent she connects to the sacred ancestors and the gods.

Below: This three-faced Maya brazier is from the Postclassic Period. Psychedelic substances powered Maya spirit journeys.

The psychedelic mushroom *Psilocybe aztecorum* also provided access to spirit realms and may sometimes have been identified with the world tree. A striking ceramic discovered at Colima, in Mexico, depicts religious celebrants dancing around a central column with an umbrella-like top, which apparently represented either the world tree or the mushroom.

Maya priests and worshippers took the *Psilocybe aztecorum* mushroom to induce a religious trance. Throughout the Maya region, archaeologists have discovered stone effigies of mushrooms set up in the period 1000BC–AD500. It was highly valued – and perhaps even worshipped – alongside tobacco flowers and morning glory flowers, for its hallucinogenic properties. Scholars believe that the Maya gained their knowledge of the bright celestial realms and of the dark underworld in the course of spirit journeys brought about through the use of psychedelic substances. Paintings on Classic Period Maya ceramics reveal that Maya nobles and priests took ritual enemas of liquids containing the peyote cactus to bring on visions.

A LUXURIOUS AFTERLIFE

Some Maya traditions held that a few lucky souls would be admitted to a heavenly realm rather similar to the Tamoanchán of the Aztecs. There they would not need to perform backbreaking work cutting terraced fields from mountainsides or thick jungle, but could rest from the hunt or the long trading journeys they had made in their lifetimes

Above: A stone depicts King Pacal's journey to the underworld in this reconstruction of his crypt at Palenque.

and simply find luxury all about them. They could lie in the sweet shade provided by the cosmic tree. When they were thirsty they could gather some cacao beans, to make chocolate drink.

THE WAY TO PARADISE THROUGH THE UNDERWORLD

Most souls were destined for the underworld. Mythical narratives such as the account in the Quiché Maya *Popol Vuh* of the Hero Twins' descent to the underworld dramatized the many tests that the spirit would have to go through there. The *Popol Vuh* tale and the Classic Period myths on which it was based were a kind of guidebook to the afterlife.

The Hero Twins' narrative ends with Hunahpú and Xbalanqué defeating death in the form of the underworld lords and rising triumphant to the heavens. It was generally understood that their triumph in the underworld paved the way for those who came after them. A tablet at Palenque shows a ruler emerging from

Above: This mask of the sun god is from an Early Classic Maya pyramid at Kohunlich, Quintana Roo.

the underworld in the appearance of the jaguar god of that realm and being greeted with an offering by his mother. Death could not hold him and that cold ogre could not expect to contain any of the ruler's descendants.

According to some scholars, the Maya believed that only the noble elite would proceed to an afterlife by way of the tests in the underworld. Other authorities argue such a religion would not have been generally sustainable and that people at all levels of society must have believed that their ancestors had somehow triumphed over death and that they themselves might do the same.

In its celebration of new life out of death the story informs a splendid late Classic Period tripod plate (*c.*AD600–900) that depicts the father of the Hero Twins' One Hunahpú being born from the cracked back of a great turtle.

According to the version given in the *Popol Vuh*, One Hunahpú is unable to leave the underworld. On this plate, however, and perhaps also in the Classic Period version of the myth, he is given new life by his sons. The Maya saw the turtle as an image of the earth and identified One Hunahpú as the Young Maize God, so the image on the plate emphasizes the myth's meaning as a celebration of the life-cycle of the maize plant. However, the plate is also a truly joyful celebration of the defeat of darkness and death and of the spirit's rebirth into light and life.

Left: A clay censer found in Yucatán bears the face of a little known Maya deity who was patron of bee-keepers.

THE JOURNEY TO MICTLÁN

Above: This jade, coral, obsidian and turquoise mosaic mask is a funerary ornament from Texmilincan, Mexico.

In the Aztec underworld, the god Mictlantecuhtli enjoyed his power in dampness and darkness. Everything in the universe had its balancing double, the other half of a perfect duality. Mictlantecuhtli and his consort Mictecacíhuatl were the underworld equivalents of Ometecuhtli and Omecíhuatl in the uppermost layers of the Aztec heaven.

THE UNDERWORLD GOD

The underworld god was skeletal because he had lost half his flesh, and his black curly hair sparkled with stars. He was often depicted dressed in clothes made from strips of bark paper. He had enormous, clawlike hands capable of tearing the underworld spirits limb from limb and was happy to see others suffer.

Mictlantecuhtli was essentially a personification of death. His liver hung from a gaping hole in his stomach. The Aztecs believed that the body had three principal parts: the head, where a person's destiny was housed; the heart, where one's consciousness lived; and the liver, home to the spirit. The liver was associated with Mictlán, realm of the spirits, by ancient Aztec tradition. Mictlantecuhtli wore sandals as a sign of his lordly standing. His consort, Mictecacíhuatl, had a fearsome skull for her face, and her thin breasts sagged despairingly. Her skirt was made of flailing fork-tongued serpents.

The underworld was the particular realm of dogs. Mictlantecuhtli was patron of the day *itzcuintli* ('dog'). Dogs were often sacrificed on their master's death and laid in his tomb, for the animals were expected to guide their masters through the ordeal after death. An underworld dog appeared to help new arrivals across the first hazard they faced.

The dead were buried with equipment to help them on their journey. They were given gifts for Mictlantecuhtli and Mictecacíhuatl, as well as paper clothes, food, water, blankets and a jade bead to serve as a replacement heart.

Below: With saucer eyes and terrible teeth, Mictecacíhuatl makes a suitably grim consort for the lord of the underworld.

TESTING THE DEAD

The soul had to negotiate different hazards at each of the nine levels of the underworld. The first was to find a way over a raging river torrent. Here a yellow or red dog appeared as a guide. The second test was to pass between towering mountains that would suddenly and terrifyingly crash together, with the noise of countless jaguars roaring as if preparing to rip flesh from bone.

The pilgrim went on through a demanding range of tests. He had to climb a mountain made of dark obsidian, the shadowy 'smoking' glass worn by the dark lord Tezcatlipoca, then survive an icy northern wind cold enough to peel the skin from the cheeks of a living man. Next he had to defeat a ravening snake, then a dread alligator, before crossing eight deserts and climbing eight great mountains. Exhaustion threatened the poor spirit, but then came a biting wind to drive him on. This gale was filled with knives of obsidian, the blades so sharp that they could slice through solid rock as easily as cut up a tortilla. Next he faced a demon named Izpuzteque, with dreadful backwards-facing legs, and then another foe who tried to blind the spirit traveller by throwing handfuls of ash in his eyes. Finally, he came face to face with Mictlantecuhtli and Mictecacíhuatl and made offerings to them. Mictlantecuhtli would rip the poor pilgrim's spirit-body to pieces. This did not end the soul's existence, for he lived on in the domain of Mictlantecuhtli and Mictecacíhuatl, in dampness and darkness, with only his companions and friends among those who had died before him to give him any pleasure or comfort. However, once a year he was permitted to return to the lands of living Mesoamerica, where his relatives would lay out earthly foods for his pleasure.

Below: A gruesome Mixtec drinking cup from Zaachila, Mexico, is intended to remind drinkers of their mortality.

Sometimes the Aztecs located Mictlán in the far north, a desolate, dry place of dreadful famines and cold winds, associated with the colours yellow and black, with the sacrificial knife and with the dark lord Tezcatlipoca. A realm of endless fear and ill-fortune, it was the northern pole balancing the mountaintop heaven situated in the far south. It was known as Mictlampa ('Abode of the Dead'), or as Tlalxicco ('Earth's Navel'). More usually it was understood to be below the earth.

Mictlán was the place where the gods stored the bones of past generations, both from this age and from previous eras. At the beginning of the current world age, Quetzalcóatl visited the underworld in the company of his dog aspect Xólotl to gather these bones in order to fashion the first people. The Aztecs' understanding of duality meant that death always included life and new beginnings. The seeds of future creation lay in the underworld, just as the seeds of future plants could be buried unseen in the earth. For this reason, skull masks used in religious rites and placed as offerings usually had bright shining eyes. These masks are usually now missing their eyes because the precious materials used have been stripped by the conquistadors or other gold diggers.

Above: Mictlantecuhtli, sunken-cheeked and horribly grimacing, keeps watch over the cold, famine-ravaged realm of the dead.

BEYOND THE WATER

The Maya underworld was ruled by the lords One Death and Seven Death. Its inhabitants roamed the underground kingdom desperately, their bodies disintegrating as they went. Images of Xibalba in codices and on Classic Period vases show spirit forms with horribly distended bellies and eyes hanging on cords from their sockets. Like Mictlantecuhtli, they found their flesh falling from their bones, allowing their stomach, liver and other organs to tumble out hideously. They could not control their bodily functions and streams of excrement and wind burst out. Some wore necklaces made from the fallen eyeballs of other poor souls.

LORDS OF THE UNDERWORLD

According to the account in the *Popol Vuh*, the Maya underworld lords had blood-chilling names and specialities. Jaundice Demon was master of that disease and climbed to earth to make people sicken, while Pus Demon followed in his footsteps and would cause people's limbs to swell and poison to seep from their bandaged wounds.

Below: This monstrous serpent appears on a late Classic Period Maya drinking cup from Motagua Valley, Guatemala.

Two other lords were Bone Sceptre and Skull Sceptre, who carried bare human bones as staffs of authority and brought wasting diseases in their train, illnesses that caused the flesh to fall away until sufferers were good for nothing but a lonely death.

House Corner and Blood Gatherer were hungry for blood, like vampire bats or leeches. Humans could not relax in their presence, for they would come out of the shadows with their sharp teeth bared to assault the soft neck and other vulnerable parts of a man or woman's body.

The Lord of Rubbish and the Stabbing Lord were found in places where people had left remains of their meals or other activities lying around the homes. These dark gods would attack from the blind side and bring their victims low with sharp stabbing pains and fierce strikes. Packstrap and Wing trailed the roads like the Aztec god Tezcatlipoca, seeking the unwary. When they struck they caused sudden death. The victim's mouth would flood and bright blood would run on to his chin, stain his chest and gush on to the ground when he collapsed. The victim would die in the roadway, alone, like a diseased dog, with the dark wind blowing desolately past.

Above: Bats were frequent tormentors of the spirit traveller in the Maya 'Place of Fright'. This urn was made in the Toltec period.

The aged god Pauahtun, one of many patron gods of scribes, was also strongly associated with the underworld. His old and sunken face surrounded a gap-toothed mouth and Pauahtun also wore a net head-wrapping in which the tools of his scribal arts sometimes appear. According to one tradition, Pauahtun supported the weight of the earth above him and so he was from time to time depicted with one hand above his head.

CHALLENGES FOR THE DEAD

Like the Aztecs, the Maya believed that the road to the underworld was full of challenges for the spirits of the deceased. When One Hunahpú and Seven Hunahpú, the father and uncle of the Hero Twins, made their descent to Xibalba in the *Popol Vuh*, they began by going down a sheer rockface. Then they came to a roaring torrent of water where a great river ran through a narrow canyon. They made a makeshift bridge to get across, but were no sooner safely over than they came to another waterway. This river was made up of spinning knives. Because they were such agile sportsmen, highly practised players of the ball game, they managed to get across to the far bank without being cut to pieces. Next they came to yet another river, this one filled with blood. They swam across, taking care not to drink, then came to a stream of pus. They made it across this as well and went on their way. When they came then to a place called the Crossroads, four ways beckoned: one red road, one yellow, one white and one black. They took the black road.

WATER IMAGERY

Images on Classic Period vases and in codices make it clear the Maya associated Xibalba with water. Fish, water lilies, shells and sea creatures appear as decorative features in representations of the underworld. The Maya also connected the moment of death with sinking into water. A carved bone found at Tikal depicts a canoe paddled by two gods with an important passenger and four animal companions; an iguana, a parrot, a spider and a dog. The passenger, who may be either a ruler of Tikal or the Young Maize God himself, holds his hand extended flat in front of his forehead in a way that represents approaching death. The image on a second carved bone shows the canoe sinking into the water as the travellers make the descent towards Xibalba.

Although it was a liquid realm, Xibalba also contained buildings, trees and solid ball courts like the world above. Once spirit travellers reached the land of One Death and Seven Death, they had to brave houses containing terrifying conditions or hungry armies of predators.

Right: This late Classic Period Maya vase shows gods in a boat, symbolically bound for the underworld.

Above: Quetzal feathers, emblems of kingship, decorate the lid of a Classic Maya funerary urn from El Quiche, Guatemala.

One house was filled with the deepest, blackest darkness. Those forced to spend time there soon lost all sense of their bearings and began to despair of ever seeing light again. Another building swamped people with cold rather than darkness. Those forced into this place shivered and tried vainly to escape drafts and the sudden lashing showers of hail that somehow managed to fall indoors. A third house was full of fierce and restless jaguars, whose slavering jaws were wet with the blood of their victims. Another was filled from top to bottom with screeching bats. The air inside a fifth building was thick with blades moving everywhere, sharp enough to cut out the heart or skin their victims. Only the Hero Twins Hunahpú and Xbalanqué knew how to tame these terrors.

THE HERO TWINS AND THE UNDERWORLD

The Quiché Maya sacred book the *Popol Vuh* relates how the terrifying lords of Xibalba were no match for the Hero Twins Hunahpú and Xbalanqué. The Hero Twins descended into the underworld to avenge the deaths there of their father One Hunahpú and their uncle Seven Hunahpú.

ONE DEATH AND SEVEN DEATH ARE ANNOYED

The primal couple Xpiyacoc and Xmucané, the grandfather and grandmother diviners who approved Huracán and Gucumatz's plan to make people from wood in an earlier age, had two children, One Hunahpú and Seven Hunahpú. They were great gamblers who loved throwing dice, but their main passion in life was the Mesoamerican ball game. They practised for long hours until they could stun onlookers with their skill. One frequent visitor to the court was a falcon, a messenger of the great god Huracán.

Below: This ceramic vessel from El Petén is delicately painted with birds. They play an important messenger role in the Popol Vuh.

In time, One Hunahpú married a longhaired maiden of striking beauty named Xbaquiyalo and the couple had a pair of twins, One Monkey and One Artisan. These boys enjoyed learning the ball game from their father, but they devoted most of their time to the arts, becoming proficient at singing, playing the flute, making jewellery, carving wood and working metal. Their grandfather died and then their mother Xbaquiyalo also died, so the boys had only Xmucané, their grandmother, to provide a woman's guidance.

One Monkey and One Artisan grew very close to their widowed grandmother, because after Xbaquiyalo had died they did not see very much of their father. He spent more and more of his time playing the ball game with his brother at their court on the far eastern rim of the flat earth, in a place called Great Abyss. Their incessant playing made a thumping noise that reverberated through the earth and made the very foundations of Xibalba shake. This annoyed the underworld lords One Death and Seven Death.

The lords of the underworld decided the time had come to take on these terrestrial athletes on the Xibalba ball court, so they sent four hideous owls from the shadowy dark places to issue a challenge. 'Come down below and show your mettle', the birds sang, 'our masters summon you; bring your equipment, your ball, your yokes and your armguard down with you.'

One Hunahpú and Seven Hunahpú agreed to come, but first they went home to tell their grandmother Xmucané of their departure. As she wept, they told her they would return to see her and that they were not going down to the underworld to die.

Above: A ball player decorates this black jug from Copán (c.AD600–900).

One Hunahpú and Seven Hunahpú cannily decided not to take their own ball game equipment with them and instead hid it under the rafters of Xmucané's home. They told One Monkey and One Artisan to use their artistic skills to soothe Xmucané's spirits, then they departed, following the owl-messengers down to the lower realms.

ONE HUNAHPÚ AND SEVEN HUNAHPÚ ARE DOOMED

The brothers went down a steep cliff face and across a number of rivers, then chose the black road at the crossroads. They came at last to the council rooms of Xibalba and entered the presence of two august lords. One Hunahpú and Seven Hunahpú assumed that these people must be the rulers of Xibalba and they greeted them by name. 'Hail, One Death', 'Greetings, Seven Death.' But the figures were lifeless, mere wood carvings set there as a trick. The true underworld lords then emerged,

Above: *The Maya goddess of the night takes the form of an owl, watcher and predator in the dark hours of silence.*

roaring with laughter, delighted to have won the first victory against One Hunahpú and Seven Hunahpú.

Next the underworld lords offered One Hunahpú and Seven Hunahpú seats on a bench in the room. The two visitors sat, and immediately leapt up again, clasping their bottoms, for the bench was burning hot. It was another low trick. The underworld lords were almost helpless with laughter, wheezing and gasping in a way that seemed to unpeel the flesh from their bodies, allowing the blood and skeleton to show through. They laughed and laughed, congratulating one another on their trickery.

One Hunahpú and Seven Hunahpú were next ushered into a house filled to the beams with darkness. Meanwhile the lords of Xibalba were plotting. They decided that they should play the ball game with their guests on the next day using the fearsome White Dagger ball, a sphere of hard bone concealing a lethal blade. The game would be quickly over; their guests would be dead in an instant. They sent two lighted cigars and a burning torch to cheer One Hunahpú and Seven Hunahpú in the Dark House. However, they said that the guests must return the lighted cigars and the flaming torch entirely unchanged on the following day. They could not put them out and they could not let them burn down.

Of course, the torch and the cigars burned down and One Hunahpú and Seven Hunahpú were defeated again. When they went to see One Death and Seven Death the following morning they had nothing to show them except the sooty remnants of the torch and the tiny stubs of the smoked cigars. They had failed and One Death and Seven Death declared that they must be put to death. The two ball players had promised Xmucané that they would return, but they were doomed.

The underworld lords sent One Hunahpú and Seven Hunahpú to be executed. One Hunahpú had his head cut off and placed in the fork of a tree growing by the roadside, while the remainder of his corpse was buried with the body of his brother Seven Hunahpú. This tree flourished. One Death and Seven Death were astounded to see that the tree was suddenly covered with so many calabashes that the head was no longer visible. They decreed that no one in all of Xibalba should go near this miraculous tree. However, one young maiden broke this rule and her act of disobedience made possible the ultimate defeat of the dark powers of the underworld.

Below: *The maize god celebrated so beautifully in stone at Copán has now been identified as the father of the Hero Twins, One Hunahpú.*

RISEN FROM THE UNDERWORLD

Above: The Hero Twins made monkeys of their brothers and the survivors of the wooden people took monkey form.

The underworld lord Blood Gatherer had a fair daughter named Blood Maiden. She was curious to taste the fruit of the calabash tree, which had suddenly flowered after the head of the terrestrial ball player One Hunahpú was put in its branches. She knew that the lords One Death and Seven Death had forbidden all the inhabitants of Xibalba to touch the tree, but she went to look at it anyway.

A MIRACULOUS CONCEPTION

One Hunahpú's head was still among the branches, hidden by the great number of calabashes. When Blood Maiden stretched out to reach the fruit, the head of One Hunahpú spat in her palm. She felt the spittle land there and pulled her hand away, but when she looked at it she could see nothing unusual. Her hand looked exactly as it always did. Then One Hunahpú spoke to her, explaining that even though he was nothing more than a bare skull, his likeness would soon return to life in the face of his son.

Blood Maiden went away and soon afterwards discovered that she had become pregnant. There was no other possible father: it must be the spittle of One Hunahpú that lived in her. When Blood Maiden's father Blood Gatherer discovered that she was with child, he was angry and asked her who the father was. She denied that she was pregnant. Blood Gatherer sent her away to be executed, instructing the owl messengers to kill her and bring back her heart in a bowl. However, on the way Blood Maiden explained to the executioners that they must not kill her, for the child in her belly had been miraculously conceived. She fashioned a block of red sap from a croton tree into the shape of a human heart and gave it to the executioners to carry back to Blood Gatherer.

One Death, Seven Death and Blood Gatherer inspected the object and appeared satisfied that it was the girl's heart. They hung it over the fire and stood round expectantly as it cooked, savouring the aroma. Meanwhile, the owls flitted away and guided Blood Maiden to the surface of the earth. It was a fateful moment when she escaped from the plots and tricks of One Death and Seven Death, because the children she would bear on the earth's surface would be the undoing of those underworld lords.

A SUSPICIOUS GRANDMOTHER

Blood Maiden came to the house of the grandmother Xmucané to explain who she was and why she had climbed to the earth's surface. At first Xmucané would not believe that Blood Maiden was pregnant with One Hunahpú's children. As a test, the grandmother sent Blood Maiden to gather a netful of food in the farm-plot kept by One Monkey and One Artisan. When Blood Maiden arrived there she found only one clump of corn plants and despaired: how would she fill a large net with corn? However, she did not give up. She began a magic song, calling on the patrons of food, Harvest Lady, Cornmeal Lady and Cacao Lady, to help her. The corn plants miraculously provided her with enough corn to fill her net.

When Blood Maiden returned with so much food, Xmucané was suspicious. She hurried to the garden to see how the underworld maiden had gathered so much food there. The grandmother found things just as they should be and saw an imprint of the net in the mud. This

Below: The calabash, fruit of a tropical American tree, grows large enough to be likened to a human head.

convinced her that Blood Maiden was mother of her new grandchildren. This element in the story appears to be a pun on one of the Maya day names, 'net'. The story is an embodiment of the cycle of Venus and this event corresponds to the rising of Venus as evening star, which should take place, according to the almanac, on the day 'net'.

BIRTH OF THE HERO TWINS

Blood Maiden gave birth to twin boys, Hunahpú and Xbalanqué, in the mountains and carried them down to Xmucané's house. The babies cried loudly by day and night and Xmucané banished them from the house. Blood Maiden made a soft bed for them, first on an anthill and then in some brambles. The twins made their own good luck by fitting in and making the best of what life offered.

Below: A ceramic vase identified by scholars only as an 'aged god' (c.AD450) was found in the jungle city of Tikal.

SIBLING RIVALRY

The twins received little love from either their grandmother or from their elder brothers One Monkey and One Artisan. The elder boys were very wise, great artists and seers. From the first day, the elder brothers could see that Hunahpú and Xbalanqué had a wonderful destiny and they became wildly jealous of their younger brothers.

While One Monkey and One Artisan stayed home practising their music and fine art, the younger twins went hunting for meat with their blowpipes. Before they had grown beards, they were already bringing home great sacks full of birds for the family pot. Xmucané, One Monkey and One Artisan just accepted it. They treated Hunahpú and Xbalanqué almost like slaves.

Finally, Hunahpú and Xbalanqué got their own back. They tricked One Monkey and One Artisan into climbing a tree to fetch food, and then turned them into monkeys. Hunahpú and Xbalanqué told Xmucané what had happened: her favourite grandsons had abandoned the family home for a life in the trees as monkeys. The boys offered to tempt One Monkey and One Artisan back with music.

Above: A late Classic Maya painted earthenware vase depicts waterbirds and their hunter – perhaps one of the Hero Twins.

So Hunahpú and Xbalanqué took their flutes and drums and played a lively song that brought the monkey men back. They looked so funny, with their long tails and little bellies that Xmucané could not help laughing. At once the monkeys fled. Three more times Hunahpú and Xbalanqué tried the music and twice more the monkeys returned, but Xmucané could not keep a straight face and the monkeys left again. The last time the monkeys would not return. They disappeared into the forest. Now the younger twins Hunahpú and Xbalanqué were ready to fulfil their destiny by returning to the underworld realm in which their father had died.

RETURN TO XIBALBA

The Hero Twins Hunahpú and Xbalanqué found their father's ball game equipment hidden under the rafters of Xmucané's house. A rat they had caught in their farmfield told them where to find it and helped them to get it down. They went to play on their father's favourite court, out at the far eastern edge of the earth. They had a good game there. All the patience, trickery and athleticism they had developed as hunters served them well on the ball court.

ONE DEATH AND SEVEN DEATH ARE ANNOYED AGAIN

Just as before, when their father had played, the game disturbed the underworld lords One Death and Seven Death. They sent their messengers once again to deliver a summons. The messengers followed the path that led them directly to the Hero Twins' house, so the challenge was delivered to Xmucané while the boys were away playing. The underworld lords expected the ball game players to come to Xibalba within seven days.

Xmucané was very upset. Although she had never shown any affection to the Hero Twins, she loved them very deeply and could not bear for them to follow in their father's footsteps down to the dark underworld. Nevertheless, she passed the message on. She gave it to a louse she found on her arm. The louse set off for the eastern rim of the earth bearing the message. On the road he met a toad who swallowed him and continued on the way to the eastern ball court himself. After a little while the toad was swallowed by a long snake, who went on with the journey. High in the mountains, close to the ball court, the snake was eaten by a laughing falcon, who made the last part of the journey to the place where Hunahpú and Xbalanqué were playing.

Above: This arresting, lifelike head (c.AD700–900) is from Copán, a centre for gifted sculptors for many years.

Below: Twin dancers and a Plumed Serpent are delicately rendered on this terracotta vase from Ulua, Honduras (AD600–900).

The laughing falcon flew over the court. When they heard its cry, the Hero Twins threw down their gaming equipment and took up their blowpipes. One shot was all they needed to shoot it in the eye. They ran over to where the falcon lay and asked it its business. 'I will tell you if you heal my wounded eye', said the bird. So the Twins picked some rubber off their ball and used it to heal the bird. For this reason it has a patch of black around its eye.

Then the falcon spat out the snake. The Twins asked the snake what it wanted and the snake spat out the toad. Again the Twins asked the purpose of the creature's visit. The toad tried to vomit the louse, but his belly was empty. The Twins pried open his mouth and eventually found the louse, stuck fast in the toad's teeth. The louse delivered the message exactly as he had been told.

The Twins went home to Xmucané and made their farewells, then travelled to the underworld. They passed safely across the rivers of water, spinning knives and blood and pus, then paused at the crossroads. They sent a mosquito ahead of them to investigate. They told it to bite any underworld lords it met. Its reward was that ever afterwards it could suck the blood of travellers and those out at dusk. The Hero Twins followed the mosquito and witnessed everything that happened. It bit all the 14 underworld lords who had gathered to play tricks on the new arrivals. Two lords, of course, did not respond. The Hero Twins could see that these were mere wooden mannequins, so they did not fall for the trick that had caught their father out. All the other lords were unsettled by the mosquito's bite and addressed one another by name. The Hero Twins listened carefully and afterwards they introduced themselves to the lords one by one.

One Death and Seven Death then tried to trick the twins into sitting on the red-hot bench that had discomfited their father, but the trickster boys refused to sit. They had the upper hand and the underworld lords were as good as beaten already. Dispirited, they led the twins into the Dark House and set them the same task that had been the undoing of One Hunahpú and Seven Hunahpú. The Hero Twins must return two newly lit cigars and a freshly burning torch in the morning.

The Hero Twins were equal to this test as well. They put a red macaw tail on the end of the torch in place of the flame and a firefly at the tip of each cigar. When they returned the cigars and torch in the morning, all three appeared to have been freshly lit. The underworld lords were really troubled now. These newcomers seemed different in appearance and in their hearts from any who had come down from the earth before.

The next challenge was to play the ball game. Hunahpú and Xbalanqué came into the court against the top Xibalban players. They agreed to use the Xibalbans' own ball, which they could tell was no more than a human skull. As soon as the skull-ball was in play, it split open and the Xibalbans' sacrificial knife, the White Dagger, came shooting out. The knife whirled around the court, seeking to strike and kill the Twins, but they managed to stay out of its way.

The Hero Twins now put their own ball into play. The Xibalbans and the Twins played a close game, but in the end Hunahpú and Xbalanqué allowed themselves to be defeated. They knew where their destiny lay and that there would be more tests to undergo.

Below: Two go as one – a Maya whistle is carved in the form of a couple with linked hands.

Above: A jaguar head on this Maya terracotta incense burner might summon the jaguar god of the underworld.

XIBALBA TAMED

After the ball game, the Hero Twins Hunahpú and Xbalanqué were shown into a house filled with flying razors. It was a fearsome place indeed, for the air was thick with blades. However, the Twins tamed the flying razors by promising them the flesh of animals to slice, from that day forward and for all time.

FINDING THE PRIZE

The Twins owed the Xibalban lords the prize that had been agreed for the ball game of four bowls of flowers. How could they find these when they were stuck in the Razor House?

They summoned the ants from the fields of Xibalba to do the job on their behalf. They sent the labouring creatures to snip the flowers from the gardens of the underworld lords. That night, while the lords were enjoying the evening air in their gardens and the Hero Twins were confined in the Razor House, the ants nibbled away enough flowers to fill the four bowls required. The lords One Death and Seven Death had set some birds – the poorwills and whippoorwills – to guard their gardens, but the birds took no notice as the ants did their work.

The next morning, Hunahpú and Xbalanqué sent the four bowls of flowers to the lords One Death and Seven Death. It was obvious where the flowers had come from. It was another embarrassing defeat for these proud underworld rulers to be presented with the flowers from their own gardens as the prize. The underworld lords punished the birds who had proved such inattentive sentries by splitting their beaks, and ever afterwards poorwills and whippoorwills have had a wide open mouth.

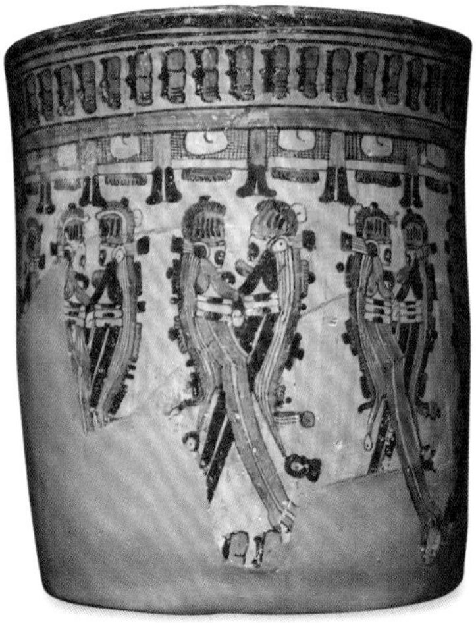

Above: This Classic Period Maya painted terracotta vase from Travesia in Honduras depicts dancing twins.

Below: Scholars have not determined whether the face on this Maya incense burner is of a deity or a common man.

MORE TESTS FOR THE TWINS

The Twins were sent to the Cold House but they were so full of vitality and energy that they survived a night in that freezing place. They spent the next night in the Jaguar House, but tamed the ferocious beasts by scattering bones on the floor. The following dusk saw them entering the House of Fire, but they survived the inferno and were safe and well the next morning.

The next test was the Bat House, which was full of shrieking bats. The Twins survived most of the night by hiding inside their blowpipe, but after waiting through many hours of darkness, Hunahpú grew impatient and stuck his head out to see if it was dawn. In that moment, a bat snatched off his head, which rolled on the hard floor of the house, out of the door and on to the underworld ball court. The underworld lords called for a game, excited that they had finally won a victory over the Twins.

SUN, MOON AND VENUS

The *Popol Vuh* stories might reflect Spanish influence and distort earlier Maya tradition.

Some scholars believe that the older Maya tales described the Twins as rising to become the sun and the planet Venus, who were regarded as brothers.

In the great majority of Maya stories, the moon is regarded as female. The male moon of the *Popol Vuh* could be a misrepresentation of the older tradition. These scholars generally identify Xbalanqué with the sun and Hunahpú with Venus.

However, the Twins go through many transformations in the course of their heroic lives and it might be that the Maya did not narrowly identify them with a particular heavenly body but rather with different phases or apparent movements of Venus, the moon and the sun.

One alternative theory is that Hunahpú became the sun by day and Xbalanqué the sun by night, when it travels through the underworld.

Left: This stucco relief of the Maya sun god is from a pyramid in the Campeche region. In ancient Maya myth the Hero Twin Xbalanqué returned from the underworld to light the world as the Sun.

ANOTHER BALL GAME

One Death and Seven Death wanted to use Hunahpú's head as the ball. Then Xbalanqué called on the animals of the world to bring their foodstuffs for him. When the coati, a mammal like a raccoon, brought a squash, Xbalanqué saw that he could use it to fashion a new head for Hunahpú. Equipped with his makeshift head, Hunahpú came on to the ball court with Xbalanqué ready for a new game.

The first time they used Hunahpú's real head, Xbalanqué hit it so hard that it flew out of the ball court into a stand of oak trees alongside. A rabbit burst out of the trees, distracting the underworld lords, and Xbalanqué and Hunahpú were able to switch the squash head for the real head.

The Twins called back the underworld lords and the game began again, this time using the squash as the ball. After a couple of hits, the squash began to break up and its seeds flew out. The lords could see that they had been outwitted again by the trickster Twins.

VICTORY OVER DEATH

The Twins were put through many more underworld tests, but were victorious every time, exhausting the ingenuity of One Death and Seven Death. They decided to demonstrate their victory over death by returning from annihilation. Invited to a feast by the Xibalban lords, the Twins leapt into the oven and were burned alive. The Xibalbans were beside themselves with delight at this unexpected victory. They hauled the Twins' bones out of the ashes, ground them up and sprinkled them on the waters of the underworld river.

Just five days later, the Twins returned, in the form of twin catfish. The Xibalbans saw them and were amazed. The following day, the Twins came once more in human form, pretending to be travelling entertainers. They performed several tricks, the most dramatic when Xbalanqué performed the rites of human sacrifice on Hunahpú then brought him back to life. He took off Hunahpú's head, rolled it out of the door and tore out his heart. The next moment Hunahpú stood there, whole and well. One Death and Seven Death were in a frenzy of delight and asked the twins to perform the magic on them. This time, however, the sacrifice was made for real. The twins sacrificed One Death and Seven Death. All the other Xibalbans fled in terror. The twins' victory in the underworld was complete. They told the Xibalbans that from this day they would not receive human hearts and blood in sacrifice, only sap from the croton tree and the flesh of forest animals.

Before the twins left the underworld, they reassembled the butchered body of their father. He would remain in Xibalba, they told him, and would be honoured by men for all time. Then the Twins rose into the sky. They became the sun and the moon and they light human activities by day and by night. At this time the Four Hundred Boys also appeared in the sky as the Pleiades constellation.

Right: Like the Hero Twins, Quetzalcóatl rose from the underworld to the night sky. In this late Classic Period carving (c.AD600–900), a priest of Quetzalcóatl emerges from the jaws of the Plumed Serpent.

QUETZALCÓATL AND HIS TWIN IN MICTLÁN

The Plumed Serpent Quetzalcóatl braved the trials of the Aztec underworld, Mictlán, to gather the raw materials for the creation of the human race. He returned with the bones of the pre-human ancestors and shed his lifeblood to make the flesh of humans.

SEARCHING FOR OLD BONES

These events took place after the fourth world age, *Nahui Atl* ('Water Sun'), had been destroyed in a great flood by the goddess Chalchiúhtlicue. Quetzalcóatl and Tezcatlipoca set about creating a new world. First they made the earth and the heavens from the body of the Earth Monster Tlaltecuhtli. Then Quetzalcóatl voyaged to the underworld to search for the bones of the previous race to have inhabited the earth; the fish and many other water creatures that lived in Chalchiúhtlicue's creation. In some versions he was accompanied by his twin aspect Xólotl, who was god of monsters and who often took dog form.

Below: The Plumed Serpent, depicted here in a Maya codex, underwent many trials to make the creation of humans possible.

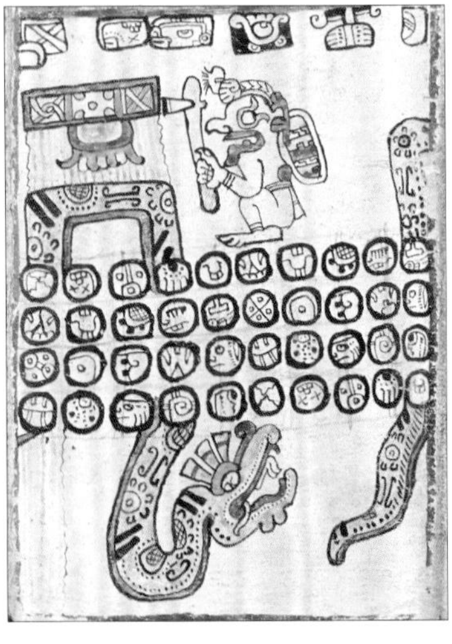

Quetzalcóatl went through many tests in the underworld, Mictlán. According to the pictorial account in the *Codex Borgia*, the god entered Mictlán through the body of the earth goddess Coatlícue. He is depicted being burned to death in the east on a pyre, the windblown ashes of his body transforming into swift, strong-winged birds. This refers to the Quetzalcóatl story in which the god was identified as prince Topiltzin, the wise ruler of Tollán who was disgraced, who left the city heading east and who offered himself in penitential sacrifice.

In the south, the Place of Thorns, he faced the threat of dismemberment or beheading, but passed unscathed through the body of Tlazoltéotl. In the west, he encountered a temple, honouring the souls of women killed by their unborn warrior-sons in childbirth. In the east he found a temple that was a tribute to the heroes of the battlefield. Here he passed through the body of the Earth Monster, Tlaltecuhtli, emerging in twin forms as Red Tezcatlipoca and Black Tezcatlipoca. In the north, Black Tezcatlipoca made a sacrifice of his red twin then cast himself on to a pyre. He rose from the pyre as Venus the morning star.

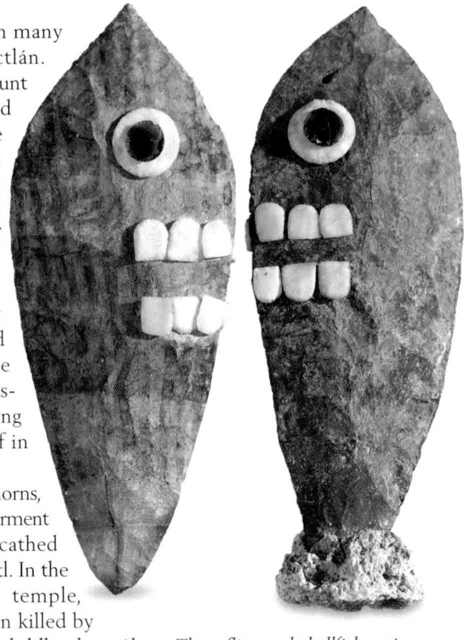

Above: These flint and shellfish votive offerings were used in Aztec religious rites as sacrificial knives.

AN IMPOSSIBLE TASK

Quetzalcóatl held to his human form when he met the underworld lord Mictlantecuhtli. The north was the darkest, foulest part of Mictlán and here Quetzalcóatl discovered the skeletal lord with his consort Mictecacíhuatl. The Plumed Serpent asked Mictlantecuhtli for the bones of the previous earth-race of fish and water mammals. The dark lord was unwilling to let the materials go, so he set what he considered to be an impossible task: Quetzalcóatl must travel four times around the underworld while trumpeting on a conch shell that had no holes drilled in it. Quetzalcóatl proved equal to the test. He summoned underworld worms to drill the holes he needed to make the conch shell sound and then made a swarm of bees enter the shell. The buzzing made a satisfying song.

Mictlantecuhtli had to hand over the bones, but he bitterly resented it, so he ordered his subjects to dig a hole in Quetzalcóatl's path. When the Plumed Serpent arrived at the place, a flock of quails swept at his face, startling him and making him fall into the hole and drop the bones. He recovered in time to gather the bones and effect his escape from Mictlán. However, because he dropped the bones, they were broken. It is for this reason that the people later made from them came in a variety of shapes and sizes.

Above: In an image from the Codex Vaticanus, *Quetzalcóatl in Plumed Serpent form rides the sky as Venus.*

A NEW CREATION

Quetzalcóatl took the bones to the gods assembled in the heaven of Tamoanchán. He gave them to the mother goddess, who ground them into a powder and asked the other deities to provide some of their blood so that a paste could be made from the bones. They gathered around and performed autosacrifice, passing thorns through their tongue or earlobes to drip blood on to the mixture. According to one version, it was Quetzalcóatl alone who provided the blood for the mixing of the paste. The gods waited and watched. They needed to be patient. After four days a male human child emerged from the paste and after four more days a girl appeared.

Another of the *Codex Borgia* images shows Quetzalcóatl as the wind god Éhecatl sitting back to back with the underworld lord Mictlantecuhtli, suggesting the duality of life and death. The tale of the god's movement through the underworld also celebrates the religious understanding that life is given meaning and context by death. The accounts of Quetzalcóatl's heroic travels end with the god rising to become Venus. The cycles of that planet repeat and celebrate Quetzalcóatl's descent to the realm of death, his outwitting of the underworld lord and his ascension in life to create the human race.

Like the *Popol Vuh* of the Quiché Maya, the tale is a celebration of the underground germination of the maize plant and its journey to the light in spring. Some scholars also see an account of the travails that await each human spirit after death in the myth of Quetzalcóatl's descent to the underworld: a sacred myth comparable to the accounts of the afterlife in the holy books of ancient Egypt, Tibetan Buddhism and the Judaeo-Christian tradition.

Below: A detail of a mural of c.AD900 *from Cacaxtla shows the head of the Plumed Serpent Quetzalcóatl.*

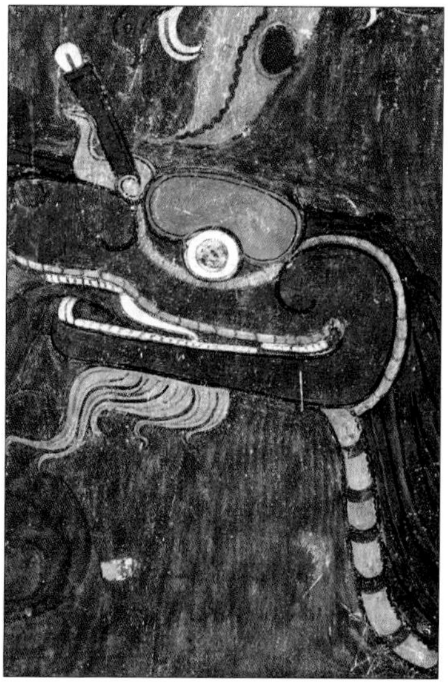

CHAPTER TWELVE

MYTHS AND HISTORY

Mesoamericans created narratives not only about the world's beginnings and the deeds of the gods, but also about the origins of their own people and the history of the tribe. Indeed the Aztecs and other Mesoamericans often took a creative approach to history, blending fact and narratives of the past in a way designed to establish political and religious points in the present.

According to an origin narrative shared by the Aztecs and many of their neighbours, the earliest human ancestors emerged from a collection of sacred caverns known as Chicomoztoc ('Seven Caves'). The Aztecs believed that the seven womb-like caves radiated out from a central chamber and that one people or tribe emerged from each cave.

Chicomoztoc was generally understood to be in the north and was associated with dryness, darkness, barrenness and lack of civilization; it was a good place to leave behind. Several attempts have been made to identify both this place of origin and the place known as Aztlán ('Land of the Cranes') from which the Aztecs claimed to have started out when they made a southward pilgrimage to the Valley of Mexico. The story appears to express the tribes' feeling that they were born from and belong to the mother goddess. However, some historians suggest that the myth is symbolic of the transition from a nomadic hunting lifestyle to a more settled lifestyle of farming supplemented by hunting; a change that equated to a rebirth and gave the former nomads a new connection to the land.

Left: This Codex Durán *image depicts Moctezuma leaving on a retreat after hearing of the Spanish landing.*

TOLTEC WANDERINGS

The Toltecs, so revered by the Aztecs as the builders of the wondrous city of Tollán, were probably the first of many tribes who travelled southward from the wasteland of the north, beginning as nomads but settling in the more fertile lands further south and learning the skills of settled life. According to one account given by the chronicler Fernando de Alva Ixtlilxóchitl, the Toltecs came south by sea, following the coastline presumably in large sea-going Mesoamerican canoes, until they came to the mythical land of Tlapallán ('Land of Bright Colours'). Scholars regard this version of events as highly unlikely, preferring a more probable land route, but they do note that in some traditions the god Quetzalcóatl was regarded as an expert in navigating a canoe and that on the eastern edge of Mesoamerica Maya traders proved themselves capable of covering large distances by sea canoe.

DISPLACEMENT OF A PEOPLE

The Toltecs began their journey because they were displaced by a stronger, better-equipped or more warlike people, setting the pattern for generations of brief settlements and enforced migrations. Ixtlilxóchitl's chronicle records that the Toltecs landed in Tlapallán in the year 1-Técpatl, identified by scholars as AD387. The chronicle then suggests that they were driven out from Tlapallán around 50 years later, in AD439, after rebelling against the king's authority. They settled nearby for eight years, then travelled to Tlapallantzinco, where they rested for three years. Afterwards they began a long migration along the Pacific coast and across northern Mexico. According to Ixtlilxóchitl's chronicle, the Toltecs at last found the appointed place to establish their wondrous city of Tollán in AD566.

Below: The Aztecs looked back to the Toltecs with the awe they felt for the grave offerings of Teotihuacán. This stone mask was placed on the face of a buried Teotihuacán noble.

Above: The Toltecs' travels to find a homeland lasted more than 100 years and included 13 brief periods of settlement.

FOUNDING OF A CITY

The myth of Tollán is based on the history of the city of Tula, which lies around 80km (50 miles) north of Mexico City. The date of Tula's founding is not certain. It may have been as late as the 10th century AD, more than four hundred years later than the date given in Ixtlilxóchitl's account.

The location for the city was chosen by the Toltecs' priest-leader Hueymatzin ('Great Hand'). In that place he saw the future; the wonderful era of peace and self-expression that would come to the Toltecs in Tollán; but also the ineffably sad departure of the priest-king Topiltzin.

The site to which Hueymatzin gave his blessing lay in a valley that was so fertile that it became known as 'The Place of the Fruits'. The Toltec people were very glad to end their migrations, and they poured all their energy into building a truly magnificent city. For six long years they laboured, laying out the most luxurious palaces, expansive plazas and towering temples with great pillars honouring brave Toltec warriors. In the seventh year they elected a king named Calchiuh Tlatonac ('Bright Precious Stone') who ruled for 52 years. Under his wise governance, in an era of peace and prosperity, the Toltecs developed great artistic skills.

The stonemasons of the Toltecs were to produce carving of the very finest quality and they raised walls literally covered in sparkling gems. The Toltecs were famed for the temple complex in their capital. The inner sanctum contained four rooms of astonishing beauty. One had walls covered with gold, the second used precious jewels for decoration, the third was covered with seashells and the fourth was carved from a red stone and also had delightful shell ornaments.

Travellers from near and far were also astonished to see the Toltecs' House of Feathers. This magnificent building also had four main rooms, each decorated with hangings and tapestries woven from feathers of different colours. In the first room these feathers were yellow, and in the second they were made from the precious blue-green feathers of the quetzal bird. The third room in the House of Fearthers was decorated with pure white feathers, not a grubby or misshapen one among them, while the fourth was hung with cloths made from red plumage. So delicate and finely wrought were their artistic creations that their neighbours began to use the term *toltec* to mean an artist.

Above: Magnificent Toltec warrior figures stand on the Temple of Tlahuizcalpantecuhtli or Venus the morning star at Tollán.

Left: Toltecs believed that warrior-gods like this used their strength to support the universe.

THE GOLDEN REIGN OF TOPILTZIN

One body of stories concerning the wondrous age of the Toltecs in Tollán celebrates the golden achievements and eventual decline of their priest-king Topiltzin. He was one of a succession of priestly rulers dedicated to the cult of the Plumed Serpent, Quetzalcóatl. This group were known after their divine inspiration as 'the Quetzalcóatls'.

Above: A carving of the birth of Topiltzin emphasizes the king's association with the Plumed Serpent Quetzalcóatl.

A TIME OF PLENTY

Topiltzin's reign, like that of Calchiuh Tlatonac before him, was remembered as a time of great plenty. Nobody needed to go without in the Toltec realm: ears of maize were so heavy and long that farmers had to use their arms to cradle them, while calabashes were the size of a man's lower leg. There was no need laboriously to dye cotton, for it grew in all the colours of the rainbow. The songs of brilliantly feathered birds hung sweetly in the clear air. A walker in the hills could easily gather gems and pieces of gold and silver, for they were as plentiful as flowers. People picked up the sparkling stones if they wanted to set them in a necklace or make an offering to the gods

The people of Tollán pioneered all the great arts in this wondrous era. They understood mining, stone cutting and masonry and developed delicate skills as carpenters. They were the first in America to practise weaving, painting, music and writing. The priests invented the ritual calendar, so the passing of time could be measured and marked in the gods' honour. They were to develop the secret science of divining the future, the throwing of seeds and the interpretation of day-names and year-names to discover the hidden destiny that governed an individual's life.

The Toltecs built observatories and watched eagerly at night to plot the movements of the stars and planets. They were rewarded for their devotion with hidden knowledge. On shamanistic journeys they encountered the creator himself, lodged both beyond the farthest star and deep in their own hearts, and they understood the secrets of the ever-changing universe. They discovered the religious uses of such alcoholic drinks as *pulque* and of mind-altering substances such as the psychedelic mushroom *Psilocybe aztecorum* and the morning glory flower.

Right: This magnificent feathered fan is thought to have once been used by Moctezuma II.

Above: The Aztecs honoured the Toltecs and other ancestors during the Festival of Huey Miccailhuitl's pole-climbing ceremony.

TOPILTZIN'S ORIGINS

There are several accounts of Topiltzin's origins, some of which seek to establish his divine status or to identify him as an incarnation of the god Quetzalcóatl. In one of these, his mother gave birth to him after she swallowed an emerald. His miraculous birth associated him with Huitzilopochtli, born after a ball of birds' down landed in his mother's bosom. According to another account, he was the son of the earth mother goddess, just as Queztalcóatl was.

RELIGIOUS REFORM

Yet another version emphasized Topiltzin's human origins. According to this account, Topiltzin was originally a warrior, brave in battle, but he was drawn away from the cult of violence and of human sacrifice to the worship of the benevolent Quetzalcóatl, provider of good things to the human race. At this time the Toltecs' chief god was Tezcatlipoca, a patron of war and sower of disharmony. Topiltzin, it is said, undertook seven years of penances to cleanse his soul of the stain of other men's blood. He then established a religious community in a Toltec city named Tulantzinco. He taught that the gods did not require the slaughter of victims on the sacrificial stone, but were far happier with the pious and peaceful offering of animals or of a worshipper's own blood drawn from the earlobes, tongue, cheeks or penis.

The Toltecs asked him to become their ruler and to bring his religious reforms to Tollán. He became a deeply loved ruler and the cult of Quetzalcóatl increasingly eclipsed that of Tezcatlipoca. However, the remaining core of the war god's followers rose up to reassert their religious tradition and its dominance. Their approach was more forceful than that of the peace-loving Quetzalcóatl priests and Topiltzin was driven from Tollán, accompanied by a band of his followers.

Below: The Toltec potter who made this ceramic Tláloc emphasized the god's curling snake 'moustache'.

Just as their distant ancestors had done, Topiltzin and his loyal followers embarked on a nomadic voyage of discovery. They may have settled on the Mexican Gulf Coast. In one account, they stopped for a while at Chapultepec ('Hill of Grasshoppers') near the site on which the Méxica/Aztecs would later build Tenochtitlán. They may have gone as far as the northern Maya city of Chichén Itzá and made it a major centre for the worship of the Plumed Serpent (who was known as Kukulcán to the Maya).

There is certainly evidence of Toltec/Mexican influence in Chichén Itzá. Traditional histories put this down to the migration of Toltec groups driven out of their Mexican homeland, but some scholars now argue the Toltec elements found in the city may be the result of trading contacts and cultural influence.

THE DIVINE PRINCE

The Aztecs, like their Mesoamerican contemporaries, were keen to associate themselves with the achievements and history of the Toltecs.

When the Aztecs first settled in the Valley of Mexico they made many marriages with noble Culhúa women of Toltec descent and told elegaic legends about the lost glory of the priestly prince Topiltzin. Over the course of time, this semi-historical figure became identified with the god he worshipped.

The story of Topiltzin's religious reforms, his conflict with the warrior elite who worshipped Tezcatlipoca, his defeat and exile all became part of the cycle of legends that describe the conflict between the god Quetzalcóatl and his dark brother Tezcatlipoca.

THE FALL OF QUETZALCÓATL

According to these stories, Tezcatlipoca was jealous of the glory of Topiltzin-Quetzalcóatl's reign in Tollán and was angry that his own cult was being marginalized by the priest-king's religious reforms. Tezcatlipoca appeared in Tollán and began his shadowy scheming to unseat Topiltzin-Quetzalcóatl from the throne.

In one account, Tezcatlipoca descended from the thirteen heavens in the form of a spider on a dark thread. He came into Topiltzin-Quetzalcóatl's chamber and offered the Plumed Serpent a drink of *pulque*. One drink became many and, in time, Topiltzin-Quetzalcóatl became confused, then angry, then wild. In his drunkenness he forgot himself and violated his sister Quetzalpetlatl. The following day Quetzalcóatl felt his disgrace very keenly and declared that he would leave the city he had governed so well. After banishing the bright-voiced, brilliantly feathered birds of Tollán, burning his palace complex and burying his silver and gold for future generations of miners to find, he departed in the company of a select band of mournful followers. He either sacrificed himself on a great pyre or set sail into the Gulf of Mexico on a raft of serpents.

In another version, Tezcatlipoca persuaded Topiltzin-Quetzalcóatl to play the Mesoamerican ball game. They played long and hard, astounding the people of Tollán who had gathered to watch, delivering impossible balls from end to end through the ring mounted high on the side of the court. Topiltzin-Quetzalcóatl, though a peace-loving and retiring man, was at least the equal of his dark adversary on the ball court. At the height of the match, however, Tezcatlipoca used his dark arts to transform Topiltzin-Quetzalcóatl into an ocelot, a smaller cousin of the jaguar, and drove the creature out of the city of Tollán.

Left: The often peaceable Plumed Serpent Quetzalcóatl did take pleasure in human sacrifices from time to time.

Above: An alabaster disc from Teotihuacán represents the planet Venus, a key aspect of Quetzalcóatl, as a deity controlling waters.

Yet another account explains how the Lord of the Smoking Mirror, Tezcatlipoca, used the device with which he is associated. He gained access to the inner chamber of Topiltzin-Quetzalcóatl and showed the prince his reflection in the dark shadow-mirror. The power of this mirror was extraordinary: it provided both deceptive and unpleasantly truthful reflections, giving access directly to the dark side. The distortion of his image that Topiltzin-Quetzalcóatl saw in the mirror unnerved him. He wandered all night long, plagued with doubt and driven by a desire to return home to the place from which he had come to bring knowledge and culture to Mesoamerica. In the morning he left.

Still another account has it that Tezcatlipoca came to visit Topiltzin-Quetzalcóatl on his sickbed. For this purpose the Lord of the Smoking Mirror had transformed himself into a kind-faced elderly man. At first, Topiltzin-Quetzalcóatl's palace staff turned the

Above: This detail of a Quetzalcóatl head is from Xochicalco, a city at its peak in the early Postclassic Period.

visitor away but he used all of his dark trickery to gain admission. He found Topiltzin-Quetzalcóatl was seemingly exhausted, as if his life energy could no longer support him. 'My body is unwound, undone,' the king said. 'My hands and feet are weak. Getting up to attend to my business is too much for me. I cannot do it.' The disguised Tezcatlipoca came gently to the ruler's bedside. 'Try this potion,' he said in a soft voice. 'It brings fire to your veins and restores vitality. You will feel strong enough to spring up and don your ball game equipment. Nothing will seem impossible any more.'

At first Topiltzin-Quetzalcóatl resisted the drink, but at last he gave in. The potion was in fact the strong alcoholic drink *pulque* and as Tezcatlipoca plied the aged ruler with it, Topiltzin-Quetzalcóatl became drunk. In his drunkenness he was lost and the aftermath of the incident was that he no longer had any appetite to govern. He felt he must return whence he had come. The era of his glorious governance could not endure, for the world cannot support timeless perfection. Quetzalcóatl-Topiltzin had grown old.

ALL GOOD THINGS MUST END

The elegiac note in the legend of Topiltzin-Quetzalcóatl in Tollán captures the human sense that nothing good can last. Both in the account of Tezcatlipoca's visit to Topiltzin-Quetzalcóatl's sickbed and in the tale of the god-king's departure from Tollán, there is an awareness that the goodness of his blessed reign has been exhausted. The king is worn out; his youthful vigour has gone and death looms. The myths embody the experience of ageing and the need for reconciliation with mortality.

Above: An image of Quetzalcóatl from the Codex Durán *(1579–81) shows him in human form with a warrior's shield.*

Some scholars argue that the legends also embody a celebration of the martial vigour and physical force of the bands of Chichimec ('Sons of the Dog'), invaders who swept away the Toltecs in the mid- to late-12th century. The priest-king is exhausted because his time, like that of the Toltecs, is up: a new force has arrived. The elegiac note appears because the invaders who developed the myths were aware of the greatness of Toltec culture and were keen to build on it.

HOW THE TOLTECS FELL

Left: The Toltecs' Chichimec enemies were as fierce as the jaguar. This painted creature is from Chichén Itzá in Yucatán.

The legends of Topiltzin and Quetzalcóatl account for the decline of the Toltec state following the abdication of its divine ruler. Another body of legends describes the same events from a different perspective, portraying the Toltec fall as a divine judgement on a king, Uemac or Huemac II, who had fallen into wicked ways.

According to this account, Huemac II became Toltec ruler in AD994. In his first years on the throne he was an exemplary king and a pious worshipper of the great Mesoamerican pantheon of gods. However, he was tempted into wrongdoing and the vices he acquired gripped his soul so tightly that he could not find his way back to virtue. The provincial cities under the rule of Tollán rose in a weak and finally inconsequential revolt. Although it came to nothing, the revolt was a sign that his stature as king was badly diminished by his sins and that his subjects neither honoured nor feared him.

A SORCERER ARRIVES

The arrival in Tollán of a great sorcerer named Toveyo made matters worse. This expert in the dark arts caused havoc among the people. On one occasion he lured a great number of Toltec people on to a stone bridge high above a riverbed. Then, using shadowy invocations, he made the bridge crack, tremble and collapse, causing the people to tumble to their deaths far below.

The story was also told that Toveyo invited the populace to a dance in the city's main plaza, but maddened the people by making the music swirl faster and faster. He finally drove the crowd into such a frenzy that the people rushed from the square into a nearby crevasse. They died as they bounced off the sides of the ravine and their corpses turned to stone when they finally came to rest at the bottom of the incline.

Toveyo appears to be a thinly veiled version of Tezcatlipoca, who was the dark hero in a whole range of tales of Tollán's downfall. The myth of the maddening music was also told of Tezcatlipoca.

Terrible apparitions began. The volcanoes visible from the city began to growl and belch flames in which the Toltec priests saw wild, threatening figures. When Huemac ordered a great sacrificial offering to the gods, a blood-chillingly awful portent was seen. At the climax of the ceremony, the priests bent the chief victim, a high-ranking noble from a rival city, over the sacrificial stone and opened his chest cavity with the sacred flint knife. But inside they could find no heart. For a few terrible moments, in chill silence, they patted at his chest and innards looking for the heart. They realized that his veins were dry and empty and that no precious blood was spilling on to the stones of the temple pyramid. Yet just a few seconds before the man had been walking and talking. In that terrifying moment a terrible stink began to rise from the body. The priests and people fled from the temple, but many were killed in an epidemic of foul wasting diseases seemingly caused by the stench of bloodless death.

PUNISHED FOR SELF-INTEREST

While out hunting in the forest, Huemac encountered the divine *tláloques*, the rain god's fleet-footed helpers. He fell on to his face, but not to honour them. Rather, he begged to be spared and to be allowed

Below: The myth tells that Huemac was punished by the rain god's helpers. This clay image of Tláloc is from Teotihuacán.

to maintain his position of wealth and importance. The *tláloques* were enraged by his rank self-interest and declared that six years of plagues would punish the Toltec people. They were as good as their word. Huemac's unfortunate subjects endured terrible, crop-killing frosts followed by summer droughts, then destructive floods and wild storms. They were plagued by thousands of toads and locusts that poured across the fields and swamped the city markets.

Huemac abdicated and placed his illegitimate son Acxitl on the throne. Like his father, Acxitl began his reign well but soon slipped into decadence and corruption. The austere city of Tollán became known as a city of vice.

Below: To the west of the Temple of Tlahuizcalpantecuhtli at Tollán are rows of columns, probably part of a palace.

Two outlying provinces rose in revolt, and they sent an army led by a nobleman named Huehuetzin to attack the city of Tollán. The soldiers and their leader were bought off with the city's great riches, but by now it had become known far and wide across Mexico that the Toltec people did not have a leader worthy

Left: This terracotta brazier from Teotihuacán represents quetzal birds, which were associated with royal authority.

of the name and that their power was on the wane. The northern nomads, who were known as the Chichimec ('Sons of the Dog') began to make raids into Toltec lands. Huehuetzin attacked again, this time with the backing of groups of Chichimec. The Toltec people, once the most widely feared warriors of the region, now had to patch together a makeshift defence force that included a company of the women of Tollán. For three years, a Toltec army led by Huemac and Acxitl held the invaders at bay. Finally, the defences broke and the Toltecs fled.

The empire was broken. The Chichimecs flooded across the land, occupying and rebuilding Toltec cities.

THE ORIGIN OF THE MÉXICA

The Méxica/Aztecs claimed that they originated on an island surrounded by reeds in a lagoon, in a place called Aztlán ('Land of the Cranes') somewhere in the far north. Its location was never identified, even by the Aztecs. (They themselves were curious and sent an expedition to attempt to find the lagoon-island in the 15th century.) From this unknown place they set out on a long and circuitous migration in search of a land in which to make permanent home. The journey, like that of the Toltecs before them, lasted more than 100 years.

The Aztecs also said they emerged from the womblike caverns of Chicomoztoc ('Seven Caves'). According to the account given by Fray Diego Durán in *The History of the Indies of New Spain*, the seven caves were in the region of Aztlán. Other accounts suggest that the Méxica/Aztecs came to the place of the seven caves in the course of their lengthy migration.

MAN OR GOD?

Seven tribes emerged from the seven caves and left the region one by one. The first six tribal groups to depart were the Alcolua, the Chalca, the Tecpaneca, the Tlalhuica, the Tlaxcalteca and the Xochimilca. The Méxica/Aztecs remained behind, instructed to do so by a divine vision. Diego Durán reports that the Aztecs left the caves 302 years after the last of the other tribes had departed. They set out to look for a fertile land in which, their god had promised, they would flourish.

Below: This intricate wooden carving of a prone Aztec warrior was used as a drum. It was found at Tlaxcala.

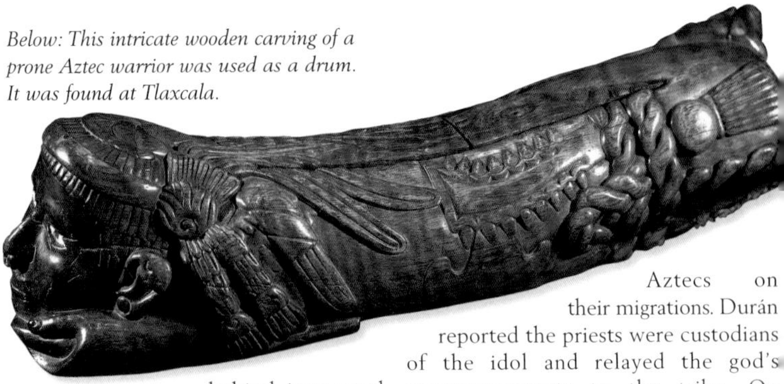

A number of scholars believe that Huitzilopochtli, revered as the Aztecs' tribal god, might originally have been a historical figure, a leader who inspired the Aztecs to leave their original home and travel south. He may have been deified after his death and his cult promoted to a position where it rivalled that of much more ancient Mesoamerican gods. In Diego Durán's account, however, Huitzilopochtli was an idol carried by the Aztecs on their migrations. Durán reported the priests were custodians of the idol and relayed the god's pronouncements to the tribe. On Huitzilopochtli's orders, the Aztecs carried the characteristic tools of nomads; nets, bows and arrows. However, they were not always on the move. In some places they stayed for as long as 20 years and built temples and even ball courts. They laid out fields and raised maize, squash, beans, chillies and chia. They also hunted in the hills and valleys around their settlement to supplement their diet with meat. However, they did not put down permanent roots and when the god told them to move on, they obeyed. Often the old and sick members of the tribe were left behind when the more vigorous set off.

Above: Aztec carvings represent the cihuateteo, *spirits of women who had died in desperate or prolonged childbirth. They became the goddesses of crossroads.*

SPIRIT VOYAGE

According to the chronicler Fray Diego Durán, Moctezuma I, *tlatoani* of Tenochtitlán, dispatched an expedition sometime in the 1440s to try to find the Méxicas' original tribal home in Aztlán.

The exploratory group consisted of 60 shaman-priests who were equipped by their supernatural shape-shifting powers to see to the very heart of whatever they encountered. They headed north, past the Toltecs' great city of Tollán, and came to the mountain they knew as the birthplace of the tribal god Huitzilopochtli. Here they met a shrouded divinity who transformed them into birds for the next stage of their journey.

They arrived by air in Aztlán, where they returned to human form. Here they were introduced to an ancient relative of Huitzilopochtli who observed these formerly tough nomads had allowed themselves to be softened by their settled life in the comfortable surroundings of Tenochtitlán. He brought them to see Coatlícue, Huitzilopochtli's mother. They made obeisance before her and presented gifts they had carried from their capital, proudly telling her of the extent of the Aztec empire and the vast amount and wide variety of tribute they received each year from subject peoples. In reply, however, she prophesied that the conquering Aztecs would themselves be conquered. The travellers thus returned with unsettling news for Moctezuma. The fact that this adventure was presented as a spirit voyage to a place inhabited by the gods betrays the fact that the Aztecs considered Aztlán, their mythical place of origin, to be less a physical location than a place of spiritual birth.

Some scholars believe that the seven caves of Chicomoztoc can be identified as Mount Culhuacán ('Curving Mountain'), one of the Aztecs' most important stopping points on their journey. This peak may be a mountain near San Isidro Culhuacán. From ancient times, Mesoamericans understood caves to be holy places and believed life could be brought forth from the heart of the sacred mountain. In one myth, Quetzalcóatl discovers the maize plant in the heart of Mount Tonacatépetl. One theory says the Aztecs came to an existing ancient cave shrine in Mount Culhuacán and performed religious rites there. Perhaps they already shared the common Mesoamerican origin myth of emerging from the place of seven caves.

Above: Ancestors are honoured in this Mixtec codex, which records the genealogies of a place called Belching Mountain.

Below: This mural of deities in procession is from the Palace of Tepantitla at Teotihuacán.

THE CACTUS AND THE EAGLE

The Méxica/Aztecs made many stops before they found the ordained site for a permanent settlement, the place in which their god Huitzilopochtli had promised they would find wealth and glory.

They came to an island in Lake Texcoco after fleeing the fury of the Culhua. On Huitzilopochtli's orders, the Méxica/Aztecs had taken the daughter of the Culhua king and sacrificed her in a fertility rite, provoking the rage of the king and his warriors. The Méxica had retreated from the place near Culhuacán where they had made their home and were hiding in the marshes and reed beds around Lake Texcoco.

FOUNDING TENOCHTITLÁN

Before sunrise the next morning, they canoed across the lake to the islands they could dimly see in mid-water. As they reached land, a priest of Huitzilopochtli had a blinding vision of his god declaring that the Méxica should look for a place where an eagle perched on a large cactus holding a writhing snake in its talons. This would be the spot where they should build their permanent home. Although it was still just before sunrise, light was blazing in the priest's vision; he was trembling, and collapsed into a pool. His assistants hauled him back to safety, but he appeared oblivious to their attentions, jabbering, 'This is the spot, this is the spot!'

The settlers looked around and a cry went up. Sure enough, there was an eagle perched on a cactus holding a snake at its mercy. At that moment the sun rose and its light caught the eagle's feathers as the bird extended its wings. The Aztecs saw the light of the sun fall on the spot like a blessing from their sun god and leader, Huitzilopochtli. They ran to the place and threw themselves down, praising and thanking the god. They built a platform around the cactus and raised a temple house in which they placed their idol of Huitzilopochtli. From these humble beginnings rose the Great Pyramid at the heart of Tenochtitlán's temple precinct While they were seeking building materials for the platform they found springs of blue and red water; to Mesoamericans, this was a well-known sign that a place was blessed.

THE DEFEAT OF COPIL

The priest's vision indicated that the cactus on which the eagle alighted was growing in the place where Huitzilopochtli had flung the heart of Copil after defeating and sacrificing him. The reference to Copil is to an earlie episode in the foundation legend According to a mythologized account the Aztec group had quarrelled and spli in the years when they were making thei first settlements near Lake Texcoco. One group of Aztecs remained under the

Below: Once the Aztecs had found the right place, they set to work to build their capital This illustration is from the Codex Durán.

Left: The Aztecs raised a platform around the cactus where the eagle landed and founded the city of Tenochtitlán.

guidance of Huitzilopochtli, here cast as a historical leader of the tribe, while a rival faction went their own way under the control of Huitzilopochtli's sister, Malinalxochitl. The breakaway group left the area of Lake Texcoco altogether and settled in mountains to the southwest. However, Malinalxochitl's son, Copil, returned to lead a force against the Méxica when they encountered trouble during their stay at Chapultepec.

On that fateful day, Copil's army was triumphant but he himself was waylaid in the marshes by the invincible Huitzilopochtli. The war god trounced Copil, then took his still-living body and performed a brisk ritual sacrifice. He tore the heart from Copil's chest cavity and hurled it out across the water. It landed on the island in Lake Texcoco where Tenochtitlán would later be built.

A number of variant foundation stories were told. In one version, Copil had been put to ritual death on a sacrificial stone on one of the islands in Lake Texcoco. When the Aztecs came to the island, they found a nopal cactus growing from the spot in the stone where Copil's lifeblood had been spilled. They saw the eagle, symbol of Huitzilopochtli himself, alight on the cactus, seize a serpent from the ground nearby and proceed to tear the creature to pieces. In some accounts the people all heard Huitzilopochtli's voice crying from the spirit realm that this was the place to build their city.

A MESSAGE FROM THE RAIN GOD

This proclamation from the war god was backed up by a message from the rain god. A priest maddened by religious ecstasy impulsively leapt into a pool nearby, where he sank to the murkiest depths. There he encountered Tláloc, god of rains, and received the word of the deity that the place was blessed and that any who built there would receive glory, a great empire and the tribute of countless subject peoples. In some versions of the story, the cactus on which the eagle perched bore red fruit. This symbolized the many human hearts that would be torn from their bodies and offered to Huitzilopochtli in the years after the establishment of Tenochtitlán.

Below: The eagle was a symbol of the sun, of human sacrifice and of the military prowess embodied by warriors.

THE QUICHÉ MAYA SEEK A HOME

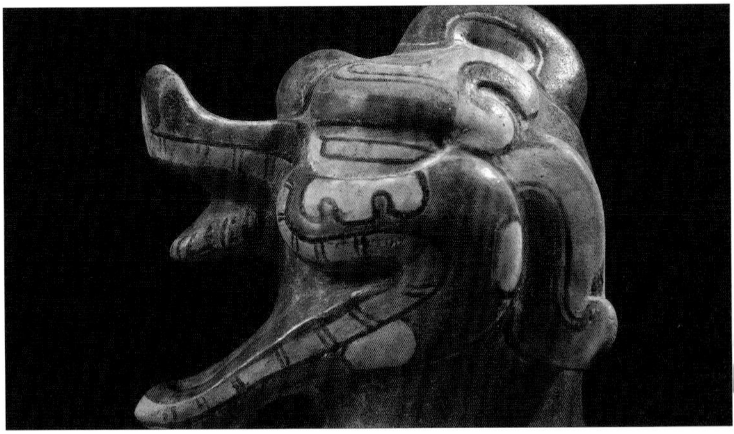

Above: In the Quiché story, the sudden appearance of Tohil froze the creatures of the forest to stone. This animal's head decoration adorns a pot found at Tikal.

Like their Aztec counterparts, the Maya told of an epic migration by their ancestors. The Quiché Maya *Popol Vuh* recounts how the early men and women lived in perpetual darkness and prayed devoutly to the creator gods Huracán and Gucumatz to provide a sun to give them light and to make their world safe.

The first created men and women – Jaguar Quitze and his wife Celebrated Seahouse, Jaguar Night and Prawn House, Mahucutah and Hummingbird House, True Jaguar and his partner Macaw House – had many children and grandchildren. They lived expectantly, facing to the east as often as possible, watching for the rising of Venus the morning star and the sun that would follow shortly afterwards.

When the sun did not rise, they began a pilgrimage that took them to a great city called Tulan Zuyua, ('Seven Caves, Seven Canyons'). Scholars note that this may have been the revered Tollán built by the Toltecs at Tula or the older city of Teotihuacán. The Maya thus shared the Aztecs' reverence for a place of seven caves that played an important part in the early lives of the first tribal ancestors.

GIFT OF FIRE

In the city of Tulan Zuyua, the main Quiché lineages were given the gods that they were to worship. The principal one was Tohil, who gave human beings fire. He has been identified as the Classic-Period deity Tahil ('Obsidian Mirror'), who is represented in carvings at Palenque with a 'smoking mirror' in his head; a Maya equivalent of the Aztec god Tezcatlipoca.

Right: The head of a Maya ceremonial spear found at Copán is carved with the heads of seven kings.

In the very first days, people had all spoken a single language, but while the Maya ancestors were living in Tulan Zuyua, different groups began speaking in different tongues. The Maya had great need of the fire given to them by Tohil, for it was cold in the time before the sun rose and they would huddle around bonfires to try to keep warm. It so happened that a hail storm swept across the dark sky, drenching the people and putting out all the fires. Tohil relit the Quiché fire by rotating on the spot inside his sandal so as to make a spark of fire, rather in the way that a fire can be started by rotating a fire drill in its base.

A DARK PACT

The other Maya groups now clamoured to Tohil to renew their fires. He agreed to supply the golden flame on condition that, at a future date, they would embrace him and allow themselves to be 'suckled by him'. It seemed a harmless request and the other Maya agreed, little realizing that the hidden meaning of being 'suckled' was that they would one day be sacrificed to the god by the Quiché and have their hearts torn from their chests in his honour.

Tohil instructed the Quiché to leave Tulan Zuyua. They were greatly saddened that they would not be in that wonderful city when the sun finally rose, but they obeyed the divine command.

The Quiché resumed their pilgrimage, visiting a place named Rock Lines, Wrinkled Sands and then the Great Abyss, where One Hunahpú and Seven Hunahpú had their ball court. They eventually arrived at a mountain named

Place of Advice in the Guatemalan highlands, where they halted and awaited the dawn once more.

At last their patience was rewarded. They saw the morning star rise and they rejoiced. They burned sacred incense to honour Tohil and the other gods. Then the sun climbed into the sky. His first appearance was unlike any other. He was seen in his full body length and gave off so much heat that he scorched the surface of the earth and turned the idols of the Quiché and the snakes, jaguars and pumas of the forest to stone.

One god named White Sparkstriker escaped the effect of the sun by hiding among the trees. Ever since, White Sparkstriker has been known as a divine gamekeeper, the patron of the wild beasts of the forest. The Quiché were filled with joy at the sunrise. Then they recalled their brothers among the Maya, the groups from whom they had been separated, and this caused sadness in their hearts.

The Quiché settled at this place and they built a fortified settlement. While they were there, they began to sacrifice humans to Tohil and their other principal gods, catching their victims on the mountain roads and offering their hearts and lifeblood to the stone idols of their gods in the jungle. Then they rolled the heads of the dead strangers on to the lonely roads. The local peoples attacked the Quiché stronghold, but they were foiled by a combination of Tohil's magic and the martial force of the Quiché.

Left: This Maya noble wearing body armour with large ear decorations and helmet is part of a ceramic lid from Copán.

Above: With Tohil's blessing, the Quiché established a great settlement and dynasty. At Copán, a sculpted bench panel marks the accession of King Yax-Pac. He called his nineteen predecessors back from the afterlife to honour his occupation of the throne.

In the aftermath of this triumph the great ancestors Jaguar Quitze, Jaguar Night, Mahucutah and True Jaguar removed themselves to the land of the dead. Their sons led another great pilgrimage to the east, in the course of which they met a being named Nacxit, who was a form of the Plumed Serpent. Nacxit honoured them with gifts and titles indicating their high rank and they returned to the highlands in great splendour.

VISIONS OF TRIUMPH AND DOWNFALL

Above: The key reason for Spanish success was that Cortés was able to persuade native soldiers to fight against the Aztecs.

Stirring visions of future glory and ominous warnings of impending disaster are common occurrences in the mythical history of the Aztecs and the Maya. The visions clearly bear the sign of having been inserted into narratives or added to traditions at a later date in order to provide a justification or celebration of particular events. Some narratives, which celebrate Christianity or use Christian imagery, were added by Spanish priests or by converts to the new religion.

DIVINE PROPHECIES

One of the most celebrated of these visions was the god Huitzilopochtli's prophecy of greatness for the Aztec people. As the Méxica/Aztecs made their southward voyage in search of a place to build a great settlement, they were driven on by the urging of Huitzilopochtli. According to chronicle accounts, he promised the Méxica that they would conquer all the peoples of the world and be blessed with subjects beyond counting. The tribute from these subject tribes would be in gold, coral, emeralds, multicoloured cotton and magnificent quetzal feathers, and would allow the conquerors to dress in utmost splendour. They would also receive abundant supplies of rich-tasting cacao beans. They would be kings of the world.

However, others knew, even if Huitzilopochtli did not, that the Aztecs' time was limited. According to Diego Durán's account of the tribe's search for Aztlán, their mythical place of origin, Huitzilopochtli's mother Coatlícue troubled her listeners by prophesying a terrible and humbling end for the empire.

A RESURRECTION

In the months before the arrival of the Spanish invaders under Hernán Cortés, there were many troubling omens and portents. Not the least of these was the return from the land of the dead of Moctezuma's sister Papantzin and her prophecy of the Spaniards' arrival.

Papantzin was a dearly loved princess who was married to the governor of Tlatelolco. When she died she was mourned by Moctezuma and the extended family and laid to rest in a tomb of magnificent splendour with many supplies for her journey through the land of the underworld lord Mictlantecuhtli. However, early the next morning she was seen back in Tenochtitlán, awaiting the dawn in the gardens of the *tlatoani*'s residence. There was no doubt in anyone's mind that she had been dead and her body prepared for the afterlife, yet here she was, returned to earth.

When she walked into her brother's chamber he needed the support of his aides to prevent him collapsing. He tried to speak, but she held up her hand to silence him and told her remarkable tale. In a steady voice she reported that after she died she went from Tenochtitlán to a wide valley flanked by tall mountains. She saw a river to the east and approached it because she knew that the underworld must lie beyond the water

Below: By the time of the Spanish Conquest, the war god Huitzilopochtli was worshipped mainly by members of the Aztec elite.

Above: Troubling portents of Aztec decline and ruin included a dazzling comet witnessed by Moctezuma himself.

crossing. However, a youth with fair skin and emerald eyes stopped her. He was wearing a long cloak fastened by a diamond brooch and had an upright cross marked on his forehead. From his back sprouted great wings that glowed with myriad colours.

The youth led her around the valley, in which lay the disjointed remnants of many human skeletons, and showed her a site nearby where men with cloven feet were building a house. On the river she saw several white-skinned sailors voyaging in boats, carrying banners and wearing battle helmets. Then the young man explained all that Papantzin had seen. It was not time, he said, for her to cross the river to the land of the dead. Her destiny lay back in Tenochtitlán where she would witness the arrival of the bearded men and take pleasure in the blessing of the god they worshipped. The bones she saw were the sad remains of her countrymen who rejected the new religion and so died without the blessing of the new god. The house being erected was for the many Aztecs who would die at the hands of the newcomers. She must return and tell her people of the coming events; the joyous arrival of the word of God in Tenochtitlán.

Moctezuma was greatly troubled by his sister's tale. She was certainly no ghost, for having returned from the land of the dead, she remained in the *tlatoani*'s palace. When the white-skinned men arrived and began to preach the good news of their religion – as she had foretold – she was one of the first Aztecs to convert to Christianity.

MAYA FOREBODING

The *Books of Chilam Balam* – an unsettling mix of prophecy, mythology and history kept by members of the Yucatec Maya – also appeared to prophesy the Spaniards' victory. One of the books declared that 'bearded men of the east' would arrive with violence but carrying the 'signal of god', and that they would impose their will on the Maya. The natives would lose touch with their own culture and have to speak the language and wear the clothes of the invaders.

Right: Very few surviving solid representations of Huitzilopochtli survive, so scholars must rely on codex images.

AN EMPIRE LOST, AN EMPIRE WON

Both native and Spanish accounts of the Conquest mythologize events in order to suggest that the Spanish victory was preordained and so explain the Aztecs' less than vigorous response to the conquistadors' arrival.

The accounts claim that many portents and omens troubled Moctezuma and his people in the years before the Spaniards' arrival. A full decade before Cortés and his troops arrived, they say, a brilliant comet lit the skies.

Tzocoztli, who was the earthly representative of Huitzilopochtli and who lived in his temple, was first to see it. He was greatly amazed and informed Moctezuma, who waited up the following night to witness it. When Moctezuma saw the celestial phenomenon, his blood ran cold, for Netzahualpilli, the sorcerer-visionary *tlatoani* of Texcoco, had warned him that the Aztec people would be overcome and their ruler would see 'signs in the sky' when the catastrophe was near.

In a frenzy, Moctezuma called Netzahualpilli into his presence to ask what the omen might mean. The sorcerer-prince could give him no comfort. He said that death was coming to sweep them all away, and that the Aztecs' land would be filled with misfortunes.

Below: An image from the Codex Tlaxcala *depicts a clash of warring cultures as Spaniards and Aztecs compete for glory.*

Above: A Codex Durán *image shows Moctezuma briefing ambassadors before sending them to greet the invaders.*

Neztahualpilli declared that he himself was to travel very soon to the land of the dead, for he wanted to escape the terrors that were to come. After he left, Moctezuma was plunged into a deep depression. When Moctezuma heard, shortly afterwards, that Netzahualpilli had indeed died, his spirits fell lower still and he expected the worst.

AN ATTEMPT TO AVERT DISASTER

Moctezuma now decided that it was not too late to make lavish sacrifices to the gods in the hope of averting the predicted calamities. He sent for a new and larger sacrificial stone, but when his men found a suitable rock they were unable to move it. Reinforcements were sent for and at last they were able to shift the great rock. After many hours of hauling they stopped for the night and slept very deeply after their labours. However, in the morning they were once again unable to move the great boulder. For many hours they tried until finally the stone spoke, in a grating voice that struck fear into the hearts of all who heard it. The labourers must abandon their efforts and go and tell their ruler that it was indeed too late. The stone would not come to Tenochtitlán, it said, because it wanted to avoid the terrible events about to hit that city. Moctezuma was to be swept away, the stone said, because the ruler, in his vanity, had wanted to claim more adoration than the living God.

Moctezuma's men finally got the rock moving again and carried on hauling it towards Tenochtitlán. However, when they came to a wooden bridge across a canyon, the rock broke the timbers and tumbled into the river far below. Many of the rock-cutters, stonemasons and porters were killed. When Moctezuma heard the news, he ordered divers to look for the great boulder in the water but they found nothing. Eventually they heard a report that the stone had miraculously returned to the place in which it had first been found. Moctezuma himself went to see the rock and was astounded to find it there. He returned to Tenochtitlán even more badly shaken than before.

UNSETTLING EVENTS

Terrifying occurrences came thick and fast. A fire exploded in the temple of the tribal god Huitzilopochtli, high on the Great Pyramid. Bystanders reported that it had been started by a lightning strike from a clear sky. On a still day waves arose on Lake Texcoco and threatened to engulf the city, while at night the people of Tenochtitlán were awakened by wailing voices, the shrill cries of supernatural women telling of impending death and the demise of the empire. One day it snowed in Tenochtitlán, which it had never done before. A man was seen with two heads. A pillar of fire arose from the land, sending a host of new stars up into the heavens and the volcano Popocatépetl began erupting after long years of quiet.

Below: With an interpreter at his left hand and armed men at his back, Cortés meets the ambassadors sent by Moctezuma.

As well as all these unsettling events, a year of great import was approaching. By tradition, when Quetzalcóatl departed to the east on a raft of snakes he prophesied that he would return in the same year as his birth (1-Reed). According to the Aztec calendar, 1-Reed could fall in 1363, 1467 and 1519.

Moctezuma was thrown into fearful confusion as the year approached and the omens piled up. He increasingly neglected his state duties and spent his time in the company of priests and shamans, seeking reassurance and advice on ways to win the gods' favour. It did not help that when he performed a rite involving a mirror-headed bird, he saw a vision of unfamiliar armed men bearing down on his lands.

Scholars have established that the prophecy of Quetzalcóatl's return in the year 1-Reed was not originally part of native accounts of the Topiltzin-Quetzalcóatl legend and that it appears

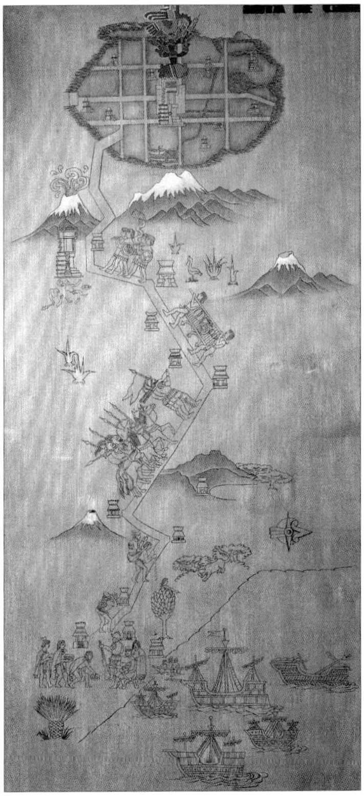

Above: Between mountains to the lake city – this schematic map shows the route taken by Cortés from the coast to Tenochtitlán.

to have been added after the Conquest to explain away the Aztecs' defeat by the small Spanish invasion force. The argument was that the Aztec collapse was inevitable because it was part of a divine plan and, moreover, part of a repeating pattern of history set in motion in the hallowed era of the Toltecs. History moved inexorably on. The great Aztecs were humbled, not by the European invaders but by the great Mesoamerican gods who had granted life, land and maize to Moctezuma's distant ancestors and who now chose to withdraw their gifts.

INDEX

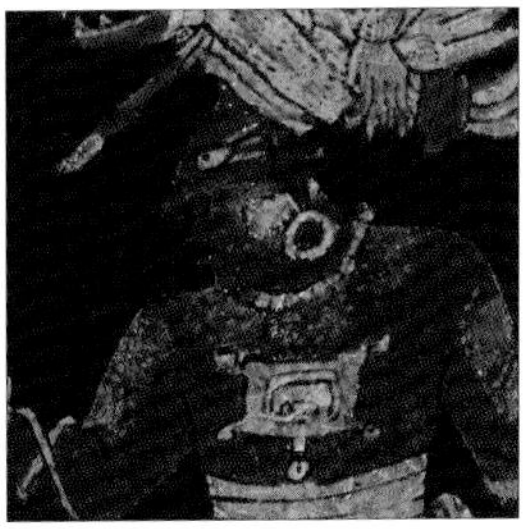

This edition is published by Lorenz Books, an imprint of Anness Publishing Ltd, Blaby Road, Wigston, Leicestershire LE18 4SE; info@anness.com

www.lorenzbooks.com; www.annesspublishing.com

Anness Publishing has a new picture agency outlet for images for publishing, promotions or advertising. Please visit our website www.practicalpictures.com for more information.

A CIP catalogue record for this book is available from the British Library.

Publisher: Joanna Lorenz
Editorial Director: Helen Sudell
Editor: Joy Wotton
Designer: Nigel Partridge
Maps: Peter Bull Art Studio
Illustrations: Vanessa Card
Production Controller: Wendy Lawson

PUBLISHER'S NOTE

Although the advice and information in this book are believed to be accurate and true at the time of going to press, neither the authors nor the publisher can accept any legal responsibility or liability for any errors or omissions that may have been made.

p. 1. A fine mask of Xochipilli, the Aztec god of flowers, from the ruins of Teotihuacan.
p. 2. Steep stairs ascend the Temple of the Count at the Maya city of Palenque.
p. 3. A golden Mixtec necklace displays their belief that the gods were inspired metalworkers.

PICTURE ACKNOWLEDGEMENTS

The Art Archive: 15t, 83bl, 183l, 188l, 189t, 200l, 205t and b, 206t, 208b, 214r, 226t, 232r, 241t, 248l, /Bodleian Library, Oxford: 81b, 115b, 209r, /Album/Joseph Martin: 142l, 234t, /Museo de America, Madrid: 187t, 228l, /Nicolas Sapieha: 160b, /Dagli Orti: 3, 4br, 5bl, 5.5, 5.6, 24t, 30b, 38t, 54t, 63l, 65b, 66t, 67b, 72, 81t, 82b, 83t, 85t, 88, 89t, 90b, 94b, 95b, 98l and r, 99b, 100l, 104l, 105b, 111b, 115t, 120b, 130r, 131l, 132b, 139t, 141t, 147b, 148t, 149b, 161l, 166t, 172t, 178bl, 184t and bl, 192r, 193b, 194r, 195t and r, 196l and r, 197t, 198r, 202t, 203l, 206l, 207r, 210–11, 214l, 215t and b, 216l, 218l and r, 219t and b, 220bl, 220r, 221t, 222t and r, 223l, 224t and l, 225l and r, 227l and r, 228r, 229b, 230–1, 233b, 234bl, 235l, 236r, 237r, 238l and r, 239t and b, 240t and b, 241b, 242b, 243b, 244l and r, 245l, 247t, 248t, 249l and r, 250t, 251b, 252tl, 253t, /Eileen Tweedy: 59b, 143b, 226b, /Mireille Vautier: 4.6, 13t, 73b, 79b, 87t, 90t, 116–17, 139bl, 190–1, 199l, 201l and r, 204l, 213t, 229t, 235r and b, 236l, 246l, 247r, 252b, 255tr.

The Bridgeman Art Library: 39t, 65t, 79t, 86t, 106l, 107, 109t, 114l, 129t, 138r, 146t, 148b, 151b, 152b, 164l, 176l, 223r, /Archives Charmet: 68b, /Brooklyn Museum of Art, New York: 178br, /Giraudon: 37t, 126r, 143tr, 146b, 193tl, /Index: 104tr, /Lauros/Giraudon: 102, /Ian Mursell/Mexicolore: 34t, 161t, 184br, /Banco Mexicano de Imagenes/INAH: 84, 109r, 140t, 159t, 162l, 167t, 172b, 174r, 177l and r, 183t, 185t, 188t, /Sean Sprague/Mexicolore: 5.3, 170–1, /The Stapleton Collection: 103t and b.

Corbis: 118l, /Archivo Iconografico, S.A.: 5.2, 106r, 124–5, 154–5, 156, 158r, /Yann Arthus-Bertrand: 166b, /Bettmann: 5.4, 9t, 15b, 207t, /Anna Clopet: 93t, /Randy Faris: 18–19, 51t, 256, /Arvind Garg: 4.2, 45b, /Bettmann: 198l, /Historical Picture Archive: 192l, /Kimbell Art Museum: 101b, 151tr, /Danny Lehman: 6t, 68t, /Charles and Josette Lenars: 1, 16t, 17t and b, 32t and b, 78t, 173t, /Macduff Everton: 105t, 134–5, Gianni Dagli Orti: 12l, 26t, 33l and r, 52t, 53b, 64b, 85b, 94t, 95t, 112r, 113tr and b, 145b, 175, 180b, 187l, Enzo & Paolo Ragazzini: 44b, /Gian Berto Vanni: 8b, /Nick Wheeler: 86b.

Werner Forman: 62b, 73t, 110tr, 122t, 128b, 158b, 185b, 213b, 254t, /Anthropology Museum, Veracruz University, Jalapa: 138l, 217r, /David Bernstein, New York: 62t, 111t, /Biblioteca Nacional, Madrid: 37t, /Biblioteca Universitaria, Bologna: 71, 80b, 118t, 123t, 176r, /British Museum, London: 38b, 58, 66b, 70b, 168b, 169b, 174l, 180t, 182r, 189l, 204t, 221r, 245r, /Dallas Museum of Art: 74l, 110b, /Field Museum of Natural History, Chicago: 80m, /Philip Goldman, London: 194t, /Liverpool Museum, Liverpool: 5.1, 59t, 136–7, 140b, 153t, 203t, 209l, /Edward H. Merrin Gallery, New York: 100r, 152t, /Museo de America, Madrid: 127t, /Museum of the Americas, New York: 13b, /Museum of Fine Arts, Dallas: 108l, /Museum für Völkerkunde, Basle: 34b, 63r, 132t, 186r, 199r, 212r, /Museum für Völkerkunde, Berlin: 67t, 69tr, 126l, 141b, 163b, /Museum für Völkerkunde, Hamburg: 163t, /Museum für Völkerkunde, Vienna: 35t, /National Museum of Anthropology, Mexico: 78b, 87b, 91b, 93b, 119tl and r, 133t, 144t, 145t, 151tl, 162r, 168t, 169t, 181l and r, 186l, 212l, 216r, 217l, /National Museum of Denmark, Copenhagen: 144bl, /Pigorini Museum of Prehistory and Ethnography, Rome: 37b, 64t, 82r, 157t, /Portland Art Museum, Oregon: 114t, /private collection: 30t, /private collection, London: 44t, /private collection, Mexico City: 99t, /private collection, New York: 12r, 91r, 100l, 128t, 130l, 149t, 178t, 232l, /St Louis Art Museum, MO: 167b, /Smithsonian Institution, Washington: 120t, 164t, 200tr, /Sotheby's, New York, 142t, /Dr Kurt Stavanenhagen Collection, Mexico City: 55b, 160t, 208t.

N.J. Saunders: 8t, 20tr, 28t, 35b, 40–1, 45t, 46b, 165b, 179.

South American Pictures: 131tr, /Robert Francis: 20tl, 26br, 31b, 42t, 46t, 49t, 54b, 55t, /Tony Morrison: 2, 4.1, 4.3, 4.4, 4.5, 6b, 7b, 10–11, 21tr, 22–3, 24l, 25b, 29t and b, 39b, 42bl, 47l, 50t, 51b, 56–7, 70t, 76–7, 96–7, 108r, 121t, 132r, 159b, 197l, 255tl, /Iain Pearson: 14b, /Chris Sharp: 14t, 21bl, 25t, 26bl, 28b, 31t, 47r, 48l and r, 49b, 50b, 52b, 69tl, 74r, 75t and b, 89b, 92l and r, 112l, 133b, 150b, 182b, 233t, 237l, /Rebecca Whitfield: 42br.